New York University School of Social Work

Groh Compton

MANUAL OF READINGS (1994-1995)

Social Welfare Programs and Policies I

FOURTH EDITION

G I N N   P R E S S

Printed in the United States of America

10 9 8 7 6 5 4 3 2 1

This publication has been printed using selections as they appeared in their original
format. Layout and appearance will vary accordingly.

ISBN 0–536–58514–8

BA 5314

GINN PRESS

160 Gould Street/Needham Heights, MA 02194
Simon & Schuster Higher Education Publishing Group

Copyright Acknowledgments

Table of Contents

Perspectives on American Social Welfare
Winifred Bell

American and European social welfare systems have many specific programs in common. Yet the total systems add up to something very different. Why should this be true? Quite simply because like other major social institutions, social welfare reflects its host society. Nations have different historical experiences, attitudes toward government, economic systems, and cultural values. Their populations may be homogeneous or heterogeneous, relatively stable for generations or constantly replenished by newcomers who arrive with varied backgrounds, ideologies, and expectations.

The U.S. has been described as the "contrapuntal civilization . . ., a land of polarity and paradox" (27), "high ideals and catchpenny realities . . ., piety and advertisement" (15), diversity and conformity. In the same vein, Americans are known for their godly materialism, conservative liberalism, and pragmatic idealism. In contrast to other western peoples, they are said to be more preoccupied with personal and private values than social and political ones, and hence to be more competitive. While many European nations also have capitalist economies, the U.S. is proud of its quintessential capitalism.

Furthermore, the migration to the U.S. and westward was selective. The journey, the struggle, and the challenge appealed to some more than others, and not all stayed. Those who did shaped the new society in their own diverse images.

The hallmarks of the American experience and their influence on social welfare are examined in the following discussion of (a) economic individualism and social welfare, (b) universal and selective organizing principles, and (c) the role of government in redistributing income.

Economic Individualism and Social Welfare

The folk heroes of America were pioneers, cowboys, and captains of industry. They are honored for their rugged individualism and resourcefulness in wresting the land from the original inhabitants, opening up the west to European immigrants and their descendants, and building unparalleled industrial empires. They left to generations of young Americans a legacy of romance, fabulous fortunes, and violence that obscured the drab harshness of frontier poverty and the fear and misery of disease-infected, teeming, lawless eastern slums (5, 21). Steeped in economic individualism, American youth were imbued with a zest for competition and the optimistic belief that strength of character, self-reliance, hard work, and noninterference by government were the keys to their heroes' success. If a great deal of luck in being in the right place at the right time, generously larded with more than their share of greed and ruthlessness, also played a role, such faults were soon turned into virtues.

Economic individualism had a profound influence on how social welfare was viewed and organized. Not until the great Depression of the 1930s did a rival ideology seriously challenge our traditional assumptions about poverty and the role of social welfare. The result was still another polarity— residual versus institutional conceptions of social welfare (25, 48).

Beliefs of Residual Role

The Residual role of Social Welfare. The centuries-old conception of the residual role of social welfare reflects belief in the economic logic of free enterprise and unbounded faith that American capitalism will thrive to the benefit of all so long as it remains sufficiently unfettered by government and undiluted by social welfare benefits to keep the spirit of competition alive. In this conception, the economic market and the family system are viewed as the primary structures of support. Together, they are all that most people need to prosper and succeed. Only when these basic structures break down does social welfare have a "residual" role to play in human affairs. When economic recessions put people out of work or wage earners die, short-term reliance on public aid may be necessary. But long-term dependence is an anathema except for vulnerable groups like orphaned children, the aged, or the severely disabled.

Residualists view poverty in individualistic terms as due to personal weakness, improvidence, immorality, and indolence (6). The worst sin is to discourage incentives to work, an ever-present threat, it is claimed, when social welfare enters the scene. Adversity, far from breaking the human spirit, is believed to strengthen character and stimulate heightened efforts toward self-support. Proponents of this view chronically mistrust the poor. They are always trying, it is said, to "get something for nothing," but if they are in want they have "no one to blame but themselves." In this climate, when cash or services are provided, programs are overrun with controls to prevent fraud and abuse.

Wherever the residual view holds sway, social welfare programs tend to be scarce and mean. Not only is poverty stigmatizing, so is the mere act of asking for help.

Beliefs of Institutional Role

The Institutional Role of Social Welfare. This school of thought believes that social welfare plays a major role, equal in importance to the economic market and the family system, in meeting normal, everyday needs of average citizens, as well as helping vulnerable populations (24, 26). In fact, the two so-called primary institutions cannot hope to satisfy all human needs; nor do they succeed in doing so. In a wage economy when full-time, year-round workers earn too little to support families decently, and the economic market generates too few jobs to go around even in good times, people cannot fairly be blamed for their poverty. Nor can they be expected to resolve independently the problems it creates. Furthermore, if the family system is to thrive in complex, rapidly changing, urban societies, a wide range of services is essential. And sharing their cost so that everyone can use them is often the most sensible solution.

In addition, while many services are provided in the economic market and the voluntary nonprofit market, as well as the public social welfare market, some services like education are regarded as too vital to the general welfare or, as with child care institutions and nursing homes for the aged, too risk-laden to operate without the restraining influence of state standards and inspection to protect access, safety, and quality. State licensing of professions, foster homes, and day-care centers, are an endorsement of this principle.

To institutionalists, providing and using community services are intelligent responses to commonly encountered needs. Services should be readily accessible, it is emphasized, and offered in ways that protect self-esteem and promote self-mastery; also, citizens should be closely involved in their planning, delivery, and evaluation (45).* Frankel (18) believed that this attitude accounted for much of the resistance to the institutional view. "The policy of helping others while allowing them to retain their self-respect," he wrote, "has not been . . . usual in human affairs."

Background of the Residual Institutional Conflict. The residual view has been strongly entrenched in the U.S., and has persisted much longer here than in Europe, where it originated. It existed in its purest form in the old Poor Laws of England, which were codified in 1601 and soon exported to the colonies. They marked the first acceptance of public responsibility for the relief of poverty. But they were very much the product of a propertied class. For the law also marked the first time in Anglo-Saxon law that primary responsibility for support was placed squarely on the family system. If families proved incapable of support, only the most vulnerable members — the aged, disabled, and blind — were eligible for public aid. Alternative arrangements like indenture of children and provision of work materials for adults in times of extreme hardship were also provided. Thus, for the able-bodied, work and welfare were inseparable, but even these conditional public responsibilities were extended only to town residents (43). Centuries were to pass before nations broadened the scope of responsibility or recognized that industrial societies required an educated, skilled, mobile labor force and an institutional structure designed to accommodate these needs.

In colonial America if fathers died prematurely or were killed, widows and children might be lodged temporarily with neighbors at public expense, if necessary. Occasionally, intact families were given temporary aid in their own homes. But if after a few months they still had no plans for self-support, they could be indentured, auctioned off to the lowest bidder, or let out on contract to the town (3, 16). Town fathers zealously protected their private fortunes as well as the public till. Even if strangers arrived with money and possessions, they were often required to post bond. Deutsch (17) reports on the frequent practice of spiriting away mentally ill paupers and abandoning them in distant towns in order to avoid the burden of support.

The belief that poverty is due to personal weakness, and the willingness to help neighbors but not strangers, have shown remarkable staying power in the U.S. For centuries marked by wars, frontier tragedies, epidemics, repeated crop failures, economic panics, and depressions, these views neatly rationalized decisions to share little with the poor and hapless. In the process, waves of immigrants and black and native Americans were victimized (13, 21). Why was reform so long in coming? Why was the labor movement that pressed European nations toward an institutional role for social welfare still so minuscule and faltering in the U.S.? Thernstrom (39) explains part of the lag by the selective pattern of migration to the U.S. and westward. Those immigrants who suffered the most extreme hardships and had the greatest reason to feel outrageously exploited — the Irish in

*The Task Force for the Reorganization of the Social Services, appointed by the U.S. Department of Health, Education and Welfare in late 1967, brought together a number of proponents of this view. The final report, submitted just before Administrations changed in Washington in 1969, was never published. A brief summary and appraisal appeared in *Social Work* (9).

the 1840s and 1850s, the French Canadians in the 1870s, and the Italians and various East Europeans in later years — came from peasant societies. American tenements might be deathtraps, the work brutal and underpaid, but what they found was a "damn sight better" than what they left behind. Under the best of circumstances, organizing collectivist movements was difficult when people spoke so many different languages and rarely knew any but their own. But having escaped famine and persecution, thousands of immigrants became fanatically loyal Americans, resentful of any criticism of their adopted land, and inevitably an important source of conservatism. In this climate, even investigating and exposing visible shortcomings in economic and social arrangements became "unpatriotic." They invested their energies in improving their personal lot, settled among others of similar ethnic origin, religion, and perspectives, and too often constituted themselves as "super-patriots," impervious to the man-made misery around them, oblivious to the lessons of history, insistent on a static society. All of which added up to something very different from the insights, personal qualities, and public conscience required to organize an effective labor movement in those harsh and unwelcoming years. Different, too, from the resilience, compassion, aspirations, courage, and deep involvement that with all its imperfections had caused America to be perceived as the "promised land" by millions of immigrants.

Then too, Thernstrom adds, those who pressed on toward the West were disproportionately failures in the East. But while horizons beckoned and free land was in the offing, they served as both safety valve and promise. And if nothing else had impeded their development, strong labor unions were not likely in such a highly mobile society. Finally, unlike the politicized labor movements spreading over Europe, protest and organization died aborning when "returning home" in failure was so intolerable to proud people.

It has been observed that in the excessively competitive, success-oriented climate in the U.S., as poor immigrants "made it" into the main stream, they, too, joined the pecking order and perceived the next arrivals as outsiders threatening the purses, lives, and customs of "good, hard-working Americans." The Chinese Exclusion Act of 1882 was an extreme example. The Chinese were lured to America to build our railroads, but when the hardest work was done chauvinistic alarms about the Yellow Peril spread across the land. The result was a series of laws that greatly reduced the influx from China and finally halted it entirely for a generation after 1924 (30). Another illustration is the discriminatory treatment of recent immigrants and blacks in the small Mothers' Pension programs organized in the first quarter of the twentieth century. Blacks were rarely admitted to this elite program for fatherless families, and as late as 1922 social workers reported that "low-type" families like Mexicans, Italians, and Czechoslovakians were seldom helped. If they were, they usually received lower grants than "high-type" Anglo-Saxons (47).

By far the greatest damage was done to black and native Americans who, except for the stream of immigrants, might well have received a warmer welcome in the industrial labor force. Exploited by southern landowners until they were pushed aside by the mechanization of agriculture, and neglected and harassed when they migrated to cities, blacks were poorly educated, often denied the right to vote, and were virtually always consigned to decaying urban and rural slums and dead-end jobs (33, 34). As for native Americans, they became the poorest Americans whether the index used is health, education, income, a sense of belonging, or mastery over their own destiny and culture.*

Virulent racism and the arrogance, indifference, and greed that have characterized our relationships with minorities have all played a key role in keeping the residual conception of social welfare alive. Some progress toward an institutional role has been made in the U.S., but mainly in behalf of workers with a long, steady attachment to the labor force. The great breakthrough came with the Depression of the 1930s, which put enough citizens out of work to assure passage of the Social Security Act in 1935. Two decades later, well after European nations launched comprehensive "cradle-to-grave" programs covering entire populations, the civil rights movement finally forced Americans to confront the issues of unequal rights and maldistributed services. Dr. Martin Luther King, Jr., gave his life attempting to unite his people and all poor Americans in efforts to achieve social justice. Poverty lawyers in the 1960s challenged discrimination on many fronts and won impressive victories. Walter Reuther, before his death in 1970, struggled with indifferent success to persuade unions to join in a genuine war on poverty. In their various ways, all endorsed a broader institutional role for social welfare, and all were keenly aware of the many forces beyond individual control that determined whether people are poor or rich, employed or unemployed, sick or well.

[handwritten margin notes: Institutional — Depression of 1930's put people out of work to assure passage of the SSA 1935. - Dr. Martin Luther King Jr. - Walter Reuther — Civil rights movt. forced Americans to confront the issues of unequal rights & maldistributed services. - Dr. MLK ing tried to achieve social justice - Walter Reuther war on poverty - realized forces beyond indiv. control are responsible for their conditions]

Organizing Principles — Universal or Selective

Social welfare programs are either universal or selective. The key distinction is that the former provide benefits irrespective of income while selective measures are designed solely for the poor (40).

Their relative merits have been debated almost unceasingly for the past two decades. While all industrialized nations rely more heavily on universal measures, few people question that a small selective program is essential to help households with extraordinary or emergency needs and to bring the poorest of the poor up to an acceptable income floor. But the problems seemingly inherent in the selective approach are widely felt to make it inappropriate for large-scale programs. There is no question that universal measures have been far more popular with users, program administrators, and the general public. As differences are reviewed in the following pages, it would be well to keep an open mind about feasible ways of neutralizing or correcting weaknesses so that both approaches might become better social policy instruments.

[handwritten margin notes: Universal benefits no matter income, - industrialized nations more popular | Selective - inappropriate for large-scale programs. | Universal - provide services for poor regardless of their income. Selective - measures designed only for the poor.]

The Eligibility Determination Process. Eligibility is generally much easier, simpler, and less costly to determine in universal than selective measures. Universal programs provide benefits to certain statuses or groups of people, like retired, disabled, or unemployed workers, survivors of deceased workers, veterans, children under sixteen years of age, workers injured on the job, or miners with black lung disease. For the most part, so long as beneficiary groups can be defined precisely in the parent legislation, verifying membership in the group is a fairly straightforward task. Age, of course, is the simplest criterion. This is one reason why family allowances cost so little to administer. But death of a wage earner, loss of a job, and retirement as criteria are usually close seconds. Even if people retire from regular jobs and work elsewhere for a while, "retirement tests"

[handwritten margin notes: Universal provide benefits - Age criterion why family allowances cost so little to administer]

---

*In recent years the reorganization and improvement of medical care have brought about significant reductions in infant mortality rates among native Americans.

can prescribe earnings levels or maximum hours of work that distinguish the "truly retired" (7). In the U.S., determining occupational disability often causes headaches, primarily because so many actors become involved, including doctors, state vocational rehabilitation agencies, lawyers, and program administrators. But this difficulty cuts across both selective and universal measures and has no bearing on programmatic differences between the two.

Conversely, determining eligibility for selective benefits is complex, time-consuming, abrasive, error-prone, and expensive. First, poverty must be defined. Then methods must be devised for separating the poor from the nonpoor. Together, these steps are often referred to as the "means test."

Defining poverty may sound like a simple task, but it rarely proves to be, since it always involves politically sensitive and emotionally laden judgments about the relative needs of poor families and public treasuries. The first step in the process is to set upper limits on household assets and current income. Historically, these have usually been set as low as possible to make certain that families who qualify are indeed impoverished.

Few subjects are more vexatious than assets tests. Traditionally, welfare investigators were required to search for every conceivable resource. In fixing the value of resources, arguments proliferated over whether the proper reference was the original price, current value, or equity (28, 29, 32). After settling this issue, appraisers often had to be consulted to fix the exact value. As time passed, some assets like homegrown produce, small savings accounts for a child's education, burial lots, and owner-occupied homes were partly or wholly disregarded. In 1981, in addition to settling on equity value as the appropriate measure, the list of exempt assets was narrowed in AFDC to include only an owner-occupied home, burial lots and funeral arrangements up to $1,500, essential personal belongings and household furnishings of "limited value," and an automobile with an equity value no higher than $1,500. Simultaneously, the family ceiling for nonexempt assets was dropped from $1,500 to $1,000 — or less if states preferred. In some situations a grace period was allowed for the sale of excess property like livestock for farm families or a reliable car for working mothers with no access to public transportation. Otherwise, when limits were exceeded, applications were summarily denied, even though disposing of the property often greatly increased the risk of long-term dependency.

The same process must be repeated in sorting out whether family income is within bounds. Most AFDC families have very little, but for those who have other income, the most likely sources are earnings and child support payments from absent fathers. During the 1960s, when ending poverty was a national objective, federal law was amended to require states to exempt a share of earnings sufficient to cover work expenses, including child day care, and a cash work incentive amounting to about a third of earnings. Also, states were required to disregard the earnings of children who were full-time students, on the theory that their money was essential for current and future school expenses. This package of disregards made work affordable for more welfare families and resulted in more consistent work patterns (8). Child support payments were treated in a similar spirit. When only one of several children in a family, for instance, received support money, it could be disregarded so long as the child was not included in the AFDC application. Still another pitfall for poor families was outlawed in the 1960s: assumed income policies, which permitted welfare agencies to assume that all *expected* income actually arrived, as with child support, or later during the 1970s the low-wage earner's tax credit.

When the Reagan Administration took office, it soon became apparent that the liberalized policies of the 1960s were slated for repeal or retrenchment. Although some of the resulting cutbacks were modified in 1984, the main thrust survives. Now all children in the home must be included in the AFDC application, and only fifty dollars of child support a month can be disregarded. As for earnings and smaller disregards, some were eliminated, others were reduced, and a few crucial ones were redefined as temporary, not permanent, exemptions.* In the process, a gross income ceiling representing a percentage of the state's welfare standard was set so low as to disqualify most families with a full-time worker, and "assumed income" policies were reinstated.

Other complications face welfare applicants who live with relatives defined as "liable" or "responsible" for family support by welfare law (38). In this situation, *all* household assets and household income must fall below welfare ceilings in order for any member or members to qualify for public aid. Both are subject to the usual disregards, but everything left over is assumed to be available to the entire household — at welfare standards. Whole kinship networks have been impoverished by provisions of this kind over the centuries. Young, ambitious, striving members are particularly vulnerable. Money set aside for college is suddenly confiscated, in effect, by welfare agencies for family support. To some Americans, this is as it should be: it is better for entire families to be poor than for family bonds and responsibilities to be overlooked or "spurned." In the 1960s, a consensus of citizens disagreed with the proposition that this was good anti-poverty policy, let alone good family policy. But the Reagan Administration would have us believe the mood has changed. In this connection, it is significant that *welfare* concepts of liability do not necessarily coincide with those in the General Statutes of the various states. When the two are not congruent, welfare may be denied on the assumption that a "responsible" relative will support the children; but the relative in question may not be sued for nonsupport.

Since World War II at least, most modern nations, including belatedly the U.S., progressively narrowed the list of liable relatives to include only (1) natural and adoptive parents for their minor children — unless the latter were "emancipated" — and (2) spouses for each other. In 1981, federal law reversed its direction. Now when AFDC applications are made in behalf of children, their stepparents, "blood-related" siblings (including half siblings), and grandparents are liable when they share a home with the young family. This means in the first instance that welfare agencies must hold these relatives liable, even if the states in which they reside do not. By the same token, such policies also expand the income pool that must fall below welfare ceilings. The inclusion of half siblings has the anomalous result of diverting court-ordered support from the intended child to the entire household. The inclusion of grandparents is the Administration's answer, apparently, to teenage pregnancy. Introducing this new social control means that young mothers may no longer apply for aid in behalf of themselves and their children; only the teenagers' parents may do so. Nor may teenagers move from home in order to qualify for AFDC. Infusing selective measures with social controls is an old habit, which sociologists usually find is more successful at spreading poverty than changing behavior.

---

*For current information regarding federal regulations, state plans, standards of need, maximum money payments, and federal reimbursement rates, see the federal government's yearly publication, *Characteristics of State Plans for Aid to Families with Dependent Children* (46).

Finally, another Administration cost-saving device was to lower the upper age limit of eligibility for AFDC. Raised from eighteen to twenty-one during the 1960s when older children were full-time students, it was cut back to eighteen unless school children were confidently expected to complete a course of study by their nineteenth birthday. Since many poor children are two years behind normal grade placement by their high school years, this means that more will leave before graduating. This is one reason for the surge in school dropout rates in many large cities.

While the Reagan policy shifts have been illustrated by referring to AFDC, they have been extended, whenever relevant, to all selective programs, including higher educational grants and loans to low-income students, food stamps, school lunches, and so forth.

Finally, pervading the administration of selective programs is a ubiquitous fear of fraud, which generates horrendously detailed procedures for verifying everything. The paper work itself is staggering, and the procedural labyrinth invites high error rates.* But while Americans continue to distrust the poor, the price will have to be paid, both in errors and in hard cash. Unfortunately, human nature being what it is, no measures yet devised succeed in totally eliminating fraud—in welfare, tax systems, or private business.† In welfare, the typical pattern involves many charges of fraud for very small sums and a fair number of dismissals for want of evidence. A case in point occurred in 1977 when former Secretary of the U.S. Department of Health, Education, and Welfare (HEW), Joseph Califano, proclaimed a "crackdown on welfare cheats." Ten months later he happily announced the names of fifteen current or former HEW employees who had been indicted on felony charges. After another ten months it was revealed—but not by the Secretary or HEW—that five cases had been dismissed and in four the charges were reduced to misdemeanors. Federal judges were unimpressed with government cases against the remaining six women who pled guilty to felonies. Only $2,000 repayment was ordered for the entire group (23). As usual in situations of this kind, the cost incurred in the process was not made public. Often it is never computed. But it would certainly far exceed $2,000 if investigative, administrative, and court costs are taken into account.

Benefit Structures. Universal programs pay standardized benefits that are spelled out precisely in the parent legislation. This means that in social security, for instance, everyone earning the same amount, working the same number of years, and retiring at the same time receives the same benefits. If programs pay dependents' allowances, these, too, are standardized. This means that benefits are calculated by computers in seconds.

Selective benefits are less standardized and far less predictable. In SSI and food stamps, "standards of need" (as income ceilings are usually called in public aid) are set and updated by the federal government. For AFDC this is a state prerogative. Standards supposedly reflect what officials regard as the cost of essential maintenance items for different-sized families. Paradoxically, having set standards, about three fifths of the states

---

*By far the most accurate account of the process is found in Edgar May's Pulitzer prize-winning book (31) on public welfare.

†The IRS estimates that in 1981, $82 billion was lost in tax revenues because of the underreporting of income. By 1985 it was expected the figure would exceed $100 billion (14). Employees are reported to steal about $3 billion of their employers' property yearly (20). The rising flood of evidence of corporate crime—against stockholders, consumers, and government—also confirms that the inclination to commit fraud is no respecter of income levels.

appropriate too little money to meet them. This, in turn, gives rise to "maximum money payments," which become the effective income ceiling.

In 1985 maximum AFDC payments for a mother with two children varied from $96 in Mississippi (25 per cent of the state standard) to $555 in California. Thirteen states paid less than $250; five paid over $500. But no one can predict how long payment levels will remain constant, a fact of life that makes family budgeting very difficult for the poor.

A special problem plagues working mothers of AFDC today— "retrospective budgeting." First mandated in 1981,* this budgeting method requires welfare agencies to base money grants on family needs and financial circumstances during the *previous* month, not the *current* month. Inevitably, this makes for a very slow response to family crises, which abound in the lives of the poor. A case illustration will show how this budgeting approach works.

> Mrs. Brown, with two elementary school children, earned enough to meet two thirds of the family's needs. Their AFDC check made up the balance. She was laid off, with no advance notice, in early January, and called the welfare agency the next day. But her welfare check could not be increased to reflect this midwinter crisis until the family had survived on her current AFDC check and a few days' pay for a full month. Only then did the loss of earnings signal the need for a higher AFDC grant.

Incidentally, like all families with earnings, Mrs. Brown must file a monthly report with the welfare agency; if she forgets to do so, her grant will be discontinued.

Treatment of Beneficiaries. Universal programs like social security and public employee pensions have earned a far better reputation for courteous, fair, and thoughtful treatment of recipients and the general public. In part this reflects the greater respect for "earned" benefits than for the "dole," a distinction that was vigorously reinforced by social security enthusiasts.†

But there is apparently a great deal more to be said for programs that serve all income classes. With a mix of recipients, sheer numbers tend to be larger which makes for a larger concerned public, including a fair proportion with well-developed instrumental skills that help them negotiate successfully with government bureaucracies. Often, too, recipients represent natural groups that organize around common interests—like the countless organizations of retired people or the labor unions, which play such strategic roles in bringing about legislative and administrative reforms in social security. The mere fact that when recipients represent a broad population spectrum, a higher share will have long-established reading habits or be more likely to read, speak, and comprehend English, gives them added power. Between having more complex programs to master and having less education, the poor are signally handicapped in confronting government bureaucracies. All of these factors contribute to the dismal conclusion, well documented over the years, that programs for the poor soon become poor programs.

---

*It applied to the entire caseload until late 1984.

†Ozawa (35) and widespread informal reports suggest that since the Social Security Administration became responsible for the means-tested SSI program, the favorable image is becoming somewhat tarnished.

10

Economic Efficiency. Many economists prefer the selective approach because of its greater *economic efficiency*. This term refers to the share of program costs that goes directly to poor households (10). Unless administrative expenses are exorbitant, as was sometimes true in earlier years when welfare agencies hired special investigators to "stake out" the homes of suspect families for weeks on end, programs designed exclusively for the poor are always more economically efficient than those extending over all income classes.

Yet universal measures have had far more impact on poverty rates in the U.S. than selective programs. One reason is that, thriving better, they can afford higher benefits, thereby lifting more households out of poverty and preventing millions of others from sinking below poverty levels. In this connection, it should be kept in mind that in choosing groups to be targeted by universal cash transfers, planners have concentrated on poverty-prone segments like retired, disabled, or unemployed workers, and widows and orphans, whose median incomes tend to be very modest. Certainly, the very wealthy are few and far between. All of this means that if the goal is to reduce poverty rates, doubts have to be raised about measuring economic efficiency solely in terms of the share of program expenditures going yearly into the pockets of the poor. At least as important is the proportion of eligible people who move or stay out of poverty over one, five, or ten years *because of each program*. It is fairly clear by now that less "economically efficient" universal programs that consistently prosper and win friends have far more impact on both the level and distribution of poverty than highly "efficient" but constantly threatened selective measures that do little but help some of the poor become somewhat less poor. For this and many other reasons, the search continues for universal solutions to the "welfare mess" (19).

The Role of Government in Redistributing Income

Many people seem to believe that the only direction in which government redistributes income is downward, from the rich and middle class to the poor. Some years back, Titmuss (42) of England tried to correct this misconception. His efforts resulted in a tripartite analysis of social policy, designed to demonstrate how governments actually affect the distribution and redistribution of household income. He identified three types of "welfare": fiscal, occupational, and public. Each is financed in different ways, which greatly affects their relative visibility; and their primary beneficiaries come from different income classes.

Fiscal Welfare. This package consists of tax exemptions, deductions, and credits as well as special tax treatment of certain types of income like capital gains, all of which are particularly helpful to upper-income households. Titmuss points out that whether income redistribution is achieved by tax policy — commonly referred to as "tax expenditures" in this context — or by "public expenditures" is simply a matter of national style. If $1,000 is conserved by one family through tax policy while $1,000 is received by another family from AFDC, both families are equally beneficiaries of government policy. They both have $1,000 more to spend and they both cause the public treasury to be $1,000 poorer (1, 37). Despite their equivalence in this regard, families receiving "welfare" through the tax system get the better bargain by far since tax shelters are relatively

invisible as compared with AFDC grants, and exploiting all possible tax loopholes elicits very different responses from those elicited by being on welfare. Then, too, once incorporated into tax law, loopholes may remain forever; but public expenditures are reviewed and appropriated yearly (4).

Identifying the fiscal welfare package soon led others to point out a host of government policies that redistribute income, although not necessarily or ostensibly as a primary objective (12, 36). Futurist Henderson (22) observes that both government action and government inaction affect the distribution of pretax household income. Her list includes government subsidies to the sugar and tobacco industries, farmers, airlines, and so on, and the failure of our government (unlike its European counterparts) to curb the propensity of large corporations for deploying facilities and resources to cheaper labor markets and lower-taxing jurisdictions. Governments also have a marked effect, she notes, on employment and unemployment patterns that determine both initial distribution and redistribution of income. Government purchasing decisions, the habit of "bailing out" some but not all hard-pressed industries, defense contracts, subsidized research, and protective tariffs are other cases in point. The current trend to cut back civil service employees by contracting with private firms to carry out long-standing government functions is another example.*

While the total redistributional impact of all such policies has never been determined, there is no disagreement that they funnel money primarily toward the well-to-do. A 1975 study of federal subsidies, which then totalled some $96.1 billion, concluded that "they redistribute money to the affluent and in too many cases their costs far exceed their benefit to society as a whole" (44). Using an equivalent definition, the 1984 federal budget listed "tax expenditures" of $388.4 billion, $100 billion of which represented tax loopholes, which could be "closed to good advantage," as Joseph Pechman (4), well-known economist at the Brookings Institution commented, "if there were a will to do so." Instead, they have remained intact or increased yearly — although lawmakers are now determined to reform the tax code.

Occupational Welfare. This second part of Titmuss's tripartite scheme includes a long list of fringe benefits workers qualify for as a result of their occupational status. These comprise the largest share of income distributed through social welfare programs. The chief beneficiaries are not the chronically poor or the occasionally employed but regularly employed workers and their families. In the "occupational welfare" system, benefits rise with earnings. Employed millionaires pile up infinitely larger pensions than average workers. The list of benefits will sound familiar:

- social security (cash benefits and Medicare).
- unemployment compensation.
- workers' compensation (cash benefits and medical care).
- public and private employee pensions and health insurance.
- veterans' pensions and other benefits.
- railroad retirement benefits.
- sick and vacation pay.
- low-cost meals in employer's cafeteria.

*The most conspicuous losers in this instance may well be blacks since they have been more heavily represented in the government labor force than in the reasonably well paid commercial labor force.

- credit unions.
- group life insurance.
- dental and vision insurance.
- related benefits like entertainment expenses, use of company automobiles and airplanes, free tuition at some universities for professors and their families, sabbatical leaves, and free or low-cost employer-sponsored cultural and athletic events.*

This generous group of fringe benefits underscores the importance of steady work and the hardship of unemployment. Pensions grow in value with the length of employment, whereas unemployment causes many benefits to stop entirely and interrupt "coverage" in others, thus ending health insurance and reducing delayed benefits like retirement pensions. In nations where full employment is the goal and is usually achieved, attaching so many benefits to the workplace may make good sense and reflect widely shared views of social justice. But in the U.S., where millions of workers have been unemployed every year since World War II, deploying resources so heavily in this direction can only enhance the poverty and alienation of groups who cannot work, cannot find work, or are always among the "first fired and last hired." One obvious way to correct the skewed impact of government measures that redistribute income, intentionally or not, is to include in the social welfare package some universal, non-work-related cash benefits, like children's and youth allowances or flat old age pensions as in Canada.

Public Welfare. Finally, the third sector of Titmuss's scheme consists of the bundle of selective programs providing cash grants and in-kind benefits like food stamps and social services to the poor. For years they have commanded less than one fifth of social welfare expenditures in the U.S. and a much smaller share of the total cost of government policies that redistribute income. In the interest of equity and social justice, this fact deserves far more attention than it receives.

*Only part of this group is reflected in social welfare expenditures, but all are financed or subsidized by public funds.

References

1. Aaron, Henry J. "Tax Exemptions—the Artful Dodge." *Trans-action,* **6** (March 1969), pp. 4–6.
2. ———. *Why is Welfare So Hard to Reform?* Washington, D.C.: Brookings Institution, 1973.
3. Abbott, Grace. *The Child and the State.* Chicago: University of Chicago Press, 1938, Vol. 1, Pt. 3.
4. Alperovitz, Gar and Jeff Faux. *Rebuilding America.* New York: Pantheon Books, 1984, p. 123.
5. Asbury, Herbert. *The Gangs of New York: an Informal History of the Underworld.* New York: Alfred A. Knopf, Inc., 1927, pp. 1–20.
6. Axinn, June and Herman Levin. *Social Welfare: A History of the American Response to Need.* New York: Harper & Row, Publishers, 1975, pp. 39–45.
7. Ball, Robert M. *Social Security Today and Tomorrow.* New York: Columbia University Press, 1978, p. 269.

8. Bell, Winifred. "Relatives' Responsibility: A Problem in Social Policy." *Social Work,* **12** (January 1967), pp. 32–39.

9. ———. "Services to People: Appraisal of the Task Force on Reorganizing the Social Services." *Social Work,* **15** (July 1970), pp. 5–12.

10. ——— and Dennis M. Bushe. "The Economic Efficiency of AFDC." *Social Service Review,* **49** (June 1975), pp. 175–190.

11. ——— and Dennis M. Bushe. *Neglecting the Many, Helping the Few: The Impact of the 1967 AFDC Work Incentives.* New York University, Center for Studies in Income Maintenance Policy, 1975.

12. ———, Robert Lekachman, and Alvin L. Schorr. *Public Policy and Income Distribution.* New York: New York University, Center for Studies in Income Maintenance Policy, 1974.

13. Billingsley, Andrew and Jeanne M. Giovannoni. *Children of the Storm: Black Children and American Child Welfare.* New York: Harcourt Brace Jovanovich, Inc., 1972, passim.

14. Bradley, Bill. *The Fair Tax.* New York: Pocket Books, 1984, pp. 12–13.

15. Brooks, Van Wyck. *America's Coming of Age.* New York: B. W. Huebsch, 1915, pp. 7, 9.

16. Coll, Blanche D. "Public Assistance in the United States: Colonial Times to 1860." In E. W. Martin, Ed., *Comparative Development in Social Welfare.* London: George Allen & Unwin, Ltd., 1972, pp. 128–158.

17. Deutsch, Albert. *The Mentally Ill in America.* Garden City, N.J.: Doubleday, Doran & Co., 1938, pp. 44–45.

18. Frankel, Charles. "The Welfare State: Postscripts and Prelude." In Charles I. Schottland, Ed., *The Welfare State.* New York: Harper & Row, Publishers, 1967, pp. 207–214.

19. Garfinkel, Irwin. "What's Wrong with Welfare?" *Social Work,* **23** (May 1978), pp. 185–191.

20. Goode, William J. *The Celebration of Heroes — Prestige as a Control System.* Berkeley: University of California Press, 1978, p. 250.

21. Handlin, Oscar. *The Uprooted.* Boston: Little, Brown & Co., 1951.

22. Henderson, Hazel. *Creating Alternative Futures: The End of Economics.* New York: Berkley Publishing Co., 1978, pp. 93–105.

23. Hendricks, Evan. "How Not to Catch Welfare Cheats." *Washington Post,* July 8, 1979.

24. Kahn, Alfred J. *Social Policy and Social Services,* 2d ed. New York: Random House, Inc., 1978, pp. 11–32.

25. ———. Ed. *Issues in American Social Work.* New York: Columbia University Press, 1959, Ch. 1.

26. ——— and Sheila B. Kamerman. *Not for the Poor Alone: European Social Services.* New York: Harper & Row, Publishers, 1977, pp. 171–179.

27. Kammen, Michael. Ed. *The Contrapuntal Civilization: Essays Toward a New Understanding of the American Experience.* New York: Thomas Y. Crowell Co., 1971, pp. 3–30.

28. Lurie, Irene. "Income, Asset and Work Tests in Transfer Programs for Able-Bodied, Nonaged Individuals." In Institute for Research on Poverty, *The Treatment of Assets and Income from Assets in Income Conditioned Government Benefit Programs.* Washington, D.C.: Federal Council on the Aging, 1977, pp. 52–90.

29. MacDonald, Maurice. *Food, Stamps, and Income Maintenance.* New York: Academic Press, Inc., 1977, pp. 27–38.

30. Marden, Charles F. and Gladys Meyer. *Minorities in American Society,* 5th ed. New York: D. Van Nostrand Co., 1978, p. 280.

31. May, Edgar. *The Wasted Americans.* New York: Harper & Row, Publishers, 1965, Ch. 6.

32. Moon, Marilyn. "The Treatment of Assets in Cash Benefit Programs for the Aged and Disabled." In Institute for Research on Poverty. *The Treatment of Assets and Income from Assets in Income-Conditioned Government Benefit Programs.* Washington, D.C.: Federal Council on the Aging, 1977, pp. 15–51.

33. Myrdal, Gunnar. *An American Dilemma: The Negro Problem and Modern Democracy,* rev. ed. New York: Harper & Row, Publishers, 1962, pp. 205–219.

34. Newman, Dorothy, et al. *Protest, Politics, and Prosperity: Black Americans and White Institutions, 1940–1975*. New York: Pantheon Books, 1978.

35. Ozawa, Martha. "SSI: Progress or Retreat?" *Public Welfare,* **32** (Spring 1974), pp. 33–40.

36. Rein, Martin. "Equality and Social Policy." *Social Service Review,* **51** (December 1977), pp. 565–587.

37. Surrey, Stanley S. "Federal Income Tax Reform: The Varied Approaches Necessary to Replace Tax Expenditures with Direct Government Assistance." *Harvard Law Review,* **84** (1970), pp. 352–408.

38. tenBroek, Jacobus. "California's Dual System of Family Law: Its Origin, Development, and Present Status." *Stanford Law Review,* **16** (January, July 1970), passim.

39. Thernstrom, Stephan. "Urbanization, Migration, and Social Mobility." In Barton J. Bernstein, Ed., *Towards a New Past: Dissenting Essays in American History*. New York: Random House, Inc., 1978, pp. 158–175.

40. Titmuss, Richard M. *Commitment to Welfare,* 2d ed. London: George Allen & Unwin, Ltd., 1976, pp. 113–123, 188–199.

41. ———. *Essays on "the Welfare State,"* 2d ed. London: George Allen & Unwin, Ltd., 1963, pp. 215–243.

42. ———. "The Role of Redistribution in Social Policy." *Social Security Bulletin,* **28** (June 1965), pp. 14–32.

43. Trattner, Walter I. *From Poor Law to Welfare State,* 2d ed. New York: The Free Press, 1979, pp. 18–19.

44. U.S. Congress, Joint Economic Committee. *Federal Subsidy Programs.* Staff Study prepared for the use of the Subcommittee on Priorities and Economy in Government. Washington, D.C.: U.S. Government Printing Office, 1974, pp. 1–5.

45. U.S. Department of Health, Education, and Welfare. "Services for People." Report of the Task Force on the Reorganization of the Social Services. Mimeographed. Washington, D.C.: Office of the Secretary, 1978.

46. U.S. Department of Health and Human Services. *Characteristics of State Plans for Aid to Families With Dependent Children.* Washington, D.C.: U.S. Government Printing Office, 1985.

47. U.S. Department of Labor. *Proceedings of Conference on Mothers' Pensions,* Providence, Rhode Island, June 28, 1922. Children's Bureau Publication #109. Washington, D.C.: U.S. Government Printing Office, 1922, p. 2.

48. Wilensky, Harold L. and Charles N. Lebeaux. "Conceptions of Social Welfare." In Paul E. Weinberger, Ed., *Perspectives on Social Welfare,* 2d. ed. New York: Macmillan Publishing Co., Inc., 1974, pp. 23–30.

Social Control:
A Rationale for Social Welfare
Charles D. Cowger
Charles R. Atherton

From a functional sociological perspective social control is the primary function of social welfare. Is this a legitimate rationale or an inappropriate one? Social workers have tended to view it as inappropriate. Part of the problem lies in the term *social control*, which to many has become equated with the arbitrary exercise of power by an elitist group. This view is unfortunate because, sociologically, it does not necessarily have this meaning. An obvious solution is to use a less loaded term. Parsons, for example, uses "boundary maintenance," but such semantic substitution avoids the issue.[1]

As a sociological term, *social control* refers to those processes in a society that support a level of social cohesiveness sufficient for the survival of the society as a recognizable functional unit.[2] Basically, social control takes three forms:

- *Socialization.* As children grow, the family, the educational system, and the religious institutions in the society teach them the ways of their culture. The norms or standards that are inculcated help regulate social behavior within culturally desirable patterns.
- *Direct behavior control.* The formal laws of the society backed by the police power of the state define and enforce the limits of behavior.
- *Resocialization.* Social welfare agencies, mental health facilities, and other psychological and social services help solve social problems for those having difficulty in coping with life situations.

Although it is possible to separate these three forms of social control for the purpose of analysis, they are closely intertwined. Each has preventive as well as corrective aspects.

MISGIVINGS OF SOCIAL WORKERS
Because of their orientation to humanistic values, social workers may view social control as antithetical to social work practice although they must concede that social control is a necessary and important element of any culture. In contemporary articles in a recent issue of *The Humanist,* Callahan and Kurtz agree that the advances of science have created ethical problems that need normative answers.[3] Both are disturbed by the lack of clear ethical guidelines on which to base decisions. Callahan calls for a reexamination of normative ethics and even public morality. Kurtz fears public morality since it could lead to tyranny, but he does not deny the need for some form of moral or normative order. At some point, normative boundaries are necessary and social control must exist to provide coherence and consistence in a society.

In his presidential address to the American Psychological Association, Clark—hardly a reactionary—called as follows for more emphasis on control:

> The critical questions for a contemporary science of psychology and for other behavioral sciences are: What are their contributions to the understanding and control of the behavior of human beings? How can the knowledge, the insights, and the related technology contribute directly or indirectly to effectiveness of individual human beings, to stability in human society, and increase the chances of survival of the human species?[4]

Although social control is inherent in organized social life and is necessary if a society is to survive, it does not follow that any specific control mechanism is part of the process. Different societies go about the business of maintaining their boundaries in characteristic ways. No society has absolute boundaries. Even totalitarian societies allow some leeway. It is true that the limits in a totalitarian society are much more narrow, but such a society often plays a reasonably fair game within its rules and may provide significant "payoff" for its citizens. Failing to do so requires an enormous investment in repression, which in the long run of history has been counterproductive. Easton's comments on the necessity of government support this position:

> Whatever the form of government it must also possess some moral authority and be acceptable either to a majority of the people or to a minority that commands enough moral or material resources to enable it to coerce the majority. No government, whether by one man or by many, can survive without some support and acceptance.
>
> A government, to ensure its acceptance by any of the people, cannot behave in an arbitrary and unpredictable manner. It must make clear what its policy is in matters of daily concern to the people. This need for certainty is satisfied by the establishment of law, which explains to the people what is expected of them and decrees penalties for the behavior it defines as unacceptable. Law is essentially the regulation of the public behavior of human beings in an organized society and it is enforced by the power of the government as long as the government is able to maintain its authority.[5]

Such discussion regarding the regulation of behavior is not characteristic of social work. Social workers do not like to entertain the idea of social demands on behavior. Nor do they like to think that their work is part of a process to produce social competence for the good of the society. Nevertheless, whenever a social worker, parent, educator, physician—anyone—engages in an activity to modify or set boundaries on human conduct according to valued norms, that person is engaging in social control. When, for example, a mother teaches a child manners, arithmetic, or health habits, she is engaging in social control as she passes on through the socialization-education process a set of rules or values that are part of our civilization.

Psychotherapy is a form of social control to the extent that it encourages a patient to give up one set of behaviors (for example, delusions, compulsions) for another set considered more appropriate in the society. Family counseling is a form of social control in that it encourages family members to temper certain interactions that are judged faulty in favor of more normative behavior that will enable them to get along with each other with less friction and pain. When social workers assist clients to find a job, apply for public aid, or manage the use of alcohol or other drugs, they are engaging in the process of social control. The objective in all these instances is to enable clients to get along better within the social order.

The concept of social action is not antithetical to this rationale of social welfare. Social action involves strategies and tactics that individuals or groups in society may undertake to change norms. When people embark on social action, they are not denying the reality of normative behavior. Those who seek to change society (with the exception of anarchists) do not seek to end all norms, but to substitute different ones.

CRITICISM OF SOCIAL CONTROL

Miller has argued that, to protect the dignity of man, social casework should deal only with the voluntary client.[6] He is markedly uncomfortable with the control aspects of practice in child welfare and corrections.

Piven and Cloward criticize the control aspects of public assistance as follows:

> Historical evidence suggests that relief arrangements are initiated or expanded during the occasional outbreaks of civil disorder produced by mass unemployment, and are then abolished or contracted when political stability is restored. We shall argue that expansive relief policies are designed to mute civil disorder, and restrictive ones to reinforce work norms. In other words, relief policies are cyclical—liberal or restrictive depending on the problems of regulation in the larger society with which government must contend.[7]

To Piven and Cloward, the use of public welfare to dampen civil disorder is questionable social policy.

Gyarfas questions using the knowledge of social science in social work practice. She holds that there is a possibility, particularly in behaviorism, that the use of such knowledge would limit individual freedom and self-determination. However, her argument for the "self-determined client" asks for social control over certain processes that she considers inimical to the interests of citizens and indirectly inimical to society.[8]

Confusion arises in that these writers actually support social control as legitimate while they are seemingly writing *against* the idea of control. They do not maintain that social control is objectionable, but rather they protest who is doing the controlling and according to what value system.

In his stance of advocacy, Miller suggests that social workers should influence society to conform to certain moral norms that he considers of value. He contends that social workers should challenge social institutions on behalf of clients, should try to persuade institutions to change the rules—but change to another set of rules, not to a system of no rules.[9]

Piven and Cloward urge that society deal with the problem of poverty. They espouse social action designed to get society to live up to certain values. They insist that harmful deviance from these values (deviance by institutions, but still deviance) should be controlled so that the poor are not excluded. In their view, excluding the poor from equal access to the benefits of society results in harmful consequences to the society as well as to the poor.[10]

Miller, Piven and Cloward, and Gyarfas do not reject social control as such. They do reject one set of rules or values in favor of others. They prefer that society live up to the values that they themselves espouse, and they naturally want these values to prevail. They propose that the moral authority of government and the force of law support the values they promote. In supporting justice—ephemeral as this concept is—over special privilege, these writers are engaging in social control.

WHO DECIDES VALUES?

The real issue, then, is not whether social workers engage in social control. Clearly they are engaging in it, as the term is defined sociologically. The questions are to decide what values to support and how to support them.

Who decides which behaviors are the norm? How do social workers guard against the danger that an elite will decide what behavior is to be controlled? These questions are not affected by defining social welfare in the context of social control. They exist now as legitimate concerns regardless of how social welfare and social work are defined.

Callahan's concern for normative ethics grows out of his observations of the variety of bases on which scientists and physicians make ethical decisions. His discussion that follows is important:

A number of schools of popular ethical thought can be distinguished. In the "religious" school, ethical decisions are made out of the context of a tradition of religious morality. If asked for a reason why he thinks some particular act is "right" or "good," a person in this school is likely to reply, "because I am a Christian," or "because I am an Orthodox Jew," and so on. The "emotive" school believes that certain acts are right or wrong because they "feel" they are. "Gut reactions" are taken to be normative. The "conventionalist" judges acts to be right or wrong on the basis of accepted conventions or mores. An acceptable reason for a certain type of behavior is, for instance, because "that's what everyone does," or "it's always been done that way." Another school might be called "empirical conventionalism," which relies on the results of public opinion surveys. If a majority of persons thinks something is right, then it must be right. "Simple utilitarians" believe that acts are good because they are conducive to the greatest good for the greatest number.

If these are representative of the kinds of reasons given for personal behavior, another related cluster of schools can be found to classify judgments about public behavior and social conflicts. For example, the "barefoot civil liberties" school allows everyone to be free to "do his own thing" or to "make up his own mind." It is not necessary for people to justify their conduct; it is enough if they are honest, sincere, or authentic. Another school, "gross majoritarianism," judges public acts and laws as right if they command majority support. If it is legal, then it must be morally acceptable. Still another criterion of judgment is "primitive cost-benefit analysis," which says that if the public will save x dollars by carrying out a certain policy, then that must be the ethically correct policy.

Finally, there are some expressions that are variants of "professional ethics"; "That's not our responsibility"; "If we don't do it, then someone else will"; "I'm not a philosopher or theologian"; "That's a political (or ethical, or social, or theological) question." [11]

Callahan traces the rise of this diversity to the liberal movements of the past—"individualism, libertarianism, affluence and all forms of liberation." He offers the following recommendation:

In handling the ethical problem of the life sciences, it is quite possible that the democratic political method is the best we have and all that we should aspire to. It does provide a procedure for resolving public disputes and, together with the courts, ways of adjudicating conflicting values. If that is the case, then the best path to follow would be to attempt to maximize public information and debate, submit vexing issues to the courts and legislators, and hope for the best. [12]

Kurtz recognizes the diversity of ethical positions and echoes Callahan's faith in the democratic process. He rejects, as follows, normative decisions made by various categories of the elite, but renders his insistence on democracy less convincing by putting his trust in other elitists:

I would resist entrusting our destiny to a group of behavioral scientists, Pentagon experts, party bureaucrats, or philosopher kings who claim to know what is best for individuals without their consent. . . .
In the last analysis the best guarantee against abuse [of sciences] is full initial discussion by the community of scientists and the educated public. [13]

Clark has perhaps the most startling answer to the question of who decides and who ought to decide normative behaviors. His conclusion, recommendation, and explanation of his position, are as follows:

It is a fact that a few men in the leadership position in the industrialized nations of the world now have the power to determine among themselves, through collaboration or competition, the survival or extinction of human civilization. . . .
Given these contemporary facts, it would seem logical that a requirement imposed on all power-controlling leaders—and those who aspire to such leadership—would be that they accept and use the earliest perfected form of psychotechnological, biochemical intervention which would assure their positive use of power and reduce or block the possibility of their using power destructively. . . .
In medicine, physical diseases are controlled through medication. Medicines are prescribed by doctors to help the body

overcome the detrimental effects of bacteria or viruses—or to help the organism restore that balance of internal biochemical environment necessary for health and effectiveness. Medicines are not only used to treat the diseases of individuals, but are also used preventively in the form of vaccines. All medicines are drugs—and all drugs used therapeutically are forms of intervention to influence and control the natural processes of disease. Selective and appropriate medication to assure psychological health and moral integrity is now imperative for the survival of human society. [14]

Clark does not say how he would persuade the leaders who control power to try his remedy. Fortunately for human society it is unlikely that his recommendation will be carried out. Any power strong enough to force us to take our medicine would not need to give it.

A provocative forecast for the future is offered by Bell, chairman of the Commission on the Year 2000 of the American Academy of Arts and Sciences. He expects the emergence of a "knowledge class" composed of scientific, technological, administrative, and cultural professionals as the highest and most powerful class in the post-industrial society. He foresees the following complexities with respect to power in determining normative behavior:

If one turns, then, to the societal structure of the post-industrial society . . . two conclusions are evident. First, the major class of the emerging new society is primarily a professional class, based on knowledge rather than property. But second, the control system of the society is lodged not in a successor-occupational class but in the political order, and the question of who manages the political order is an open one. [15]

Bell thinks that (1) contending political parties, (2) various mobilized groups such as labor unions, ethnic minorities and the poor; and (3) elites in science, the academic world, business, and the military will make the decision through contest and conflict in the political arena.

What is normative? Clearly, the question is still open. The strong hopes for its resolution expressed by Callahan, Kurtz, and Clark indicate that this is an uncomfortable situation. The diversity of their proposals shows that it cannot be easily resolved. Bell's forecast of a fluid pluralism, if correct, does not suggest any immediate relief.

ACCOUNTABILITY

In exploring social control as an explicit rationale for social services, one is confronted with this problem: What is the appropriate relationship between the social services and society? To whom are the providers of social services accountable?

The authors' answer is that those who provide social services are accountable to their constituency—the legislators, the donors and the citizens who support agencies and programs, and the consumers who use the services. The providers of services are responsible for helping people resolve the problems of their lives in ways that permit them to get along better in society. This concept is not revolutionary, nor does it need to be. But as soon as one takes this position one returns to the original theme: The primary function of social welfare is social control. Social workers—and others in the helping professioins—are free, in most societies at least, to define normative behavior compassionately but are less free to espouse values independent of their constituency. The answer to the question "Who decides normative behavior?" is thus answered as best it can be within the framework of the constituency concerned.

Social agencies are funded and chartered to achieve certain ends. Social programs are funded and designed to attain specific objectives. For example, family agencies are expected to strengthen family life. This expectation does not impose such a severe limit that the family agency cannot be innovative or accepting toward changes that have taken place in relations between men and women. However, it is doubtful whether a family agency could continue to operate if the staff decided that elimination of family life was their mission.

What would be the advantages if social workers openly embraced the concept of social control as a primary rationale of social welfare? The authors believe that their constituency would better understand what social workers are trying to do. Social control has more honesty and integrity than the notion that social services are based on simple altruism and good will. It is not enough to tell people that social workers' hearts are pure. People are now asking embarrassing questions about the benefits that social services provide and for whom they are provided. No longer are social workers automatically seen as the "good guys in the white hats."

In today's cynical society, altruistic rationales are not marketable. Good intentions are not enough to earn sanction for social welfare programs. Dependence on altruistic rationales rather than concrete contributions to society may have helped social workers win the sarcastic sobriquets of "do-gooder" and "bleeding heart."

The concept that social control is the primary function of welfare and that social control involves providing constructive services—this is a marketable idea. People can understand being responsible to a constituency. Such a rationale is realistic in the contemporary sociopolitical arena. Social work could move from idealistic, well-intentioned moralism about the nature of man to rational and pragmatic provision of evidence that social services contribute significantly to society in terms of desired outcomes—for example, less child abuse, fewer family breakdowns, and less class and racial discrimination. Unless the social worker thinks in terms of such specific accomplishments, social work will no longer be sanctioned and funded even at present levels.

Pincus and Minahan have suggested that "the credibility of the profession of social work rests on its ability to demonstrate that it can bring about the changes it claims to be able to make." [16] This is good advice. Can it best be followed in the context of social control?

SOCIAL SERVICES VERSUS POLICE POWER

In an advanced industrial society, social and economic situations are constantly changing, with new social and economic needs continually appearing. Rapid technical changes, discrimination against minorities, relocation of industries, and governmental anti-inflation programs that accept 6 percent unemployment as a situation not requiring rectification—all these increase social and economic inequality. If society does not meet the needs of the people who are adversely affected by these factors, deviance is likely to continue and multiply, and greater social unrest and disorder are probable.

Societies have attempted to exercise social control in a variety of ways as a response to deviance, social unrest, and disorder. Some societies have relied heavily on the perpetual threat or use of police power. Some have relied on elaborate systems of social welfare. Most have relied on both. It would appear that our society is not finally convinced that the development of social welfare services is a satisfactory means of social control in some problem areas. Therefore, when dealing with these areas it fluctuates between police power and the provision of social services. This is the current response to drug abuse. Is there a trade-off between social welfare services and police power as two of the predominant mechanisms for the control of deviance? Is it not true that the primary options available for attaining social control in our society are often either police power or social services? This seems most obvious in problem areas such as drug abuse, alcoholism, mental illness, and juvenile delinquency.

Social workers can contribute significantly to an orderly society by helping to seek and provide remedies or solutions for the dysfunctions in the social and economic system. Their contribution would include helping the poor, minorities, and other disfranchised people participate actively in the social and economic system of the society. This is not to suggest a new thrust for social welfare services. The task of the social services should involve the provision of evidence that the best way to control disorder and deviance in the society is by responsive, universal, and flexible social services focused on (1) alleviation of individual problematic behavior, and (2) intervention in the ongoing process of the society. This may be done by direct service to individuals and groups, social change strategies, and planning. As the social services are able to demonstrate that their approach to disorder and deviance is effective, the approach will be more universally sanctioned and provide a viable alternative to the direct behavior control of police power.

NOTES AND REFERENCES

1. Talcott Parsons, *The Social System* (Glencoe, Ill.: Free Press, 1951), pp. 482–483.

2. For a full exposition of this point, *see* John W. Bennett and Melvin M. Tumin, "Some Cultural Imperatives," in Peter B. Hammond, ed., *Cultural and Social Anthropology* (New York: Macmillan Co., 1964).

3. Daniel Callahan, "Normative Ethics and Public Morality in the Life Sciences," and Paul Kurtz, "The Uses and Abuses of Science," *The Humanist*, 32 (September/October 1972), pp. 5–7 and 7–9, respectively.

4. Kenneth Clark, "The Pathos of Power: A Psychological Perspective," *American Psychologist*, 26 (December 1971), pp. 1047–1057.

5. Stewart Easton, *The Heritage of the Past* (New York: Holt, Rinehart & Winston, 1964), p. 4.

6. Henry Miller, "Value Dilemmas in Social Casework, *Social Work*, 13 (January 1968), pp. 27–33.

7. Frances Piven and Richard A. Cloward, *Regulating the Poor* (New York: Pantheon Books, 1971), p. xiii.

8. Mary Gyarfas, "Social Science, Technology and Social Work: A Caseworker's View," *Social Service Review*, 43 (September 1969), pp. 259–272.

9. Miller, op. cit.

10. Piven and Cloward, op. cit.

11. Callahan, op. cit., p. 5.

12. Ibid., pp. 6–7.

13. Kurtz, op. cit., p. 8.

14. Clark, op. cit., pp. 1056 and 1057.

15. Daniel Bell, *The Coming of Post-Industrial Society* (New York: Basic Books, 1973), p. 374.

16. Allen Pincus and Anne Minahan, *Social Work Practice: Model and Method* (Itasca, Illinois: F. E. Peacock Publishers, 1973), p. 273.

Charles D. Cowger, MA, is Instructor, Jane Addams School of Social Work, University of Illinois, Urbana, Illinois. Charles R. Atherton, Ph.D., is Associate Professor, School of Social Work, University of Alabama, University, Alabama.

The Significance of Welfare History
Michael B. Katz

Public policy often is made on self-interest and sold on myth. This is one reason why history is important. Without historical analysis it is hard to see the recurrent connections between welfare policy and strategies of social discipline or to appreciate the stale, repetitive, and self-serving quality of myths about the poor. Without history, it is hard to understand why a welfare system that nobody likes or trusts is so resilient to change. History serves, too, to undercut any lingering notions of the inevitability of progress or improvement in the lives of the poor. A few benefits may have passed from the category of charity to entitlement, but most are still fragile. They have been rolled back before, and they will be rolled back again.

Welfare in America is a historical product, the accretion of layers over time. There is, in fact, an identifiable style of welfare policy and practice in America with 12 major characteristics:

1. The individual and degraded image of the poor. It is the fault of individuals that they are poor. America is a land that offers work and at least modest rewards to all who try. The poor lack the moral fiber of respectable, hard-working citizens.

2. The division of the working class into two groups. These have been called the worthy and the unworthy poor, the working and the non-working poor, or the working class and the lumpen proletariat. The result is the same, whatever the terms: to set off people who receive welfare as outside the working class, as, in fact, in drain upon those who work, and, hence, to divert working-class sympathy away from welfare measures.

3. The gap between images of poverty or dependence and demography. Wherever contemporaries, historians, or social scientists have examined the demography of dependence with care, the characteristics of the poor have not matched their image. The causes of poverty have had little to do with individual moral weakness and much to do with the organization of economic and political life. Periodic dependence has been a predictable, structural feature of working-class life throughout most of American history.

4. The punitive character of policy. Welfare policy has penalized the poor even more than it has helped them. One explicit purpose of early poorhouses was to discourage the working poor from seeking welfare. The degrading, punitive features of contemporary welfare policy have been documented over and over again.

5. The reversibility of progress. There is nothing inevitable about the welfare state. Welfare has been decreased or restricted at various points in the past, and there is every reason to believe that it will be cut back again.

6. Welfare policy as part of a strategy of social discipline. Every generation has had its characteristic style of social discipline. In the 1870s it

was repression; by the early decades of the twentieth century, it was welfare capitalism. Welfare policy is one key component of the strategy, and one whose study shows the assumptions and styles of an era with special force and clarity.

7. Welfare policy is dialectical. Policy emerges not only from a series of political, social, and economic forces but also from an internal process. Policies create administrative structures and officials whose aspirations and interests help shape or resist innovation. Social scientists and other academics have acquired a stake in policies that depend on experts and technical advice.

8. The early and pervasive role of the state. There has never been a golden age of voluntarism in America. Some level of government always has been active, usually providing most of the money. Voluntarism never has proven adequate to the problems of urban welfare.

9. The intermixture of public and private. Despite the attempt to differentiate public and private spheres in the nineteenth century, the two never became distinct. Groups with power and resources have used the state to advance their own interests in welfare policy as well as in other areas of public life. The irony of welfare reform is that it usually has meant lowering taxes by taking away benefits from poor people.

10. The achievement of progress through conflict and coalition. The poor have gained very little through the disinterested benevolence of individuals or the state. Gains have come through the formation of coalitions based on various interests, the attempt to win votes, and the fear of radicalism and violence.

11. The activity of the poor on their own behalf. The poor have bent institutions and policies to their own purposes. There has always been a difference between the purposes for which policies were adopted and the uses to which they were put. In every era the poor have created strategies of survival whose resourcefulness belies the images of passive degradation with which poor people so often are portrayed.

12. Welfare policy is not inevitable. There is no set of arrangements that magically fit any state of industrialization or modernization. At every point in its history, welfare policy has been the result of compromise and choice. And at every stage those choices have been controversial. Sane, reasonable people have seen the self-serving myths that have undergirded descriptions of the poor, the punitive nature of policy, and the interests really served by welfare. The existence of this alternative vision and its message that another way is possible is the only truly hopeful aspect of welfare in American history.

A Feminist Perspective on the Welfare State
Mimi Abramovitz

Gender, like race and class, structures the organization of social life. Its study only recently taken into account by students of the welfare state, is critical for it changes our perception of reality. Using a gender-lens uncovers previously ignored information, introduces new understandings of social interactions, and exposes how the construction of knowledge itself supports the *status quo*.[1] The two major political theories of modern times—liberalism and Marxism are gender-blind and uninformed by an understanding of patriarchy, and have consequently failed to explain women's experience. However, growing out of (and perhaps in spite of) these theories is a range of new and exciting feminist analyses which address women's oppression and begin to explore the relationship between women and the welfare state.

The first part of this chapter reviews the traditional political theories and the responses to them by liberal, radical, and socialist feminists. It gives special attention to the socialist-feminist perspective which informs this book. The second part the chapter moves from the theory of the welfare state to the ideology of women's roles, positing an important and largely unrecognized relationship between the two. It is argued that the ideology of women's roles, referred to here as the "family ethic," became encoded within the rules and regulations of the welfare state where it, along with the work ethic, has shaped public policy and regulated the lives of thousands of women who, from colonial times to the present, have turned to social welfare programs for support.

Traditional Political Theories: Liberalism and Marxism

Liberalism and Marxism are critical to our understanding of the political economy. Like other political theories, they analyze and explain regularly observed societal patterns. One such pattern, the role and function of the government or "the state," is especially relevant to social welfare policy which operates within and presumes the existence of the state. The following brief review of these two theories seeks to place the emerging feminist views of the welfare state into an historical and theoretical context. By no means does it capture the full complexity of each school of thought, do justice to the many important internal debates within each, or to provide a major critique of them.

Liberalism

Classical liberalism[2] originated in seventeenth-century England, took root in the eighteenth century, and with the rise of industrial capitalism, became the dominant political theory of twentieth-century Western societies. Reflecting new views of human nature which placed selfishness, egoism, and individualistic self-interest at the center of the human psyche, liberalism held that the competitive pursuit of individual self-interest in a market free of government regulation would maximize personal and societal benefits. In *The Wealth of Nations* (1776),[3] Adam Smith described the market as an "invisible hand" impartially channelling naturally selfish motives of human beings into mutually consistent and complementary activities that would best promote the welfare of all. Smith's views were soon expanded into what became known as laissez-faire doctrine, the view that the market, rather than the state, should be the regulator of society.

The pressure to limit state power arose, in part, because the prevailing philosophy of more active government involvement, known as mercantilism, had begun to impede the development of the capitalist economy. Government subsidies, the granting of state charters and monopolies, the imposition of high tariffs, the seizing of overseas markets, and other interventionist practices which had usefully promoted trade and commerce now operated as a constraint. Earlier experiences with despotic monarchs and undemocratic parliaments also inspired opposition to state activism.

Laissez-faire doctrine restricted the responsibilities of the state without eliminating its regulatory role as protector of capital, property, and national security. The new doctrine defined legitimate state activity to include (a) securing the country against internal disorder and external threats; (b) protecting private property, enforcing contracts, and maintaining public institutions necessary for commerce but too costly for single firms to operate; (c) using naval and military power to control trade routes and develop an overseas empire; and (d) guaranteeing individuals freedom from undue interference and their right to be represented in government, to form associations, and to travel, speak, worship, and publish freely.

Liberalism also defined the state as the arbiter of societal conflict, a role that became necessary because the possibility of such conflict existed within the principles of liberalism itself. Indeed, one person's right to individual freedom might contradict another's, as might the maximization of individual self interest. To promote social cohesion, liberalism charged the state with setting and enforcing the general conditions governing social relations, establishing the means to reconcile various differences, and the methods for enforcing compliance. Classical liberalism, in effect, asked the state to do what the market could not do—to act as a neutral mediator, to reconcile competing interests on behalf of the common good.[4]

Liberty, was the political value that gave liberalism its name. But as it evolved, the complex and never singular political theory of liberalism also embraced the values of equality and justice, which were potentially competitive with the value of liberty. Departing radically from earlier political philosophies that accepted social hierarchies as natural and God-given, liberal theory opposed political institutions that treated individuals unequally by subordinating them to the will or judgment of another. Thus, it also charged the state with assuring formal or legal equality and with promoting justice, ie., the social distribution of economic benefits and obligations. Since nineteenth-century liberalism tolerated government regulation but discouraged direct state involvement in the political economy, the distribution of economic resources was left to the market. When it failed, these social welfare activities were picked up first by local and then state governments and private charitable agencies.

As liberalism evolved, the unregulated "liberty" of the twentieth century produced unequal access to economic resources and interfered with the individual's ability to maximize self-interest and to secure the liberty, equality, and justice that liberalism promised. As liberalism began to call for a broader state role in managing this and other problems, the nineteenth-century view of the "night watchman" or non-interventionist state became known as conservatism. Twentieth-century or contemporary liberalism, in turn, gradually accepted more government involvement on behalf of business, but also the working class and the poor. It began to justify limited state intervention to mitigate the worst effects of the market economy on business and industry and to provide a minimum standard of living for the poor. While the idea of state regulation, rather than direct intervention, remained a central feature of contemporary liberal thought, the shift toward a more active state became the ideological basis for the acceptance of state-provided social welfare benefits as a way to promote economic justice. According to liberal theory, the essence of the welfare state is government-protected minimum standards of income, nutrition, health, housing, and education assured to every individual as a political right, not as charity.[5] Viewing the rise of the welfare state in terms of collective responsibility, Richard Hofstadter, a liberal historian, stated that

> It has been the function of the liberal tradition in American politics...at first to broaden the numbers of those who could benefit from the great American bonanza and then to humanize its workings and help heal its casualties. Without [the] sustained tradition of opposition and protest and reform, the American system would have been, and in times and places it was, nothing but a jungle, and would probably have failed to develop into the remarkable system for production and distribution that it is.[6]

Marxist Political Theory

Marxists dispute liberalism's definition of the origins, functions, and political neutrality of the state. Marxist political theory views the state as pro-capital, not a neutral mediator of conflicts whose only interest is to allow all individuals their private pursuits. The state, according to Marxism, is the institution through which those with power rule; it helps to create the conditions necessary for the profitable accumulation of capital and for the legitimization of a social structure based on unequal social economic and political power relations. With the emergence of classes based on private ownership, the state was needed to maintain the power of the dominant class. Because the rule of the owning class was neither immutable nor self-maintaining, state power was necessary to protect it.[7] In addition to the use of force and repression, the modern state strengthens the dominance of the ruling group by creating the conditions necessary for profitable economic activity, citizen loyalty, and class harmony. James O' Connor, a Marxist economist, calls these economic and political activities of the state its accumulation and legitimization functions.[8] Although contemporary Marxists agree that the state serves capital, they debate whether it does so as a "handmaiden" taking instructions from the dominant class or as a "relatively autonomous" body that looks past the short-term interests of individual capitalists and their internal rivalries to act on behalf of the long-term interests of the capitalist class as a whole.[9]

In either case, and contrary to liberal theory, Marxists believe that the welfare state arose, not to cushion individuals against the worst excesses of the market economy, but to protect prevailing class and property relations. The state's accumulation and legitimization functions became necessary due to troublesome contradictions that Marxists define as built into the system of capitalist production. According to Marxist theory, the welfare state appeared when the imperatives of capitalist production contradicted the requirements of accumulation, stability, but also reproduction, creating problems that became too expensive, economically and politically, for individual capitalists to absorb.

The problems giving rise to the welfare state centered on what Marxists call, "the reproduction and maintenance of the labor force:" the need found in all societies to develop and maintain a healthy and productive labor supply that is properly socialized and readily available for work and to provide for the care of those who cannot support themselves. The incessant drive to accumulate capital necessary for the survival of capitalism, they say, intensified the processes of production in ways that often generated social unrest and interfered with the reproduction and maintenance of the labor force, including both the working class' ability to labor, procreate, properly socialize family members, and otherwise maintain itself and its non-working members.

According to British Marxist, Ian Gough,[10] the defining feature of the welfare state is "the use of state power to modify the reproduction of labor power (the capacity to perform labor) and to maintain the non-working population in capitalist societies."[11] The expansion of the welfare state, he says, shifted the costs of socializing and maintaining workers from private capital to the public sphere. These publicly-supported services are made available (a) through tax-supported programs of cash and in-kind assistance that enable families to purchase the food, housing, education, training, health care, and other services needed to bear and raise children and to prepare all family members for another day of productive labor; and (b) through publicly subsidized services that enforce patterns of thinking and behavior appropriate to the needs of a capitalist economy. These same welfare state programs maintain the non-working population by absorbing the costs of home or institutional care of those unable to support themselves due to old age, poor health, childcare responsibilities, or market dislocations. At times, the provision of these social welfare benefits operates as a concession in the face of mounting social unrest.

Building on Gough, James Dickinson,[12] a Marxist sociologist, argues that the welfare state became necessary to capital because the changing requirements of production gradually undermined the ability of the working class to carry out its reproductive and maintenance tasks. He argues that although capital accumulation depends on the supply and regeneration of labor in households, capitalism has not always generated the levels of wages and employment needed for the successful formation and maintenance of families. Instead, changes in the system of production designed to increase profits and labor productivity and to lower production costs frequently produced negative consequences that undercut the health, economic security, and general fitness of workers and their families. Low wages, illness, and unemployment, for example, not only deplete the ability of workers to labor, but historically have diminished the working class' ability to carry out its reproductive role in the home.[15] Influenced by the feminist thinking described below, which argues for attention to the family as well as the market, Dickinson's analysis suggests that the welfare state lowered the reproductive costs to capital by mediating tensions between family and the economy on behalf of capitalist reproduction.

Drawing on the British experience, Dickinson's description of the welfare state's evolution suggests a periodization that can be applied to the United States. In the pre-industrial United States, when both production and reproduction occurred within the home, the state, operating through colonial governments (there was no welfare state *per se*), helped to assure the formation of families, an adequate supply of labor, and the productivity of all community members. In the early nineteenth century, once industrialization separated household and market production, changing demands on the family and the development of an industrial labor force led the state to become more involved in enforcing ideas of proper family functioning and in disciplining the labor force. A century later, the negative consequences of capitalist development on labor productivity, and on the health, safety, and economic security of the working-class family combined with workers' demands for protection against abusive working conditions, to produce social legislation. Statutory protections such as Workers' Compensation, Protective Labor Laws, and Mothers' Pensions began to limit the over-exploitation of labor and to strengthen the reproductive capacity of the household. The modern welfare state emerged in the United States in 1935. The signing of the Social Security Act that year signaled acceptance of the idea that the state had to transfer at least some economic resources from households in surplus to those in deficit if the market's failure to provide enough income and jobs was not to become too disruptive to the smooth functioning of the political economy.

In contrast to liberal political theory which suggests that the welfare state represents collective responsibility and the public interest, Marxists argue that the welfare state arose to protect capital from the negative effects of the "class struggle." The class struggle is inherent to the capitalist system because, in the Marxist view, the structure of capitalism produces two opposing classes: a ruling class whose members own and control the means of production and a working class whose members, lacking such ownership, sell their labor power to capital in order to survive. Because profit depends on the owners' ability to exploit the workers, the interests of these two classes are in fundamental conflict. Members of the working class have collectively fought low wages, unemployment, occupational illness, and other negative consequences of capitalist production. Their unions, strikes, political candidates, and street protests represent a potential challenge to prevailing property relations that capital wants to preserve. The welfare state developed, in part, because capital, at various times and under various conditions, seeking to maintain internal harmony and the political loyalty of the working class, concedes to such pressure with economic and social reforms. According to Paul Sweezy, a Marxist economist,

> economic legislation has. . . had the aim of blunting class antagonisms so that accumulation, the normal aim of capitalist behavior, could go forward smoothly and uninterrupted. . . For the sake of preserving domestic peace and tranquility, blunting the

edge of class antagonisms, and ultimately avoiding the dangers of violent revolution, the capitalist class is always prepared to make concessions through the medium of the state.[14]

State-sponsored programs, developed in response to the demands of disadvantaged groups for a greater share of the economic pie, also promote the political and economic stability necessary for the smooth functioning of production. At any moment in time, however, the likelihood of state action and the nature of the reform that results is not predetermined. Rather, it reflects the outcome of a contest between the demands of capital and those of labor as mediated by the state as well as the relative power of labor and capital at the particular historical moment.[15]

For this reason some contemporary Marxists now define the welfare state as an arena for class struggle and argue that social welfare provisions, while pro-capital, are not without benefit to the working class.[16] Welfare state programs are seen as having paradoxical outcomes that simultaneously enhance and negate human potential. On the one hand, the welfare state intervenes in daily life to reproduce the conditions necessary for the perpetuation of capitalist social, economic, and political relations. On the other hand, programs that benefit the "powers that be" also meet "common human needs." If social welfare benefits absorb the cost to industry of reproducing the labor force and maintaining the non-working poor, they also help individuals and families to survive. Secondly, to the extent that welfare state programs emerged from struggles waged by workers, people of color, women, and the poor, they not only produced a redistribution of income, however slight, but also empowered members of the labor, civil rights, women's liberation, and community organizations whose actions often create "pressures from below" that can force social change.[17] Third, the resulting package of benefits, which the British call a "social wage," operates as economic leverage, increasing the bargaining power of workers relative to capital. The social wage enables workers to take the economic risks involved in fighting for improved wages and working conditions and to consider resisting pressure to take any availiable job to survive. Thus, it is in their interest to fight for more generous social welfare benefits and to demand that capital, not labor, absorb the cost.

The Feminist Response To Liberal and Marxist Political Theory

The gender-neutrality of liberal and Marxist political theory has elicited responses from liberal, radical, and socialist feminists. Each feminist school has applied a gender-lens to their respective theoretical heritages and contributed to a new understanding of women's oppression and the welfare state.

Liberal Feminism

Liberal feminism[18] accepts liberal political theory but argues that its practice excludes women. The denial of equal rights to women and their differential treatment on the basis of sex without regard to individual wishes, interests, abilities, or merits interferes with women's free pursuit of self-interest, constrains their economic opportunities and deprives them of the benefits of full political participation. Arguing that this societal treatment of women violates liberalism's guarantee of liberty, equality, and justice for all, liberal feminists maintain that every individual must receive equal consideration regardless of sex, except when sex is relevant to the ability to perform a specific task or to take advantage of a certain opportunity. Extending the idea of the state as a guarantor of rights to include women's rights and family life, liberal feminists call on the state to take positive steps to compensate women in the market and at home.

Liberal feminists see blocked opportunities, the denial of rights, and sex discrimination as the keys to women's oppression. They historically have fought for formal equality under law including the right to vote, to enter the market, to receive an education, to own property in marriage, and to control their own bodies. Since the mid-nineteenth century, liberal feminists have also called for the elimination of protective labor laws that barred women from better paying jobs, the end to special exemptions from jury duty, and greater access for women in business, politics, and education. Their agenda has included laws that prohibit discrimination against women in relation to wages, hiring, promotions, credit, and social welfare programs, among other things. The capstone of these campaigns for gender-blind laws is the not yet ratified Equal Rights Amendment (ERA) to the Constitution which states that "Equality of rights under the law shall not be denied or abridged by the United States or any State on account of sex."

Reflecting a belief that the attainment of liberty, equality, and justice depends on the presence of certain material pre-conditions, traditional liberalism concluded that poverty may prevent individuals from exercising their rights. In this spirit, liberal feminists have stressed that the historic "feminization of poverty" has left women economically dependent, socially unfree, and unequal to men in most arenas. Their political goals include improvements in public programs serving women and expansion of the welfare state. Trusting to "reasoned" arguments and legislative change, liberal feminism relies heavily on the state to incorporate women into mainstream contemporary society. Viewed as a neutral arbiter of conflicting interests, the state is assumed to be the proper and the only legitimate authority for enforcing justice.

Liberal feminists accept considerable state intervention in family life. In addition to economic and political rights for women, they have fought for day care centers, reproductive freedom, maternity leaves, and more equitable divorce laws, and against pregnancy discrimination, rape, incest, wife battering, and other features of family life that negatively effect women. Moving still further away from traditional liberal concepts, some liberal feminists argue that the achievement of equality of opportunity for women requires an end to unfair social expectations and to exclusive childrearing by women.

The impact of the liberal feminist agenda on family life has led Zillah Eisenstein to suggest that it harbors a radical potential.[19] Arguing that liberal feminism contains an implied and often undefined analysis of women's oppression as flowing from their status as a distinct sex-class, Eisenstein suggests that the logical conclusion of liberal feminism is that liberty, equality, and justice for women requires an end to patriarchal arrangements in the market and the home. Their demand for laws that guarantee women the same opportunities as men promotes equal opportunity but also the conditions for women's economic independence which contains the potential for destabilizing patriarchal power relations. Their call for state protection against domestic violence, marital rape, and other issues of family life extends the realm of public concern to matters traditionally regarded as private and beyond the realm of state intervention.[20] While the demands of liberal feminism do not directly challenge the state, Eisenstein also concludes that their thrust may be incompatible with aspects of liberal theory and the operation of the state. Liberal feminists' heavy reliance on legislative redress reflects the definition of the state as a neutral protector of all citizens' rights. But their strong dependence on government action contradicts the liberal tenet that state interventions undercut individual freedom and their demands risk exposing the state as biased against women.

Radical Feminism

Radical feminism emerged in the late 1960s as a break with both liberal feminism and traditional Marxism. Its understanding of women's oppression as rooted in patriarchal power relations of male domination and female subordination has forced a new conceptualization of the state. In contrast to liberal feminism which sees the denial of rights and blocked opportunities as the source of women's oppression, radical feminism points to the domination of women by men. Locating the imbalance of power between women and men in the biological differences between the sexes, most radical feminists ground male domination or patriarchy in the social relations of reproduction, i.e. the work women do bearing and raising the next generation. Male control of institutional arrangements, but also of women's bodies, enables men to define women's roles and traits, to exploit women's labor and sexuality, and to diminish women's control over their choices about childrearing, mothering, laboring, and loving. Viewed as "other," women have been excluded and devalued.

In this analysis, gender, more than race or class, structures every aspect of human nature and social life. It becomes the most important determinant of a woman's life experience. The gender-based division of society is patriarchy's overarching tool. The distinction between the sexes, according to radical feminism, pre- and post- dates capitalism, making it the deepest and most decisive social division. The resulting assignment of public and private life to men and women respectively appears in different forms in different societies, but everywhere it legitimizes excluding women from the public arena of the market and politics, privatizing family life, and ultimately devaluing all that is associated with women.[21] The gender division of labor also creates a social relationship of dependency between biological females and males capable of reproducing offspring together and thus enforces marriage, heterosexuality, and the nuclear family system.

The radical feminist analysis of women's oppression focuses primarily on the private sphere and the gender domination of women's reproductive capacity, sexuality, mothering, family life, interpersonal relations, and culture. Here, the private and the personal is defined as political. In its illumination of the power of patriarchal arrangements and its development of a woman-centered perspective, radical feminism has focused special attention on male violence against women (rape, incest, wife abuse, pornography), homophobia, and sexual politics at home and on the job. It supports the creation of an alternative women's culture and in some cases espouses female separatism. Radical feminism's biological explanation of the gender division of labor, its tendency to universalize the female experience, to posit the moral superiority of women, and to focus nearly all its attention on the private and personal spheres of life has resulted in criticism of its analysis as veering toward biological determinism, ignoring differences of race, class, and ethnicity among women, and divorcing its under-standing of patriarchy from other features of the political economy. But implied in the radical feminist analysis, if not yet fully developed, is an account of the state as a patriarchal substitute for male control of women in the family. Whether it is a welfare mother referring to "the state" as "The Man" or Mary Daly claiming that "patriarchy appears to be everywhere,"[22] the idea that patriarchy is the cause of women's subor-dinate status has become part of feminist consciousness.

Socialist Feminism

The socialist-feminist response to the theories of liberalism and Marxism integrates the radical feminist analysis of patriarchal power relations and the Marxist analysis of capitalist class and property rela-tions. The resulting understanding of female oppression helps to pave the way for a feminist analysis of the welfare state. The emerging syn-thesis locates the oppression of women in the ways that the power rela-tions of capitalism (class domination) and patriarchy (male domination) together structure ideology, the social relations of gender and class, and the overall organization of society. The dynamics of racism have also recently begun to be factored into this complex equation.

Socialist feminists share the Marxist critique of liberal political theory as obscuring the class relations of the state. However, they find the Marxist analysis limited by its failure to include the experience and perspective of women. The lack of attention to women in Marxist theory is problematic, both descriptively and analytically, according to socialist feminists. Descriptively, it ignores that from colonial times to the present many women received social welfare benefits. Moreover, most of the reproductive tasks assumed by the welfare state correspond to those historically assigned to women in the home. Analytically, the Marxist analysis pays too little attention to the private sphere of reproduction in the home and to the overall role of patriarchy, both of which struc-ture the lives of women. Although Marx and his followers did consider the "woman question,"[23] they focused primarily on the dynamics of capitalist production and did not develop their rudimentary discussion of patriarchy, reproduction, and the labor of women into a full account of female oppression. To correct for this, socialist feminists expanded the Marxist analysis to include the impact of patriarchy, the gender division of labor, and the sphere of reproduction.

Patriarchy

The early Marxists understood patriarchy and what they called the "world-historic defeat of women," as a product of the emergence of private property, the state, and class relations at a particular point in capitalist development. Under a system of private property, women as a group became property, that is, "mere instruments of production" to men who owned women's ability to labor. The oppression of women and their status as the property of men derived from their exclusion from the process of production which left women economically de-pendent and thus vulnerable to exploitation. The emergence of private property, classes, and the state also gave rise to monogamy and the nuclear family to assure the inheritance of individually-owned wealth by male offspring. Only the elimination of class and the private owner-ship of property would eliminate women's "wage slavery" in the market and their "domestic slavery" in the home. Viewing capitalism as the source of male domination, Marxists did not consider patriarchy to have an autonomous influence on women's lives.[24]

In contrast, socialist feminism, influenced by radical feminism, gives patriarchy equal standing with capitalism as a source of female oppression. While radical feminists stress the direct, personally exer-cised, and legitimized dominance of individual men over women, socialist feminists expanded the concept of patriarchy to include the male dominance that is structured into social arrangements, that in-directly secures male interests, and that gives men control over women. This broadened terrain permits a discussion of both the individual and society, and focuses on both the private and the public sphere. As a result, the influence of patriarchy in the home, on the job, in societal institutions, and throughout the wider social order is explored. More historical than radical feminism, socialist feminism also examines how patriarchy changes over time.

Patriarchy is grounded in relations of power as well as in the biological differences between the sexes. It consists of a social system that establishes the shared interests and interdependence among men that enables, if not requires, them to dominate women. Characterized by male domination and female subordination, patriarchy permits men as a group to control women's sexuality as well as their productive and reproductive labor. Under patriarchy, some men have more power than others and while all men benefit from patriarchy, privileges vary sharp-ly by class and race.

Socialist feminism defines patriarchy as an autonomous system of social relations but insists on its inseparability from capitalism. The societal divisions by gender, class, and race thus reflect a synthesis of patriarchy and capitalism and are not determined primarily by one or the other alone. So for example, socialist feminists suggest that capitalist production is shaped by the forces of male dominance and that male dominance is organized by capitalist class relations. By insisting on the inseparability of capitalism and patriarchy, socialist feminism articulates the need to struggle against both. The understanding of the differential impact of capitalism and patriarchy on women of color that is now emerging (see below) provides a way to incorporate the dynamics of racism into this analysis.

The Gender Division of Labor

Patriarchal dominance is established and maintained by a gender-segregated society which assigns certain spheres and tasks to women and others to men. The early Marxists acknowledged this but did not develop the concept of patriarchy or the gender division of labor very fully. They viewed pre-class gender divisions as a "natural" (ie. biologi-cally based) product of the sex act which extended outward to organize the rest of society. With the development of classes and the transfor-mation of the family into an economic unit, the class structure became dominant. That is, instead of the gender division of labor shaping socie-tal patterns, capitalist class relations now determined the gender division of labor.[25] Making gender division secondary to capitalist class relations prevented the early Marxists from seeing the social order as structured both by capitalism and patriarchy, and recognizing gender divisions as an independent source of female oppression.[26]

Socialist feminism makes society's gender division co-equal with its class divisions and central to its analysis of the political economy. In this view, when the rise of capitalism moved economic production from the househod to the market, domestic and economic production were separated. Patriarchy then caused the resulting division of *production* to be structured by gender: the assignment of the private sphere of family and reproduction to women and the more power-laden public sphere of market and production to men. Furthermore, the work within each sphere was divided along gender lines as well.[27] The new gender divisions and the accompanying ideology which sanctioned a public\private split served capital's need for discrete "homemakers" and "breadwinners" (see Chapter Four). At the same time they sustained patriarchal authority, which the rise of capitalist social relations threatened to undermine.[28]

The Sphere of Reproduction

The identification of the gender division of society as central to female oppression led the socialist feminists to examine the labor of women in the home as well as in the market. Their analysis of women's oppression forced them to look at women's domestic labor and the sphere of reproduction—both largely ignored by the early Marxists and other economists. Although most economists recognized that all societies needed to reproduce the labor force, they did not think of the family as the place where daily and generational reproduction of labor took place. Instead they analyzed reproduction as a characteristic of production. In standard Marxist usage, reproduction refers to the reproduction of capital (the replacement of machinery and capital equipment), the reproduction of wage laborers as factors of production, and to the reproduction of capitalist social relations by cultural and ideological institutions such as the family, education, and religion which, among other things, socialize individuals to capitalist norms.[29]

If the early Marxists had pursued their insights about the reproduction of labor further, they might have developed an understanding of the importance of women's reproductive labor in the home and uncovered the relationship between women's domestic labor, the process of capitalist production, and the oppression of women.[30] Their singular interest in the system of production, however, led them to focus only on the reproduction of wage laborers on the job, that is, the means by which the relationship between wage laborers and the capitalist employers is sustained. They asked what amount of labor must workers as a group expend and what wages must they be paid to assure that they will recreate themselves and continue to participate regularly in the process of production.

With regard to women's domestic labor in the home, the early Marxists recognized the importance of "individual consumption" to the reproduction of labor, assumed it took place in the working-class family, and suggested that the breadwinner's wage included a payment for the domestic labor of his wife. Indifferent to reproduction in the home, they failed to understand the ways in which the daily maintenance of workers depended on women's domestic labor and the structure of the family system. Thus, their analysis did not include the relationship of women's domestic labor to capitalist production, nor did it define the reproductive sphere as a potential source of female oppression.[31] While contemporary Marxists such as Gough and Dickinson pay more attention to reproduction in the home, they still fail to account for women's experience because they continue to subsume reproduction to production and to ignore patriarchy altogether.

Socialist feminists expanded Marxism by analyzing the sphere of reproduction in its own right. Instead of examining the dynamics of reproduction as a *response* to the needs of production or *vice-versa*, socialist feminists give equal attention to both spheres. They do so on the grounds that the survival of human society depends on the reproduction of the species as well as the production of commodities, that humans require the satisfaction of material, social, and emotional needs, and that attention to home and family life better explain women's experiences.[32] Production occurs primarily within the market and is the means by which society organizes and distributes the goods and services necessary for survival and for leisure. Reproduction, occurring within the family, organizes and distributes the means of satisfying the needs of procreation, socialization, sexuality, daily maintenance, and emotional nurturance.[33]

The earliest socialist-feminist discussion of the reproductive sphere stayed close to the Marxist focus on production. It analyzed women's unpaid domestic labor as essential to capital's need to reduce the costs of reproducing and maintaining the labor force and held capitalist relations responsible for the oppressive economic dependence of women on men.[34] But as socialist feminists incorporated ideas about patriarchy into their analysis, they began to examine the contribution of women's domestic and market labor to both systems. They found that women's labor provided benefits to individual men and employers, but also to the more systemic arrangements of patriarchy and capitalism. They concluded that the dynamics of women's home and market labor enforced female subordination in both spheres.[35]

More specifically, they argued that the need for women's labor in the home reinforced their exploitation in the market while their exploitation in the market helped to maintain their subordination in the home.[36] In its need for low paid workers, capitalism has maintained women (and other groups) as a reserve pool of labor that can be drawn into and out of the labor force as needed. The ready availability of cheap female labor benefits capital by exerting a downward pressure on wages, while the possibility of displacement helps to keep currently employed workers in line. The requisites of patriarchy, particularly the idea that women's primary place is in the home, act to reinforce this dynamic. At the same time, when women enter the market, employers rationalize paying them less for work in the least stable and most uninteresting jobs on the grounds that they are secondary earners, working temporarily or just for "pin money."

From the start, women's employment outside the home has also challenged the underpinnings of patriarchy. The early development of a sex-segregated labor market, however, helped to restore male domination and female subordination in the world of work. The sex-segregated labor market operates to keep labor costs down and to uphold male domination. By crowding large numbers of female workers into a small number of "women's jobs," occupational segregation increases competition among women, reduces their wages, and raises their unemployment rates. Occupational segregation by sex also supports the male\female wage gap, maintains male-dominated job hierarchies, and prevents women from competing with men for higher paying jobs.

The economic vulnerability resulting from work in low paid, low status women's jobs, in turn, helps to enforce women's subordinated place in the home. It promotes the economic, if not psychological, dependence of women on men, necessitates entrance into marriage, and locks women into their subordinate domestic roles. When women work without pay, doing the household and childcare tasks that assure the daily and generational renewal of the labor force, their labor benefits both men and capital.

Poor Women, Immigrant Women and Women of Color

While the socialist-feminist analysis has advanced the understanding of women's oppression in several ways, it has been accurately criticized for inadequately addressing the experiences of women from different racial, ethnic, and class backgrounds. To generalize from the lives of middle-class, native-born, white women to other groups of women as if no differences existed, creates distortions similar to those that result when scholars generalize research on male subjects to women. In recent years, socialist-feminist researchers, both white and women of color, have begun to reformulate their concepts by combining them with theories of racial oppression. Evelyn Nakano Glenn and Bonnie Thornton Dill,[37] for example, argue that the distinctions between public and private spheres and between productive and reproductive labor, drawn by socialist feminists, do not adequately reflect the experience of women other than middle-class white women. They re-examine these ideas to make them more applicable to the experiences of women with other backgrounds. Both Glenn and Dill point out that the notion of separate spheres is less useful for understanding the experiences of women whose poverty caused them to work for wages outside the home. Drawn by capital's need for cheap labor, women and children from native-born, immigrant, and families of color without means were a substantial part of the wage labor force. For these working women, the lines between private and public were not so distinct.

Glenn and Dill maintain that the line between productive and reproductive labor all but disappeared for the female members of oppressed groups. Like other members of racially subordinated groups, white society valued them primarily for their ability to work. During slavery, the reproductive labor of black female slaves belonged to their masters, who owned them as well as their children. Since then, the wage labor of women of color has continued to take precedence over their domestic labor. Viewed as workers rather than homemakers, the maternal and reproductive roles have been diminished and ignored. While patriarchal society "protected" white middle-class women as wives and mothers, women of color received little recognition, respect, or support for these roles. The family system of women of color, moreover, was regularly assaulted by the dominant society which not only refused to recognize its needs but often tore it apart. The slave trade, followed by certain immigration policies sometimes prevented and/or disrupted family formation among black as well as Chinese and Mexican-American workers. Low wages, irregular employment, and intensive internal labor mobility futher hindered the development of families among oppressed groups. Frequently these families, experiencing extreme exploitation on the job and having to struggle for cohesion in family life, were important sources of resistance to the *status quo*.

Finally, this analysis raises the issue of racial divisions among women.[38] As slaves and as domestic servants, women of color historically performed reproductive labor for white women and their families. When women of color entered the wider labor market, their jobs became tightly stratified by race.[39] Their nearly exclusive employment in the most menial personal service and cleaning jobs left more satisfying work for white women. Moreover, during economic downturns when jobs were few, white women often displaced women of color. Such labor market patterns led Glenn to argue that in the exploitation of women, race becomes a "second axis of oppression"—one that frequently brings benefits to white women. She maintains, however, that despite the benefits of racial oppression to white women and those of patriarchal oppression to men of color, white men remain the dominant exploiting group.

Socialist Feminism and the Welfare State

Socialist feminists have begun to apply their analysis of women's oppression and of the political economy to the welfare state. Elizabeth Wilson,[40] Mary McIntosh,[41] Hillary Land,[42] Carol Brown,[43] Zillah R. Eisenstein,[44] and Allison M. Jaggar[45] from the United States, Jane Ursell,[46] from Canada and others with an interest in the role of the state have started to account for complexities of the welfare state that contemporary Marxists and other gender-neutral theorists neither saw nor addressed.

Building on the Marxist analysis of capitalism and the radical feminist analysis of patriarchy, socialist feminism maintains that the state is neither a neutral mediator of interest group conflict nor simply pro-capital. Rather, the state protects the interests of both capital and patriarchy by institutionalizing capitalist class and property relations and upholding patriarchal distinctions. According to Zillah Eisenstein,

> The formation of the state institutionalizes patriarchy; it reifies the division between public and private life as one of sexual differences...The domain of the state has always signified public life and this is distinguished in part from the private realm by differentiating men from women...The state formalizes the rule by men because the division of public and private life is at one and the same time a male-female distinction...The state's purpose is to enforce the separation of public and private life and with it the distinctness of male and female existence.[47]

The state protects capitalism and patriarchy by enforcing their respective requirements, but also by mediating any conflicts that arise from the state's simultaneous commitment to both. The state steps in to create order and cohesion especially when the heterogeneous and frequently divided dominant class cannot agree on how best to resolve these tensions.[48]

Including patriarchy complicates the otherwise useful analysis of the origins and development of the welfare state put forward by Gough, Dickinson, O'Connor, and other contemporary Marxists who suggest that the welfare state operates to mediate conflicts between the capitalist requirements of production and reproduction. They see the welfare state as assisting capitalist accumulation and the legitimacy of the prevailing social order by assuring the reproduction of the labor force, the maintenance of society's non-working members, and securing the social peace. If Marxism argues that the welfare state arose to mediate reproductive relations on behalf of the productive needs of capital, socialist feminism holds that the welfare state originated to meet the changing requirements of patriarchy *and* capitalism and to mediate their conflicts. Drawing on various parts of the socialist-feminist discourse, a new but far from singular and still incomplete perspective can be envisioned which suggests that the origins and functions of the welfare state represent not only the need to reproduce and maintain the labor force as observed by the Marxists, but also to uphold patriarchal relations and to regulate the lives of women. From this perspective, the welfare state operates to uphold patriarchy and to enforce female subordination in both the spheres of production and reproduction, to mediate the contradictory demands for women's home and market labor, and to support the nuclear family structure at the expense of all others.

Upholding Patriarchal Control in the Family and the Market

Socialist feminists maintain that state intervention in work and family life reflects the changing requirements of patriarchy as well as those of capitalism and the historical intervention of the state on behalf of "proper" family life. Both Brown and Ursel[49] argue that the advance of capitalism gradually shifted the center of patriarchal control from the private family headed by a man to the state. In pre-industrial society, where the household was both the productive and reproductive unit, patriarchal authority was private or familial, that is, grounded in the gender organization of the family. Public or social patriarchy, rooted in the state, was more facilitative than direct, providing only the structural supports for private patriarchy in the home. By law, custom, and economics, male heads of household controlled the labor of women and other family members as well as their access to most economic resources. Marriage, property, inheritance, and public aid laws were local and operated primarily to enforce such control by the patriarch who, in turn, was obliged to maintain the nuclear family and women's place in the home.

Public or social patriarchy became stronger as the rise of industrial capitalism began to weaken the economic and political underpinnings of male authority. The separation of production and reproduction, the growth of factories, the creation of a wage labor force (which employed women and children as well as men), and the emergence of new ideas about individual freedom, equality, and opportunity shifted the basis of patriarchal authority from the male head of household to the employer and the state. As market relations slowly lessened men's ability to control the labor of family members and increased their wives' and children's access to economic resources, familial patriarchy alone no longer sufficed to maintain male domination and the gender division of labor.

The decline of patriarchal authority modified the state's relationship to private family life. As familial patriarchy gave way to social or public patriarchy, the state assumed regulatory functions previously confined to the family including greater regulation of marriage, inheritance, child custody, and employment.[50] The growth of the social welfare system and its "reform" in the early nineteenth century also marked the shift from familial to social patriarchy, at least for the poor. The transition, signaled by an attack on public aid (outdoor relief) and the rise of institutional care (indoor relief) made public aid very harsh and punitive. The Marxist explanation of these "reforms" suggests that

state-regulated deterrence became necessary to discipline the newly industrialized labor force. The feminist analysis adds that the social welfare changes also operated to enforce new ideas about proper family
life. Punitive relief programs assured that women chose any quality of
family life over public aid. Welfare recipients whose families did not
comply with prevailing norms were considered undeserving and treated
even more poorly by the system. Given women's responsibility for
maintaining the home, poor, immigrant, and female-headed
households suspected of being unable to properly socialize their
children were frequently defined as unworthy of aid. If an institutional placement resulted, it could tear "undeserving" families apart, often
for reasons of poverty alone.

In the early twentieth century, the entry of more women into the
labor force challenged patriarchal patterns and was viewed as competitive with men. The new labor and social welfare legislation that
emerged enforced the gender division of labor and otherwise re-as-
serted patriarchal structures in the family and the market (see Chapter
Six). Protective labor laws, Mothers' Pension programs, and other new
social legislation excluded women from the labor market and relegated
them to the home where they worked to reproduce and maintain the
labor force. These and other laws also supported a sex-segregated occupational structure and established male-dominated hierarchies at the
workplace (which mirrored and reinforced those already in place in
the home).

During the rest of the twentieth century, the expanding welfare
state continued to support patriarchal dominance while mediating
reproductive relations on behalf of the productive needs of capital (see
Chapters Seven through Ten). The emergence of the modern welfare
state, marked by the enactment of the 1935 Social Security Act, signaled
the institutionalization of public or social patriarchy. Instead of simply
assuming patriarchal control, the state began to systematically subsidize
the familial unit of production through the provision of economic
resources to the aged, the unemployed, and children without fathers.
The major income maintenance programs of the Social Security Act also
incorporated patriarchal family norms. They each presumed and reinforced marriage, the male breadwinner/female homemaker household
type and women's economic dependence on men. Mary McIntosh,[51]
points out that even the special programs for female heads of
households indirectly buttressed the ideal family type by substituting
the state for the male breadwinner. By helping this "deviant" family ap-
proximate the "normal" one, programs for female-headed families
"solved" one of patriarchy's major problems, that of the so-called
"broken home" or female-headed home. At the same time, the
program's low benefits and stigma penalized husbandless women for
their departure from prescribed wife and mother roles. This kept unmarried motherhood and the breakup of the two-parent family from
appearing too attractive to others. Until very recently, when they began
to falter in this regard, the programs of the Social Security Act implicitly supported family structures that conformed to the patriarchal model
and penalized those that did not. The historical intervention by the state
on behalf of "proper" family life suggests the family's importance to the
survival of capitalism and patriarchy. Indeed, families absorb the cost
and responsibility for bearing and socializing the next generation, for
managing consumption and other household matters, for organizing
sexual relations, for providing care to the aged, sick, and young who
cannot work, and for producing income to meet all these needs. The

1980 attack on the welfare state (described in Chapter Eleven), can be understood partly as an effort to restore the ability of the welfare state to uphold traditional patriarchal arrangements in face of recent threats derived from major changes in both the family system and the political economy.

Regulating The Labor of Women

Socialist feminists agree with contemporary Marxists that the welfare state helps to assure the reproduction of the labor force and the maintenance of the non-working members of the population. But they stress that from the start, programs serving women have had a more complicated role. The activities necessary to secure the physical, economic, and social viability of the working class depend heavily on women's unpaid domestic labor as do prevailing patriarchal family patterns. But because this competes with capital's ongoing demand for women's low paid market labor, socialist feminism forces us to see that the welfare state must regulate the lives of women in a unique way.

The demands for women's domestic and market labor have contradicted each other since the separation of household and market production in the early nineteenth century. Women's domestic labor assures capital fit, able, and properly socialized workers on a daily and a generational basis as well as the care of those unable to work. This unpaid domestic labor absorbs the costs that industry or government would otherwise have to pay to reproduce and maintain a productive labor force. Women's domestic labor also reinforces patriarchal arrangements. It relieves individual men of household tasks, services their physical, sexual, and emotional needs, keeps women economically dependent, stops them from competing with men in the job market, and defines women's place in the home. By the end of the colonial period, however capital's need for cheap market labor had combined with the impoverishment of the working class to draw increasingly large numbers of women into the wage labor market. Paradoxically, their entry conflicted with the benefits received by capital from women's unpaid domestic labor. Combined with fewer marriages and more female-headed households, the growing labor force participation of women, which held the possibility of greater economic independence, also contained a challenge to male dominance and patriarchal family patterns.

Socialist feminism argues that, from colonial times to the present, social welfare programs serving women have had to deal with these contradictory pulls. Given the twin benefits of female labor, the welfare state, in most historical periods, has played a central role in mediating the resulting conflict, especially among poor and working-class women. As this book details, social welfare policies have always regulated the lives of women, channelling some into the home to devote full time to reproducing and maintaining the labor force and others into the labor market where they also create profits for capital. By distinguishing among women as "deserving" and "undeserving" of aid, the policies also reinforced divisions among women along lines of race, class, and marital status.

Arena of Struggle

Like some Marxists, some socialist feminists conclude that the paradoxes of the welfare state make it a productive arena for feminist as well as class struggle. On the one hand, welfare state policies assist capital and patriarchy by reproducing the labor force, regulating the competing demands for female labor, enforcing female subordination, maintaining women's place in the home, and sustaining the social peace. On the other hand, welfare state benefits threaten patriarchal arrangements. They redistribute needed resources, offer non-working women and single mothers a means of self-support, and provide the material conditions for the pursuit of equal opportunity. Welfare state benefits that help women to survive without male economic support subsidize, if not legitimize, the female-headed household and undermine the exclusivity of the male-breadwinner, female-homemaker family structure. As a social wage, welfare state benefits increase the bargaining power of women relative to men. Eisenstein[52] argues that the very existence of the welfare state, especially its deep involvement in family life, is potentially subversive to capitalism, liberalism, and patriarchy. Whether or not and how the welfare state carries out its abstract tasks or exposes its roots in patriarchal capitalism, however, is not predetermined. Rather it reflects the degree of prevailing struggle over who (capital or labor) "pays" for these benefits and the extent to which the welfare state policies can be made to change rather than reproduce the conditions necessary to perpetuate patriarchal capitalism. In the final analysis, the outcome of the struggle reflects the relative power of the contesting forces at any moment in time.

The Role of Ideology: The Family Ethic and the Regulation of Women

The welfare state functions identified by socialist feminists are carried out, in part, by the codification of the family ethic or the ideology of women's roles in its rules and regulations. Indeed, the family ethic is one way in which the welfare state regulates the lives of women. Ideology, or the relatively coherent system of beliefs and values about human nature and social life generated by a society for itself, is found in the realm of ideas, the actions of individuals, and in the practices of societal institutions, including the welfare state. The power of ideology lies in its ability to influence the thinking and behavior of individuals, the practices of institutions, and the organization of society. In the case of women, the family ethic, articulates expected work and family behavior and defines women's place in the wider social order. Embodied in all societal institutions, this dominant norm is enforced by the laws and activities of the state.

The family ethic derives from patriarchal social thought that sees gender roles as biologically determined rather than socially assigned and from standard legal doctrine that defines women as the property of men. It is grounded in the idea that natural physical differences between the sexes determine their differential capacities. The idea of natural differences between the sexes causes individuals to see their femininity and masculinity solely as part of human nature[53] rather than as the product of socialization. The sense of "naturalness" legitimizes socially constructed gender distinctions and enables individuals to participate, without question, in gender-specific roles. The implication that biology is destiny also obscures the historical impact of differential socialization and unequal opportunities on the choices made by individuals of different sexes, races, and ages. By making these choices seem natural and rational, the family ethic helps to justify discrepancies between societal promises and realities, to rationalize prejudice, discrimination, and inequalities, and to promote the acquiescence of the oppressed in their oppression. Finally, the direct appeal to nature as the source of gender differences minimizes the cultural determination of women's sexuality, the significance of changes in women's position over time, and the importance of women's private domestic labor to both capitalist production and patriarchal arrangements.

Like most ideologies, the ideology of women's roles represents dominant interests and explains reality in ways that create social cohesion and maintain the *status quo*. The family ethic articulates and rationalizes the terms of the gender division of labor. Despite its long history, the lynchpin of the family ethic—the assignment of homemaking and childcare responsibilities to women—has remained reasonably stable.

A family ethic telling women about their proper place existed in colonial America. This pre-industrial code placed women in the home and subordinate to the male head of household. Women were expected to be economically productive, but to limit their productive labor to the physical boundaries of the home. Between 1790 and 1830, changes in the political economy that accompanied the rise of industrial capitalism caused a dramatic shift in women's roles. The emerging market economy removed production from the home and created gender-based separate spheres. As men took their place in the market, the work ethic followed them there; but the new "industrial family ethic" continued to define women's place as in the home.

The industrial family ethic resembled its colonial predecessor in many ways, except that it denied women a recognized productive role. Told not to engage in market labor at all, the family ethic defined women's place as exclusively in the home. Reflecting the needs of the new social order, their domestic work included creating a comfortable retreat for the market-weary breadwinner, socializing children to assume proper adult work and family roles, managing household consumption, offering emotional nurturance to family members, caring for the aged and the sick, taming male sexuality, and providing moral guardianship to the family and the wider community. At the same time, and reflecting patriarchal rules, women were viewed as the "weaker sex" in need of male support and protection. The subordination of women became grounded in their economic dependence on men and in the law. The latter continued to define women as male property and to grant men control of women's labor and access to resources.

The idea of the family ethic draws on what other scholars have labeled the "cult of domesticity" or the "cult of true womanhood."[54] But as developed here, the concept goes beyond earlier descriptions, to examine the codification of the ideology of women's roles in societal institutions and to analyze its regulatory powers. Indeed, the family ethic which "protects" the white middle-class family also operates as a mechanism of social regulation and control.

On the individual level, the family ethic keeps women in line. Fulfilling the terms of the family ethic theoretically entitles a woman to the "rights of womanhood" including claims to femininity, protection, economic support, and respectability. Non-compliance brings penalties for being out of role. Encoded in all societal institutions, the family ethic also reflects, enforces, and rationalizes the gender-based division of society into public and private spheres and helps to downgrade women in both. The ideology of women's roles helps to keep women at the bottom of the hierarchies of power in both the public and the private spheres.

Indeed, the idea that women belong at home has historically sanctioned the unequal treatment of women in the market. The resulting economic insecurity has channelled them back into the home. The need for women's domestic labor and the ideological presumption of a private sphere to which women rightfully belong has helped to rationalize their subordination in the public sphere. When industry's need for inexpensive labor drew women out of their "proper place," the idea that they belonged in the home justified channelling them into low-paid, low-status, gender-segregated sectors of the economy and into jobs whose functions paralleled those tasks traditionally performed by women at home. Women's inability to earn a livable wage made men, marriage, and family life into a necessary and a more rational source of financial support. Lacking a material basis for independence, women easily became economically, if not psychologically, dependent on men which, in turn, created the conditions for women's subordinate family role.

In brief, the family ethic, which locked women into a subordinate family role also rationalized women's exploitation on the job. By devaluing women's position in each sphere, the ideology of women's work and family roles satisfied capital's need for a supply of readily available, cheap, female labor. By creating the conditions for continued male control of women at home and on the job, the economic devaluation and marginalization of women also muted the challenge that increased employment by women posed to patriarchal norms.

Targeted to and largely reflecting the experience of white, middle-class women who marry and stay home, the family ethic denied poor and immigrant women and women of color the "rights of womanhood" and the opportunity to embrace the dominant definition of "good wife" and mother because they did not confine their labor to the home.[55] Forced by dire poverty to work for wages outside the home, they also faced severe exploitation on the job, having to accept the lowest wages, longest hours, and most dangerous working conditions. Instead of "protecting" their femininity and their families' social respectability, the notion of separate spheres placed poor and immigrant women and women of color in a double bind at home and reinforced their subordinate status in the market. Separate spheres, which recognized and sustained the household labor that white women performed for their families, offered no such support to non-white women.[56] Both Dill and Glenn point out that society's treatment of women of color clearly indicated that their value as laborers took precedence over their domestic and reproductive roles. On all fronts, the families of poor and immigrant women and women of color experienced a series of assaults not faced by middle-class white women.

Perhaps this is why some of the families of poor, employed, husbandless, immigrant women, and women of color tried so hard to comply with the terms of the family ethic. Indeed, working-class men struggled to keep their wives at home even when this involved major sacrifices in the organization and comfort of their family life. To stay out of the labor force, working-class women typically limited family consumption, sent their children to work, sacrificed the privacy of their homes to take in boarders, increased the production of household goods and/or took in paid piece-work which burdened their already long work day.[57]

The ideology of women's roles is deeply encoded in social welfare policy. It is well-known that social welfare laws categorize the poor as deserving and undeserving of aid based on their compliance with the work ethic. But, as this book suggests, the rules and regulations of social welfare programs also treat women differentially according to their perceived compliance with the family ethic. Indeed, conforming to the ideology of women's roles has been used to distinguish among women as deserving or undeserving of aid since colonial times. Assessing women in terms of the family ethic became one way the welfare state could mediate the conflicting demands for women's unpaid labor in the home and her low paid labor in the market, encourage reproduction by "proper" families, and otherwise meet the needs of patriarchal capitalism. Recognizing the role of the family ethic in social welfare policy permits us to uncover the long untold story of the relationship between women and the welfare state, to which we now turn.

1. Virginia Held, "Feminism and Epistemology: Recent Work on the Connection Between Gender and Knowledge," *Philosophy and Public Affairs*, 14(3) (1985), pp. 296-307.

2. This discussion of liberal economic and political theory draws heavily from E. K. Hunt, *Property and Prophets: The Evolution of Economic Institutions and Ideologies* (New York: Harper & Row Publishers, 1981), pp. 36-50; and Alison M. Jaggar, *Feminist Politics and Human Nature* (Totowa, New Jersey: Rowman & Allanheld, 1983), pp. 27-50.

3. Adam Smith, *The Wealth of Nations* (New York: Modern Library, 1937), pp. 420-423.

4. For a clear contemporary presentation of this view, see Milton Friedman, *Capitalism and Freedom* (Chicago: University of Chicago Press, 1962), Ch. 2, "The Role of Government in a Free Society."

5. Harold L. Wilensky and Charles N. Lebeaux, *Industrial Society and Social Welfare* (New York: Russell Sage Foundation, 1965), p. xii.

6. Richard Hofstadter, *The Age of Reform* (New York: Vintage Books, 1955), p. 18.

7. Hal Draper, *Karl Marx's Theory of Revolution I: State and Bureaucracy* (New York: Monthly Review Press, 1977), pp. 237-262.

8. James O'Connor, *The Fiscal Crisis of the State* (New York: St. Martin's Press, 1973), pp. 5-10.

9. For this debate see Ralph Miliband, *The State in Capitalist Society* (New York: Basic Books, 1969); Ralph Miliband, *Marxism and Politics* (Oxford: Oxford University Press, 1977); Ralph Miliband, "Poulantzas and the Capitalist State," *New Left Review* 82 (1973), pp. 83-91; Nicol Poulantzas, "The Problem of the Capitalist State," *New Left Review* 58 (November/December 1969), pp. 67-78; Nicol Poulantzas, *Political Power and Social Classes* (London: Verso, 1978); Fred Block, "The Ruling Class Does Not Rule: Notes on the Marxist Theory of the State," *Socialist Revolution* 7(3) (May-June 1977), pp. 6-28; Paul M. Sweezy, *The Theory of Capitalist Development* (New York: Modern Reader Paperbacks, 1942); Paul A. Baran and Paul M. Sweezy, *Monopoly Capital* (New York: Modern Reader Paperbacks, 1966); Theda Skocpol, "Political Response to Capitalist Crisis: Neo-Marxist Theories of the State and the Case of the New Deal," *Politics and Society* 10 (2) (1980), pp. 155-201.

10. Ian Gough, *The Political Economy of the Welfare State* (London: MacMillan Press, 1980), p. 49.

11. *Ibid.*, pp. 44-45.

12. James Dickinson, "From Poor Law to Social Insurance: The Periodization of State Intervention in the Reproduction Process, " in James Dickinson and

Bob Russell (eds.), *Family, Economy, & State* (New York: St. Martins Press, 1986), pp. 113-149.

13. James Dickinson and Bob Russell, "Introduction: The Structure of Reproduction in Capitalist Society," in Dickinson and Russell (eds.) *op. cit.*, (1986), pp. 9-10.

14. Sweezy (1942) *op. cit.*, p. 249.

15. *Ibid.*, pp. 58-62.

16. Paul Corrigan, "The Welfare State as an Arena of Class Struggle," *Marxism Today* (March 1977), pp. 87-93; Gough, *op. cit;* Frances Fox Piven and Richard A. Cloward, *The New Class War* (New York: Pantheon Books, 1982).

17. Thomas Weisskopf, "The Current Economic Crisis in Historical Perspective," *Socialist Review* #57 (May-June 1981), pp. 9-54.

18. Jaggar (1983) *op. cit.*, pp. 34-35, 173-185.

19. Zillah Eisenstein, *The Radical Future of Liberal Feminism* (New York: Longman, 1981), pp. 4, 201-219.

20. Conversation with Joan Tronto, May 1987, Political Science Department, Hunter College, New York, NY.

21. Hester Eisenstein, *Contemporary Feminist Thought* (London: G. K. Hall, 1983), pp. 15-26.

22. Mary Daly, *Gyn/Ecology: The Metaethics of Radical Feminism* (Boston: Beacon Press, 1978), p. 326.

23. See *The Woman Question: Selections from the Writings of Karl Marx, Frederick Engels , V. I. Lenin and Joseph Stalin* (New York: International Publishers, 1951).

24. Natalie J. Sokoloff, *Between Money and Love: The Dialectic of Women's Home and Market Work* (New York: Praeger, 1981), pp. 115-119, 144-145.

25. *Ibid.*, p. 18.

26. *Ibid.*, p. 146.

27. *Ibid.*, p. 151; Jaggar (1983) *op. cit.*, p. 127.

28. Elizabeth Fox-Genovese, "Placing Women's History in History," *New Left Review* no. 133 (May-June 1982), pp. 22-23.

29. Louis Althusser, *Lenin and Philosophy* (New York: Monthly Review Press,1971), pp. 127-189; Jaggar, *op. cit.*, p. 156.

30. Sokoloff (1981) *op. cit.*, p. 12.

31. *Ibid.*, p. 120.

32. Jane Ursel, "The State and the Maintenance of Patriarchy: A Case Study of Family, Labour and Welfare Legislation in Canada," in James Dickinson and Bob Russell (eds.) (1986) *op. cit.*, pp. 150-192.

33. Jaggar (1983) *op. cit.*, p. 159; Sokoloff (1981) *op. cit.*, pp. 120-124; Ursel (1986) *op. cit.*, pp. 150-152.

34. For a review of the long theoretical debate among Marxists about the meaning of women's domestic labor see Sokoloff (1981) *op. cit.*, pp. 112-140 and references therein.

35. Jaggar (1983) *op. cit.*, pp. 139, 144-147; Sokoloff (1981) *op. cit.*, p. 145.

36. Sokoloff (1981) *op. cit.*, pp. 203-251.

37. This section draws heavily on: Bonnie Thornton Dill, *Our Mothers' Grief: Racial Ethnic Women and the Maintenance of Families*, Research Paper #4, May 1986, Center For Research on Women, Memphis State University, Memphis Tennessee 38152; Evelyn Nakano Glenn "Racial Ethnic Women's Labor: The Intersection of Race, Gender and Class Oppression," *Review of Radical Political Economics*, 17 (3) (Fall 1985), pp. 86-108.

38. Glenn, *op. cit.*, pp. 104-106.

39. Bette Wood and Michelene Malson, *In Crisis: Low Income Black Employed Women in the U.S. Workplace*, Working Paper No. 131, 1984, Wellesley College Center For Research On Women, Wellesley, MA 01281.

40. Elizabeth Wilson, *Women and the Welfare State* (London: Tavistock Publications, 1977).

41. Mary McIntosh, "The State and the Oppression of Women," in Annette Kuhn and Ann Marie Wolpe (eds.), *Feminism and Materialism: Women and Modes of Production* (London: Routledge and Kegan Paul, 1978), pp. 254-289.

42. Hillary Land, "Women: Supporters or Supported?" in Barker, D. L. and Allen, S. (eds.), *Sexual Divisions in Society* (London: Tavistock Publications, 1976); Hillary Land, "Who Cares For The Family," *Journal of Social Policy* 7 (3) (1978), pp. 357-384; Hillary Land, "The Family Wage," *Feminist Review,* 6 (1980), pp. 55-57; and Parket, R., "Implicit and Reluctant Family Policy—United Kingdom," in Kamerman, S. B. and Kahn, A. J. (eds.), *Family Policy: Government and Families in Fourteen Countries* (New York: Columbia University Press, 1978).

43. Carol Brown, "Mothers Fathers and Children: From Private to Public Patriarchy," in Lydia Sargent (ed.), *Women and Revolution: A Discussion of the Unhappy Marriage of Marxism and Feminism* (Boston: South End Press, 1981), pp. 239-267.

44. Zillah R. Eisenstein, *Feminism and Sexual Equality: Crisis in Liberal America* (New York: Monthly Review Press, 1984).

45. Jaggar (1983) *op. cit.*

46. Ursell (1986) *op. cit.*

47. Z. Eisenstein (1984) *op. cit.*, p. 92.

48. *Ibid.*, pp. 89-92.

49. Ursell (1986) *op. cit.;* pp. 154-155, 157; Brown (1981) *op. cit.*, pp. 239-267.

50. Ursell (1986) *op. cit.*, p. 158.

51. McIntosh (1978) *op. cit.*

52. Z. Eisenstein (1981) *op. cit.*, pp. 104-105.

53. Julie A. Matthaei, *An Economic History of Women In America* (New York, Shocken Books, 1982), pp. 3-7.

54. See for example: Nancy F. Cott, *The Bonds of Womanhood: "Woman's Sphere" in New England, 1780-1835* (New Haven: Yale University Press, 1977); Barbara Welter, "The Cult of True Womanhood: 1820-1860," in Michael Gordon (ed.), *The American Family in Socio-Historical Perspective* (New York: St. Martin's Press, 1978), pp. 313-333; Barbara Epstein, "Industrialization and Femininity: A Case Study of Nineteenth Century New England," in Rachel Kahn-Hut, Arlene Kaplan Daniels, Richard Colvard (eds.), *Women and Work: Problems and Perspectives* (New York: Oxford University Press, 1982), pp. 88-100; Barbara J. Harris, *Beyond Her Sphere: Women and the Professions in American History* (Westport, Ct: Greenwood Press, 1983), pp. 32-72; Laurel Thatcher Ulrich, *Good Wives: Image and Reality in the Lives of Women in Northern New England* (New York: Oxford University Press, 1982).

55. Dill (1986) *op. cit.*, pp. 48-49.

56. Glenn (1985) *op. cit.*, pp. 86-109.

57. Dill (1986) *op. cit.*, p. 15.

The Colonial Family Ethic: The Development of Families, the Ideology of Women's Roles, and the Labor of Women
Mimi Abramovitz

Recruiting Women to North America

Only a few women accompanied the first exploring parties and trading companies that reached North America. Several dozen female names appeared on the passenger lists before 1616, but not until 1619 did the numbers begin to grow. The European nations and commercial trading companies expected to reap quick profits from the riches of America.[1] Presuming no need for permanent migration, they typically sent male traders, explorers, and fortune hunters to the New World. But once they discovered that commercial profits and economic development required stabilized communities rather than rapid exploitation,[2] the trading companies began to bring women to America to stimulate the formation of families. The need for women's reproductive and productive labor led to the recruitment of wives, indentured servants, and slaves to the colonies. Only a few settlers married Native American women who already lived on and worked what, for the European explorers, was a new land.

White Wives

The first free white women came to the New World with those male explorers who brought their families with them.[3] To induce bachelor farmers to marry and settle down and to keep unmarried fortune hunters from returning home, colonial leaders began to devise ways to increase the supply of free white women. The owner of the Virginia Trading Company of London, for example, proposed that brides be sent to the Virginia planters. "He wished that a fit hundred might be sent of women, maids young and uncorrupt, to make wives to the inhabitants and by that means to make the men there more settled and less moveable who by defect therefor (as is credibly reported) stay there but to get something and then to return to England." Such instability it was feared would "breed a dissolution and so an overthrow of the plantation."[4]

Trading companies devised a variety of incentives to induce men to marry and to attract white women to the New World. They paid the transportation costs for planters who took a recruited wife, provided additional land to men who married, and promised servants to new couples to help "preserve families and proper family men before single persons." In 1619, the Virginia House of Burgess allotted husbands an equal land share for their wives, declaring, "in a newe plantation it is not knowne whether man or woman be the most necessary." In all, the

Virginia company sent 140 women to the colony between 1620 and 1622.[5]

Other colonies enticed women with the promise of property rather than a breadwinner. Pennsylvania offered seventy-five acres to women who came at their own expense and Salem, Massachusetts offered "maid lotts" to women without husbands.[6] This inducement had to be eliminated, however, when some independent female landowners chose not to marry. The Maryland legislature in 1634 introduced a bill threatening to repossess land from women who did not marry within seven years after receiving it.[7] The governor of Massachusetts refused land to Deborah Holmes, "being a maid"; he wanted to avoid "all presedents and evill of graunting lotts unto single maidens not disposed of." Holmes got a bushel of corn instead.[8] Georgia, settled a hundred years later, not only refused to grant women land, but denied them the right to inherit.[9]

The great need for women in the colonies also encouraged the "sale" of wives. A sea captain in the early seventeenth century brought 144 single women looking for husbands to Virginia and sold them as "wives" for 120 pounds of leaf tobacco—or about $80. While this captain advertised for women looking to marry, others simply kidnapped young women off the streets of London for sale as wives or indentured servants to men in the American colonies.[10]

White Indentured Servants

The indenture system accounted for one-third to one-half of all immigrants to North America until the American Revolution.[11] Owing to the scarcity of labor prior to slavery, female and male indentured servants from Europe became an important labor supply, especially in the middle-Atlantic and southern colonies. Forty percent of Virginia's population of about 1,100 were indentured servants in 1625.[12] By 1671, the colony's population of 40,000 persons included 2,000 black slaves and 6,000 white servants. In Maryland, too, nearly all the newly arrived unmarried women were indentured.

Many women voluntarily took advantage of colonial shortages of women and labor by agreeing to "indenture" themselves to a prosperous person for a fixed period of time (typically four to seven years) in exchange for transportation to America. Others, as noted above, arrived involuntarily, victims of organizations that kidnapped and sold servants in the colonies. The British government also "banished" displaced agricultural workers, felons, convicts, vagrants, prostitutes, and other "undesirables" into servitude in the colonies where they worked for the Crown.[13] In 1635, Charles I ordered the sheriff of London to send nine female convicts to Virginia to be sold as servants. In 1692, a judge ordered "fifty lewd women out of the house of corrections and thirty others who walked the streets at night" to be sent to America.[14] Britain used this colonial labor to develop its trade and commerce, to supply raw materials to the mother country, and to purchase finished products from it at a good price. Britain also used the colonies as a dumping ground for those who might cause social unrest.

Most indentured servants traveled to the New World on overloaded vessels, crowded beyond capacity by shipmasters to assure that deaths en route did not lower their profits. One traveler reported that:

During the voyage there is on board these ships terrible misery, stench, fume, horror, vomiting, many kinds of seasickness, fever, dysentery, headache, heat, constipation, boils, scurvy, cancer, mouth rot, and the like of which comes from old and sharply salted food and meat, also from the very bad and foul water, so that many die miserable...Add to this want of provisions, hunger, thirst, frost, heat, dampness, anxiety, want, afflictions and lamentations, together with other trouble as e.g. the lice abound so frightfully, especially on sick people, that they can be scraped off the body. The misery reaches a climax when a gale rages for two or three nights so that everyone believes that the ship will go to the bottom with all human beings on board. In such a visitation the people cry and pray most piteously.[15]

Upon arrival in America, passengers paid their transportation before leaving the ship. Unlike free white women recruited to form families as well as to work the land, the colonies treated indentured servants as individual laborers. Buyers separated husbands from wives, and parents often had to sell their children into service never to see them again. "Soul Drivers" purchased other passengers, driving fifty or more servants through the countryside like cattle, offering them for sale to the highest bidder.[16]

Black Female Indentured Servants and Slaves

With the development of a large-scale plantation economy and the end of the Royal African Company's monopoly on the slave trade, slavery superceded white indentured servants as a profitable and sure source of labor.[17] However, the first black women to arrive in America were indentured servants. Twenty blacks, including three black women, traveled on a Dutch ship to Jamestown in 1619, a year before the *Mayflower* voyage. Prohibited by law to sell baptized blacks into slavery, the government bought their contracts and sold them as indentured servants to colonial administrators.[18] When their contracts expired, the early African arrivals became farmers, artisans, and landowners who voted, had servants, and even some slaves.[19] Former black servants contributed to the rise of a free black population in America. Representing 7.9 percent of all blacks in 1790, the free black population grew faster than the slave population until the 1820s and consisted as well of West Indian refugees and American slaves who gained their freedom by flight, purchase, or release from conscientious masters.

Most Africans, however, arrived in America as slaves. Philip Curtin, the first person to systematically analyze the available evidence, estimates that British North America imported about 5 percent of the nine to ten million Africans who reached the New World in the 350 years of transatlantic slave trade.[20] The majority of Africans went to Brazil and the Caribbean. Most slaves—the prisoners of tribal wars, those sold by chiefs to black slave merchants, and those kidnapped by white slavers—came from the West African coast between Senegal and Angola, a region extending 300 miles inland, whose rich culture was strongly influenced by that of the western Sudan, an important center in the development of human culture.[21] Those Africans who survived the voyage to America brought a multitude of languages, skills, crafts, and cultural heritages to the New World. The black population in the colonies (both free and slave) rose from twenty in 1619 to 16,700 in 1690 to 325,000 in 1760 when blacks accounted for 22 percent of the nation's population.[22] Like indentured servants, slaves were imported to the colonies to work. For black women this meant working the fields and reproducing the slave labor force. Instead of assisting the formation of families as colonial society did for free whites, the imposition of slavery tore black families apart.

The long journey to America was an extremely harsh one for black women and men. Unlike the trip by free whites and many indentured servants, the trip from Africa was involuntary, deliberately brutal, and, in effect, the initial stage of an indoctrination process meant to transform the free African into a docile and marketable slave. After examining Africans for health and physical prowess, slave traders, often Arab or black, marched their captives long distances to coastal warehouses where they were stored until a shipload was amassed.[23] Aboard ship the slaveowners chained their "cargo" in pairs and forced them to lie on their backs or on their sides in cramped spaces often only eighteen inches high. Lack of space, mobility, fresh air, and food killed 6 to 16 percent of the slaves en route.[24] Schools of sharks often followed slave ships across the Atlantic, feeding on the bodies of the dead and the sick thrown overboard to check the spread of infection, and those who tried to escape by jumping ship.

The first ships contained only a few African women, but over time their numbers grew to about one-third. Their experience aboard ship, like that of black men, foreshadowed the conditions of slavery in America. Both sexes were stripped and branded, although at times the women were freed from the chains used to confine black men. Some traders branded black women under the breast with smaller irons, so as not to jeopardize their future marketability and readily whipped women who cried out in pain or resisted the hot iron. The nakedness of the African females served as a constant reminder of their sexual vulnerability to any white male who might choose to physically abuse and torment them. According to one witness," The younger women fared best at first as they were allowed to come on deck as companions for our crew...Toward the end of the run, which lasted nearly six weeks, the mortality thinned out the main hold, and some scores of women were driven below as company for the males."[25] The crew often raped black women to torture them or to subdue the recalcitrant. Slavers also ridiculed captured women contemptuously, often brutalizing children just to watch the anguish of their mothers.

While some women were pregnant prior to their purchase, one observer explained that "...many a Negress was landed upon our shores already impregnated by someone of the demonic crew that brought her over."[26] Women who survived the early stages of their pregnancy received little food or exercise and gave birth in the scorching sun or freezing cold without any assistance during labor.[27] One traveler noted, "I saw pregnant women give birth to babies while chained to corpses which our drunken overseers had not removed."[28] The number of black women who died in childbirth or lost their babies will never be known, but a ship doctor reports high insanity rates, especially among the women:

> One day at Bonny I saw a middle-aged stout woman, who had been brought down from a fair the proceeding day, chained to the post of a black trader's door, in a state of furious insanity. On board the ship was a young negro woman chained to the deck, who had lost her senses soon after she was purchased and taken on board. In a former voyage we were obliged to confine a female negro about 23 years of age, on her becoming a lunatic. She was afterward sold during one of her lucid intervals.[29]

Many plantation owners continued to torture and terrorize slave women and men to force them to suppress their own needs, to accept their inferiority and dependence, to ally themselves with the will of the master, and to accede to their own enslavement.

The Colonial Economy

The work and family life of women in the colonies was shaped by the imperatives of the agricultural economy, the institution of slavery, and the ideology of women's roles. Nearly all of the initial white women and men who came to America settled in rural areas and engaged in farming and other agricultural pursuits. However, as increasing numbers of Dutch, English, German, and Scot-Irish immigrants established new settlements farther South, North, and West, colonial villages became diverse ranging from new outposts to century-old communities.

The shock of entry into a wilderness vitally conditioned life in this pre-industrial society. Some families lived in log cabins, lacked the equipment needed to weave, to make candles, or even to grind flour, and like Native Americans wore skin clothing and used grease and rags to provide light. By the end of the seventeenth century, improved production techniques permitted New England farmers to live in more substantial quarters and to grow some surplus for export. During the eighteenth century, men farmed and fished while women manufactured a variety of goods for both use and trade. A rural class structure composed of a landed gentry, small landowners, yeoman farmers, and landless peasants emerged.

Larger cities such as Philadelphia, New York, Boston, and Charleston also sprung up in the mid-eighteenth century around Eastern seaboard centers of commerce and manufacturing. Here, the merchant elite, the upper crust of "urban" society, exchanged the products of American farms and forests for English, European, and West Indian food and African slaves. Craftpersons, retailers, innkeepers, and small jobbers comprised the middle class, while the working class consisted of sailors, unskilled workers, and some artisans.[30]

The South was shaped by the plantation economy and the institution of slavery. Slavery became a key factor to both American industry and European commerce when colonial economic development, especially in the South, suffered from British economic restrictions, widespread labor shortages, and the refusal of the Native American population to be enslaved. Slavers imported more than two million Africans to the West Indies and America between 1680 and 1786, including many women.[31] The inhumane slave trade itself became extremely profitable with gains ranging from one-third to one-half or more on original investments.[32] That the English enslaved Native Americans and Africans but never their white captives suggests that racism was deeply ingrained in America prior to slavery.[33] To the Puritans, blacks were barbarians, uncivilized, unchristian, and inferior persons not entitled to the same human rights as whites.[34]

Virginia, whose court records showed blacks in hereditary life service by 1640,[35] legalized slavery in the mid-1650s followed by Massachusetts, Maryland, New York, the Carolinas, Pennsylvania, Delaware, and Rhode Island. Most slaves worked on southern plantations. But slaves, distributed widely among small slaveholders, also began to supplement free white labor in northern cities.[36] Between 1710 and 1742, the number of slaves in Boston quadrupled, reaching 8.5 percent of the city's population, while the white population only doubled. Black slaves comprised more than 18 percent of New York's population in 1731 and over 21 percent in 1746.[37]

In both the North and the South, the pre-industrial household functioned as the center of economic production and social reproduction. Until the manufacturing economy of the early nineteenth century separated household and market activities, the colonial household was the basic unit of economic production as well as the place of procreation, socialization, maintenance, consumption, and recreation. It relied heavily on the labor of free white women, white indentured servants, and black female slaves. The nature and meaning of women's productive and reproductive labor in colonial society was governed by gender, race, class, marital status, and degrees of servitude; and by the colonial family ethic, that is, the prevailing ideology of women's roles.

The Colonial Family Ethic

The colonial settlers brought patriarchal ideas about the proper role of women with them to the New World. Although the intense interest in the ideals of male and female temperament, which accompanied the rise of industrialization did not yet exist, the European settlers did subscribe to an array of feminine stereotypes and role prescriptions including—women as the "weaker vessel," the seductive Eve, the loose-tongued gossip—as well as notions of female meekness, wifely obedience, and the injunction to be a sturdy, orderly, and industrious helpmeet. Referred to here as the colonial family ethic, these ideas informed women (and men) about their proper work and family roles. Fulfilling the terms of the colonial family ethic established a woman's femininity, her womanhood, and her social respectability, and non-compliance brought penalties. Directed primarily toward white, married, middle-class homemakers, the colonial family ethic largely reflected their experience. As the dominant ideology encoded in the rules and regulations of most societal institutions, the colonial family ethic exerted considerable influence over the entire social order. Indeed, colonial society measured, valued, and rewarded indentured servants, free black women, and black female slaves according to their conformity to its terms.

The Family

Colonial society placed the patriarchal family at the center of the social order. Defined as "little cells of righteousness" that held a "watchfulle eye" over the conduct of every individual and enforced the laws of God,[38] families assumed the responsibility for teaching religion, morality, the work ethic, obedience to the laws, deference to authority, and general good conduct at home. Supported by prevailing norms and laws, the colonial family operated as the key unit for survival, socialization, and social stability.[39]

In this view, the father's unquestioned rule was the only assurance of a proper discharge of the family's obligations. A leading Puritan theologian of the time wrote, "in the good man or master of the familie resteth the private and proper government of the whole household, and he comes not unto it by election as it falleth out in other states, but by the ordinance of God settled even in the order of nature. The husband indeed naturally beares rule over the wife, parent over their children, master over their servants."[40] Colonial society expected free white women to marry, to bear and raise children, and to manage a household in which they were economically productive, but faithful, obedient, and subordinate to men. To be proper helpmeets, colonial women each had to acquire a husband and a family, and had to take up homemaking in her own home.

Marriage

Marriage became the lynchpin of the colonial family ethic. "True womanhood" required the presence of and dependence on a male breadwinner.[41] The association between women and wife was so close that in some English dialects the two words had the same meaning. In northern New England, for example, between 1650 and 1750, most women were called "Goodwife," usually shortened to "Goody," as in Goody Prince, Goody Quilter, or Goody Lee.[42] Reflecting the economics of survival as well as patriarchal rules, colonial laws encouraged white women and men to marry, divorced persons to remarry, and required bachelors, spinsters, and other unmarried persons to live within an established household. A 1669 Plymouth statute read:

> Whereas great inconvenience hath arisen by single persons in this colony being for themselves and not betaking themselves to live in well-governed families. It is enacted by the Court that henceforth no single person be suffered to live of himself [sic] or in any family but such as the Selectman of the Town shall approve of; and if any person or persons shall refuse or neglect to attend such order as shall be given them by the Selectman, that person or persons shall be summoned to the Court to be proceeded with as the matter shall require.[43]

Town courts fined single persons and couples who lived apart, and taxed bachelors and self-supporting single women for evading their civic responsibilities.[44] Unmarried women, in addition, faced social disapproval as dependent girls and incomplete women. Without a husband, a colonial woman was not a "real" woman. Single women with means and widows were respected somewhat more, but newspapers and town gossips often characterized single females as unattractive, disagreeable "old virgins" unable to catch a man.[45]

Subordination

Colonial society expected married women to be subordinate to their husbands who by law and custom controlled women's labor and access to economic resources. According to one historian,

> Control rested with the male head to whom all others were subordinate. His sanctions were powerful; they rested upon traditions that went back beyond the memory of man [sic]; on the instinctive sense of order as hierarchy, whether in the cosmic chain of being or in human society; on the processes of law that reduced the female to perpetual dependence and calibrated a detailed scale of female subordination and servitude; and above all on the restrictions of the economy which made the establishment of independent households a difficult enterprise.[46]

Justified by the Old Testament's patriarchal model and prevailing cultural assumptions of female weakness and inferiority, religious leaders held that submission to God and submission to one's husband were part of the same doctrine. Economics and civil law further enforced female subordination. The exclusion of women from economic activity independent of their husbands or fathers left them financially dependent and poorly positioned for self-support. Colonial law acknowledged women's economic importance in deeds and wills that typically granted some resources to wives, but this recognition did not extend to the basic rights of land ownership, political participation, or social equality.[47]

English Common Law, the basis of much American law, caused married women to suffer "civil death" by holding that in "marriage, the husband and wife are one person in law; that is, the very being or legal existence of the woman is suspended during the marriage, or at least is incorporated and consolidated into that of the husband; under whose wing, protection, and cover she performs everything."[48] A married woman's inheritance, property, income, and even her clothing belonged to her husband, who could sell her possessions without her consent. She could not buy or sell, make contracts, sue in court, or be sued without her husband's permission. Married women could not even claim their children in cases of legal separation.[49]

The obedience and submission of women to men was also evidenced in laws that required female chastity and sexual fidelity. According to religious doctrine, God told Eve, "Thy desire shall be to thy husband and he shall rule over thee."[50] Colonial society openly acknowledged female sexuality, including the sexual needs of married women whose "intemperate longings" a husband was duty-bound to gratify. Failure to do so, be it due to impotence or willful denial, could be grounds for separation.[51] The community, however, did not condone extra-marital sex. Harsh laws severely penalized adultery, pre-marital sex, and out-of-wedlock births.

Within the law, however, a double standard prevailed. Adulterous relations by or with a married woman received the most severe penalties and could result in a death sentence. Sex between a married man and a single woman or between two single persons received a harsh but lighter response. Public opinion also tolerated greater violation of sexual norms by men than women. Popular magazines advised women to conceal their husband's infidelities while engaging in none of their own. A 1771 issue of the *Ladies Journal* stated:

> A licentious commerce between the sexes. . .may be carried on by the men without contaminating the mind so as to render them unworthy of the marriage bed, and incapable of discharging the virtuous and honorable duties of husband, father and friend...[But] the contamination of the female mind is the necessary and inseparable consequence of an illicit intercourse with men...[W]omen are universally virtuous or utterly undone.[52]

According to Dr. Samuel Johnson, the double standard protected propertied men from passing their wealth along to a child fathered by someone else. He explained that "Confusion of progeny constitutes the essence of the crime; therefore a woman who breaks her marriage vows is much more criminal than a man who does it."[53]

Economic Productivity

Private homemaking became the centerpiece of colonial womanhood. The colonial family ethic defined free white women as industrious helpmeets, placed a great value on the average woman's productive labor in the home, and called upon them to make an economic contribution to the family and the community. The expectation of such productivity from women meshed with the household economy's needs but also with Puritanism's strong negative sanction against idleness.

Household work followed a clearly defined but flexible gender division of labor.[54] Men worked largely outdoors and in the fields while women worked closer to home. Colonial homemaking included the supervision of the home, the manufacture of household goods, the planting and preparation of food, and the spinning and weaving of cloth. Women also assisted with the harvest, helped in the family store, and produced crafts. In cash poor and frontier families, men struggled to produce for the market, to build up capital goods, and to save cash income for future investment. Wives contributed by reducing family expenditures and providing for most of the family's basic subsistence needs. They fed, clothed, and cared for their large families, made household furnishings, and often defended their frontier homes against attack.[55] Many colonial women also functioned as "deputy husbands," shouldering male duties from the most menial to the management of the family's external business affairs. Women could assume almost any task as long as it furthered the good of their family, was acceptable to their husband, and remained close to the confines of the home. But in all cases, women's productive labor was defined as secondary to that of male providers.[56] Any income that resulted from women's work was seen as saving money by reducing the demand on their husband's overall capital.[57]

Reproductive Tasks

As caretakers of the family and the community, colonial wives attended to the ill, aged, young, and disabled family members as well as to the widowed, orphaned, and destitute. Childbearing, a central part of women's homemaking role, conferred status upon women in a world where high infant mortality rates and a heavy dependence on child labor dictated large families. While bearing many children helped to perpetuate the family and to strengthen the community, infertility signaled female failure. Given the limits of prevailing medical knowledge, however, childbearing was dangerous work. One out of every five women in seventeenth-century Plymouth, Massachusetts died from causes associated with childbirth.[58]

While pregnancy and childbirth occupied many of a woman's adult years, seventeenth- and eighteenth-century America did not idealize motherhood.[59] Expected to show affection and sentiment, colonial society discouraged undue indulgence as a troublesome invitation to disorder and disobedience. Puritan ministers warned against "a Mother's excessive fondness" and the tendency of mothers to spoil their children. The conditions of colonial life reinforced these views. High infant mortality rates and large families left mothers with little time to dote on their children or to become too emotionally involved with them.[60]

Except for childbearing, breastfeeding, and the preliminary education of the very young, social conventions assigned few childrearing tasks exclusively to mothers. In wealthy families children were suckled and raised by wet nurses, servants, and black slaves. In all classes, considerable responsibility for parental governance also rested with fathers[61] who disciplined children and supervised their education, religious instruction, and vocational training.[62] This pattern meshed with the authority attributed to the patriarch and with the Puritan devaluation of women as less rational and requiring the guidance of men. The structure of the home economy also permitted these parenting arrangements. Men worked in sufficient proximity to their children to become involved in their development. Colonial women who lacked time for extensive involvement could care for infants while cooking, weaving, and keeping an eye on farm animals.[63] With both economic and domestic activities taking place in the home, there was no obvious line between women's productive and reproductive labor. Productive tasks associated with economic matters were intermingled with reproductive tasks associated with childrearing, consumption, and home maintenance.

Class Differences

Both geography and the class position of a free white woman's husband determined the character of her work.[64] Less marked than in Europe, class distinctions in the colonies were based on differentials in wealth and landholdings. Indeed, in the middle class and upper class, a second image of woman as a decorous object and charming companion began to emerge. Unlike the later Victorian lady of "leisure," however, the image of the colonial gentlewoman meshed with society's demand that women be industrious. What differentiated her from lower classes of colonial women was the greater availability of resources, greater household help, and greater attention paid to grace and style.[65]

Instead of producing food and clothes themselves, the homemaking duties of wealthy colonial wives involved purchasing goods and services in the market, managing the many details of a large household, and supervising the work of servants and slaves. Feminine graces and the charms of female social companionship also added to their utility.[66] Taught to be charming, fashionable, and accomplished in drawing, painting, and French, upper-class housewives also played a social, entertaining, and decorative role.[67]

In sum, colonial society expected white women to marry, to make an economic contribution to the family and the community, to bear and raise children, to remain morally pure, and to manage a household under male authority and control. Those who followed the rules—acquired a family and pursued homemaking according to the needs of the household economy and the norms of patriarchy—won social approval as a "true woman." Because profits and economic growth required the formation and protection of white families, colonial leaders encouraged their organization and development.[68] Although white women were not granted equal rights and full social participation, colonial society acknowledged and supported the contribution their productive and reproductive labor made to the growth and stability of the family, the community, and the wider social order.

White Servants, Black Slaves, and Colonial Womanhood

The structure of colonial society denied the stamp of respectable womanhood to unfree women, both white indentured servants who were owned temporarily and black female slaves who were locked into involuntary and lifelong bondage. The same profitable development of colonial society which necessitated granting the "rights of womanhood" to free white women, led owners to refuse them to servants and slaves, along with their legal and economic rights.

Colonial norms which encouraged white women to develop their own families defined female servants and slaves first and foremost as individual units of labor. Indeed, the productive labor that female servants and slaves performed for their master's household took precedence over the productive and reproductive activities conducted on behalf of their own families. Prevented by law from marrying, their own mothering and homemaking roles were subsumed to their laboring tasks and accorded little recognition or support in white society. Colonial society left servants and slaves vulnerable to sexual exploitation and rationalized this by viewing them as sexually available and morally impure.

Female Indentured Servants

The female servant's productive and reproductive labor was almost completely controlled by the master for the term of the indenture. Masters prevented servants from marrying, leaving, or even buying anything without permission.[69] Although practices varied by region, typically indentured servants were poorly compensated and deprived of good food and privacy. Servants who tried to escape, and many did try, faced severe punishment, including fines, whipping, and branding for a second offense, as well as extended service. They received similar penalties for theft and laziness. Unlike slaves, however, the white indentured servant received some protection under the law which specified the provision of certain amounts of food and clothing, banned corporal punishment,[70] and permitted servants to sue their owners, with the courts granting freedom or shortened service.[71] Most critically, the servitude of indentured servants was contracted and ended after a stipulated period of time.

The rules of indenture barred servants from doing anything that threatened to impair or interrupt their productive labor. A female servant who became pregnant, thus degrading her productivity, faced heavy fines and possible whipping for failure to pay. To compensate for her reduced service and to punish the sin, her term might be extended as much as two years, if the father of her child did not purchase her remaining years of labor. If impregnated by her master, as frequently happened, the town denied extra service to him, selling it to the town instead.[72]

Some women escaped servitude when prospective husbands purchased the remainder of their time,[73] but most completed their contracts. At the end of the indenture period, servants were entitled to freedom dues, typically a few barrels of Indian corn, some clothing, or a small parcel of land. Although written into the contract, such freedom dues were not always paid.[74] Given the shortage of women, former indentured servants tended to marry quickly. Some married "up"; others entered the working class as wives or as domestic servants; still others drifted off and joined the ranks of the colonial poor along with formerly indentured men.[75]

Black Female Slaves

White colonial society simply denied the "rights of womanhood" to black female slaves. The very notion of black womanhood under slavery contradicted the prevailing ideology of women's proper role. Enslaved black women never possessed the right to legal marriage, to family integrity, or to protection against economic or sexual abuse. In an economy dependent on subordinated labor, female slaves worked outside their own families and outside of a woman's homemaking role.

The productive and reproductive labor of black women, central to the slave labor system, was owned and regulated by white masters who used force or the threat of force to extract as much work as possible from them. Female slave labor contributed to the master's economic well-being in both the "big house" and in the field, while the capacity of black women to reproduce guaranteed the growth of the slave labor force.[76] On the large plantations, 70 to 90 percent of the slaves of both genders worked in the fields. Black women hoed, shoveled, plowed, planted, and harvested; they felled trees, split rails, drove and loaded carts, and otherwise assumed tasks defined by white society as "men's" work. According to one ex-slave, "it was usual for men and women to work side by side on our plantation; and in many kinds of work, the women were compelled to do as much as the men."[77] Indeed, planters considered the sexual division of labor to be economically inefficient and disregarded it when organizing the tasks of slaves.[78] With the rise of industry, some slave-owners began to "rent" female slaves to the builders of southern roads, canals, levees, and railroads and to owners of mines, iron works, factories, and lumbering companies.[79]

Less than 5 percent of all adult slaves worked in the elite corps of trained household servants, the advantages of which were exaggerated by whites, according to slave narratives. In the "big house," where labor was more likely to be gender-typed, black women worked as nurses, cooks, seamstresses, washerwomen, and dairy keepers, and provided the elbow grease for most domestic chores, although during harvests they were frequently sent into the fields. Housework was backbreaking, closely supervised, and as fast-paced as work in the fields. The black woman's proximity to the master in the "big house" created special problems for slave women. Masters sometimes kept them "on call," forced them to remain standing in the presence of whites, and made them sleep on the floor at the foot of their mistress' bed. Under these conditions, white owners could also rape and sexually assault their female house slaves more easily and with impunity.[80]

Minor infractions or failure to accomplish the expected amount of work might result in severe chastisement in both the field or the manor. Masters whipped black female slaves for burning the waffles or oversleeping. One female fugitive slave reported:

One day I set the table and forgot to put on the carving-fork—the knife was there. I went to the table to put on a plate. My master said,—"Where's the fork?" I told him, "I forgot it." He says,—"You'd d— black b——, I'll forget you!"—at the same time hitting me on the head with the carving knife...I was frequently punished with raw hides,—was hit with tongs and pokers and anything. I used when I went out, to look up at the sky and say, "Blessed Lord, oh do take me out of this." It seemed to me I could not bear another lick. I can't forget it.[81]

According to another slave woman:

When dey ready to beat you dey'd strip you stark mother naked and dey'd say, "Come here to me, God Damn you. Come to me clean! Walk up to dat tree and damn you, hug dat tree!" Den dey'd tie your hands round de tree, den tie you feets, den dey's lay de rawhide on and cut your buttocks open. Sometimes they's rub turpentine and salt in de raw places, and den beat you some more.[82]

The reproductive labor done by female slaves for their masters was indistinguishable from their productive labor. After the slave trade became illegal in 1808, the line blurred even more as plantation owners placed increased value on the fertility of their female slaves and "breeding" became more common. A southern white traveler observed:

In the states of Maryland, Virginia, North Carolina, Kentucky, Tennessee, as much attention is paid to the breeding and growth of negroes as to that of horses and mules. Further south, we raise them both for use and for market. Planters command their girls and women (married or unmarried) to have children; and I have known a great many girls to be sold off because they did not have children. A breeding woman is worth from one-sixth to one-fourth more than one that does not breed.[83]

Owners often bribed or coerced female slaves to reproduce rapidly, although repeated pregnancies without proper care resulted in numerous miscarriages and sometimes death. Masters promised freedom to slave mothers who gave birth to ten or fifteen children. Slave women were given extra food, special clothes, small sums of money, or were physically coerced to reproduce regularly. Some masters mated black women with white men, as mulattoes often brought a higher price or were easier to sell.

The economic benefits of the female slave's productive and reproductive labor at times, contradicted each other. The extraction of maximum physical labor produced immediate profits, but long hours of back-breaking work could damage a woman's reproductive system and undermine the owner's long-term investment in black female slaves as childbearers.[84] To preserve their ability to breed, some slave-owners gave pregnant and post-partum women fewer or lighter tasks and limited their workloads or floggings. But others forced female slaves to work through most of their pregnancy and put them back to work shortly after their delivery. One ex-slave told of a master who beat nursing mothers whose full breasts slowed them down, "with raw hide so that the blood and milk flew mingled from their breasts."[85] Another tells of an overseer who stripped, tied, and beat a slave woman in an advanced state of pregnancy for three days in a row because she failed to complete her assigned task.[86]

In contrast to the support given to the formation and maintenance of white families, slave-owners and government officials ignored and, in some cases, destroyed the black family. A combination of economics, racism, and fear led slave-owners, particularly those with large plantations and many slaves, to callously separate black family members in sales and estate settlements, to deny recognition of slave marriages, to sexually exploit female slaves, and to degrade all slaves by preventing them from defending family members from abuse.[87] Not all slave-holders engaged in these severe practices or carried them out with the same brutality, but the practices were condoned by the law.

After working in the master's house, fields, and factories, slave women returned home to carry out the reproductive work needed by their family and community. But black women's own homemaking came second and took place under a wide range of cultural assaults.[88] To begin with, the black woman's double day left her chronically over-worked. A former slave recalls,

> I never knowed what it was to rest. I just work all de time from mornin' till late at night. I had to do everythin' dey was to do on de outside. Work in de field, chop wood, hoe corn, till sometimes I feels like my back surely break...In de summer we had to work outdoors, in de winter in de house. I had to card and spin till ten o'clock. Never get much rest, had to get up at four de next mornin' and start again.[89]

Another slave described her work: "What did I do? I spun an' cooked, an' waited, an' plowed; dere weren't nothin' I didn't do."[90]

Black women's work in the slave quarters followed a traditional gender division of labor in which women cared for children and maintained the house. Where the constraints of slavery permitted, men functioned as providers and household heads.[91] Some[92] but not all[93] historians argue that black women were subject to chauvinism from black men. However, the subordination of both the slave homemaker and her husband to their owner renders the discussion of marital inequality difficult. Such subordination left both husband and wife powerless and introduced a strange equality to the slave marriage that was based on shared oppression. Often unable to carry out the role of family provider and protector and lacking the resources of patriarchal society, black men, even when they wanted to, were poorly positioned to turn gender distinctions into female subordination.[94]

Gender distinctions were, however, very significant when it came to white men's treatment of black women. In this relationship, black women were exploited not just because of their race but also because of their sex. Slavery denied black women the rights of motherhood and accorded them virtually no protection against sexual assault by white men. White male ownership of slave children made mothering by slave women a painful and complicated task and allowed a mother to protect her child only so far. In the words of a former slave: "Many a day my ole mama has stood by an' watched massa beat her chillun 'till dey bled an' she couldn' open her mouf."[95] Female slaves also risked losing their offspring to high infant mortality rates or sale in the slave market. Some mothers killed their babies to keep them from being sold down the river; others "descended into madness" or "donned a mask of stoicism" to conceal their inner pain.[96] Still others desperately tried to prevent the sale. Moses Grandy, born a slave, told how his mother resisted the sale of one of his brothers: "My mother, frantic with grief resisted...she was beaten and held down; she fainted, and when she came to herself, her boy was gone. She made much outcry, for which the master tied her up to a peach tree in the yard and flogged her."[97]

The threat of sexual assault from white masters and overseers constantly confronted the female slave. Virtually all the slave narratives contain accounts of the sexual victimization of slave women. One ex-slave reported,

> Ma mama said that a nigger 'oman couldn't help herself, fo' she had to do what de marster say. Ef he come to de field whar de women workin' an' tel gal to come on, she had to go, He would take one down in de woods an' use her all de time he wanted to, den send her on back to work. Times nigger 'omen had chillun for de marster an his sons and some times it was fo' de ovah seer.[98]

Slave narratives refer to Henry Bibb's master who forced one slave girl to be his son's concubine; M.F. Jamison's overseer who raped a slave girl; and Solomon Northrup's owner who forced one slave, "Patsy," to be his sexual partner.[99] Without the right of choice or refusal, virtually any sexual contact between black female slaves and white men with power over them became a form of rape. The child of a slave recounted what happened when his mother tried to choose:

> I don't like to talk 'bout dem times 'cause my mother did suffer misery. You know dar was an overseer who use to tie mother up in the barn wid a rope aroun' her arms up over her head, while she stood on a block. Soon as dey got her tied, di block was moved an' her feet dangled, you know, couldn't tech de flo'. Dis ole man, now would start beaten' her nekked.'til the blood run down her back to her heels. I asked mother 'what she done fer 'em to beat and do her so? She said, 'Nothin 'other dan 'fuse to be wife to dis man.'[100]

The sexual exploitation of black women by white men differentiated their oppression from that of male slaves. The sexual abuse of black female slaves by white men became a weapon of domination that worked to extinguish the slave woman's will.[101] According to Susan Brownmiller, "Rape in slavery was more than a chance tool of violence. It was an institutionalized crime, part and parcel of the white man's subjugation of people for economic and psychological gain [in which] the black woman's sexual integrity was deliberately crushed in order that slavery might profitably endure."[102]

Despite these many assaults and contrary to popular stereotypes, black slaves achieved considerable family stability. Recent research by Gutman and others has uncovered evidence of strong and enduring family ties among slaves.[103] A strict set of kinship norms prescribed sexual mores, marriage ceremonies, and kinship patterns.[104] Most slave families tried, within the limits of the system, to maintain the two-parent, male-headed household quite prevalent in the Afro-American culture. Unions between husbands and wives, and parents and children endured for many years. Even when separated by owners over long distances and great time spans, slave family members, when possible, reunited.

The relationship between the slave family and their masters was a contradictory one. The slave family simultaneously supported and threatened the institution of slavery. Stable slave families, it was hoped, would socialize children to their subordinate status[105] and enhance the productivity of the master's workforce. At the same time, strong family ties among slaves promoted allegiances other than to the slave-master. The wide protective kinship networks formed in the slave community created pride, cohesion, and also became a breeding ground for resistance.[106]

Black slaves—both women and men—resisted their subordination by preventing the full use of their labor, by organizing revolts, and by running away. Resistance began on the slave ships where slaves tried to escape by jumping overboard, drowning themselves, or organizing sometimes successful mutinies.[107] On the plantations, slave women and men deliberately withheld their labor by feigning illness, slowing down their work pace, destroying crops and equipment, and even injuring themselves, all the while assuming an obedient, compliant posture. One ex-slave reports, "I knew a woman who could not be conquered by her mistress, and so when her master threatened to sell her to New Orleans Negro traders, she took her right hand, laid it down on a meat block and cut off three fingers, and thus made the sale impossible."[108] Slaves also taught themselves to read and write in clandestine "midnight schools" often run by women.[109] But perhaps the most dramatic and least known act of resistance among slave women was their refusal to perform their most essential role, producing slave babies. Slave women fought forced mating and used contraceptives and abortive agents to resist the system.[110]

More direct forms of resistance included fighting with their masters or overseers, running away, and organizing slave revolts.[111] Though no one knows for sure, between 40,000 and 100,000 slaves escaped to the North and Canada via the Underground Railroad during the years preceding the Civil War. Harriet Tubman, the Railroad's most famous conductor, made nineteen journeys to the South after her own escape in 1850, bringing over 300 slaves out of Maryland alone.[112] Numerous revolts and rebellions and riots by free blacks during the 1700s and 1800s left the colonists in constant fear of slave insurrections.[113]

Because of their ties to children, slave women ran away less often than men. But from New York to New Orleans they became actively involved in slave uprisings where they fought alongside men, often with guns and knives, and at times committed suicide rather than face capture and execution. Women also committed arson, sabotage, and on occassion poisoned their owners.[114] In 1681, a Massachusetts town court tried a slave named Maria and two male companions for trying to burn down their master's home. One man was banished from the colony, the other hanged; but the town burned Maria at the stake because "she did not have the feare of God before her eyes," and her action seemed to be "instigated by the devil."[115] A small band of slaves who killed seven whites in Newton, Long Island in 1708 included one woman. In 1712, twenty-three armed male and female slaves prepared to set fire to a slave-holder's house in New York City; they killed nine whites and injured six others. A visibly pregnant black slave woman was among those arrested. Black female slaves were known to be involved in slave plots in Louisiana (1730, 1732), in Charleston, South Carolina (1730), in Charlestown, Massachusetts (1741) and many others up until the end of the Civil War.[116] Frequently caught, the men were banished or hanged but women such as Maria, having a "malicious and evil intent," often were burned at the stake—a hideous torture no doubt meant to deter women from participating in these revolts.[117]

Summary

Colonial leaders and traders brought women to the New World as wives, servants, and slaves because their productive and reproductive labor was needed for family formation and economic development. Upon arrival and thereafter, women's experience reflected the demands of the household economy, the strength of patriarchal norms, and their relationship to the institution of slavery. In addition to gender, the character and scope of women's productive and reproductive labor was shaped by their race, class, marital status, and degree of servitude. These characteristics determined not only the personal and economic safety and security of women, but also the value, respect, and support accorded to their reproductive and productive labor. The traits also governed white women's ability to fulfill the terms of the colonial family ethic and reap its rewards. For black women, denied even the opportunity to comply, the family ethic—the white family ethic—only deepened their oppression as women as well as blacks.

Poor women, whose numbers continued to grow despite the contribution of women's labor to the nation's economic growth, confronted the colonial family ethic in the rules and regulations of public relief to which they often turned for help. Embedded in the institutions of public welfare, the colonial family ethic became a means of determining which poor women were aided and how much help they received. By treating women who conformed to the terms of the family ethic more favorably than those who did not, could not, or chose not to do so, the colonial poor laws responded to women differentially. They also helped to support patriarchal family governance and the ideology of women's roles. Chapter Three, which explores the colonial poor laws, presents the first segment in the untold story of the relationship between women and the U.S. social welfare system.

1. June Axinn and Herman Levin, *Social Welfare: A History of the American Response to Need* (New York: Harper and Row, 1975), p. 16.

2. Susan Estabrook Kennedy, *If All We Did Was To Weep At Home: A History of White Working Class Women in America* (Bloomington: Indiana University Press, 1979), pp. 3-4.

3. Barbara M. Wertheimer, *We Were There: The Story of Working Women in America* (New York: Pantheon Books, 1977), p. 7. The first white woman settler in America was the wife of a Spanish soldier who traveled with her husband to Florida and who later died in an Indian raid in 1541. White women, along with black male artisans and agriculturalists, participated in the Spanish and Portuguese colonizing expeditions that, in 1565, founded St. Agustine, the first permanent mainland settlement in the United States. Still others were among the 150 families who, in 1598, accompanied 400 Mexican soldiers into what became the southwestern United States. Seventeen women disappeared between 1587 and 1591. Kennedy (1979) *op. cit.*, p. 4. The second supply ship sent to Jamestown, Virginia in 1608 included at least two women: Lucy, the wife of Thomas Forest and her thirteen year old maid, Anne Buras.

4. Julia Cherry Spruill, *Women's Life and Work in the Southern Colony* (New York: W.W. Norton & Company, 1972), p. 8.

5. *Ibid.*, p. 9.

6. Alice Kessler-Harris, *Out To Work: A History of Wage-Earning Women in the United States* (Oxford: Oxford University Press, 1982), pp. 10-11.

7. Spruill (1972) *op. cit.*, p. 11.

8. Kessler-Harris (1982) *op. cit.*, p. 11, citing Robert B. Morris, *Studies in the History of American Law* (New York: Octagon Books, 1963 [1930]) pp. 131, 134.

9. Spruill (1972) *op. cit.*, p. 17.

10. Carol Hymowitz and Michael Weissman, *A History of Women In America* (New York: Bantam Books, 1980), p. 3; Axinn and Levin (1975) *op. cit.*, p. 17.

11. Wertheimer (1977) *op. cit.*, p. 11.

12. Lois Green Carr and Lorena S. Walsh, "The Planter's Wife: The Experience of White Women in Seventeenth Century Maryland," in Jean E. Friedman and William G. Shade (eds.), *Our American Sisters: Women in American Life and Thought* (Lexington, Mass.: D.C. Heath and Co., 1982), p. 55; Mary P. Ryan, *Womanhood in America: From Colonial Times to the Present* (New York: New Viewpoints, 1975), p. 24.

13. Marcus W. Jernegan, *Laboring and Dependent Classes in Colonial America, 1607-1783* (Chicago: The University of Chicago Press, 1931), pp. 46-48.

14. *Ibid.*, p. 48.

15. Rhea Dulles Foster, *Labor in America*, (New York: Thomas Y. Crowell Co., 1966, third edition), p. 6, cited by Wertheimer (1977) *op. cit.*, p. 11.

16. Jernegan (1931) *op. cit.*, p. 51.

17. August Meier and Elliot Rudwick, *From Plantation to Ghetto* (New York: Hill and Wang, 1976, third edition), pp. 42-43.

18. Paula Giddings, *Where and When I Enter: The Impact of Black Women on Race and Sex in America* (Toronto: Bantam Books, 1985), p. 34.

19. *Ibid.*

20. Julie Matthaei, *An Economic History of Women In America* (New York: Schocken Books, 1982), pp. 74-75; Wertheimer (1977) *op. cit.*, p. 27.

21. Meier and Rudwick (1976, third edition) *op. cit.*, pp. 3-26.

22. Axinn and Levin (1975) *op. cit.*, p. 17.

23. Cited by Meier and Rudwick (1976, third edition) *op. cit.*, p. 38.

24. *Ibid.*, p. 38.

25. Eleanor Flexner, *Century of Struggle: The Women's Rights Movement in the United States* (New York: Antheum, 1968), p. 19, citing George F. Dow, *Slave Ships and Slaving* (Salem, Mass., 1927), p. 242.

26. Bell Hooks, *Ain't I A Woman: Black Women and Feminism* (Boston: South End Press, 1981), p. 18.

27. *Ibid.*

28. Flexner (1968), p. 19, citing Dow, *op. cit.*, (1927), p. 242.

29. *Ibid.*, citing Dow (1927), p. 151.

30. Matthaei (1982) *op. cit.*, pp. 22-23.

31. Wertheimer (1977) *op. cit.*, pp. 29, 109.

32. Meier and Rudwick (1976, third edition) *op. cit.*, p. 40.

33. Gerda Lerner, *Black Women in White America: A Documentary History* (New York: Vintage Books, 1973), p. 5; June Schoen, *Herstory: Record of the American Woman's Past* (Palo Alto: Mayfield Publishing Company, 1981) p. 23; George Brown Tindall, *America: A Narrative History* (New York: W.W. Norton & Co., 1984), Vol. I, p. 100.

34. Lerner (1973) *op. cit.*, p. 5.

35. Tindall (1984) *op. cit.*, p. 98.

36. Meier and Rudwick (1976, third edition) *op. cit.*, pp. 27-28, 40.

37. Gary Nash, *The Urban Crucible: Social Change, Political Consciousness, and the Origins of the America Revolution* (Cambridge: Harvard University Press, 1979), p. 107.

38. Barbara A. Hanawalt, "Women Before The Law: Females as Felons and Prey in Fourteenth-Century England," in D. Kelly Weisberg (ed.), *Women and the Law: The Social Historical Perspective* (Cambridge: Schenkman Publishing Co., 1982), Vol. I, p. 186.

39. Kessler-Harris (1982) *op. cit.*, p. 4.

40. Robert H. Bremner (ed.) *Children and Youth in America: A Documentary History, Vol. I: 1600-1865* (Cambridge: Harvard University Press, 1970), p. 27.

41. Matthaei (1982) *op. cit.*, p. 51.

42. Laurel Thatcher Ulrich, *Good Wives: Image and Reality in the Lives of Women in Northern New England, 1650-1750* (New York: Oxford University Press, 1982), p. 6, xiii.

43. William Brighan (ed.), *The Compact with the Charter and Laws of the Colony of New Plymouth* (Boston 1836), p. 156, excerpted in R. Bremner, Vol. I (1970) *op. cit.*, p. 49; Robert W. Kelso, *The History of Public Poor Relief in Massachusetts 1620-1920* (Montclair, N.J.; Patterson Smith, 1969), p. 31.

44. Ryan (1975) *op. cit.*, p. 38; Mary Sumner Benson, *Women in Eighteenth Century America* (New York: Columbia University Press, 1966), p. 233; Spruill (1938) *op. cit.*, p. 137.

45. Spruill (1938) *op. cit.*, p. 138.

46. Nancy Folbre, "Patriarchy in Colonial New England," *The Review of Political Economics,* 12(2) (Summer 1980), p. 6, citing Bailyn, B., *Education in the Forming of American Society* (Chapel Hill: University of North Carolina Press, 1969), p. 16.

47. Ryan (1975) *op. cit.*, pp. 26, 29-30.

48. Ulrich (1982) *op. cit.*, p. 7, citing Sir William Blackstone, *Commentaries on the Laws of England* (Oxford: Clarendon Press, 1765-1769), Vol. I, p. 442.

49. Carol Brown, "Mothers, Fathers, and Children: From Private to Public Patriarchy," in Lydia Sargent (ed.), *Women and Revolution: A Discussion of the Unhappy Marriage of Marxism and Feminism* (Boston: South End Press, 1981), pp. 250-251.

50. Matthaei (1982) *op. cit.*, p. 49, citing Cotton Mather, *Ornaments to The Daughters of Zion* (Boston: Kneeland and Green, 1741, third edition), p. 94.

51. Ryan (1975) *op. cit.*, p. 52.

52. Spruill (1938) *op. cit.*, pp. 172-173.

53. *Ibid.*, p. 173.

54. Historians of colonial America do not agree as to the status of women or the presence of a gender division of labor. Some such as Alice Clark, Elizabeth Dexter, and Alice M. Earle stress the presence of women in traditionally masculine jobs in this period and conclude that women did not suffer the confines of the division of labor in colonial America. Another group of historians, including Edith Abbott and Robert Smuts, finds a simple strict division of labor which assigned women to the home and men to the fields. Examples of women and men doing the same work are dismissed as exceptions. A third group, which includes Mary Ryan, ignores the issues of the presence of a gender division of labor and points instead to an economic partnership between women and men characterized by an equality that was lost when nineteenth century development excluded women from work.

55. For more discussion of frontier women, see John Mark Faragher, *Women and Men on the Overland Trail* (New Haven: Yale University Press, 1979) and Joanna L. Stratton, *Pioneer Women: Voices From the Kansas Frontier* (New York: Simon and Schuster, 1981).

56. Ulrich (1982) *op. cit.*, pp. 13-34.

57. *Ibid.*, pp. 37-38.

58. Matthaei (1982) *op. cit.*, p. 38; Kessler-Harris (1982) *op. cit.*, p. 4.

59. The following discussion draws heavily from Ruth H. Bloch, "American Feminine Ideals in Transition: The Rise of the Moral Mother, 1785-1815," *Feminist Studies,* 4(2) (June 1978), pp. 101-127.

60. Ulrich (1982) *op. cit.*, p. 54.

61. *Ibid.*, pp. 157-158.

62. See also Ryan (1975) *op. cit.*, p. 60; Laural Thatcher Ulrich, "Virtuous Woman Found: New England Ministerial Literature, 1668-1735," in Nancy F. Cott and

Elizabeth H. Pleck, *A Heritage of Her Own* (New York: Simon and Schuster 1979), p. 39.

63. Ulrich (1982) *op. cit.*, pp. 145-164.

64. The following discussion draws heavily from Matthaei (1982) *op. cit.*, pp. 15-49.

65. Ulrich (1982) *op. cit.*, pp. 68-86.

66. Bloch (1978) *op. cit.*, pp. 102-103.

67. Matthaei (1982) *op. cit.*, pp. 36-50; Spruill (1938) *op. cit.*, pp. 64-85.

68. Bonnie Thornton Dill, *Our Mother's Grief: Racial Ethnic Women and the Maintenance of Families*, Research Paper 4, May 1986, Center for Research on Women, Memphis State University, Memphis, Tenn. 38162, p. 6.

69. Jernegan (1931) *op. cit.*, p. 54.

70. Kessler-Harris (1982) *op. cit.*, p. 10.

71. Jernegan (1931) *op. cit.*, p. 54; Wertheimer (1977) *op. cit.*, p. 21.

72. Carr and Walsh (1982) *op. cit.*, p. 59; Kessler-Harris (1982) *op. cit.*, p. 9.

73. Carr and Walsh (1982) *op. cit.*, p. 60.

74. G.B. Brown (1984) *op. cit.*, pp. 13-15.

75. Wertheimer (1977) *op. cit.*, p. 21.

76. Angela Y. Davis, *Women, Race and Class* (New York: Vintage Books, 1983), p. 7.

77. Matthaei (1982) *op. cit.*, p. 87, citing Austin Steward, *Twenty-Two Years a Slave and Forty Years a Freeman* (New York: Negro Universities Press, 1968\1856), p. 14.

78. Jacqueline Jones, "'My Mother Was Much Of A Woman': Black Women, Work, and the Family Under Slavery," *Feminist Studies*, 8(2) (Summer 1982).

79. Wertheimer (1977) *op. cit.*, p. 118; Davis (1983) *op. cit.*, p. 10.

80. Jones (1982) *op. cit.*, pp. 243-245.

81. Hymowitz & Weissman (1980) *op. cit.*, p. 43, citing Norman Yetman (ed.), *Voices from Slavery* (New York: Holt, Rinehart and Winston, 1970), p. 121.

82. Benjamin Drew (ed.), *A Northside View of Slavery: The Refugee, or the Narratives of Fugitive Slaves in Canada, Related by Themselves* (Boston: John P. Jowett, 1896), pp. 31-32.

83. Hooks (1981) *op. cit.*, p. 39.

84. Jacqueline Jones, *Labor of Love, Labor of Sorrow: Black Women, Work and the Family from Slavery to the Present* (New York: Basic Books, 1985), p. 19.

85. Hymowitz & Weissman (1980) *op. cit.*, p. 45; Hooks (1981) *op. cit.*, p. 37; Wertheimer (1977) *op. cit.*, p. 111.

86. Hymowitz & Weissman (1980) *op. cit.*, p. 45; Hooks (1981) *op. cit.*, p. 37; Wertheimer (1977) *op. cit.*, p. 111.

87. Jones (1985) *op. cit.*, pp. 33-37.

88. Dill (1986) *op. cit.*, p. 2; Elizabeth Higginbotham, "Work and Survival For Black Women," Research Paper 1, September 1984, Center for Research on Women, Memphis State University, Memphis, Tenn., 38162, p. 4.

89. Hymowitz & Weissman (1980) *op. cit.*, p. 43.

90. Matthaei (1982) *op. cit.*, p. 94.

91. Jones (1982) *op. cit.*, pp. 235-36; Jones (1985) *op. cit.*, pp. 36-38.

92. Hooks (1981) *op. cit.*, p. 4; Rennie Simson, "The Afro-American Female: The Historical Context of the Construction of Sexual Identity," in Ann Snitow, Christine Stansell & Sharon Thompson (eds.), *Powers of Desire: The Politics of Sexuality* (New York: Monthly Review Press, 1983), pp. 229-235.

93. Davis (1983) *op. cit.*, pp. 7, 12, 18.

94. Dill (1986) *op. cit.*, p. 24.

95. Jones (1985) *op. cit.*, p. 36.

96. *Ibid.*

97. Cited by Wertheimer (1977) *op. cit.*, p. 109.

98. Dorothy Sterling, *We Are Your Sisters: Black Women in the Nineteenth Century* (New York: W. W. Norton & Company, 1984), p. 25.

99. Davis (1983) *op. cit.*, p. 25.

100. Sterling (1984) *op. cit.*, pp. 25-26.

101. Gerda Lerner, *The Majority Finds Its Past: Placing Women in History* (Oxford: Oxford University Press, 1981), pp. 71-72.

102. Susan Brownmiller, *Against Her Will: Men, Women and Rape* (New York: Simon and Schuster, 1975).

103. Dill (1986) *op. cit.*, p. 20; see also Herbert Gutman, *The Black Family in Slavery and Freedom: 1750-1925* (New York: Pantheon, 1976).

104. Herbert G. Gutman, "Marital and Sexual Norms Among Slave Women," in Nancy F. Cott & Elizabeth H. Pleck (eds.), *A Heritage of Her Own* (New York: Simon and Schuster, 1979), pp. 298-310.

105. Matthaei (1982) *op. cit.*, p. 81.

106. Jones (1985) *op. cit.*, p. 31.

107. Meier and Rudwick (1976, third edition) *op. cit.*, p. 36.

108. Sterling (1984) *op. cit.*, p. 57.

109. Davis (1983) *op. cit.*, p. 22.

110. Giddings (1984) *op. cit.*, pp. 45-46.

111. Matthaei (1982) *op. cit.*, p. 77-78; for a brief discussion of the debate over the extent and meaning of slave resistance, see Meier and Rudwick (1976, third edition), pp. 80-86.

112. Wertheimer (1977) *op. cit.*, p. 145.

113. David M. Schneider, *The History of Public Welfare In New York State, 1609-1866* (Montclair: Patterson Smith, 1969), p. 86.

114. Wertheimer (1977) *op. cit.*, p. 34.

115. Giddings (1984) *op. cit.*, p. 39, citing Lorenzo Johnston Greene, *The Negro in Colonial America* (New York: Atheneum, 1968, 1969, 1971, 1974), p. 154.

116. Herbert Aptheker, *Essays in The History of The American Negro* (New York: International Publishers, 1964), pp. 16-23.

117. Giddings (1984) *op. cit.*, pp. 40-41.

The Constant Crisis of Welfare Values
John E. Tropman

OVERVIEW

The basic premise of this volume focuses on cementing values to which each of us is committed. This approach is useful in understanding the constant crisis that seems to characterize provision of aid to the disadvantaged. On the one hand, society wants to provide assistance and help. On the other, there is a great concern that this help may, in the process of its provision, corrupt the giver and harm the recipient. Part of the explanation for welfare antipathy is that the implementation of values supporting aid for the disadvantaged threaten (or appear to threaten) other values we also hold. Chapter 4 looks at the set of value pairs identified in Chapter 3 from this perspective and explicates a series of welfare threats.

The value dimension also gives rise to different and conflicting attitudes about the disadvantaged. Chapters 5 seeks to lay out some of these conflicts and to describe them.

Programs and services for the disadvantaged can also be considered in terms of competing value claims. Chapters 6 and 7 outline some of the main dilemmas and opposing orientations within the system of help. Chapter 8 discusses policy dilemmas and Chapter 9 administrative dilemmas. Chapter 10 briefly examines cultural contradictions and cultural dissonance issues.

Throughout this section, several goals are in the forefront. One is to apply the value conflict approach and to demonstrate the utility of its application to programs and problems of the disadvantaged in American society. The second goal is to make some organized and comprehensible pattern out of the confusion of values and approaches that characterize the programs and services directed toward the disadvantaged. The accomplishment of these goals should result in a clearer picture of why we think, act, and react as we do.

INTRODUCTION

The juxtaposed values scheme is useful for analyzing social welfare policy. In recent years there has been a clamorous complaint that the welfare system is in a state of crisis. The "crisis" is multidimensional: lack of adequate programs, programs that are too adequate; recipients who do not deserve money, deserving individuals who do not receive money; administrative failures, and so on. A quick survey of almost any local newspaper reveals some new article detailing some new difficulty in the programs designed to help the poor. Yet, crises in welfare are nothing new; welfare has always been in a state of crisis.

The constant crisis that envelops welfare within this country derives from American society's perception of the welfare poor as constituting a major threat to its integrity: The poor are disliked, even hated, by all social classes (Tropman, 1976). Poverty status is as threatening to the middle class as to the working class and the "near poor" (Feagin, 1975). While the aversion is moderated by charitable feelings, a portion of the welfare crisis involves a clash between our sympathy toward the poor and our resentment.

AMERICAN WELFARE PROBLEMS

Many writers have attempted to explain why Americans feel threatened by the poor.[1] The dependent poor are stigmatized because Americans generally perceive dependency as bad. Rein (1970) argues that all people are interdependent, and progress increases dependency; thus, we should not hate the poor. His argument, however, is likely to convince only those who wish to be convinced. We know, for example, that the majority of welfare recipients consist of the aged, the disabled, and dependent children—a point made repeatedly. Yet, the complaints persist, as though the welfare rolls are filled with "sturdy beggars" (Mayhew, 1861/1968). Apparently, the myths about welfare defy even rudimentary facts. This situation, too, requires explanation.

Heilbroner (1970, p. 20) offers four reasons to explain this phenomenon:

1. Racism—the poor are identified as primarily black, and we do not want to help blacks
2. A tradition of limited government
3. Lack of social magnanimity
4. Lack of a political party to advance specifically the lower class cause

Though these reasons make intuitive and theoretical sense, there are some problems with each of them.

It is partially correct to postulate that antiwelfare attitudes specifically, and antipoor attitudes generally, are expressions of racism. Race does appear to be a specific factor in negativism concerning specific elements of the welfare system, especially regarding the level of grant support and willingness of communities to undertake urban renewal (A. Hudson, 1973; Tropman and Gordon, 1978). The general population, though, does not seem to characterize the poor (defined as the lowest class) as racial minorities (Tropman, 1977). Additionally, negative feelings toward the poor existed long before blacks became a focus. It could even be argued that racism is actually in part classism.[2]

Heilbroner's second statement—that our limited governmental programs in welfare result from a tradition of limited government—is partially tautological. It also overlooks the fact that some states provide more generously than others.[3] In addition, until the Social Security Act, the federal government has generally hung back from interfering with the states. This was manifest as early as the mid-nineteenth century when President Franklin Pierce vetoed the bill initiated by Dorothea Dix to care for the indigent insane (Manning, 1964).

On the question of social magnanimity, the American society is certainly ambivalent. Herbert Spencer (1865) argued that "poor laws" would be objectionable even if they accomplished their distress-relieving goal—and they did not even do that. Yet, as he condemned organized charity (governmental or voluntary), he found room to approve those judicious charities that "help men to help themselves" (p. 152). He anticipated, perhaps, the outpourings of sympathy and assistance Americans give to the "100 Neediest Cases," published in *The New York Times* at Christmas and the millions of dollars that are donated to the annual United Way campaign (which someone once defined as a campaign that "puts all of its begs in one ask-it"). Our lack of magnanimity is, thus, more on the institutional side than in terms of personal relationships.

Perhaps Heilbroner's most powerful argument relates to the absence of a political party based upon class interests. This argument has implications for the limited governmental effort within the welfare area for the lack of institutionalized magnanimity. The individual and individual social mobility are extremely important in American society. Rischin (1965) observes that this striving for success is a personal one in which citizens constantly try to better themselves over the course of their lifetimes while hoping for even greater achievements from their sons and daughters. Americans, anticipating the achievement of success, are socialized to purchase and display the cars, clothes, and other items that are characteristic of those groups to which they aspire. Indeed, Harrington (1962) has pointed out that the poor have become in many instances indistinguishable from the mass of citizens. Thus, no one would want to proclaim membership in the "lower class," even for political reasons.

Additionally, consider the case of the young man newly graduated from high school who believes in the ethic of personal mobility and is faced with the choice of Home Town Community College or Harvard. He would be foolish to cast his lot with the Home Town Boosters. His goal is to leave Home Town and the old neighborhood. It is not to join them. As Heilbroner suggests, the impetus within the political system to develop a political association of the poor has not matured. As a result, there has been limited political support for poverty programs.[4]

Another explanation for the persistence of negative views might lie in the functions the poor perform. Sullivan (1980, p. 390) provides a list of such functions. These include doing unpleasant work, providing jobs for social workers, and absorbing through unemployment the brunt of the costs of technological change. Perhaps the guilty knowledge of these services means that we view the poor in a hostile way.

And, of course, the poor may very well represent substantive conditions that the nonpoor wish to deny. The question remains, however, why such hostility continues to exist especially as the country does better and better. So, too, does the question of why these negative views fly in the face of ameliorating and balancing evidence. Another type of answer is that the poor frighten us.

THE WELFARE THREAT

Basically, our deep seated hostility toward the poor, and especially the welfare poor, probably exists because the poor represent threats to other classes along several distinct value dimensions. This hostility may be an attempt to deny the reality of the poor person's problems while reinforcing the integrity and stability of the nonpoor person. The hostility, therefore, has less to do with the poor than it does with the nonpoor. As long as the poor interact with society in such a way as to threaten dominant values, they will constitute a perceived danger to that society. The response of the society will be as it would be to any threat: attack and destroy it. As the threat really reflects the anxieties present in the nonpoor, a case of constant crisis develops. In the words of the comic strip character, Pogo, "we have met the enemy, and he is us."[5]

Welfare, therefore, as a means of ameliorating poverty generates deep social resentment because it challenges dominant values. Arguments in its favor are neither as wide-ranging nor as powerful as the conflicts it generates. Hence, occasional and episodic charity poses no systematic threat to established values.[6] Organized, institutional charity, however, does provide a continuous challenge to the more powerful values of achievement, mobility, and so on. In the case of our specific sets of value pairs, improvement of the condition of the poor threatens— or potentially threatens—the dominant value in each value pair. While balance does occur, it does not mean (1) that this accommodation solves the inherent conflict between values, (2) that continual reminders of the value conflict do not occur, or (3) that pressures do not develop over time to change the level of equilibrium implicit in the current accommodation. Each of these issues surfaces periodically in the constant crisis of welfare. Let us consider each value pair specifically and explore how this threat works.

Work Threat (Job Orientation Threatens Career Orientation)

Purposeful activity is the key to this value arena, and work is a primary example of it. Because we value work, we look down upon those who seem to reject work or who do not put in their full measure of activity and contribution.

Job orientation is a threat to career orientation because it suggests that there are no transcendent goals toward which one is working—an element of career orientation. Rather, the individual is secure, perhaps has a sinecure, and does not need to produce any further. Job orientation may imply focused motivation and a job-description orientation to productivity. People often question positions that carry rewards but do not require a continuous level of productivity. University tenure and seniority in civil service or union activities are typical examples, though the complainers often seek to become part of these systems.

The poor threaten the dominant value system to the extent it is perceived that they are entitled to benefits without work. Welfare becomes a sort of job that one does without contributing anything. For this reason, there is constant talk about "workfare" programs, about schemes to have recipients earn their benefits.

Mobility Threat (Sponsorship Threatens Contest)

Because people achieve status in this "land of opportunity" through contest, it is important for the players to believe that the rules of the contest are fair and that the contestants are adhering to those rules. If the rules are unfair, or if some players have an edge, the sense of achievement will diminish for those who win, and if one wins in spite of these obstacles, victory and its meaning are proportionally enhanced.

By their very presence the poor provide evidence that the system produces both losers and winners. The nonpoor can feel comfortable as long as they are convinced that the poor demonstrate less skill or exert less effort. Let them doubt the integrity of the contest, however, and their victory is rendered less legitimate. In addition, the possibility of becoming a "loser" looms more conspicuously. Thus, the poor and the welfare poor threaten the credibility of the contest rules and, therefore, the personal and social meaning and integrity of the results.

A second problem resides in the possibility that some players have unfair advantages. Too many poor create the need for too much sponsorship, and too many welfare poor means too much welfare sponsorship. In the mobility contest, only a certain percentage of the players are permitted a "handicap." It is significant that the categorical approach to public relief (in which certain groups of people are identified as needing aid) always seems to develop categories of persons who are also free from the mobility contest. Women with young children, the aged, the blind, and the disabled are in this category. In some sense, perhaps, misery frees people from feeling impelled to compete for success.

The categories of the public welfare system thus introduce a third feature of the contest system: the individual who declares him- or herself a nonplayer. Persons on welfare tend to be those from whom mobility is not expected. Entering the welfare rolls may even indicate that someone is no longer "eligible" for the game of mobility, and, to have someone "pull out" of a game threatens those left as players. While their action may mean there is more left for other players, it undermines the value basis of success orientation.

Summing up, then, the poor represent three specific types of mobility threats: They cast doubt on the fairness of the mobility contest; they raise questions concerning the fairness of the players in the contest; and they remind players that at some point, they can elect to leave the game. But the alternatives to leaving welfare—homelessness, perhaps—are not very attractive.

Status Threat (Equality Threatens Achievement)

The poor and the welfare poor pose a threat to the achievement basis of status within the American value system. The claim of equality generates several specific concerns for the citizen-at-large. First, status, like money, can suffer from inflation; and long-sought prestige can be rendered useless if attained by too many. As W. S. Gilbert observed in *The Goldoliers*:

> When you have nothing else to wear
> But cloth of gold and satins rare,
> For cloth of gold you cease to care—
> Up goes the price of shoddy.

The improvement of the condition of the poor can diminish the gap between their status and one's own achievements, much as the granting of bachelor degrees in one year instead of four would diminish the stature of degrees granted under the old system.

A second type of status threat is status erosion. Status is secured through association: One seeks to interact with people of equal or higher status and to avoid those of lower status. This practice extends beyond personal interaction to affiliation with prestige organizations, business firms, universities, communities, and so on. Those who associate with the poor by fostering their participation in college programs, housing assistance, and other forms of advocacy seem to be threatened with downward mobility.[7] Thus, socially conscious citizens may refrain from championing the cause of the poor for fear their own status will be diminished by the association.

Finally, the poor—especially those on welfare—may violate norms of distributive justice in which rewards are supposed to equal contribution (Alves and Rossi, 1978; Walster, Walster, and Berscheid, 1978; Grosskind, 1987). In all justice one's social standing, it seems, should be "functionally" related to the contributions one makes to society as a whole. We feel a humanitarian desire to assist the poor, but not too much. To bestow too many benefits without reciprocation offends our sense of fairness.

Wortman (1976) observes that the social psychological theory of equity suggests that people have a strong tendency to believe the rules are fair, to ascribe causal relationships to chance events, to overestimate the extent to which they control uncontrollable events (like disasters), and to underestimate the extent to which their behavior is controlled by luck and chance. She states that in order to maintain a sense of control when confronted with suffering, one will often

> be motivated to believe that the victim earned his suffering. He will either blame the person for the outcome or (if the victim is clearly innocent) derogate the personal characteristics of the victim. (p. 26)[8]

In fact, the relationships are more complex than that. When people think of their achievements, they think of themselves in relationship to those ahead of them and those behind them. If they were to believe that those ahead of them are there due to luck and chance and those behind them are there due to merit, they can then, if they choose, think of themselves as at the top of the achievement heap. Anyone who is ahead is just plain "lucky." Anyone who happened to be behind is deserving of his or her fate. College students tend to view evaluations of their own performance in this manner (Tropman, 1979). A student who works extremely hard for an "A" would not consider some form of academic welfare as an option.[9] That is one reason why even people with ample resources resent welfare. If one views rewards that are not tied to contributions as "unjust," recipients of such rewards are both bad in themselves and bad because they threaten the "justice system."

Independence Threat
(Interdependency Threatens
Self-Reliance)

America is a land of do-it-your-selfers. Americans believe that very little cannot be improved if one does it alone. Interdependence, the recognition that one cannot do it all alone, threatens that sense of self-reliance, of personal, wholistic integrity. Interdependence means claims and demands. It thus becomes a limitation of freedom. That may be why fictional heroes frequently have companions who make few demands (Tarzan's chimp, Cheeta; the Lone Ranger's horse, Silver; Sergeant Preston's dog, King) or have sidekicks who can be ordered around (the Lone Ranger's Tonto, Batman's Robin, Matt Dillon's Chester). These heroes, of course, depend on their sidekicks, but such dependence is shrouded in power relationships.

Interdependence not only takes away from the personal ownership of results—and thus threatens their meaning—but the reciprocity implied in interdependence may emerge in ways and forms that are less convenient, less possible, and more time-consuming than one wants. It may also require the commitment of resources that one would rather spend elsewhere.

Interdependency threatens self-reliance, and the interdependency of all of us on each other raises a set of uncomfortable questions. The disadvantaged, however, raise an additional set of concerns about the balance of parity within the exchange system. From the perspective of society, they become special problems because their contribution to society—the return on society's investment—is seen as minimal.

Self-reliance is, of course, the presumed actuality of independence. It is also the sense of self, the feeling that one can do it. Dependency, when applied to the poor, connotes giving up, lack of trying, settling for something that should not be settled for and that ultimately may control the individual. Programs that take dependency as their point of departure are closely watched so that only those who are really dependent use them. The idea of threat here is particularly obvious. Why people in general should fear that there will be a "rush to welfare" is, when viewed dispassionately, mysterious since that social problem, like many others, is surrounded by negative opinions and views.

Individualism Threat (Other Direction
Threatens Inner Direction)

The poor illustrate several ways in which other direction may prevail over inner direction. The goal of inner direction is to have a set of internal guidance mechanisms to provide the criteria through which one goes about life. Recipients of social programs threaten this goal. The act of becoming a recipient means that one's own ability to control decisions and actions comes into question. In a job one gets a salary, and he or she can do with it as he or she wishes. In a welfare program there is on-going debate about whether the cash should be given to the individual directly or whether it should be paid on behalf of the individual to landlords, doctors, supermarkets, and so on. This problem is solved in different ways in different parts of the program—from cash grants to Medicaid to food stamps—but the very doing of it takes away from and, therefore, threatens inner direction.

It is not only the components of the program but the size and requirements of that program that threaten inner direction. Small-town charity was thought to be flexible and innovative. Large bureaucratic welfare programs come with books of policies thicker than fat dictionaries. The very size and complexity of the program make it difficult to understand and administer for both recipients and workers. The program comes to represent the other direction of bureaucratic life to which one must apply and by which one must be guided.

These programmatic manifestations of threat imply a greater one—that welfare recipients will give over control of their lives to external, bureaucratic forces. Not only is it threatening to have a program that tells people what to do; they may come to like being told what to do. Welfare make this threat even more real because there are, at that point in people's lives, few alternatives. If the nonpoor individual does not like the job, another job can be found. The poor person on welfare, however, is trapped; there are no alternatives. And, rather than generate sympathy in the minds of the nonpoor, it reminds the nonpoor of the extent to which they, themselves, might become trapped. This shock of recognition generates hostility.

Moral Threat (Control Threatens Permission)

The poor also represent a moral threat implicit in the many meanings of the word *poor*. The poor and the welfare poor are unpleasant reflections of the "sacred" side of the system of social status—the fact that the social ladder is also "Jacob's Ladder (the ladder to heaven)."[10] At an earlier point in the history of the social welfare profession, people were more verbal about the "low quality" of those at the bottom of the social ladder (Mayhew, 1861/1968; Spencer, 1865). Today, it is less popular to express this view (Hardin, 1969). Still, the poor pose images of low quality and low status. This moral overtone creates a situation in which the poor threaten the values of permission and freedom by generating the need for societal controls within the social system. If we place a doubt in the moral fiber of the poor, we must rely on external, not internal, means of controlling them. External controls conflict with the value of freedom.

The dislike of systemic external controls may be one of the reasons why the United States was so tardy in moving even to quasi-national systems of public relief or welfare. As long as the system could get by on charity, the value of freedom was not threatened; no controls were necessary either to maintain it or to secure taxes to support it. Government intervention implied an unacceptable level of control.

One of the moral concerns raised by the welfare system has been that in supporting fatherless children, it has condoned illicit sexual activity. Historically, sexual permissiveness has been frowned upon in American society. This view may be becoming less potent as sexual mores change, but the belief that welfare allotments support promiscuity is still a source of resentment. Regardless of whether or not greater sexual freedom exists among them, the poor might well be stigmatized as a means of reinforcing the norms of sexual control and the old-fashioned values of marriage, family, and "proper" sexual conduct (Day, 1976).

Finally, the presence of AFDC for single women and children threatens the family system myth. Society may not want too many sources of support for single women because it may require recognizing the subordination of women that marriage often involves.[11] Society will need to reject continually the image of the "welfare mother" to neutralize the fears she generates and to reassert the "traditional" role of women in society.

Ascriptive Threat (Quality Threatens Performance)

The poor also threaten society at large because they are predominantly composed of groups who have been discriminated against: women, children, minorities, the aged, the ill, the handicapped. They are people who have not been fairly judged by their performance but by their sex, age, race, or infirmity. They have not been given a "fair chance" to perform. Society knows that this is true, although elaborate mythologies have been developed to deny it, including "blaming the victim" him- or herself for poverty (Ryan, 1971). The poor are a constant reminder that there are sizeable numbers of citizens who have not been treated equally. Indeed, as mentioned previously, Miller and Roby (1970, p. 3) argue that poverty is simply a euphemism for inequality that we cannot really acknowledge. We need to believe that performance is rewarded by advancement. Olneck and Crouse (1978) observe:

> We are most puzzled not by our results, but by the belief others appear to hold in the propositions we tested. When empirical propositions are widely held and advanced without substantial scholarly confirmation, their acceptability itself should become an object of interest. The logical appeal of the ideologies of equal opportunity and advancement according to merit for legitimizing the present distribution of rewards and structure of work is apparent. The attractiveness of these ideologies to individuals nourishing hopes of success for themselves and their progeny may also be assumed. However, these possible functions of ideologies are not *explanations* for the acceptance of tenets of belief. (p. 33, emphasis in original)

CONCLUSION

The dualistic/multiplistic values scheme is one that contains some threatening elements when applied to social problems. While the dominant values link to the more major institutions in society, social welfare programs must rely for support and legitimacy on subdominant values. As social welfare seeks to expand and to make those values concrete, it threatens the more dominant values in many specific ways. It is for this reason that welfare programs—and, indeed, the poor themselves—are in a state of constant crisis. The pattern of values of social welfare, the cultural system, is subdominant. This situation creates a series of difficult problems that extend beyond threat. For one thing, it may explain in part why there is not a political movement of the poor. For those who hope for acceptance in majority values, building on subdominant ones is hardly the way to go. Furthermore, this conflict not only operates on a cultural level but on the social psychological level as well. Within the social work profession, there is a sense of conflict and ambivalence about the poor. There is, therefore, an internal threat to the self-esteem of both the social welfare recipient and the social welfare professional. The constant crisis is not only programmatic; it also lies within the helper and the recipient.

1. See, for example, Cameron (1975) for a comprehensive review up to 1975, Grosskind (1987) for recent material.

2. In a country characterized by "equality" (but only partially, as we shall see), the inequality implicit in poverty and represented by the poor becomes hard to admit.

3. States, however, do not have as much uniqueness as some of the Canadian provinces. See S. M. Lipset, *Agrarian Socialism* (1971). Certain tendencies in this direction in the United States (as conceived and operationalized by such luminaries as William Jennings Bryan, Robert LaFollet, and Huey Long) never progressed (see Williams, 1960; Koenig, 1971).

4.. This dilemma may be most acute in the racial minority communities where upwardly mobile people of color are pressured to retain identification with their racial compeers.

5. The social psychology of attribution is too complex to detail here, but it's consistent with this line of argument. We tend to believe, for example, in a just world where

people deserve what they get (because of their good qualities or because they control their environment and are responsible for—and, thus, deserving of— what results from this control). While we may be aware in general of external elements and luck (Jencks, 1972), there is also a tendency for people to "under-estimate the extent to which their behavior is controlled by situational or external forces" (Wortman, 1976, p. 28). People also apparently seek to define things in ways that create the illusion (if not the reality) of control. This personal control hypothesis was suggested by Walster (1966) and in a piece on images of the poor by Tropman (1976). Important as these ideas are to understanding attitudes toward poverty and the disadvantaged, applications are only now beginning to be made. For a comprehensive review of attribution research, see Harvey, Ickes, and Kidd (1976).

6. This may by why the social work profession so frequently seems to adopt a posture of criticism toward the very individuals from whom it seeks support for increased welfare benefits. The profession may be in the awkward position of having to delegitimate and deemphasize major values so that there is room for the expansion of secondary values. Those who respond to this attack do so filled with righteous indignation, securely based in widely shared values of achievement, contest, and the like.

7. Evidence for this point lies in the fact that in many instances in the societal system— maximum feasible participation of the poor being only one (see Moynihan, 1969)— special rules had to be passed to insure that the poor were not completely left out.

8. Just this point is made by Susan Sontag in *Illness As Metaphor* (1978). She raises questions about the "cancer personality" as a causal factor in generating the disease. Cancer, as uncontrolled growth, raises fundamental issues of personal control.

9. Another way of looking at this situation is that status requires not only a position in some hierarchy but some distance between positions as well. When the distance lessens, the value of the position is changed.

10. "Holier than thou" becomes "wealthier than thou." Being holy is never "fun." Work in school should be unpleasant. Jencks (1972) and others note that schools become "secular churches." Jencks explains some of the unpleasantness of schools with the rationale that the expiation of sin can never be fun.

11. The "job" of wife is, like any other job, filled with frustrations and disappointment. At some point a wife may decide to "throw the rascal out." For this to occur, she needs available alternative sources of support. The level and availability of AFDC, then, may be a key factor. As grants become ever larger, the woman may decide that she's safer with regular AFDC payments than with her husband. The conventional mythology of the man in a fit of sadness leaving his wife so that she can secure more money may be completely fallacious. It may be that the wife simply decides she no longer wishes to tolerate securing achievement through an unreliable, physically abusive male, or there may be a man whom she does not wish to marry because of his problematic but not violent characteristics.

Emergence of the Concept of Public Welfare
Gerald Handel

Early Christian Charity

In the earliest days of Christianity, its adherents comprised a relatively small proportion of the population of Palestine—then called the Province of Judea by the Romans—and of the neighboring provinces of the Roman Empire to which it had spread, carried by Paul and other apostles. Christians began to differentiate themselves not only from Jews but also from other non-Christian citizens and subjects of the Roman Empire. They began to establish churches, and these became the centers of their religious and community life.

During the first three hundred years of the Christian movement, the Roman Empire was becoming increasingly corrupt, ridden by class distinctions, and demanding of tax revenues from its peoples.[18] One result of this was a significant increase in poverty. Christian churches set about taking care of Christian poor, widows, orphans, aged household slaves, shipwrecked persons, and persons imprisoned, exiled, or working in mines as punishment for their Christian beliefs. Each church member was expected to place a donation, at least monthly, in a chest kept for that purpose. This monthly collection was similar to a Roman system in which the workers in particular trades and occupations were organized into associations known as *collegia* and made monthly contributions to a common fund. In addition, contributions of bread and wine were collected at the Eucharist; what was not needed for the celebration was distributed among the poor.[19]

Charity was a prominent activity in the life of the early Christian communities. One early Christian writer said: " 'We who formerly loved money and property more than anything else now place what we have in a common fund and share with everyone in need.' "[20] The sharing of funds was voluntary and was intended for distribution only among Christian believers. Each church congregation had a presiding officer who was in charge of giving out funds to needy Christian believers. As we have seen, early Christianity's ideas about charity derive from the Judaic concepts, while the organizational arrangements for implementing the ideas resemble the practices common to occupational associations in the Roman Empire.

In the early fourth century, Christianity reached an important turning point. Having been considered illegal by Roman authorities, and having suffered numerous attempts by Roman emperors to stamp it out through persecution of its practitioners, Christianity gained new status and power under the emperor Constantine who, in A.D. 313, declared the religion legal. With this official approval, many new converts came to the movement, and the volume of donations to the churches increased. In order to cope with the growth in numbers and in wealth, a new level of organization was required. Accordingly the system of distribution of charity by individual churches acting through their deacons was replaced by one in which the bishop of a diocese had supervisory control over all the churches in his district and control over the revenues, which came to the churches in greater and greater volume.[21]

It was also during the fourth century that a different theory of almsgiving became prominent—one that held increasing importance in Christianity and that was to influence not only postmedieval Europe but the nineteenth- and early twentieth-century United States as well. Early Christian almsgiving, like the Judaic, had been based largely on the conception of charity as an expression of lovingkindness, an activity necessary to the carrying out of God's will. But this concept did not offer much help with another problem that the early church fathers struggled with as they tried to work out the doctrines of their faith. This was the problem of private property and its consequences, particularly the great disparity in wealth between the rich and the poor.

Some of the early Christian writers considered the private ownership of property to be against God's will and law, but this view did not prevail. The main body of church thought considered the ownership of private property unavoidable, even if not ideal. As Christianity came to accept private property and the disparity of wealth as aspects of the real world, it also worked out a doctrine that wealth could be ennobling because it allowed the wealthy to do good works, good works that would earn them eternal salvation in the Kingdom of God. "The idea that wealth may contribute to salvation because it allows good works to be done can be found in Luke's Gospel."[22] Somewhat later, one theologian taught that almsgiving procured for the givers rewards from God through the prayers of grateful recipients. While this point of view can be found in the earliest church writings, it did not gain prominence until the fourth century, when leading Christian thinkers began to support it and to elaborate upon it. One scholar offers a brief summary of the views on this subject of two of the most important fourth-century Christian writers:

> Chrysostom praises the presence of beggars at the church door as giving an opportunity to those entering to cleanse their consciences from minor faults by almsgiving. . . . Augustine also teaches . . . the belief that almsgiving could atone for the sins of the departed as well as for those of the living. . . . He is careful to limit the efficacy of charity to those whose lives were acceptable to God. It availed nothing for living or dead who were of evil reputation.[23]

The change in the theological justification of charity and its meritoriousness was related to the social changes that were taking place at the time both within Christianity and in the Roman Empire. Although at first a religious movement especially attractive to the lower and middle strata of society, Christianity held increasing appeal for the wealthy as well.[24] Both wealthy and poor found the new religious explanations of almsgiving helpful to their own situations. Further, the church itself was becoming wealthy and propertied, particularly after it gained the right from Constantine to receive donations and bequests. At the same time, the Empire also was moving in the direction of greater concentration of wealth and property, resulting partly from the dispossession of small farmers who were pushed into choosing between working as slaves or serfs on land they had once owned or going into the cities to work, to beg, or to rob. As one historian put it:

> While this light and frivolous class of the idle rich invaded the church from above, at the same time a horde of beggars and impostors poured into the church from below, feigning poverty and faith, attracted by the new wealth and charitable practices of Christianity. The proletariat of the great cities, accustomed to public doles, scented a new quarter of supply. In a sense the Church was victimized by

this corrupt class which Rome's vicious social and economic policy over centuries had fostered; but it is a question whether the Church did not aggravate the evil which it professed to relieve by promoting a vast system of organized mendicity through a deceived philanthropy. "Never was the greed of beggars greater than it is now," complained St. Ambrose. . . . St. Basil complained of the difficulty of distinguishing between the needy poor and these imposters. Mendicancy became a profession within the circle of the Church as it long had been practised by thousands outside in the pagan world. By the end of the fourth century the Christian beggars in Rome almost formed a caste apart.[25]

During the first three hundred years of Christianity, each church congregation took care of its own poor from its own rather meager funds. With the increase in church wealth from the fourth century on, there came a change in church organization—the development of a church hierarchy. The administration of relief to the poor was taken over by the bishop of each diocese; all the churches of a city and its surroundings were under the bishop's direction. As the Roman empire and its governmental effectiveness declined, the bishops became, in effect, the governors of their territories.[26] Power and wealth gravitated to the church and its bishops, who not only accepted gifts and donations—from which they were expected to give freely to the poor—but also solicited them. Even the most sympathetic writers about the early and medieval church acknowledge that not all bishops lived up to their charitable obligations.[27] Less sympathetic historians note that some bishops exploited the doctrine of redemption from sin to increase the wealth of the church:

> . . . avarice for centuries was to be the besetting sin of the church. The famous verse "As water extinguisheth fire, so charity extinguisheth sin" was flagrantly abused to solicit gifts from the faithful. This sentiment is to be found time and again in medieval donations of land or goods. The Christians of the patristic age gave out of their poverty—for they had little wealth—to expand the gospel, to relieve the sick, to help the poor. But from the fourth century onward too many of the donations made to the Church were not primarily for the benefit of others, but to save the souls of the givers. It was a selfish unselfishness. The day was to come when a man was required in his will to leave a portion of his property to the Church, and if he had no heirs to leave it all to the Church.[28]

MEDIEVAL SOCIETY AND CHRISTIAN CHARITY

The decline and fall of the Roman Empire constitutes one of the great turning points in the history of Western society. The date of the collapse of the Empire is usually given as A.D. 476, but this was obviously not a sudden or isolated event. Rather, it followed a series of invasions by Germanic barbarian tribes that had begun considerably earlier. The years between A.D. 400 and A.D. 1500 have come to be known as the Middle Ages. The study of the Middle Ages is a specialty in its own right. In terms of this book, the period is perhaps most significant because of the sharp contrasts between it and the period that succeeded it. Many of the changes that took place in the postmedieval period will be relevant to our discussions but for our current purposes we need only make a rough distinction between antiquity, the Middle Ages, and the modern period.

Following the collapse of the Roman Empire, western Europe was a vast territory with no strong central government. As the central government deteriorated, trade diminished and the cities shrank, until the eleventh century, when both trade and the cities began to revive. Although various kingdoms succeeded the Empire, none were effective in maintaining control over their territory.

During the Middle Ages, most people lived a rural life, with farming the dominant occupation. Because of the lack of a strong central government, people were vulnerable to economic insecurity and to attack. To protect themselves, men who felt particularly vulnerable sought out stronger men to whom they "commended" themselves. They surrendered their land to the stronger men, who became known as lords, and they surrendered their status as free people and agreed to remain attached to the land, providing to their particular lord a portion of the produce of the land. In exchange, these serfs, as they were called, received the protection of the lord and the right to stay on the land. The lord thus increased his land holdings, and acquired dependents who owed him a certain number of days of work per year and a portion of the harvest of that work, while in return he became their protector. The landed estate held by the lord came to be known as a manor. The serfs lived in houses grouped together in a village on the manor. The village included a church. The lord of the manor often had the power to appoint the priest for the village church.[29] In time, the village became a parish, one unit in the diocese of a bishop. Bishops and priests were seen as having authority over the human soul, both in its life on earth and in the hereafter. Bishops came to be "lords spiritual," in contrast with the lords of the manors, who were "lords temporal," that is, lords who governed human lives during their earthly existence.

Medieval society is, however, complicated by the fact that the churches acquired manors, so that bishops often assumed temporal power in addition to their spiritual power. One result of this was that many of the clergy developed worldly concerns, enjoying the life of well-to-do country gentlemen and neglecting their duties, including their obligations to care for the poor.

Monasticism

The increasing worldliness and materialism of the church repelled some parishioners and clergy and gave rise to efforts to rediscover religious concentration through withdrawal into secluded communities known as monasteries. Those who withdrew to the monastery and became monks sought a life of prayer and study and a revival of the early Christian concern for the poor. Monasteries were places where anyone, rich or poor, who came to the gate would be given a ration or dole of food and drink, and shelter if necessary.

Monasteries developed in somewhat parallel fashion to the church organization they were trying to escape. They evolved from single settlements into organizations of monasteries run by a particular religious order. The heads of monasteries—abbots and priors—struggled with parish priests to gain control over churches in order to enjoy the wealth accumulating from church revenues. The money left in the wills of men to be distributed to the poor or to support permanently a certain number of poor went to the churches and the monasteries. In the eighth century, churches also instituted the practice of *tithing*, that is, requiring members of the church to contribute annually a tenth of their income to the church. The church revenues were supposed to be divided into four equal parts—for the support of the bishop of the diocese, the parish clergy, the upkeep of the church, and the poor, widowed, disabled, orphaned, and aged.

Medieval Canon Law

The Roman Catholic Church was the major recognized and established religion in western Europe once the conversion of the barbarian peoples was completed around A.D. 1000. Between the fall of the Roman Empire and the rise of the colonial empires, which began around A.D. 1500, the Church also came to be the major international state in the Western world.[10] People felt they belonged to Christendom and thus to a larger, more encompassing unit beyond the local community. Except for a relatively small number of Jews and heretics, everyone belonged to the Church. The Church had its own government, courts, and taxes. The religious teachings of the Church were a major influence on what people believed. And beliefs concerning salvation were, as we have noted, a powerful inducement for the donation of charitable gifts and bequests to the Church to be used for the support of the poor.

The Church had grown into an organization whose recognized leader, the bishop of Rome, had acquired the title of pope. Yet centralized authority had not resulted in a consistent set of teachings and a consistent set of laws and regulations with respect to poverty and charity as well as other matters. The teachings of the Apostles and of the early church fathers in the first few centuries after the Apostles were not entirely consistent. Local church councils had, over the centuries, developed their own regulations. The work of eliminating the inconsistencies in canon law—the technical term for the laws of the Roman Catholic Church—was undertaken by the Italian monk Gratian, who produced his treatise known as the *Decretum* about A.D. 1140[11] Later canonists—experts in Church law—added to this basic work.

The canonists tried to resolve the issue of the cause of poverty. They made a distinction between voluntary poverty, a form of asceticism pleasing to God, and involuntary poverty. They agreed that the Church had a special duty to protect "wretched persons"—the poor and oppressed, the widowed and orphaned.[12]

A second issue addressed by the canonists was that of private property. Some of the early church fathers' statements cited by Gratian were so critical of the abuses of wealth that they could be interpreted as condemning all private property. The canonists were concerned that private property might be contrary to God's will, and felt that this possibility had to be reconciled with the existing social order, in which private property rights were valid. Their solution involved drawing a distinction between ownership of property and use of property. After a man had taken care of his own necessities out of what he owned, he was obliged to share his "superfluous wealth." A man who "accumulated superfluous wealth beyond what he needed to live in a decent and fitting fashion had no right to keep that wealth. He *owed* it to the poor."[13]

Thus, by the beginning of the thirteenth century, the Church lawyers seemed to be proclaiming a doctrine that the rich had a legal obligation to support the poor and the poor had a right to such support. In actuality, this doctrine was not legally enforceable, but it did influence attitudes toward private charity during the Middle Ages:

> The doctrine that the poor man had a right to the help he received . . . colored the whole relationship between benefactor and beneficiary in the Middle Ages, tending to discourage both sentimental self-esteem on the part of the donor and excessive humiliation in the recipient.[14]

This is a very different conception from Greek and Roman philanthropy. It also bears little resemblance to the views that developed in the eighteenth century and after, when the obligation of the rich to share their wealth with the poor disappeared in the economic doctrines that accompanied the rise of industrial capitalism. And it contrasts as well with the twentieth-century attitude that dependence upon charity is shameful and humiliating. It should be noted, however, that the medieval canonists' resolution of the problem of charity was in keeping with the property system of the time, because the right to own property was commonly accompanied by certain social obligations.[15]

The medieval canonists distinguished worthy charitable actions from unworthy ones. For example, a charitable gift made from stolen property was not worthy. Contributions that were worthy had to come from justly acquired property, and the donors had to be righteous individuals motivated by a spirit of true charity, not by a desire to gain praise or to avoid embarrassment. When these conditions were met, the almsgivers were assuring their own salvation.

The Church was concerned with the effect of charity on the soul of the donor, a concern that is much less prominent in contemporary society than it was in medieval times. But the Church was also concerned with an issue whose importance became even greater to the people of later centuries: the effect of charity on the receiver. According to some of the early church fathers, there were circumstances in which being charitable would be harmful to the recipient, and donors were urged to discriminate between situations in which charity was justified and those in which it was not. Others wrote that alms should be given to all, without investigation into circumstances or attempts at distinguishing true need from claimed need.

The thirteenth-century canonists tended to favor openhandedness in day-to-day almsgiving. They probably knew that some people would take advantage of such a practice, but they did not believe that this basic attitude would corrupt society as a whole. In understanding the sharp difference between the medieval attitude toward charity and the attitude that developed in the nineteenth century along with industrialization, it is useful to note that unemployment was rare in the thirteenth century. The majority of poorer people lived in small villages and worked their own land. Those who might become unwilling to work were subject to social pressure from priest, neighbors, and family. Thus there was little basis for concern that some people would prefer an idle life in which they subsisted on charity to a life in which they earned their own living.[16]

SUMMARY

Charity and philanthropy originated as two similar concepts that later fused into a single concept. Charity and philanthropy both refer to donations of money or property to a person or group in need. Charity originated in ancient Judaism and was incorporated into Christianity. In both religions, charity was considered a religious obligation, based on the will of God, to show lovingkindness by helping the poor and other needy individuals. Philanthropy originated in the ancient Greek city-states, particularly Athens, and was part of the concept of citizenship and civic duty. Wealthy persons contributed money to the community; in return, the community passed resolutions giving official recognition to the philanthropists, who welcomed the honor. In theory, both charity and philanthropy were voluntary, but social pressures were applied to stimulate reluctant donors.

During the fourth century A.D., the church developed the doctrine that charity could earn the donors eternal salvation of their souls. This teaching remains part of Catholic theology today. Overall, however, the concept of charity has lost favor because it calls attention to the dependent status of the receiver.

Philanthropy, a more impersonal form of giving, remains widely appreciated. Individuals often feel too proud to take charity; no one feels too proud to take philanthropy. Therefore, charitable contributions today are often called philanthropic contributions.

The early Christian churches each organized their own charitable funds. After Christianity became a legal religion in the Roman Empire, contributions greatly increased and a more complex church organization developed. Churches were grouped into districts called dioceses, each headed by a bishop, who was in charge of all contributions in his diocese. In the eighth century, churches began the practice of tithing—the requirement that members contribute one tenth of their annual income to the Church. Church revenues were to be divided into four equal parts—for the support of the bishop, the parish clergy, the upkeep of the Church, and the Church charity fund.

Church lawyers of the twelfth and thirteenth centuries concluded that the rich had an obligation to support the poor and the poor had as right to such support. This doctrine virtually disappeared after the eighteenth century, when the economic ideas of capitalism became more influential than church teachings.

Emergence of the Concept of Public Welfare

The major distinction between public welfare and charity is that the concept of public welfare involves the taking on of obligations to the needy by the public authority of the state, whereas charity rests primarily on voluntary donation. Like almost all distinctions in social welfare, the distinction between public welfare and charity is not absolute; public welfare developed gradually out of charity, and for a time during the reign of Queen Elizabeth there was a kind of intermediate stage where charity was no longer purely voluntary but was not yet quite completely public welfare either.

Public welfare is a twentieth-century term. In the nineteenth century, people spoke of public charities and private charities, not of public welfare and charity. Contemporary public welfare descends from ideas that first emerged clearly in the Tudor, and specifically the Elizabethan, period. These ideas took form in the Elizabethan Poor Law. The Elizabethan Poor Law, which reached its final form in 1601, was the model that the English colonists had in mind when they began to settle North America in the 1600s. The Elizabethan Poor Law was supplemented by additional laws in the seventeenth and eighteenth centuries, but it was not changed fundamentally until 1834. Thus the Elizabethan Poor Law is also known as the Old Poor Law, and the law of 1834 is known as the New Poor Law or, sometimes, as the Poor Law Reform. The 1834 law introduced a new harshness in dealing with the poor, and twentieth-century readers of this book will undoubtedly be as divided as were the people of the nineteenth century about the merits of the reform. Some will surely marvel at how the word·*reform* can mean such different things to different people.

The most enduring component of public welfare has been the provision of income to people unable to obtain a livelihood by means that enjoy higher social esteem, namely, by work or by inheritance. This income component has at times been broadened to include supplementing the income of "the working poor"— people whose income does not meet a certain prevailing standard of the time. In addition to the income provision—generally known today as public assistance —the concept of public welfare expanded over time to include certain kinds of care for dependent persons. Children who have no parents and no other relatives to care for them have come under the protection of the state; child welfare is thus another component of public welfare. Other categories of dependents also receive assistance from public welfare programs; such categories of people as the mentally retarded, mentally ill, blind, and elderly have come under the umbrella of public welfare.

The central relationship in public welfare is, then, between the government and members of the society who are unable to care for themselves in the ways that are considered "usual." The government assumes responsibility for providing such care and protection, in the form of income and in other forms as well: Instead of providing income directly, the government may provide some of the things income buys (known as income "in kind"), such as shelter, in the form of public housing, or free food. Various kinds of institutions to care for dependent persons have also developed as part of public welfare: Systems of foster care for children who do not have or cannot live with natural parents; special residences for mentally retarded people and for others whose social functioning is impaired. The public welfare system has at times provided jobs for the unemployed and training for employment.

Public assistance, public housing, publicly sponsored jobs and job training, public institutions for persons requiring special forms of care or protection— these are the main forms that public welfare has assumed, the forms of government obligation to those in need of special, noncustomary, care. From its very beginnings, however, government action and attitude directed toward people unable to support themselves have oscillated between punishment and help, for two basic reasons: (1) Government officials—and people in general—have not understood why some people do not or cannot support themselves; their "solutions" to the problem have changed when their explanations of the problem changed; and (2) government officials—and employers—generally want able-bodied people to support themselves through work; government therefore has not wanted public assistance to be too freely available.

This chapter will focus on the development of the enormously influential Elizabethan Poor Law. Chapter 6 will discuss the transformations of public welfare from the New Poor Law to the present.

RESTRAINT AND REPRESSION

Throughout its history, the subject of public assistance has been a thorn in the side of public authorities and of the citizens whose taxes provide the funds for it. The continuously vexing question has been: Of all those people claiming to be in need of public assistance, how many could be and should be earning their own livelihood by working? The question perhaps first arose in its modern form as medieval society was breaking up and the feudal relationship of serfdom was being replaced by free labor. Under serfdom, the laborer had been tied to the land; while he was not a slave, not the absolute property of a master, he had fixed obligations to give service to a lord who, in turn, had fixed obligations to the serf. The lord was as obligated to make land available to the serf to cultivate for himself as the serf was to contribute a certain number of days to working the lord's land. With the revival of trade and town life, the feudal social order gave way to a commercial one. Gradually the serf became an agricultural laborer, working for a cash wage; he became free of his ties to the lord's land, and the lord became free of his obligations to the serf.

Forbidding Charity

Europe was struck by a deadly epidemic, the bubonic plague (also known as the Black Plague or Black Death), during the years 1348–1349. This epidemic had two important effects on the population: (1) Many people fled from their homes and towns in an effort to escape the plague, and (2) between one fourth and one third of Europe's population was killed by the disease.[1]

The consequence of death on such a large scale, plus the departure of many people, was the development of a severe shortage of labor. Farm laborers took this opportunity to charge higher wages for their work. Others took advantage of the increased movement of the times by switching to a livelihood of begging or by otherwise profiting from the life of vagabondage. This situation led to the proclamation by King Edward III in 1349 of a law—the Statute of Laborers—that is regarded by some social welfare scholars as the first step toward the national control of poor relief. The purpose of the law was to force able-bodied men to work at prevailing wages. To accomplish this goal, the statute forbade donations of alms to able-bodied men. It stated:

> Because that many valiant beggars, as long as they may live of begging, do refuse to labor, giving themselves to idleness and vice, and sometime to theft and other abominations; none upon the said pain of imprisonment, shall under the color of pity or alms, give anything to such, which may labor, or presume to favor them towards their desires, so that thereby they may be compelled to labor for their necessary living.[2]

It is evident that the attitude toward charity in this statute represents a significant departure from the attitude held by the church. St. Augustine's distinction between the deserving and the undeserving, put forward in the fourth century, seemed not to receive much attention. But in the fourteenth century, Edward III's regulation introduced an even sharper note: Being charitable to able-bodied beggars was against the law; they were definitely undeserving of charity. Edward III began to use the powers of government to separate the deserving from the undeserving, an effort that has continued for more than six hundred years down to our own day. This was also the beginning of a new way of thinking in Western society: What is considered to be in the best interests of society, as determined by government authorities, gained ascendance over the church's conception of the obligations of Christian charity.

It should be noted that this first major secular intervention into this sphere was aimed at keeping charity from being given to those who were not "truly needy"—as the modern phrase would put it—and at getting them back to work. Deterrence of idleness has continued to be a recurrent theme in the development of public welfare, and a constant focus of attention in any discussions about developing a program of guaranteed minimal income for everybody. Public welfare, as a mode of social welfare, began, in the modern world, by the taking action against the practice of charity. This was not a total rejection of almsgiving but rather an effort to bring it under control, the control of the national government.

Punishing Begging and Vagrancy

Concern about vagrancy and begging was an intermittent theme in English government and society for more than three hundred years. The problem was at its most intense during the Tudor period (1485–1603), and from time to time over a period of four hundred years, laws were passed that sharply restricted people's freedom to move from one place to another.

Restriction of such movement became one of the lasting ways in which government authorities attempted to maintain control over segments of the population that were regarded as potential troublemakers and in which they also attempted to limit the cost burdens of providing for indigent people. English colonies in America adopted such procedures, and as recently as 1971, the governor of the state of New York attempted to reduce the migration of poor people into the state by proposing that the state not pay public assistance benefits to newcomers who moved into substandard housing. He made this proposal despite the fact that restriction of benefits on a residency basis had already been ruled unconstitutional by the U.S. Supreme Court. He must have known that he could not make his proposal stick (legislative leaders from his own party said it was illegal), but he was nonetheless giving public expression to a long-existing sentiment in Western society. It might be stated as "Go back where you came from, and stay put. Your travels and migrations are making trouble for us."[3]

Note, however, that the group being troubled by such migrations changes. The earliest laws restricting movement did so because the *district being left* suffered from labor shortages and higher wage demands. From the sixteenth century onward, however, after responsibility for the poor was assumed by the government, migration troubled the *district into which* the people were moving because the district might become obligated to provide support for them.

The 1349 Statute of Laborers (and follow-up statutes) engendered evasion; men moved from county to county to escape the laws that required them to work for whoever wanted their services and at no more than the prevailing wage for such work. In 1388, during the reign of King Richard II, Parliament passed a tightening-up measure that provided that no laborer could leave his district without a letter stating the purpose of his trip and the date of his return; the penalty for violation was placement in the stocks. The law also stipulated that beggars "impotent to serve" (that is, disabled) had to stay in the city or town in which they had been living when the law was proclaimed. The only exception was that if the city or town could not support the beggar, he could move elsewhere within the district or return to the town in which he was born; this had to be done within forty days of the announcement of the law. This law of 1388 appears to be the first that recognized that some people could not work and therefore required relief. It gave them the right to beg, in contrast to the able-bodied, who were obligated to work. But neither type of person was free to wander around according to his own preference.[4]

As noted in Chapter 3, the Tudor period had major significance for the development of social welfare. One of the reasons is that "in the sixteenth century the numbers of rogues and vagabonds were larger in proportion to the population than they [had] ever been before or since."[5] This increase in the number of people wandering about the countryside and hanging about the towns —a "rowsey, ragged rabblement of rakehelles," one commentator called them —was caused by the economic, political, and legal changes that had been taking place in English society. People whose forebears had enjoyed relative security as serfs and tenant farmers had been forced off their land. Feudal rules about a person's rights to a piece of land or a portion of what it produced changed as feudal society gave way to a new economic order which no longer recognized traditional economic rights. Henry VII's breaking up of the private bands of fighting men that had been part of the feudal organization of society further increased the number of wanderers. And "all through the Tudor reigns, the 'beggars coming to town' preyed on the fears of the dwellers in lonely farms and hamlets, and exercised the minds of magistrates, Privy Councillors, and Parliaments."[6] They spread rebellious ideas, and rebellions occurred from time to time.[7] These threats to public order prompted increasing efforts to reduce the troublemaking potential of the rogues and vagabonds. In the course of the efforts, the English government was obliged to recognize that some of the people who wandered about were not troublemakers but disabled people who had no way to gain a livelihood except by begging. But from the fourteenth through the sixteenth centuries, before this realization took firm hold, vagabonds were subjected to a variety of brutal punishments, including whipping, placement in the stocks, branding on the forehead or chest with a hot iron, cutting off of an ear, and for repeat offenders, death.[8]

THE DEVELOPMENT OF GOVERNMENT RESPONSIBILITY

The development of government responsibility for the poor took place over a period of seventy years, from 1531, during the reign of Henry VIII, to 1601, near the end of the reign of his daughter, Elizabeth I. This seventy-year period is, in effect, the beginning of public welfare as a mode of social welfare. During this period, various procedures were tried, until a basic pattern was achieved that lasted in England from 1601 until its complete revision in 1834, and that influenced poor relief in America.

From Alms to Taxes

The Tudor efforts began in 1531 with Henry VIII's law that prohibited begging by able-bodied men—sturdy beggars or valiant beggars, as they were known. This revived and extended the policy prescribed in Richard II's law of 1388. The new element in Henry VIII's law was the giving of explicit recognition and support to the right of the disabled and aged poor to beg. Local officials, particularly justices of the peace, were to search out all those in their parishes who had to subsist on alms, issue them each a letter authorizing them to beg, and assign them each to a specific area in which to beg.[9]

This was a significant development despite the fact that the law was designed primarily to limit the number of beggars rather than to provide relief to the deserving poor. In succeeding legislation, the government moved in stages from what might be called government-encouraged voluntarism to the imposition of taxes for the support of the poor, aged, and infirm in 1572. Thus, in 1536, the second Poor Law of Henry VIII's reign provided for greater support of those in need, mainly through prescribing more specific procedures: The churchwardens in each parish and the mayor of each town were charged with collecting alms every Sunday, holy day, and festival day. Casual almsgiving to individual beggars was prohibited; contributions were to be given to the common collection. Contributions were still voluntary, but the law instructed "every preacher, parson, vicar, curate of this realm" to "exhort, move, stir, and provoke people to be liberal and bountifully to extend their good and charitable alms and contributions." The clergy were to do this exhorting in all their activities: when preaching sermons, hearing confessions, and assisting people in writing their wills. Thus the concept of voluntary support of the needy through church-based charity was retained from the waning Middle Ages, but was blended, somewhat awkwardly, with the newly emerging concept of governmentally prescribed and administered provisions for the poor. This law of 1536 is innovative also in that it requires the collectors of church alms to keep records of their collections and disbursements, and specifies that the collectors will receive wages for the time spent in this work. These, then, are the first paid public welfare officials.

During the years 1551–1552, new pressures on the people to make voluntary contributions were added to the law. The collectors were ordered "to gently ask" each householder what he would contribute each week for relief of the poor, and the amount he stated was entered in a book and collected every Sunday. If a householder refused to contribute, he was exhorted by the parson, and if he still refused, the parson certified the man to the bishop, who exhorted him. In 1563, under the reign of Elizabeth, an addition to the law gave the bishop the power to compel the uncharitable householder to appear before the justices of the peace (or, in towns, before the mayor and the churchwardens). These officials were also to ask in a nice way for the householder's contribution, and if he still refused, they had the authority to decide how much he should "contribute" and to assess him for that amount. He could be imprisoned if he refused to pay it. Finally, in 1572, a tax—the poor rate—was imposed on all parishioners, who thereby took on the new role of taxpayer, or ratepayer, as it was called in England. From the first, taxpayers manifested opposition to this requirement. Such opposition between taxpayers and the poor also surfaced at later times, not only in England but in the United States, as taxpayers came to feel that taxes in support of the poor were too high.[10] The opposition from taxpayers created difficulties for the overseers of the poor, officials newly designated by the law of 1572.

Perhaps the complaints about taxes had something to do with the fact that when the Poor Law was rewritten in 1597, a provision was explicitly included that stated that parents were financially responsible for their children and children for their parents, depending upon who was able to work and earn a living and who was not. Another rewriting of the bill in 1601 extended family responsibility to grandparents and grandchildren: Thus an able-bodied grandchild was responsible for the support of an aged or infirm grandparent. Similarly an able-bodied grandparent was responsible for the support of a grandchild if the child's parents could not support him or her. Only if the family was unable to support its dependent members did parish and city poor relief become available. This is a clear example of Wilensky and Lebeaux's residual concept of social welfare: The ordinary and expected ways of gaining a livelihood are by working or, if one cannot work, by receiving aid from one's parents, grandparents, children, or grandchildren, whoever is the able-bodied member of the family. Only if there is no able-bodied family member able to support the dependent members does the social welfare system come into play.

It is noteworthy that the provision in the law requiring family members to support one another involves a recognition of social change on the part of the Parliament: there was an awareness that the traditional feudal relationships, which assured the aged or disabled serf a livelihood, had substantially passed out of existence. The traditional manorial village was being replaced by villages and towns consisting of independent household units—whose members no longer had the support of a manorial lord. Thus these last two rewritings of the Elizabethan Poor Law contain a concept of the family as distinct and separable from the community. The first line of collective responsibility had passed from the manor to the individual family. Historian Lawrence Stone has stated that "the Elizabethan village was a place filled with malice and hatred," and he further noted that "as for pregnant unmarried women, they were treated with a ruthless cruelty which only the fear that the child would become a burden on the local poor-rate can explain."[11]

Paid Welfare Officials

The Tudor Poor Laws marked the beginning of paid public welfare officials. The Statute of 1536, which required mayors and head officers in each city and churchwardens in each parish to collect alms every Sunday, holy day, and festival day, also provided that they be paid for this work.[12] For reasons that are not clear, the later Tudor Poor Laws (1572, 1597, 1601) did not include a provision for paid officials. Instead, they called for the appointment in each parish of unpaid officials known as overseers of the poor. Overseers were appointed for a one-year term by the justices of the peace; they were selected from among the members of the parish, and service in the post was compulsory even though unpaid.[13] In the middle of the seventeenth century, there was criticism of a Poor Law administration carried out by overseers who were necessarily amateurs, had no interest in their work, and were replaced every year.[14] Nevertheless, this system prevailed for a long time. And it is significant that the Poor Laws did create a category of official, the overseer of the poor, whose specific responsibility was to administer poor relief.

Localism

One of the significant features of the Tudor Poor Laws was that they took over the existing units of church organization, local parishes, and made these the units of administration of the Poor Laws. This policy continued and reinforced a longstanding emphasis on localism in English society. From the earliest days of English society,

> Every person was . . . a member of some local community, to which he owed obligations, and from which he was entitled to expect some measure of protection, and, when in need, some undefined support. An unknown person, absent without credentials from the community to which he belonged, was an object of grave suspicion, having, in early times, practically no rights.[15]

With the introduction of a tax to pay for support of the poor, each parish was concerned that it not have to support the poor from some other parishes. This concern led to some absurdities, as will be noted in the discussion of the Law of Settlement and Removal. As already indicated, the intense localism has continued into the present; the example of New York in 1971 is assuredly not an isolated one. In 1981, President Reagan's administration took the first steps toward a major revival of localism.

The Poorhouse

The Tudor Poor Laws may contain the origins of the concept of public housing. The Poor Law of 1597 empowered justices of the peace and town officials to impose a tax on the parish for the purpose of maintaining "convenient houses of habitation" for paupers. The building that served as the "poorhouse" might be an old one or one built specifically for the purpose. It provided housing for a variety of people: the widowed, aged, and sick; mothers of illegitimate children; and tramps and paupers awaiting removal to other parishes. Thousands of poorhouses were in operation from the sixteenth to the nineteenth centuries.[16]

THE NEW IMPORTANCE OF WORK

The dissolution of the feudal system and its replacement by a market economy, and the change in attitude toward indiscriminate almsgiving and *its* replacement by taxes imposed to support the poor, led to a new emphasis on putting the able-bodied poor to work. The number of unemployed idlers had greatly increased, not only because of many men being turned loose from manorial settlements but also because of an enormous increase in population. For reasons that are not fully understood, the population of Europe doubled between 1500 and 1600.[17] The attitudes toward work that developed in the sixteenth century and that were built into the Tudor Poor Laws have, in many important aspects, prevailed into the present.

Work and the Tudor Poor Laws

Before the Tudors themselves began to introduce work provisions into their national laws for dealing with the poor, efforts were made on a local level. In response to the growing number of poor people and the increasing problem of vagrants, the city of London obtained permission to take over an unused royal palace at Bridewell and turn it into a place to put idle people and those of bad character to work in such trades as cap and wire making. This was the first of a series of new institutions known as houses of correction. Its location caught on as a name for the type of institution, and any *house of correction*, in America as well as in England, might be known as "the Bridewell."

Houses of correction sometimes served more than one purpose. Willful idlers were put in them and made to work; but innocent people who were unemployed and seeking work would also be given work in these institutions. In some localities, the poor thought of the house of correction as a prison; in others, they were paid prevailing wages and thus, in effect, were being provided with secure employment in a sheltered place. However, these institutions became increasingly punitive and eventually were scarcely distinguishable from jails.[18]

The London Bridewell was one element of the efforts of the city authorities to deal with poor, sick, and idle people. However, because the effort was local, the system failed. It could not cope with the great flow of people into the city, and its funds for running the system were insufficient.[19] Within a short time, consideration of the problem moved to the national level. The legislation of the latter half of the sixteenth century made use of several approaches.

The obligation to work

An important law passed in 1563, the Statute of Artificers, assumed that employment was available for all and that all able-bodied people had an obligation to work. People between the ages of twelve and sixty who were not employed could be made to work as agricultural laborers.[20] The insistence on the obligation to work represented an important social change—for not only were there people who sought to maintain themselves entirely by begging and vagabondage, but people who did work did not do so with the regularity that later became customary. The sixteenth century was a period of transition between two different types of economy, and the attitudes toward work that were appropriate in an earlier time were becoming outmoded. As historian Christopher Hill has stated:

> To celebrate a hundred or more saints' days in a year was all very well in an agricultural society like that of medieval England. . . . But an industrialized society, such as England was becoming in the sixteenth century, needs regular, disciplined labour. . . . Holy-days, said the Order of 1536 abrogating them, are the occasion of much sloth and idleness, riot and superfluity, and lead to the decay of industrial crafts. Artificers and labourers, the Bishop of Exeter observed in 1539, still needed "spiritual instruction," backed up by punishment, to persuade them to work on saints' days.[21]

In addition to time off for many saints' days, workers had little incentive to work steadily during periods when wages were high. There were few consumer goods that ordinary people could buy. Consequently people worked "short time" when wages were high; that is, they worked only enough to pay for the basic necessities of subsistence, after which they relaxed. The Statute of Artificers of 1563 and the Poor Law of 1597 referred to idleness, drunkenness, and unlawful games as "lewd practices and conditions of life," and the laws construed these as interfering with agricultural and industrial production.[22]

"Setting the poor on work"

The laws of the Tudor period, and especially of the Elizabethan period, reflected the beginnings of a national government taking responsibility to provide work for the unemployed. As humanitarian Juan Luis Vivès had urged in 1526, and as the city of London had undertaken in 1555, the English government in 1572 passed a law giving local justices of the peace the authority to put idle rogues and vagabonds to work. The 1572 law was vague as to how the justices were to do this, and detailed procedures were written into the law in 1576. The justices were to obtain "a stock of stuff"—that is, materials such as wool, hemp, and iron —which they were to make available to all poor people, who were to be paid for the goods they made from them. The officials would sell the goods, and the proceeds would be used to buy additional raw materials. Able-bodied people who refused this work were to be put into a house of correction modeled on the London Bridewell.[23]

The law of 1572 marked a significant step in thinking about social welfare. Until that time, people who did not work were divided into two categories— those who were unable to work (the impotent poor) and those who refused to work (rogues, idlers, vagabonds). Now a third category was recognized—able-bodied people who wanted to work and could not obtain a job. It has been seen, even in the present, that many people who are working and obtaining a satisfactory livelihood do not like to acknowledge that such a third category exists because such recognition creates complications for these taxpayers, who are likely to feel reasonably satisfied with the social arrangements that enable them to sustain themselves. They do not wish to be deeply critical of those arrangements. It is much easier to blame those without work for their own situation than to blame the society for failure to assure jobs for all. It is not too great an exaggeration to say that recognition of this third category of people keeps dropping out of people's understanding of unemployment and reappears from time to time only with difficulty. As will be discussed more fully later, the sixteenth and seventeenth centuries have left a heritage of ideas and attitudes that make it hard to believe that a person who wants to work cannot find work.

Apprenticeship

The purpose of setting the poor on work, as the phrasing of the time put it, was that idle rogues would no longer have an excuse for not working. The Statute of 1576 also introduced a *preventive* concept: Setting the poor on work would not only correct the behavior of adult rogues but also instill in youth the habit of working and thus reduce the chances that they would grow up to be idle rogues. The means for assuring this were specified in the 1597 revision of the Poor Law: Poor children were to be apprenticed to learn a trade. Henry VIII's law in 1536 had specified apprenticeship for children between the ages of five and fourteen who were vagrant and begging. The statute in the Elizabethan period (1597, and rewritten in 1601) went further, in empowering the church-wardens and overseers of the poor in each parish to "bind out" as an apprentice *any* child whose parents could not, in the officials' judgment, maintain him or her. Boys could be kept as apprentices until age twenty-four, girls until age twenty-one or until they married.

The workhouse

The new emphasis on work that emerged in the Tudor period developed even further in succeeding years, eventuating in the creation of a new institution, the workhouse, which was a feature of social welfare for more than two hundred years. By the nineteenth century, the workhouse had become a horror, though it does not seem to have begun that way. The idea of the workhouse as a place where the able-bodied poor would be gathered to work seems to have originated with the Dutch, who built such a facility in Amsterdam in 1596. This was a combination workhouse for the able-bodied seeking work, house of correction for the able-bodied idle, who had to be confined in order to get them to work, and poorhouse for those too old or too sick to work.

The success of the Dutch merchant class in building up business created some envy among English businessmen, who thought that the Dutch ways of dealing with their poor contributed to their economic success and thought that England should follow the Dutch example. In the late seventeenth century, some English business leaders wrote pamphlets advocating the establishment of workhouses.

In addition, setting the poor to work on a piecemeal, individual basis had proved to be rather impractical. A further complication was that providing them with a stock of stuff in their homes sometimes resulted in theft of the materials.[24] The workhouse came to be seen as a way of achieving greater efficiency in carrying out the Poor Law, but it also had other meanings attached to it. These meanings will become clear in the next section.

Social Change and the New Emphasis on Work

Three important changes took place in the sixteenth and seventeenth centuries that gave rise to the increased importance of work. First, the Tudors tried to concentrate more power in the central government in order to establish a firm and stable national rule. As part of that effort, they stopped the nobility from conducting private wars with each other and passed laws to control vagabonds, for example, by making them work.[25] The Tudors were successful, but their successors, the early Stuarts, provoked great antagonism with their authoritarian ways. A revolution and civil war broke out; King Charles I was beheaded in 1649; the country came under the domination of the Puritans, led by Oliver Cromwell, who became the head of state under the title Lord Protector; and when, after Cromwell's death, the monarchy was restored under Charles II in 1660, it had less power than it had had under the Tudors. Men of property—wealthy businessmen and country gentlemen who owned large estates—had much power in their local areas. The pressure to work no longer came from a strong central government trying to maintain "law and order." The pressure continued, however, from two changes that were to have longer-lasting effects, mercantilism and the Protestant Reformation.

Mercantilism and the rise of business

As we noted in Chapter 2, The Commercial Revolution changed the organization of Western society from an agricultural basis to an increasingly commercial one. These changes in the ways people gained a livelihood led to changes in ideas, which in turn led to changes in social relationships. The mercantilist period (which began during the reign of the Tudors) saw the emergence of a new outlook that has been called *the capitalist spirit*. As business developed, those making money—the capitalists—became increasingly influential, and their views helped to push aside earlier medieval ideas:

> The businessman came slowly to look upon his enterprise as merely a means for making profits. In fact, his search for profits pushed into the background all thoughts of his duty to society, to God, and to his neighbors. There was a growing tendency to value all things in terms of money, to believe that success meant the heaping up of wealth, to think that riches were the chief end of life and the most certain basis of power. In the middle ages, the rich man had been suspected because he was rich. In the sixteenth and seventeenth centuries, the rich man came to be respected because he was rich.[26]

This new spirit of capitalism had an impact on public welfare, as on everything else. In the second half of the seventeenth century, businessmen viewed the unemployed able-bodied poor as an undeveloped source of profits, and they began to advocate and to organize workhouses that would be economically advantageous to them, the nation, and the poor as well. One businessman calculated that "even a blind, armless, one-legged man could, in a well-managed institution, earn sixpence a day."[27]

Business leaders of the last half of the seventeenth century—for example, Sir Josiah Child, chairman of the East India Company—wrote pamphlets advocating the establishment of workhouses as a solution to the problems of poverty, destitution, and vagrancy. They considered the parish poor relief authorities to be ineffective. As a philanthropic endeavor, businessman Thomas Firmin put the greater part of his fortune into building a workhouse. It was devoted to employing the poor at manufacturing linen, and is reported to have kept 1,700 people at a time working in various textile activities. Firmin devoted the last twenty-one years of his life (1676–1697) to running this organization and claimed that he had almost succeeded in getting it to pay its own way (including the costs of educating children and maintaining aged people). His experience helped strengthen the general belief that employment of the poor could be a paying enterprise. The mayor and alderman of Bristol, then the second-most important commercial city in England, requested and, in 1696, received authorization from Parliament to take the administration of poor relief out of the hands of the overseers in the city's nineteen parishes and place it in the hands of a new citywide "Corporation of the Poor," which built and administered a workhouse. Other cities followed this same path.

Despite the contagious optimism that spread from city to city, the effort to employ the poor in workhouses and make a profit on their work proved a total failure. Not only were the workers unskilled in their work, but the managers of the workhouses were also incompetent and not very motivated to carry out their assigned responsibilities. It proved more costly to maintain people in workhouses than to give them relief in their own homes.[28]

While the workhouse as a profit-making enterprise was a failure, the spirit that led to its creation lived on after it. The capitalist spirit endures to this day as perhaps the most significant attitude regulating the flow of energy and activity in Western society. The capitalist spirit seems to have received a boost from religion, even though the result was that the capitalist spirit pushed religious ideas and attitudes out of the dominant position they had held during the Middle Ages. Ideas that arose during the Protestant Reformation blended with mercantilist ideas about business to produce an influential set of beliefs concerning the importance of work, beliefs that continued to shape American public welfare practices into the 1960s and 1970s.

Puritanism and the spirit of capitalism

Protestantism had a profound influence on Western society, an influence that was felt in every social institution, including work and social welfare. A brief summary of key points about the Protestant Reformation will help to show the way in which this new attitude toward work came about.

The Reformation's beginning is traceable to the activities of a German monk, Martin Luther, who criticized the Roman Catholic Church in a series of pronouncements and publications beginning in the year 1517. In those days, people whom the Church called sinners could buy their redemption from sin and thus assurance of salvation in the hereafter. Luther denounced this corrupt practice, known as the sale of indulgences. As Luther developed his ideas about returning to the purity of early Christianity, he attracted many followers but was denounced by both the Church authorities and secular political authorities. Although he had initially wanted to purify the Roman Catholic Church, it became apparent by the 1530s that no reconciliation between him and the Church was possible. Separate Protestant churches—Lutheran churches—began to form. The religion of Lutheranism gained legal recognition in Germany in 1555.[29]

Luther's most important religious idea, from the standpoint of the present discussion, was that people could be assured of salvation from eternal torment through their faith in God. Those who had such faith were saved by God's grace, the freely given, unmerited favor and love that God bestowed on the believer. Salvation could not be bought. It could not even be earned by good works such as giving money to the church for charity. Nevertheless, people had to fulfill the obligations imposed on them by their position in the world; every person had a "calling," an occupation and social position to which he or she had been summoned by God.[30]

Luther's ideas of salvation through faith and of the importance of a person's calling received a somewhat changed interpretation from John Calvin, a Frenchman living in Switzerland. He and Luther were the two most influential originators of Protestantism. Calvinism became the most influential form of Protestantism outside Germany.[31] Calvin's followers in England became known as Puritans—they were people who were dissatisfied with both Henry VIII and Elizabeth I for retaining too much of Catholicism in the Church of England. Eventually, some Puritans left England to establish colonies in the New World, one group settling at Plymouth, Massachusetts, in 1620 and another establishing the Massachusetts Bay Colony in 1630.

According to Calvinism, God is all-powerful, and the purpose of all human activity is not to attain salvation but to glorify God. Since God is all-powerful, humans can do nothing to influence God, who, by his own will, predestined some people for salvation and consigned the rest to eternal damnation. Nevertheless, every Christian must work for the glory of God. Individuals must not merely accept their calling but, with self-discipline and zeal, carry out their tasks, the tasks set by God.[32] The true Christian must be industrious, thrifty, frugal, and ascetic, turning away from frivolity, sentiment, and interest in comfort and luxury.

Thus a new meaning of work was developed in the teachings of the English Puritans. As stated by historian R. H. Tawney, the Puritans idealized work and saw it as

> not simply a requirement imposed by nature, or a punishment for the sin of Adam. It is itself a kind of ascetic discipline, more rigorous than that demanded of any order of mendicants—a discipline imposed by the will of God, and to be undergone, not in solitude, but in the punctual discharge of secular duties. It is not merely an economic means, to be laid aside when physical needs have been satisfied. It is a spiritual end, for in it alone can the soul find health, and it must be continued as an ethical duty long after it has ceased to be a material necessity. Work thus conceived stands at the very opposite pole from "good works," as they were understood, or misunderstood by Protestants. They, it was thought, had been a series of single transactions, performed as compensation for particular sins, or out of anxiety to acquire merit. What is required of the Puritans is not individual meritorious acts, but a holy life—a system in which every element is grouped round a central idea, the service of God, from which all disturbing irrelevances have been pruned, and to which all minor interests are subordinated.[33]

This religious doctrine supported several social changes taking place in England during the late sixteenth and seventeenth centuries. Conscientious attention to business came to be seen as a fulfillment of the highest religious and moral virtue. The personal virtues stressed by Puritanism—industriousness, punctuality, frugality—fit well with the mercantilist emphasis on production (rather than consumption) as the main purpose of economic activity. Puritan religious writers and preachers joined with businessmen in emphasizing the dangers of pampering poverty. Economic success came to be regarded as evidence that the prosperous person was one of God's elect, predestined for salvation. The prosperous found it easy to believe that the poor—and even the entire wage-earning class—were predestined to eternal damnation.[34]

These principles of Puritanism have come to be known as "the Protestant ethic," or sometimes simply as "the work ethic." There has been much scholarly discussion concerning how important this ethic was in the development of capitalism. Some writers have pointed out that capitalism had clear beginnings and even flourished in certain Catholic countries before the rise of Protestantism. This issue is beyond the scope of this book. There is little disagreement, however, that Puritanism was influential in changing the basic attitude toward work in the Western countries in which it was followed, including the Netherlands as well as England and the United States.[35]

Before the Protestant Reformation, Christians viewed work as God's punishment for human sinfulness. It was an unwelcome burden, necessary in order to obtain a livelihood, but not virtuous in itself. Protestantism, and particularly the Calvinist branches of it (the Puritans had various disagreements among themselves and eventually divided into the Presbyterian, Congregational, Quaker, and Baptist churches, among others), saw working hard as a way of serving God, of being a moral person, of carrying out their responsibility to the community. Not less important, strictly disciplined work was a means of controlling the ever present threat of disorder in society.[36] Idleness thus became a multiple threat— to the order of the state, to the productivity that was so important to developing business, and to the carrying out of God's will, which demanded energetic labor in a calling. Political, economic, and religious ideas combined to generate a conception of work that dominated the consciousness of Western humanity until the middle of the twentieth century, when it began to lose its hold.

THE LAW OF SETTLEMENT AND REMOVAL

One of the important features of English society, as noted earlier in this chapter, was the notion that everyone belonged to a particular local community. From the middle of the fourteenth century on, as we also noted, laws were passed from time to time to keep various categories of people in their home districts or towns. During the development of the Tudor Poor Law in the sixteenth and seventeenth centuries, towns began to adopt various measures to keep out newcomers. Some towns, for example, adopted a procedure of making monthly searches for newcomers who seemed poor enough that they might become "chargeable"— that is, might become public charges who would have to be supported from the poor rates—and expelled them.[37]

The practices of a few towns, concerned with keeping poor strangers out, were made nationwide and applicable to almost everybody in a sweeping law passed in 1662, during the reign of King Charles II. The Law of Settlement and Removal was not a radical piece of legislation, since it only put into law what had in many places already been a matter of local custom. Nevertheless, it has been called by some the worst law ever passed in England.[38] The enforcement of the law resulted in enormous hardship to poor people and led to endless legal proceedings that enriched lawyers. And it put enormous obstacles in the way of people who were trying to overcome their poverty or improve their economic position by moving to an area that offered better opportunity.

The community to which a person belonged was his "settlement." The 1662 law empowered local authorities to removed *any* person who came into a parish or borough (district of a town) unless he could prove that he would *never* become chargeable. If he could not prove this, he could be removed to the place that was considered his legal settlement. Good character and conduct were not sufficient, nor did it matter that the person had not applied for relief from the poor rates. The mere possibility that the person might at some time become a pauper was sufficient reason for ejection—unless the required proof to refute this possibility could be offered. The procedure was as follows: Newcomers had to demonstrate that they were able to rent property worth £10 per year. They had forty days to establish this level of financial ability. Since the average laborer's cottage was valued at no more than a fourth of that amount, the level of financial ability required was not attainable by most agricultural laborers, manual workers, and craftsmen. A neighbor's complaint to the churchwarden or overseer of the poor was sufficient basis for the official to remove a newcomer.

But the law had a loophole, since people might slip into a parish and remain out of sight until forty days were up. Apparently some parish officers had been bribing their own poor to go into another parish and stay hidden for forty days, thus making the new parish thereafter responsible for their relief. So the law was amended to require that the forty days be counted from the time the overseer of the poor was notified of the person's arrival. This safeguard proved insufficient, so a few years later the law was amended again to start the counting of the forty days' residence from the time of a public announcement in church of the newcomer's arrival. Not until 1795 was the law changed so that people could not be removed from a parish until they actually applied for relief. The 1795 amendment did not, however, apply to pregnant, unmarried women "who were potentially the most expensive, and hence the most unpopular, of all paupers." Even in the early twentieth century, some removals were still being carried out.[39]

Since the parish officials and the taxpayers were responsible for the poor, they looked for ways to meet the responsibility at the lowest possible cost. The Law of Settlement and Removal provided the officials some legal means by which to keep costs down. For example, the law required the overseers of the poor to bind out young boys and girls as apprentices, but the overseers seldom took the trouble to look for a master craftsman who would train the youngster; in order to save money, the overseers would put the children out "to any sorry masters that [would] take them, without any concern for their education and welfare, on account of the little money that [was] given with them."[40] The law stipulated that apprentices be given a settlement from whatever parish they were placed in. Consequently, overseers tried to find masters in other parishes who would take their apprentices. This would relieve the original parish of any future responsibility for the boy, the woman he would later marry, and the children they would have. Since all parishes were resorting to the same tactics, it is doubtful that any parish actually reduced its costs for supporting the poor. This practice only guaranteed that there was not even the little supervision over the parish apprentices that the churchwardens and overseers would have exercised if the apprenticing had been done in the home parish.[41]

All in all, the Law of Settlement and Removal resulted in the compulsory moving around of thousands of people annually for more than two hundred years. A parish receiving a person removed from another parish would often dispute the claim that it was in fact the person's legal settlement. It would go to court against the removing parish and sometimes get the removed person sent back. The person had no right of appeal and might be shuttled back and forth several times while the courts decided the case. A Parliamentary report in 1837 gave this summary of the situation:

> . . . a perpetual transplantation was going forward, which set the whole country alive with the movements of vagrant carts, and filled the coaches and the inns with burly overseers and fat constables, traveling from all points between the Thames and the Tweed, from Berkshire to Leicestershire, and from Sussex to Cornwall, with laborers and laborers' wives, and astonished children. All this was managed to the great satisfaction of the vestry and overseers, and the lawyers; under whose auspices it was generally arranged that the laborers, and the wives, and the children, or some of them with many of their friends and fellow-laborers, should make a journey to the county sessions [court] as witnesses, and after the most solemn inquiry, travel back again to the place whence they came and from whence they had been "illegally" removed.[42]

The intense localism, traditional for centuries, but further intensified by the sixteenth-century Poor Laws and the seventeenth-century Law of Settlement and Removal, was carried by English settlers to the American colonies and remained a powerful element in social welfare in England and in the United States until well into the twentieth century.

THE POOR LAWS IN
THE AMERICAN COLONIES

The English people who began establishing colonies in North America, beginning with Jamestown, Virginia, in 1607, brought to the new land much of their English culture, including their concepts for dealing with dependency. As early as 1646, legislation passed in Virginia called for avoiding the sloth and idleness with which children are corrupted and gave local officials the authority to put poor children to work by binding them out as apprentices. Additional legislation in later years was prompted by concern about increasing numbers of idle and dissolute vagabonds who abandoned their wives and children.[43]

The basic principles of English poor relief became the basic principles of the colonies. The most important of these were: (1) *public responsibility* for the poor and dependent classes; (2) *taxation* of those with property to pay for support of the poor and dependent; (3) *localism*—geographic restriction of eligibility for aid to those who had established a settlement.[44] The colonists were willing to assist their neighbors who fell upon hard times. But they were as resistant as their compatriots in England to providing assistance to strangers. An example of this intense localism is the Rhode Island law of 1702, which made shipmasters responsible for chargeable passengers that they transported to the colony. The shipmaster was obliged to remove any passenger not accepted by a town, and he could be jailed if he refused or did not put up a substantial sum of money as security for the care of the person.[45]

The extreme localism broke down in many places during the Revolutionary War. The task of providing relief to refugees from war-torn areas was too great to be handled by the local system, and so, for example, New York's way of arranging emergency relief for such people was to create a category known as "the state poor," who were not chargeable to a specific local unit.[46]

A major theme in the development of public welfare from the eighteenth to the twentieth century, both in America and in England, has been the progressive shifting of responsibilities for public welfare from small local units to larger units of local government and eventually to the national government. Most of these shifts have come about because the particular local units handling public welfare at the time found their resources inadequate for coping with new problems thrust upon them by changing circumstances such as wars or major economic upheavals. Most generally, the states took over important responsibilities in the nineteenth century, and the federal government in the twentieth.

A word should be said about colonial methods of caring for the poor.[47] The dominant practice throughout the colonial period was to support the person in his or her own home; when this was not possible, a neighbor would take responsibility for caring for the person and would be reimbursed for the expenses by the parish (in the southern colonies, which followed the Church of England) or by the town (in the New England colonies, which, being Puritan, did not follow the Church of England). Poor relief in colonial times was essentially assistance to one's neighbors, and was thought of in this way. The settlement laws, of course, helped to keep it this way. Strangers coming into a town were "warned out," and townspeople who had out-of-town visitors had to give assurance to town officials that the visitors were of "good substance" and would not become chargeable.[48]

Although poor relief in colonial times had a neighborly aspect, it had a harsher side as well. As a way of minimizing the cost of poor relief, many towns adopted the practice of auctioning the poor to the lowest bidder. At the auction,

> . . . the qualities of each pauper were detailed with the same callousness as that shown in discussing the merits of a horse—or a slave. . . . To add to the festivity of the occasion (and to stimulate bidding) liquor was furnished at the expense of the town in some places.[49]

This procedure originated in New England and spread to other colonies and later to various states. It began to be outlawed in the 1830s; the last state to make the practice illegal was North Carolina, in 1877.[50] The binding out of children as apprentices was the practice used with orphans, illegitimate children, and children whose parents were considered dissolute and unfit to bring them up properly.

SUMMARY

Public welfare—the assumption of responsibility by the government for meeting the dependency needs of people unable to support themselves through the usual institutions of market and family—originated during the Tudor period in sixteenth-century England. The state's concern for public dependency can be found even earlier, in fourteenth-century measures to curtail almsgiving and punish begging and vagrancy. During the Tudor reigns, the state's responsibility was at first confined to requiring localities to take care of their own poor. This requirement strengthened an already existing tradition of localism and led to an intense concern about having to support "somebody else's poor." The concept of local responsibility has persisted for centuries, even though the concept of locality has broadened as times have changed—from parish to union of parishes (in England and from parish or township to county and state in the United

States. The legal concept of settlement did not disappear in the United States until 1969, when the Supreme Court ruled that the individual states could not require a certain period of residence in the particular state before public assistance could be received.

The Elizabethan Poor Law introduced several new concepts into public welfare that have remained influential to this day. Reliance upon voluntary charity to support the poor was replaced by taxation to provide the necessary funds. The government undertook to provide work for able-bodied people unable to find work, and it accepted responsibility for finding training situations for children deemed likely to grow up without skills to earn a living. The Poor Law made parents and grandparents responsible for children and grandchildren who could not support themselves, and able-bodied children and grandchildren responsible for parents and grandparents in need of support.

During the Tudor period, work assumed a new importance under the impact of political, economic, and religious changes. The newly strong central government of the Tudors saw idleness and vagrancy as threats to its stability and to the public order. The growing mercantilist spirit of this period led to a new emphasis on hard work and disciplined, systematic pursuit of profit. Finally, the Protestant Reformation, occurring first on the European continent and spreading to England, introduced the idea that work was a way of serving God, not a punishment for original sin as the Roman Catholic Church had taught.

All of these new ideas stressing the importance of work also called into question the traditional Christian belief that giving charity was always beneficial to the recipients. The idea began to take hold that giving help could be damaging, both to the person who received it and to the society, which suffered the loss of good workers who lapsed into sluggish dependency when sustained by alms. This idea became dominant in the nineteenth century, and has not entirely lost influence in the twentieth.

The English colonists who began establishing permanent settlements in America four years after the death of Queen Elizabeth brought the Elizabethan Poor Law with them. The principles of public responsibility for the poor and dependent classes when family responsibility failed, taxation, and localism became the foundation of American public welfare.

Notes

[1]The shift in terminology is neatly documented by a comparison of two similar publications. The *Encyclopedia of the Social Sciences*, published in 1931, includes an article on charity; the reader who seeks an article on philanthropy finds only the cross-reference: "See Charity." The successor publication, *The International Encyclopedia of the Social Sciences*, Vol. 12, published in 1968, includes an article on philanthropy (pp. 71–76) but no entry at all for "Charity."

[2]For a brief discussion of the Greek city-states, see William H. McNeill, *The Rise of the West* (New York: Mentor Books, 1963), pp. 219–226 and 281–285.

[3]A. R. Hands, *Charities and Social Aid in Greece and Rome* (Ithaca, N.Y.: Cornell University Press, 1968), pp. 34ff. Our discussion of philanthropy in ancient Greece and Rome is drawn mainly from Hands's study.

[4]W. Dittenberger, *Sylloge Inscriptionum Graecarum*, in Hands, *Charities and Social Aid*, pp. 175–176. A *deme* is a district. A *drachma* is the Greek unit of currency.

[5]Hands, *Charities and Social Aid*, pp. 41–46.

[6]*Ibid.*, pp. 51–56.

[7]The English word *metropolis* is taken directly from the Greek, where its meaning is mother-state or mother-city.

[8]James Westfall Thompson, *Economic and Social History of the Middle Ages (300–1300)*, Vol. I (New York: Frederick Ungar, 1959), p. 44. First published in 1928.

[9]Robert M. Grant, *Augustus to Constantine—The Thrust of the Christian Movement into the Roman World* (New York: Harper & Row, 1970), p. 258. See also Thompson, *Economic*

and Social History, p. 60, and R. M. Grant, *Early Christianity and Society* (New York: Harper & Row, 1977), Chap. 6.

[10]Yehezkel Kaufmann, *The Religion of Israel—From Its Beginnings to the Babylonian Exile*, trans. and abr. Moshe Greenberg (Chicago: University of Chicago Press, 1960), p. 60.

[11]*Ibid.*, pp. 73–75. The notion of the absolute power and goodness of God has led to many problems of theological interpretation in Judaism and in Christianity. For example, if God is all-powerful and also good, why are there people who suffer poverty, illness, and other misfortunes? A discussion of the theological explanations of misfortune would take us far afield. Our present concern is to describe the basic ideas from which the Judeo-Christian concepts of charity derive.

[12]*Ibid.*, p. 319.

[13]*Ibid.*, p. 320.

[14]Prov. 14:31.

[15]H. Tadmor, "The Period of the First Temple, the Babylonian Exile, and the Restoration," Part II, in H. H. Ben-Sasson, ed., *A History of the Jewish People* (Cambridge: Harvard University Press, 1976), pp. 128–130; and Kaufmann, *Religion of Israel*, pp. 347 and 366.

[16]Chester C. McCown, *Man, Morals and History—Today's Legacy from Ancient Times and Biblical Peoples* (New York: Harper & Brothers, 1958), pp. 164–168.

[17]The Judaic religious ideas received further development and elaboration in a book of commentaries on the Bible known as the Talmud. See Isidore Epstein, *Judaism—A Historical Presentation* (Baltimore: Penguin Books, 1959), pp. 150–152 and 169–170 for a discussion of charity.

[18]See Grant, *Augustus to Constantine*, p. 9, on rising taxes.

[19]C. T. Dimont, "Charity, Almsgiving (Christian)," in *Encyclopedia of Religion and Ethics*, Vol. 3 (New York: Charles Scribner, 1922), p. 362; and Grant, *Augustus to Constantine*, p. 259.

[20]Grant, *Ibid.*, p. 258.

[21]Dimont, "Charity," p. 383; and Grant, *Augustus to Constantine*, pp. 173–174.

[22]Maurice Goguel, *The Primitive Church*, trans. H. C. Snape (New York: Macmillan, 1964), p. 542.

[23]Dimont, "Charity," pp. 383–384. See Grant, *Augustus to Constantine*, p. 268, for a summary of early Christian attitudes toward property.

[24]Thompson, *Economic and Social History*, p. 64.

[25]*Ibid.*, p. 70.

[26]*Ibid.*, p. 77.

[27]See, e.g., Dimont, "Charity," p. 383.

[28]Thompson, *Economic and Social History*, pp. 76–77.

[29]Denys Hay, *The Medieval Centuries* (London: Methuen, 1964), p. 49.

[30]Harry Elmer Barnes, *An Economic History of the Western World* (New York: Harcourt, Brace, 1937), p. 120.

[31]Brian Tierney, *Medieval Poor Law—A Sketch of Canonical Theory and Its Application in England* (Berkeley and Los Angeles: University of California Press, 1959), p. 7. Our discussion of medieval canon law is drawn mainly from Tierney.

[32]*Ibid.*, p. 15.

[33]*Ibid.*, p. 37, italics in original.

[34]*Ibid.*, p. 39.

[35]A detailed account of the complexities of the obligations attached to landholding in England is given in Austin Lane Poole, *Obligations of Society in the XII and XIII Centuries* (Oxford: Oxford University Press, 1946).

[36]Tierney, *Medieval Poor Law*, pp. 62–66.

[1]The estimate of one fourth killed is given by Norman Cantor, *Medieval History*, 2nd ed. (New York: Macmillan, 1969), p. 533. The estimate of one third killed is given by Henri Pirenne, *Economic and Social History of Medieval Europe*, trans. I. E. Clegg (New York: Harcourt, Brace & World, 1937), p. 193.

[2]*Statutes of the Realm*, in Karl de Schweinitz, *England's Road to Social Security* (New York: A. S. Barnes, 1972), p. 1. First published in 1943. De Schweinitz agrees with an earlier scholar, E. M. Leonard, that this statute can be regarded as the beginning of English government efforts to deal with poverty. See Leonard's *Early History of English Poor Relief* (Cambridge: Cambridge University Press, 1900), p. 3.

[3]"Governor Weighs Drastic Changes to Curb Welfare," *New York Times*, March 10, 1971, p. 1; "City and State Officials Are Wary on the Governor's Reported Ideas on Curbing Welfare," *New York Times*, March 11, 1971, p. 27; "Welfare's Bankruptcy," editorial, *New York Times*, March 12, 1971, p. 36.

[4]Leonard, *Early History*, pp. 3–6; de Schweinitz, *England's Road*, pp. 3–8.

[5]Frank Aydelotte, *Elizabethan Rogues and Vagabonds* (Oxford: Clarendon Press, 1913), p. 3.

[6]G. M. Trevelyan, *English Social History—A Survey of Six Centuries, Chaucer to Queen Victoria* (Harmondsworth, England: Penguin Books, 1967), p. 128. First published in 1942.

[7]*Ibid.*, p. 133; Aydelotte, *Elizabethan Rogues*, pp. 52–53.

[8]Sidney Webb and Beatrice Webb, *English Poor Law History—Part I: The Old Poor Law* (Hamden, Conn.: Archon Books, 1963), pp. 23–24 and *passim*. First published in 1927.

[9]The discussion in this section of the development of the poor laws draws mainly on three sources: de Schweinitz, *England's Road*; Leonard, *Early History*; and Webb and Webb, *English Poor Law History*.

[10]Leonard, *Early History*, pp. 167–171.

[11]Lawrence Stone, *The Family, Sex and Marriage in England, 1500–1800* (New York: Harper & Row, 1977), p. 98.

[12]de Schweinitz, *England's Road*, pp. 24–26.

[13]Leonard, *Early History*, p. 76.

[14]Margaret James, *Social Problems and Policy During the Puritan Revolution, 1640–1660* (London: Routledge, 1930), p. 278.

[15]Webb and Webb, *English Poor Law History*, p. 315.

[16]*Ibid.*, pp. 212–214; de Schweinitz, *England's Road*, p. 27; Leonard, *Early History*, p. 77.

[17]John A. Garraty, *Unemployment in History—Economic Thought and Public Policy.* (New York: Harper & Row, 1978), pp. 32–33.

[18]Webb and Webb, *English Poor Law History*, pp. 49–53, 83–86.

[19]Leonard, *Early History*, pp. 39–40, 45–46.

[20]Garraty, *Unemployment in History*, p. 30. See also Richard B. Morris, *Government and Labor in Early America* (New York: Harper Torchbooks, 1965), pp. 3–4.

[21]Christopher Hill, *Society and Puritanism in Pre-Revolutionary England* (New York: Schocken, 1964), pp. 146–149.

[22]*Ibid.*, pp. 124–125.

[23]Webb and Webb, *English Poor Law History*, pp. 52–59.

[24]Garraty, *Unemployment in History*, p. 44; Leonard, *Early History*, p. 225; Samuel Mencher, *Poor Law to Poverty Program—Economic Security Policy in Britain and the United States* (Pittsburgh: University of Pittsburgh Press, 1967), p. 32.

[25]Christopher Hill, *Reformation to Industrial Revolution—The Making of Modern English Society*, Vol. I, 1530–1780 (New York: Pantheon, 1967), pp. 19–20; Trevelyan, *English Social History*, pp. 74–75.

[26]Shepard Bancroft Clough and Charles Woolsey Cole, *Economic History of Europe* (Boston: D. C. Heath, 1941), p. 151.

[27]Garraty, *Unemployment in History*, p. 46.

[28]Webb and Webb, *English Poor Law History*, pp. 101–125, 215–240.

[29]Hans J. Hillerbrand, *The World of the Reformation* (New York: Scribner's, 1973), pp. 95ff.

[30]Max Weber, *The Protestant Ethic and the Spirit of Capitalism*, trans. Talcott Parsons (New York: Scribner's, 1930), pp. 80ff.

[31]Hillerbrand, *World of the Reformation*, p. 151; R. H. Tawney, *Religion and the Rise of Capitalism* (London: John Murray, 1936), p. 102.

[32]Weber, *The Protestant Ethic*, p. 85. Tawney, *Religion*, pp. 109, 240.

[33]Tawney, *Religion*, p. 242.

[34]*Ibid.*, pp. 241, 251, 262–273.

[35]Garraty, *Unemployment in History*, pp. 39–40. For discussions on issues surrounding the importance of the Protestant Ethic, see S. N. Eisenstadt, ed., *The Protestant Ethic and Modernization—A Comparative View* (New York: Basic Books, 1968); and R. W. Green, ed., *Protestantism and Capitalism—The Weber Thesis and Its Critics* (Boston: D. C. Heath, 1959).

[36]Michael Walzer, "Puritanism as a Revolutionary Ideology," in S. N. Eisenstadt, *Protestant Ethic and Modernization*, pp. 109–134.

[37]Leonard, *Early History*, pp. 107–109.

[38]Norman Longmate, *The Workhouse* (New York: St. Martin's Press, 1974), p. 17.

[39]de Schweinitz, *England's Road*, pp. 41–42; Longmate, *The Workhouse*, p. 18.

[40]From a report written in 1732, in Webb and Webb, *English Poor Law History*, p. 198.

[41]*Ibid.*, pp. 199–200.

[42]in de Schweinitz, *England's Road*, p. 45.

[43]Marcus Wilson Jernegan, *Laboring and Dependent Classes in Colonial America, 1607–1783* (Chicago: University of Chicago Press, 1931), pp. 179–180.

[44]This summary of principles is adapted from Jernegan, *Laboring and Dependent Classes*, p. 208; Elizabeth Wisner, *Social Welfare in the South* (Baton Rouge, La.: Louisiana State University Press, 1970), pp. 3–4; and David J. Rothman, *The Discovery of the Asylum* (Boston: Little, Brown, 1971), pp. 20ff.

[45]Margaret Creech, *Three Centuries of Poor Law Administration* (Chicago: University of Chicago Press, 1936), p. 47.

[46]David M. Schneider and Albert Deutsch, *The History of Public Welfare in New York State, 1867–1940* (Chicago: University of Chicago Press, 1941), pp. 4–5.

[47]Rothman, *Discovery of the Asylum*, p. 4.

[48]*Ibid.*, pp. 20–35; Creech, *Three Centuries*, pp. 22–23.

[49]Benjamin J. Klebaner, "Pauper Auctions: The 'New England Method' of Public Poor Relief," *Historical Collections of the Essex Institute*, Vol. 91, No. 3 (July 1955), p. 1.

[50]*Ibid.*, p. 10. See also Benjamin J. Klebaner, "Some Aspects of North Carolina Public Poor Relief, 1700–1860," *North Carolina Historical Review*, Vol. 31, No. 4 (October 1954), p. 480.

Red, White, and Black:
The Peoples of Early America
Gary B. Nash

PURITANS AND INDIANS

Given the Puritan ideal of community and the centrality of the idea of reforming the world in their image, it might be thought that the conflict and limited acculturation that characterized Anglo-Indian contacts on the Chesapeake would have been replaced in New England by less hostility and greater interaction. But this was not the case.

Descendants of nomadic hunters who had come to the region 10,000 years before, the Indians of New England lived on the margin of the agricultural zone. Therefore, their economy combined hunting, fishing, and agriculture, though the latter, by the time Europeans arrived, was their primary subsistence activity. Efficiently utilizing their environment according to the season, they engaged in winter hunting, spring stream fishing and clearing of fields, summer cultivation of crops and sea fishing, and autumn harvesting and hunting. "Seasonality," writes Neal Salisbury, "provided the basis for a rudimentary but regularly recurrent annual cycle."[4]

The sexual division of labor was marked among the Algonkian tribes of New England. Men hunted but women were responsible for all phases of agriculture—planting, maintaining, and harvesting crops—as well as for fishing and gathering wild plant products. Since agriculture had become the most important component of the economy, a distinct imbalance had evolved in the productivity of the two sexes. This did not lead, as in the case of the Iroquois, to the adoption of a matrilineal kinship system or the conferring of a degree of political power upon women. In New England kinship remained patrilineal, and men continued to dominate political and religious life.

Political leadership of Algonkian tribes in New England was held by single individuals, called "sachems" in the southern region and "sagamores" in the northern region. The sachem's role was to coordinate, at the village level, activities that concerned the group as a whole—hunting, trade, the administration of justice, and diplomacy. The sachem's authority depended heavily on maintaining the consent of his people. This, in turn, depended greatly on the sachem's ability to communicate with the spiritual forces that controlled the fate of the tribe. "Their authority is most precarious," wrote one Frenchman among the Abenaki, "if indeed, that may be called authority to which obedience is in no wise obligatory."[5] Sachems and sagamores were not chiefs or lords whose title was inherited and authority unquestioned, but "coordinators and ceremonial representatives for their people."[6]

In the pre-contact period the Algonkian-speaking people of New England were more densely settled than in the Chesapeake region, probably numbering more than 100,000 between the Kennebec River and Cape Cod. Among them, the most numerous were the Abenaki, Pawtucket, Massachuset, Narragansett, Pequot, and Wampanoag. All of these groups had been in contact with Europeans for many generations. Fishermen who dried their catches and engaged in minor trade had provided the more northerly tribes with knowledge of European culture since the first quarter of the sixteenth century, and short-lived French and English attempts at settlement in the first decade of the seventeenth century gave them further understanding of the people from across the sea.

A series of English exploratory incursions and small-scale attempts at settlement occurred in the early seventeenth century. All of them had to contend with the fact that the French had already established permanent settlements and a trading network that extended from Nova Scotia to Cape Cod. This economic hegemony had been built upon a system of reciprocal relations with the natives of the region. None of the first English attempts at settlement fared well, for the English adopted a far more militaristic stance toward the Indians, typified in John Smith's formula of deception, intimidation, and unbridled force, which he recommended following his voyage to the New England coast in 1614. English expeditions attacked and kidnapped coastal Indians on a number of occasions. In 1614 one of Smith's captains captured more than twenty Indians and sold them into slavery in Malaga, Spain. Such a predatory approach guaranteed that the English, when they came in larger numbers in the 1620s, would not be welcomed as a people with whom amicable relations could be expected.

It was not brute force or superior numbers, however, that paved the way for a permanent English presence in New England. Rather it was disease. In 1616 English fishermen stopped on the coast and triggered a "virgin soil epidemic"—the implantation of viruses into a population with no immunological defense. Tens of thousands of Indians died within a single year along the New England coast. Especially hard hit was the area from Massachusetts Bay to Plymouth Bay where entire towns were swept away or abandoned. Five years later an Englishman moving through the area wrote that the Indians had "died on heapes, as they lay in their houses, and the living that were able to shift for themselves would runne away and let them dy, and let there Carkases ly above the ground without buriall. . . . And the bones and skulls upon the several places of their habitations, made such a spectacle . . . that as I travailed in that Forrest nere the Massachussetts [tribe], it seemed to mee a new found Golgotha."[7] Three-quarters or more of the native inhabitants of southern New England probably succumbed to the disease.

When the Pilgrims arrived in 1620, they disembarked in an area that had suffered catastrophic population losses just a few years before. This was crucial not only in opening up the land for them but also in greatly weakening the Indians' ability to resist the encroachers. It was the further good fortune of the English to encounter Squanto, a Wampanoag who had been kidnapped by an English ship captain in 1614. Squanto had been sold by his abductor in Spain but somehow had made his way to England where he joined an English captain on several trips to the New England coast. On the second of these trips Squanto found that most of his tribe had been killed by the plague, but he remained in the Cape Cod area and was there when the Pilgrims landed. Through Squanto's friendship the Pilgrims were rendered important assistance in the early years.

A decade after the initial settlement, William Bradford, the leader of the Pilgrim colony, wrote that the English had come anticipating the "continual danger of the savage people, who are cruel, barbarous, and most treacherous"—characteristics that made "the very bowels of men to grate within them and make the weak to quake and tremble."[8] But given the record of kidnapping and broken trust which the English had established in their periodic visits to the coast before 1620, the characterization better fitted the English than the local tribes. The local Indians were probably deeply suspicious of the Pilgrims, but no incident of violence at Plymouth occurred until after the newcomers discovered the natives' underground cold-storage cellars and stole as much of the corn, placed there for winter use, as they could carry off. Even then the Indians chose to minimize contact with the settlers, though after death had reduced the Plymouth colony to about fifty persons in the spring of 1621 the vulnerability of the English invited Indian attack.

The need of the local Wampanoags for a military ally to aid them in their struggle with the neighboring Narragansetts probably explains why they tolerated English abuses and even signed a treaty in 1621 that formed the basis for trade and mutual assistance with the precariously situated English. The logic of the Wampanoag diplomacy was revealed when Miles Standish and other Pilgrims aided them in a dispute with their enemies in 1621. The Wampanoags regarded the treaty as an alliance of equals but the English, regarding themselves as culturally superior, saw it as the submission by the Indians to English domination.

This surface amity lasted only a year, however. In 1622 the arrival of about sixty non–Pilgrim newcomers to the colony brought serious friction. The new colonists settled themselves at Wessagusset, some distance from the Pilgrim colony, stole corn from the neighboring Massachusets, and planned attacks on them when they refused to trade with the needy, but arrogant, newcomers. Under cover of a story that the Indians were conspiring against both white communities, Standish, who had long harbored grudges against several insulting Massachusets, led an offensive against the friendly Indians, killing eight of them and impaling the head of the sachem Wituwamet on top of the fort at Plymouth as a symbol of white power. Hearing of the deterioration of relations, John Robinson, formerly the Pilgrims' minister in Holland, wrote Governor Bradford in dismay, asking why the English indulged in needless violence. What was happening to "civilized" men in the wilderness? asked Robinson. Were they beginning to act like "savages," forgetting that they were supposed to represent order and piety? Robinson singled out Miles Standish, the militia captain of Plymouth, who had adopted John Smith's formula of inspiring fear and submission rather than mutual respect and harmonious relations. "It is . . . a thing more glorious, in men's eyes, than pleasing in God's, or convenient for Christians, to be a terrour to poor barbarous people. And indeed I am afraid lest, by these occasions, others should be drawn to affect [this kind of behavior] in the world."[9] As for the Indians, they "could not imagine, from whence these men should come," wrote Thomas Morton, a friend of the Indians, "or to what end, seeing them performe such unexpected actions." From that time on the English colonists were called "Wotowquenange, which in their language signifieth stabbers or Cutthroates."[10]

When the Puritan migration began in 1630, natives of the New England coast had more than a generation of experience with English ways. Little that they had encountered could have rendered them optimistic about future relations, although their own intertribal hostilities continued to make the settlers potentially valuable allies, and their desire for trade goods persisted. As for the Puritans, they were publicly committed to interracial harmony but privately preparing for the worst. The charter of the Massachusetts Bay Company spoke of the commitment to convert the Indians to Christianity. The "principall ende of this plantacion," it pronounced, was to "wynn and incite the natives of [the] country, to the knowledg and obedience of the onlie true God and Savior of mankinde, and the Christian fayth."[11] But the instructions of the Company to John Winthrop revealed more accurately what was anticipated. According to these orders, all men were to be trained in the use of firearms; Indians were prohibited from entering the Puritan towns; and any colonists so reckless as to sell arms to the Indians or instruct them in their use were to be deported to England where they would be severely punished. While ordering that the Indians must be fairly treated, the Company reflected the garrison mentality that settlers, once landed and settled, would manifest even more strongly. No missionary activity was to be initiated for thirteen years.

In the first few years of settlement the Indians did little to arouse Puritan wrath. Their sachems made overtures of friendship; they supplied the colonists with corn during the difficult first winter; and a minor trade was started. It was with surprise that one Puritan leader recounted that during the first winter, when the Puritans "had scarce houses to shelter themselves, and no doores to hinder the Indians access to all they had in them, . . . where their whole substance, weake Wives and little ones lay open to their plunder; . . . yet had they none food or stuffe diminished, neither Children nor Wives hurt in the least measure, although the Indians came commonly to them at those times, much hungry belly (as they used to say) and were then in number and strength beyond the English by far."[12]

This state of coexistence lasted only a few years. Smallpox struck the eastern Massachusetts bands in 1633 and 1634, killing thousands as far north as Maine and as far south as the Connecticut Valley. For the colonists it was proof that God had intervened in the Puritans' behalf at a time when the expansionist impulses of the settlers were beginning to cause friction over rights to land. The town records of Charlestown, for example, state that "without this remarkable and terrible stroke of God upon the natives, [we] would with much more difficulty have found room, and at far greater charge have obtained and purchased land."[13] As in Virginia, it was the need for land that provided the incentive for steering away from rather than toward equitable relations between the societies. That the population buildup came so quickly in Puritan New England only hastened the impulse to regard Indians as objects to be removed rather than subjects to be assimilated.

THE QUESTION OF LAND

Puritan theories of land possession help to clarify this tendency to classify Indians in such a way that only violence rather than assimilation or coexistence could occur. Like other Europeans, Puritans claimed the land they were invading by right of discovery. This theory derived from the ancient claim that Christians were everywhere entitled to dispossess non–Christians of their land. A second European legal theory, called *vacuum domicilium*, bolstered Puritan claims that land not "occupied" or "settled" went by forfeit to those who attached themselves to it in a "civilized" manner. Before he set foot in the New World John Winthrop wrote:

> As for the Natives in New England, they inclose noe Land, neither have any setled habytation, nor any tame Cattle to improve the Land by, and soe have noe other but a Naturall Right to those Countries, soe as if we leave them sufficient for their use, we may lawfully take the rest, there being more than enough for them and us.[14]

Thus, in Puritan eyes, entitlement to the land of New England required nothing more than the assertion that because their way of life did not conform to European norms, the Indians had forfeited all the land which they "roamed" rather than "settled." By European definition the land was *vacuum domicilium*—unoccupied. To this mental picture of an unoccupied land the awful epidemic of 1616–18 had made an important contribution.

Given the slender power of the disease-ravaged coastal tribes of the Massachusetts Bay region and the legal principles invoked under the concept of *vacuum domicilium*, the Puritans were ideally situated to establish their beachhead in the New World. The remnants of the formerly populous Massachuset and Pawtucket peoples were in no position to resist and in fact willingly consented to the settlement of their lands by the Puritan vanguard that inhabited Naumkeag (renamed Salem) in 1629 and the 3,000 settlers who came in the next four years. In return for land, of which they now had a great surplus, the Indians gained the protection of the English against their Micmac enemies to the north. Hence the Puritans quickly acquired the notion that the local Indians were properly regarded as domesticated subjects, who lived in separate villages but were to answer to Puritan concepts of government and law.

Nonetheless, by about 1634 the land question had begun to assume a central place in Puritan-Indian relations. Another epidemic in 1633 had struck down many native people throughout a wide area from the St. Lawrence River to Long Island. Once more the English saw the divine hand intervening in their behalf and Indians trembled at the power of the English God. This may have temporarily lessened the Indian sense of being overwhelmed by the steady flow of English colonists into the area. But pressure on available land resources was mounting rapidly.

The land question also became critical because in 1633 the radical separatist, Roger Williams of Salem, disputed the claim of the Massachusetts Bay leaders that their royal patent entitled them to occupy Indian land without first purchasing it from the natives. Williams had become inmersed in Indian culture shortly after his arrival in 1631—one of the few Englishmen to do so—and by the next year was absorbed in learning their language. Williams argued that the Puritans had illegally and sinfully grabbed Indian land and would have to answer for this before God and the English authorities. He also argued that the natives of the region used the land in rational and systematic ways, thus directly challenging the random use of land supposed in the legal concept of *vacuum domicilium*. The Massachusetts magistrates indignantly dismissed these ideas, ceremoniously burned the tract in which Williams advanced his arguments, and shortly thereafter banished him from the colony. Traveling to Rhode Island with some of his followers, Williams was offered land by a Narragansett sachem and found "among the savages," as he wrote, a place where he and his followers could peaceably worship God according to their consciences. Winthrop's response to Williams's argument was that "if we had no right to this lande, yet our God hathe right to it, and if he be pleased to give it us (takinge it from a people who had so long usurped upon him and abused his creatures) who shall controll him or his terms?"[15] By claiming that God directed all Puritan policy, Winthrop thus charged anyone who murmured dissent with opposing not only Puritan policy but God himself.

Nevertheless, the practice of purchasing Indian land progressed slowly as settlement continued. But the purchases were usually made in order to obtain a favorable settlement in a situation where the same tract of land was coveted by rival groups of settlers. In such cases a deed to the land in dispute from an Indian seller was the best way to convince a court of one's claim. Even in those cases where intra–European rivalry necessitated the purchase of Indian land, the sale could be accomplished through a variety of stratagems designed to reduce the cost to the white settler. Turning livestock into cultivated Indian fields over a period of time was an effective way of convincing an Indian that his land was losing its value. Alcohol was frequently used to reduce the negotiating skill of the Indian seller. Another method was to buy the land at a rock-bottom price from an Indian sachem who falsely claimed title to it and then take to court any disputing sachem who claimed ownership. Before an English court, with its white lawyers, judges, and juries, the Indian claimant rarely won his case. Perhaps most effective of all was fining an Indian for minor offenses of English law—walking on the Sabbath or illegally entering a town, for example—and then "rescuing" him from the debt he was unable to pay by discharging the fine in return for a tract of his land. None of these tactics worked in areas where Indian tribes were strong and unified. But among the decimated and divided tribes of southern New England they were highly effective.

THE PEQUOT WAR

All the factors that operated in Virginia to produce friction between the two societies—English land hunger, a deprecatory view of native culture, and intertribal Indian hostility—were to be found in New England. They were vastly augmented by another factor not present on the Chesapeake—the Puritan sense of mission. For people of such high moral purpose, who lived daily with the anxiety that they might fail in what they saw as the last chance to save corrupt Western Protestantism, the Indian stood as a direct challenge to the "errand into the wilderness." The Puritans' mission was to tame and civilize their new environment and to build in it a pious commonwealth that would "shine like a beacon" back to decadent England. But how could order and discipline be brought to the new environment unless its inhabitants were tamed and "civilized"? Governor William Bradford of Plymouth tellingly described the land he was entering as "a hideous and desolate wilderness full of wild beasts and wild men."[16] Land, beast, and man must all be brought under control. To do less was to allow chaos to continue when God's will was that Christian order be imposed. As Roy H. Pearce has explained, the Indian stood as a vivid reminder of what the English knew they must not become. The native was the counterimage of civilized man, thought to be lacking in what was most valued by the Puritans—civility, Christian piety, purposefulness, and the work ethic. If such people could not be made part of the Puritan system, then the Puritans would have demonstrated their inability to control this corner of the earth to which God had directed them. God would surely answer such a failure with his wrath. So Puritans achieved control of themselves—internal control—through controlling the external world containing forests, fields—and Indians.[17]

The greater one's doubts about the success of this utopian experiment, doubts magnified by internal dissension, the greater the inner need to stifle self-doubt through repression and extension of control. Thus in New England, Indians became obstacles in two senses: as in Virginia and elsewhere they represented a physical barrier since they possessed the land and could not easily be subjugated so as to serve English ends; and they were a psychological obstacle since, while they remained "savages," they threatened the identity of individual Puritans and the collective success of the Puritan Way.

To eliminate "savagism" one did not necessarily have to eliminate the "savages." From their writings it appears that Puritans would have preferred to convert the "heathen" to Christianity. But this could only be accomplished through great expenditure of time and effort. The Spanish and

Portuguese had sent hundreds of missionaries along with the conquistadors and settlers. But the Puritans came only with their own ministers and these men had more than enough to do to maintain piety, unity, and moral standards within the white community. Proselytizing the natives of New England never received a high priority. Much was written about foiling Satan, who had "decoyed those miserable savages hither, in hopes that the gospel of the Lord Jesus Christ would never come here to destroy or disturb his absolute empire over them," but little was done in saving the Native Americans from Satan.[18]

Rather than convert the "savages" of New England, the Puritans attempted to bring them under civil government, making them strictly accountable to the ordinances that governed white behavior in Massachusetts. Insofar as Indians were willing to subject themselves to the new white code of behavior, usually out of fear, the Puritans could prevail, keeping a close eye on all Indians within the areas of white settlement and bringing them to court for any offenses against white law. Many of the smaller bands of eastern Massachusetts, disastrously weakened by European disease or living in fear of strong and hostile neighbors, did what was necessary to satisfy the newcomers. But the question of control became a military problem when the Puritans encountered a tribe that was sufficiently strong to resist the loss of its cultural identity and political sovereignty.

Such were the Pequots—a strong and aggressive people who had migrated to southern New England in the century before English arrival. By the 1630s they had built a trading network of tributary groups and viewed the Narragansetts as their main rival in southern New England. The Pequots worked hard to convince the neighboring Narragansetts that only by uniting against the English could either tribe survive. But their arguments went unheard. Following the advice of Roger Williams, the Narragansetts agreed

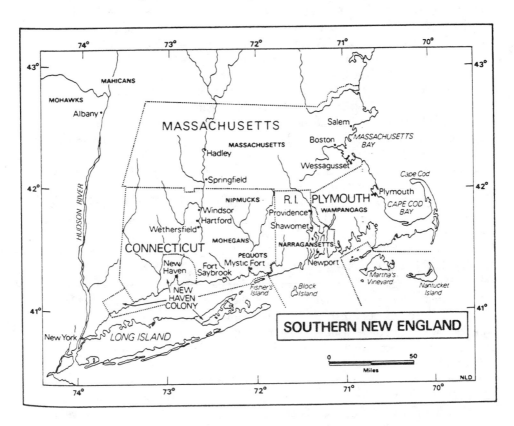

to ally themselves with Massachusetts Bay, leaving the Pequots virtually alone in their determination to resist the English.

Hostilities between the Pequots and English were ostensibly triggered by the murder of two white ship captains and their crews. One of the mariners, John Stone, was cordially hated among the English, for he had attempted to murder Governor Prence of Plymouth and had later been banished from Massachusetts for other misdeeds. Two years after Stone's death in 1634, John Oldham was found murdered on his pinnace off Block Island. Using these incidents as justification for a punitive expedition against the unsubmissive Pequots, a joint Connecticut-Massachusetts force marched into Pequot country and demanded the murderers (who, as it turned out, were not Pequots) as well as a thousand fathoms of wampum, and some Pequot children as hostages.

The Pequots understood that the issue was broader than the death of several English mariners, that in fact they were embroiled in a complicated set of disputes over land and trade. These were the real causes of the war that shortly would break out. At the center of the tensions was the English–Dutch trade rivalry and intertribal Indian hostilities. Since 1622 the Dutch in New Amsterdam had controlled the Indian trade of New England through their connections to both the Pequot and the Narragansett, the region's two strongest tribes. After the arrival of the English and their rapid expansion in the early 1630s, the Dutch perceived that their trading empire was greatly threatened. Hence, they purchased land on the lower Connecticut River—an area on which several English groups had their eyes—and built a trading post there to defend their regional economic hegemony. Some of the Pequots' discontented client tribes, however, were already breaking away, signing separate trade agreements with and ceding land to the English. Amidst such fragmentation, expansionist New England was ready, with the aid of its Narragansett allies, to drive the Dutch traders from southern New England and to subdue the Pequots who occupied some of the area's most fertile soil. The Pequots first tried to placate the English; when this proved impossible, they chose to resist.

In the war that ensued, the English found the Pequots more than a match until they were able to surround a secondary Pequot village on the Mystic River in May 1637. The English and their Narragansett allies attacked before dawn, infiltrated the town, and set fire to the Pequot wigwams inside before beating a fast retreat. In the meleé about twenty Narragansetts suffered wounds at the hands of the English, who found it difficult to distinguish between Indian enemies and allies. Retreating from the flame-engulfed village, the English regrouped and waited for fleeing survivors from the inferno. Most of the victims were noncombatants since the Pequot warriors were gathered at another village about five miles away. Before the day was over a large part of the Pequot tribe had been slaughtered, many by fire and others by guns. Those who escaped or who were not at the fort were enslaved and sold to other tribes or shipped to the West Indies in chains. One of New England's first historians, William Hubbard, wrote that dozens of captured Pequots were put on board the ship of Captain John Gallup, "which proved [to be] Charon's ferry-boat unto them, for it was found the quickest was to feed the fishes with 'em."[19] One of the militia captains wrote that at Mystic Fort "God . . . laughed [at] his Enemies and the Enemies of his People to Scorn, making them as a fiery Oven . . . [and] filling the Place with Dead Bodies." William Bradford wrote that "it was a fearful sight to see them thus frying in the fire and the streams of blood quenching the same, and horrible was the stink and scent thereof; but the victory seemed a sweet sacrifice, and they gave the praise thereof to God, who had wrought so wonderfully for them, thus to enclose their enemies in their hands and given them so speedy a victory over so proud and insulting an enemy."[20] In 1638, at the Treaty of Hartford, the Pequot nation was declared dissolved. Two generations later Cotton Mather, a pillar of the Puritan ministry, reiterated: "in a little more than *one* hour, five or six hundred of these barbarians were dismissed from a world that was *burdened* with them."[21]

Such savagery as the "civilized" Puritans demonstrated at Mystic Fort was shocking to the Narragansett "savages" who fought with the Puritans. According to one English officer, they came after the victory and "much rejoiced at our victories, and greatly admired the manner of Englishmen's fight, but cried Mach it, Mach it; that is, It is naught, it is naught [bad or wicked] because it is too furious and slays too many men." It was a poignant comment on the different styles and functions of warfare in the two societies.[22]

For the Puritans the extermination of the Pequots was proof of their political and military ascendancy. Its additional function was to provide a response to anxiety and disunity that had become widely diffused throughout the colony. These fears were associated not only with the threat of the Pequots but also with the dissensions within Puritan society. It is well to remember that the war came on the heels of three years of intense internal discord centered around the challenges to the power of the magistrates by Roger Williams and Anne Hutchinson. These challenges, in turn, involved not only theological questions but economic restrictions, the distribution of political power, and competing land claims among English settlers in Massachusetts, Connecticut, and Rhode Island. Their colonies beset with controversy, the Puritan leaders talked morbidly about God's anger at seeing his chosen people subvert the City on the Hill. In this sense, the Puritan determination to destroy the Pequots and the level of violence manifested at Mystic Fort can be partially understood in terms of the self-doubt and guilt that Puritans could expiate only by exterminating so many of "Satan's agents." Dead Pequots were offered to God as atonement for Puritan failings.

Victory over the Pequots decisively established English sovereignty over all the Indians of southeastern New England except the Narragansetts and removed the one remaining obstacle to expansion into the Connecticut River Valley. The tribes of southern New England, reduced to about one quarter of their former population, adjusted as best they could to the realities of Puritan power. The fur trade kept the two societies in touch with each other and provided the means by which English iron goods became incorporated into the material culture of the Indians. But the trade, which flourished in the 1630s, petered out by mid-century as the beaver supply in New England became depleted. In spite of these trade contacts, most of the remnant groups that had survived the coming of the English struggled to maintain their native way of life. Some of the weaker and more demoralized groups followed the handful of missionaries, finally spurred to action in 1643 by English critics, who rightly charged that conversion had been studiously ignored for more than a decade. After ten years of effort less than a thousand Indians of the region were settled in four villages of "praying Indians" and fewer than one hundred of these declared their conversion to the Puritan form of Christianity. Even among these, defections would be numerous in the 1670s when war broke out again in Massachusetts. As in the case of Virginia, the natives incorporated certain implements and articles of clothing obtained in the European trade into their culture, but overwhelmingly, even after major military defeats, they preferred to resist acculturation when it meant adopting English religion, forms of government, styles of life, or patterns of social and economic organization.

For Puritans and non–Puritans who migrated into New England in increasing numbers after mid-century, the Indians served no useful purpose. The rough balance of English males and females eliminated the need for Indian women as sexual partners. The church took only a minor interest in the Indian, who in any event could rarely satisfy the qualifications that Puritans placed upon their own people for church membership. The Indian trade withered to relative unimportance, as fishing, lumbering, shipbuilding, and agriculture became the mainstays of the colonizers' economy. This lack of function within English society, combined with the special tendency of Puritans to doubt the Indians' capacity for meeting the standards required in the New Jerusalem, made close and reciprocal contacts between the two societies all but impossible.

[4]Neal E. Salisbury, *Manitou and Providence: Indians, Europeans, and the Making of New England, 1500–1643* (New York: Oxford University Press, forthcoming).

[5]Reuben Gold Thwaites, ed., *The Jesuit Relations and Allied Documents . . . 1610–1791* (Cleveland: The Burrows Brothers Company, 1896), II, 73.

[6]Salisbury, *Manitou and Providence*.

[7]Thomas Morton, "New English Canaan," in *Tracts and Other Papers Relating Principally to the Origin, Settlement and Progress of the Colonies in North America*, Peter Force, comp. (Washington, D.C., 1836), II, No. 5: 19.

[8]William Bradford, *Of Plymouth Plantation, 1620–1647*, ed. Samuel Eliot Morison (New York: Alfred A. Knopf, Inc., 1966), p. 26.

[9]*Ibid.*, p. 375.

[10]Thomas Morton, "New England Canaan," p. 76, quoted in Neal E. Salisbury, "Conquest of the 'Savage': Puritans, Puritan Missionaries, and Indians, 1620–1680" (Ph.D. dissertation, University of California, Los Angeles, 1972), p. 86.

[11]Nathaniel B. Shurtleff, *Records of the Governor and Company of the Massachusetts Bay in New England*, 5 vols. (Boston: W. White, 1853–54), I: 17.

[12]Edward Johnson, "Wonder-Working Providence," quoted in Salisbury, "Conquest of the 'Savage'," pp. 63–64.

[13]Quoted in Alden T. Vaughan, *New England Frontier: Puritans and Indians, 1620-1675* (Boston: Little, Brown and Company, 1965), p. 104.

[14]"Generall Considerations for the Plantation in New England . . . " (1629), in *Winthrop Papers*, 5 vols., ed. Allyn B. Forbes (Boston: Massachusetts Historical Society, 1929–47), 2: 118.

[15]Quoted in *ibid.*, 534n.

[16]Bradford, *Plymouth Plantation*, p. 62.

[17]Roy H. Pearce, *The Savages of America: A Study of the Indian and the Idea of Civilization* (Baltimore: The Johns Hopkins Press, 1953), pp. 3–24.

[18]Cotton Mather, *Magnalia Christi Americana* (Hartford, Conn., 1853), II, 556.

[19]William Hubbard, *A Narrative of the Troubles with the Indians in New England* (1677), quoted in Carolyn T. Foreman, *Indians Abroad, 1493–1938* (Norman: University of Oklahoma Press, 1943), p. 29.

[20]John Mason, "A Brief History of the Pequot War," *Massachusetts Historical Society Collections*, 2d Ser., 8 (Boston: 1826): 140–41. Bradford, *Plymouth Plantation*, p. 296.

[21]Cotton Mather, *Magnalia Christi Americana: or, The Ecclesiastic History of New England* (New York: Russell & Russell, 1967), II: 558.

[22]John Underhill, "News from America," quoted in Salisbury, "Conquest of the 'Savage'," p. 81.

EUROPE, AFRICA, AND THE NEW WORLD

The African slave trade, which began in the late fifteenth century and continued for the next four hundred years, is one of the most important phenomena in the history of the modern world. Involving the largest forced migration in history, the slave trade and slavery were crucially important in building the colonial empires of European nations and in generating the wealth that later produced the Industrial Revolution. But often overlooked in the attention given to the economic importance of the slave trade and slavery is the cultural diffusion that took place when ten million Africans were brought to the western hemisphere. Six out of every seven persons who crossed the Atlantic to take up life in the New World in the 300 years before the American Revolution were African slaves. As a result, in most parts of the colonized territories slavery "defined the context within which transferred European traditions would grow and change."[1] As slaves, Africans were Europeanized; but at the same time they Africanized the culture of Europeans in the Americas. This was an inevitable part of the convergence of these two broad groups of people, who met each other an ocean away from their original homelands. In addition, the slave trade created the lines of communication for the movement of crops, agricultural techniques, diseases, and medical knowledge between Africa, Europe, and the Americas.

Just as they were late in colonizing the New World, the English lagged far behind their Spanish and Portuguese competitors in making contact with the west coast of Africa, in entering the Atlantic slave trade, and in establishing African slaves as the backbone of the labor force in their overseas plantations. And among the English colonists in the New World, those on the mainland of North America were a half century or more behind those in the Caribbean in converting their plantation economies to slave labor. By 1670, for example, some 200,000 slaves labored in Portuguese Brazil and about 30,000 cultivated sugar in English Barbados; but in Virginia only 2,000 worked in the tobacco fields. Cultural interaction of Europeans and Africans did not begin in North America on a large scale until more than a century after it had begun in the southerly parts of the hemisphere. Much that occurred as the two cultures met in the Iberian colonies was later repeated in the Anglo-African interaction; and yet the patterns of acculturation were markedly different in North and South America in the seventeenth and eighteenth centuries.

THE ATLANTIC SLAVE TRADE

A half century before Columbus crossed the Atlantic, a Portuguese sea captain, Antam Gonçalvez, made the first European landing on the west African coast south of the Sahara. What he might have seen, had he been able to travel the length and breadth of Africa, was a continent of extraordinary variation in geography and culture. Little he might have seen would have caused him to believe that a natural inferiority characterized African peoples or that they had failed to develop over time as had the peoples of Europe. This notion of "backwardness" and cultural impoverishment was the myth perpetuated after the slave trade had transported millions of Africans to the western hemisphere. It was a myth which served to justify the cruelties of the slave trade and to assuage the guilt of Europeans involved in the largest forced dislocation of people in history.

The peoples of Africa may have numbered more than 50 million in the late fifteenth century when Europeans began making extensive contact with the continent. They lived in widely varied ecological zones—in vast deserts, in grasslands, and in great forests and woodlands. As in Europe, most people lived as agriculturalists and struggled to subdue the forces of nature so as to sustain life. That the African population had increased so rapidly in the two thousand years before European arrival suggests the sophistication of the African agricultural methods. Part of this skill in farming derived from skill in iron production, which had begun in present-day Nigeria about 500 B.C. It was this ability to fashion iron implements that triggered the new farming techniques necessary to sustain larger populations. With large populations came greater specialization of tasks and thus additional technical improvements. Small groups of related families made contact with other kinship groups and over time evolved into larger and more complicated societies. The pattern was similar to what had occurred in other parts of the world—in North America, Europe, the Middle East, and elsewhere—when the "agricultural revolution" occurred.

Recent studies of "pre-contact" African history have showed that the "culture gap" between European and African societies was not as large as previously imagined when the two peoples met. By the time Europeans reached the coast of West Africa a number of extraordinary empires had been forged in the area. The first, apparently, was the Kingdom of Ghana, which embraced the immense territory between the Sahara Desert and the Gulf of Guinea and from the Niger River to the Atlantic Ocean between the sixth and tenth centuries. Extensive urban settlement, advanced architecture, elaborate art, and a highly complex political organization evolved during this time. From the eighth to the sixteenth centuries, it was the western Sudan that supplied most of the gold for the western world. Invasion from the north by the Moors weakened the Kingdom of Ghana, which in time gave way to the Empire of Mali. At the center of the Mali Empire was the city of Timbuktu, noted for its extensive wealth and its Islamic university where a faculty as distinguished as any in Europe was gathered.

Lesser kingdoms such as the kingdoms of Kongo and Benin had also been in the process of growth and cultural change for centuries before Europeans reached Africa. Their inhabitants were skilled in metal working, weaving, ceramics, architecture, and aesthetic expression. Many of their towns rivaled European cities in size. Many communities of West Africa had highly complex religious rites, well-organized regional trade, codes of law, and complex political organization.

Of course, cultural development in Africa, as elsewhere in the world, proceeded at varying rates. Ecological conditions had a large effect on this. Where good soil, adequate rainfall, and abundance of minerals were present, as in coastal West Africa, population growth and cultural elaboration was relatively rapid. Where inhospitable desert or nearly impenetrable forest held forth, social systems remained small and changed at a crawl. Contact with other cultures also brought rapid change, whereas isolation impeded cultural evolution. The Kingdom of Ghana bloomed in western Sudan partly because of the trading contacts with Arabs who had conquered the area in the ninth century. Cultural change began to accelerate in Swahili societies facing the Indian Ocean after trading contacts were initiated with the Eastern world in the ninth century. Thus, as a leading African historian has put it, "the cultural history of Africa is . . . one of greatly unequal development among peoples who, for definable reasons such as these, entered recognizably similar stages of institutional change at different times."[2]

The slave trade seems to have begun officially in 1472 when a Portuguese captain, Ruy do Sequeira, reached the coast of Benin and was conducted to the king's court, where he received royal permission to trade for gold, ivory, and slaves. So far as the Africans were concerned, the trade represented no strikingly new economic activity since they had been long involved in regional and long-distance trade across their continent. This was simply the opening of contacts with a new and more distant commercial partner. This is important to note because often it has been maintained that European powers raided the African coasts for slaves, marching into the interior and kidnapping hundreds of thousands of helpless and hapless victims. In actuality, the early slave trade was a reciprocal relationship between European purchasers and African sellers, with the Portuguese monopolizing trade along the coastlands of tropical Africa for the first century after contact was made. Trading itself was confined to coastal strongholds where slaves, most of them captured in the interior by other Africans, were sold on terms set by the African sellers. In return for gold, ivory, and slaves, African slave merchants received European guns, bars of iron and copper, brass pots and tankards, beads, rum and textiles. They occupied an economic role not unlike that of the Iroquois middlemen in the fur trade with Europeans.

Slavery was not a new social phenomenon for either Europeans or Africans. For centuries African societies had been involved in an overland slave trade that transported black slaves from West Africa across the Sahara Desert to Roman Europe and the Middle East. But this was an occasional rather than a systematic trade and it was designed to provide the trading nations of the Mediterranean with soldiers, household servants, and artisans rather than mass agricultural labor. Within Africa itself, a variety of unfree statuses had also existed for centuries but they involved personal service, often for a limited period of time, rather than lifelong, degraded, agricultural labor. Slavery of a similar sort had long existed in Europe, mostly as the result of Christians enslaving Moslems and Moslems enslaving Christians during centuries of religious wars. One became a slave by being an "outsider" or an "infidel," by being captured in war, by voluntarily selling oneself into slavery to obtain money for one's family, or by committing certain heinous crimes. The rights of slaves were restricted and their opportunities for upward movement severely circumscribed, but they were regarded nevertheless as members of society, enjoying protection under the law and entitled to certain rights, including education, marriage, and parenthood. Most important, the status of slave was not irrevocable and was not automatically passed on to his or her children.

Thus we find that slavery flourished in ancient Greece and Rome, in the Aztec and Inca empires, in African societies, in early modern Russia and eastern Europe, in the Middle East, and in the Mediterranean world. It had gradually died out in Western Europe by the fourteenth century, although the status of serf was not too different in social reality from that of the slave. It is important to note that in all these regions slavery and serfdom had nothing to do with racial characteristics.

When the African slave trade began in the second half of the fifteenth century, it served to fill labor shortages in the economies of its European initiators and their commercial partners. Between 1450 and 1505 Portugal brought about 40,000 African slaves to Europe and the Atlantic islands—the Madeiras and Canaries. But the need for slave labor lessened in Europe as European populations themselves experienced great growth beginning late in the fifteenth century. It is possible, therefore, that were it not for the colonization of the New World the early slave trade might have ceased after a century or more and be remembered simply as a short-lived incident stemming from early European contacts with Africa.

With the discovery of the New World by Europeans the course of history changed momentously. Once Europeans found the gold and silver mines of Mexico and Peru, and later, when they discovered a new form of gold in the production of sugar, coffee, and tobacco, their demand for human labor grew astonishingly. At first Indians seemed to be the obvious source of manpower and in some areas Spaniards and Portuguese were able to coerce native populations into agricultural and mining labor. But European diseases ravaged native populations and often it was found that the Indian, far more at home in his environment than the white colonizer, was a difficult person to subjugate. Indentured white labor from the mother country was another way of meeting the demand for labor, but this source, it soon became apparent, was far too limited. It was to Africa that colonizing Europeans ultimately resorted. Formerly a new source of trade, the continent now became transformed in the European view into the repository of vast supplies of human labor—"black gold."

From the late fifteenth to the mid-nineteenth centuries, almost four hundred years, Europeans transported Africans out of their ancestral homelands to fill the labor needs in their colonies of North and South America and the Caribbean. The most recent estimates place the numbers who reached the shores of the New World at about ten to twelve million people, although several million more lost their lives while being marched from the interior to the coastal trading forts or during the "middle passage" across the Atlantic. Even before the English arrived on the Chesapeake in 1607 several hundred thousand slaves had been transported to the Caribbean and South American colonies of Spain and Portugal. Before the slave trade was outlawed in the nineteenth century far more Africans than Europeans had crossed the Atlantic Ocean and taken up life in the New World. Black slaves, as one eighteenth-century Englishman put it, became "the strength and the sinews of this western world."[3]

Once established on a large scale, the Atlantic slave trade dramatically altered the pattern of slave recruitment in Africa. For about a century after Gonçalvez brought back the first kidnapped Africans to Portugal in 1441, the slave trade was relatively slight. The slaves whom other Africans sold to Europeans were drawn from a small minority of the population and for the most part were individuals captured in war or whose criminal acts had cost them their rights of citizenship. For Europeans the African slave trade provided for modest labor needs, just as the Black Sea slave trade had done before it was shut off by the fall of Constantinople to the Turks in 1453. Even in the New World plantations, slaves were not in great demand for many decades after "discovery."

More than anything else it was sugar that transformed the African slave trade. Produced in the Mediterranean world since the eighth century, sugar was for centuries a costly item confined to sweetening the diet of the rich. By the mid-fifteenth century its popularity was growing and the center of production had shifted to the Portuguese Madeira Islands, off the northwest coast of Africa. Here for the first time an expanding European nation established an overseas plantation society based on slave labor. From the Madeiras the cultivation of sugar spread to Portuguese Brazil in the late sixteenth century and then to the tiny specks of land dotting the Caribbean in the first half of the seventeenth century. By this time Europeans were developing an almost insatiable taste for sweetness. Sugar—regarded by nutritionists today as a "drug food"—became one of the first luxuries that was transformed into a necessary item in the diets of the masses of Europe. "Together with other plantation products such as coffee, rum, and tobacco," writes Sidney Mintz, "sugar formed part of a complex of 'proletarian hunger-killers,' and played a crucial role in the linked contribution that Caribbean slaves, Indian peasants, and European urban proletarians were able to make to the growth of western civilization."[4]

The regularization of the slave trade brought about by the vast new demand for a New World labor supply and by a reciprocally higher demand in Africa for European trade goods changed the problem of obtaining slaves. Criminals and "outsiders" in sufficient number to satisfy the growing European demand in the seventeenth century could not be found. Therefore African kings resorted to raids and warfare against their neighbors as a way of obtaining "black gold" with which to trade. European guns abetted the process. Thus, the spread of kidnapping and organized violence in Africa became intricately connected with the maintenance of commercial relations with European powers.

In the forcible recruitment of slaves, adult males were consistently preferred over women and children. Primarily this represented the preference of New World plantation owners for male field laborers. But it also reflected the decision of vanquished African villagers to yield up primarily their men to raiding parties because women were the chief agriculturalists in their society and, in matrilineal and matrilocal kinship systems, were too valuable to be spared.

For the Europeans the slave trade itself became an immensely profitable enterprise. In the several centuries of intensive slave trading that followed the establishment of New World sugar plantations, European nations warred constantly for trading advantages on the west African coast. The coastal forts, the focal points of the trade, became key strategic targets in the wars of empire. The great Portuguese slaving fort at Elmina on the Gold Coast, begun in 1481, was captured a century and a half later by the Dutch. The primary fort on the Guinea coast, started by the Swedes, passed through the hands of the Danes, the English, and the Dutch between 1652 and 1664. As the demand for slaves in the Americas rose sharply in the second half of the seventeenth century, European competition for trading rights on the west African coast grew intense. By the end of the century monopolies for supplying European plantations in the New World with their annual quotas of slaves became a major issue of European diplomacy. The Dutch were the primary victors in the battle for the west African slave coast. Hence, for most of the century a majority of slaves who were fed into the expanding New World markets found themselves crossing the Atlantic in Dutch ships.

Not until the last third of the seventeenth century were the English of any importance in the slave trade or in the demand for slaves in their North American colonies. Major English attempts to break into the profitable trade began only in 1663, when Charles II, recently restored to the English throne, granted a charter to the Royal Adventurers to Africa, a joint-stock company headed by the king's brother, the Duke of York. Superseded by the Royal African Company in 1672, these companies enjoyed the exclusive right to carry slaves to England's overseas plantations. For thirty-four years after 1663 each of the slaves they brought across the Atlantic bore the brand "DY" for the Duke of York, who himself became king in 1685. In 1698 the Royal African Company's monopoly was broken due to the pressure on Parliament by individual merchants who demanded their rights as Englishmen to participate in the lucrative trade. Thrown open to individual entrepreneurs, the English slave trade grew enormously. In the 1680s the Royal

African Company had transported about five to six thousand slaves annually (though interlopers brought in thousands more). In the first decade of free trade the annual average rose above twenty thousand. English involvement in the trade increased for the remainder of the eighteenth century until by the 1790s England had become the foremost slave trading nation in Europe.

THE DEVELOPMENT OF SLAVERY IN THE ENGLISH COLONIES

Even though they were long familiar with Spanish, Dutch, and Portuguese use of African slave labor, English colonists did not turn immediately to Africa to solve the problem of cultivating labor-intensive crops. When they

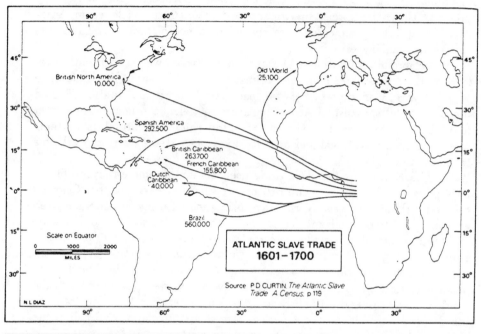

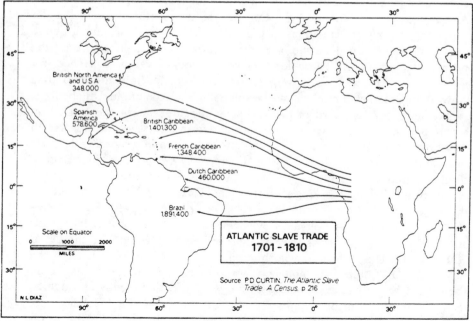

did, it could have caused little surprise, for in enslaving Africans Englishmen were merely copying their European rivals in attempting to fill the colonial labor gap. No doubt the stereotype of Africans as uncivilized creatures made it easier for the English to fasten chains upon them. But the central fact remains that the English were in the New World, like the Spanish, Portuguese, Dutch, and French, to make a fortune as well as to build religious and political havens. Given the long hostility they had borne toward Indians and their experience in enslaving them, any scruples the English might have had about enslaving Africans were quickly dissipated.

Making it all the more natural to employ Africans as a slave labor force in the mainland colonies was the precedent that English planters had set on their Caribbean sugar islands. In Barbados, Jamaica, and the Leeward Islands (Antigua, Montserrat, Nevis, and St. Christopher) Englishmen in the second and third quarters of the seventeenth century learned to copy their European rivals in employing Africans in the sugar fields and, through extraordinary repression, in molding them into a slave labor force. By 1680, when there were not more than 7,000 slaves in mainland America and the institution of slavery was not yet unalterably fixed, upwards of 65,000 Africans toiled on sugar plantations in the English West Indies. Trade and communication were extensive between the Caribbean and mainland colonists, so settlers in America had intimate knowledge concerning the potentiality of slave labor.

It is not surprising, then, that the American colonists turned to the international slave trade to fill their labor needs. Africans were simply the most available people in the world for those seeking a bound labor force and possessed of the power to obtain it. What is surprising, in fact, is that the American colonists did not turn to slavery more quickly than they did. For more than a half century in Virginia and Maryland it was primarily the white indentured servant and not the African slave who labored in the tobacco fields. Moreover, those blacks who were imported before about 1660 were held in various degrees of servitude, most for limited periods and a few for life.

The transformation of the labor force in the Southern colonies, from one in which many white and a relatively small number of black indentured servants labored together to one in which black slaves served for a lifetime and composed the bulk of unfree labor, came only in the last third of the seventeenth century in Virginia and Maryland and in the first third of the eighteenth century in North Carolina and South Carolina. The reasons for this shift to a slave-based agricultural economy in the South are twofold. First, English entry into the African slave trade gave the Southern planter an opportunity to purchase slaves more readily and more cheaply than before. Cheap labor was what every tobacco or rice planter sought, and when the price of slave labor dipped below that of indentured labor, the demand for black slaves increased. Also, the supply of white servants from England began to dry up in the late seventeenth century, and those who did cross the Atlantic were spread among a growing number of colonies. Thus, in the late seventeenth century the number of Africans imported into the Chesapeake colonies began to grow and the flow of white indentured servants diminished to a trickle. As late as 1671 slaves made up less than 5 percent of Virginia's population and were outnumbered at least three to one by white indentured servants. In Maryland the situation was much the same. But within a generation, by about 1700, they represented one-fifth of the population and probably a majority of the labor force. A Maryland census of 1707 tabulated 3,003 white bound laborers and 4,657 black slaves. Five years later the slave population had almost doubled. Within another generation white indentured servants were insignificant in number and in all the Southern colonies African slaves made up the backbone of the agricultural work force.

To the north, in Pennsylvania, New Jersey, and Delaware, where English colonists had settled only in the last third of the seventeenth century, slavery existed on a more occasional basis, since labor-intensive crops were not as extensively grown in these areas and the cold winters brought farming to a halt for a considerable part of the year. New York was an exception. During the period before 1664 when the colony was Dutch, slaveholding had been extensively practiced, encouraged in part by the Dutch West India Company, one of the chief international suppliers of slaves. The population of New York remained largely Dutch for the remainder of the century, and the English who slowly filtered in saw no reason not to imitate Dutch slave owners. Thus New York became the largest importer of slaves north of Maryland. In the mid-eighteenth century, the areas of original settlement around New York and Albany remained slaveholding societies with about 20 percent of the population composed of slaves and 30 to 40 percent of the white householders owning human property.

As the number of slaves increased, legal codes for strictly controlling their activities were fashioned in each of the colonies. To a large extent these "black codes" were borrowed from the law books of the English West Indies. Bit by bit they deprived the African immigrant of rights enjoyed by others in the society, including indentured servants. And gradually they reduced the slave, in the eyes of society and the law, from a human being to a piece of chattel property. In this process of dehumanization nothing was more important than the practice of hereditary lifetime service. Once servitude became perpetual, relieved only by death, then the stripping away of all other rights followed as a matter of course. When the condition of the slave parent was passed on to the child, then slavery had been extended to the womb. At that point the institution became totally fixed so far as the slave was concerned.

Thus, with the passage of time, Afro-Americans had to adapt to a more and more circumscribed world. Earlier in the seventeenth century they had been treated much as indentured servants, bound to labor for a specified period of years but thereafter free to work for themselves, hire out their labor, buy land, move as they pleased, and, if they wished, hold slaves themselves. But, by the 1640s, Virginia was forbidding blacks the use of firearms. In the 1660s marriages between white women and black slaves were being described as "shameful Matches" and "the Disgrace of our Nation"; during the next few decades interracial fornication became subject to unusually severe punishment and interracial marriage was banned.

These discriminatory steps were slight, however, in comparison with the stripping away of rights that began toward the end of the century. In rapid succession Afro-Americans lost their right to testify before a court; to engage in any kind of commercial activity, either as buyer or seller; to hold property; to participate in the political process; to congregate in public places with more than two or three of their fellows; to travel without permission; and to engage in legal marriage or parenthood. In some colonies legislatures even prohibited the right to education and religion, for they thought these might encourage the germ of freedom in slaves. From human status, slaves descended to property status. More and more steps were taken to contain them tightly in a legal system that made no allowance for their education, welfare, or future advancement. The restraints on the slave owner's freedom to deal with his slaves in any way he saw fit were gradually cast away. Early in the eighteenth century many colonies passed laws forbidding the manumission of slaves by individual owners. This was a step designed to squelch the strivings of slaves for freedom and to discourage those who had been freed from abetting attempts by their black brothers and sisters to gain their liberty.

The movement to annul all the slave's rights had both pragmatic and psychological dimensions. The greater the proportion of slaves in the population, the greater the danger to white society, for every colonist knew that when he purchased a man or woman in chains he had bought a potential insurrectionist. The larger the specter of black revolt, the greater the effort of white society to neutralize it by further restricting the rights and activities of slaves. Thus, following a black revolt in 1712 that took the lives of nine whites and wounded others, the New York legislature passed a slave code that rivaled those of the Southern colonies. Throughout the Southern colonies the obsessive fear of slave insurrection ushered in the institutionalization of violence as the means of ensuring social stability. Allied to this need for greater and greater control was the psychological compulsion to dehumanize slaves by taking from them the rights that connoted their humanity. It was far easier to rationalize the merciless exploitation of those who had been defined by law as something less than human. "The planters," wrote an Englishman in eighteenth-century Jamaica, "do not want to be told that their Negroes are human creatures. If they believe them to be of human kind, they cannot regard them . . . as no better than dogs or horses."[5]

Thus occurred one of the great paradoxes in our history—the building of what some thought was to be a utopia in the wilderness upon the backs of black men and women wrenched from their African homeland and forced into a system of abject slavery. America was imagined as a liberating and regenerating force, it has been pointed out, but became the scene of a "grotesque inconsistency." In the land heralded for freedom and individual opportunity, the practice of slavery, unknown for centuries in the mother country, was reinstituted. Following other parts of the New World, America became the scene of "a disturbing retrogression from the course of historical progress."[6]

The mass enslavement of Africans profoundly affected white racial prejudice. Once institutionalized, slavery cast Africans into such lowly roles that the initial bias against them could only be confirmed and vastly strengthened. Initially unfavorable impressions of Africans had coincided with labor needs to bring about their mass enslavement. But it required slavery itself to harden the negative racial feelings into a deep and almost unshakable prejudice that continued to grow for centuries. The colonizers had devised a labor system that kept the African in America at the bottom of the social and economic pyramid. Irrevocably caught in the web of perpetual servitude, the slave was allowed no further opportunity to prove the white stereotype wrong. Socially and legally defined as less than a person, kept in a degraded and debased position, virtually without power in their relationships with white society, Afro-Americans became a truly servile, ignoble, degraded people in the eyes of the Europeans. This was used as further reason to keep them in slavery, for it was argued that they were worth nothing better and were incapable of occupying any higher role. In this long evolution of racial attitudes in America, nothing was of greater importance than the enslavement of Africans.

126

[1]Sidney W. Mintz, "History and Anthropology," in *Race and Slavery in the Western Hemisphere*, Stanley L. Engerman and Eugene D. Genovese, eds. (Princeton: Princeton University Press, 1975), p. 483.

[2]Basil Davidson, *The African Genius* (Boston: Little, Brown and Company, 1969), p. 187.

[3]Eric Williams, *Capitalism and Slavery* (Chapel Hill: University of North Carolina Press, 1966), p. 30.

[4]Mintz, "Time, Sugar, & Sweetness," *Marxist Perspectives*, No. 8 (1979), p. 60.

[5]Edward Long, *The History of Jamaica* . . . (London, 1774), II, Book 2, p. 270.

Philosophical Disputes in Social Work: Social Justice Denied
Dennis Saleebey

The debate in the social work academy about the pertinence of empiricist/positivist modes of knowing and doing is epistemological in character. It is the argument of this essay that prior ontological questions must be answered before the profession of social work can profitably enter this debate. These questions center on the nature of social work, the symbolic and moral essence of the social work enterprise and what the profession is becoming.

The profession of social work as actually practiced could hardly be accused of a mania for a positivist tools for practice (Welch, 1983). The social work academy, however, is buzzing with a debate about the relevance of such tools and their accompanying presuppositions for practice (Fischer, 1981, 1984; Gordon, 1983; Heineman (Pieper), 1981; Hudson, 1982; Karger, 1983; Ruckdeschel and Farris, 1981; Brekke, 1986; Weick, 1987). The debate, now soft and insinuated, now loud and bitter, centers on selecting *either* a rigorous *or* a relevant epistemology to guide social work education, practice, and research.

It is the intent of this essay to briefly assay and critique core elements of the debate; to account for the ostensible and premature resolution of the debate; to argue that prior questions must be answered before the epistemological conflicts can be reasonably resolved; and to suggest that these prior questions are ontological and to suppose how they might be answered.

The Debate

If the debate is about the fundamental epistemology of social work knowledge and practice it is about questions of how professionals know, how professional knowing is different from mundane knowing, and how professionals come to know, evaluate, and characterize their practice. The roots of the debate extend back for centuries, fertilized extensively by Enlightenment fomenting over the best avenues to apprehend and control elements of the universe in the interest of "progress" and "freedom" (Gay, 1969). The empiricist contends that all knowledge must be based on the perceptions of the senses. Such knowledge can be systematically gathered and accumulated, and its validity put to the test by standard method and instrumentation. Rationalists on the other hand, argue that the mind inevitably enlarges, shapes, and or imbues impressions gained from sensory, empirical experience. Another related facet of the debate, again embedded in our past, is the tension between realists and idealists, the former asserting that the objects of our knowing are, in fact, real and have an existence apart from us and they can be known *as* they exist, while the latter posit that these objects are to some degree, a product of mind's intention, experience, and desire (Popper, 1982; Eccles, 1980).

In the social work academy, this hoary debate can be exemplified by the exchange between Martha Heineman-Pieper (1981; 1985) and Walter Hudson (1982). Others have contributed to this occasionally acrimonious dialogue, not the least of whom are Joel Fischer (1981, 1984) and William Gordon (1983, 1984) (although the irony of their particular foofaraw is that they both, as Haworth (1986) has pointed out, are empiricists). Heineman-Pieper believes that the positivist approach to understanding human experience is naive, inadequate to such a task and may even falsify, in its reliance on measurement, the essence of human experience. She asserts, in summarizing critiques of positivism from a variety of fields, that what is unique about human experience is that it is formed and can only be known in interaction, participation, and dialogue (Heineman-Pieper, 1985). Hudson (1982), on the other hand, puts it quite directly: "Constructs that cannot be defined, operationalized, and then measured are mentalisms that are useless to an understanding of the world in which we live" (p. 256).

This pale summary on the central issues at hand indicate that its substance is, in fact, epistemological, although there are those who have tried to extend the argument beyond questions of knowing (Weick, 1987). Confusions and conflicts over the nature of practice knowledge and the state of mind of the practitioner have obscured prior questions that must be analyzed, appreciated, and answered before the epistemological issues can be reasonably grappled with: questions about the very nature of social work and what social work is becoming; that is to say, what exactly is the essence of the profession of social work's being?

These are ontological questions; and require inquiry directed to the existential basis of the profession. If social work as a profession, merely deals with questions about knowing, however constructively, we stand in danger of the tail wagging the dog, the method dictating the meaning, a prospect that forebodes the devolution of social work into technique or technology. To embarrass an old biological saw, in this case ontology must precede epistemology.

The Debate: Resolution by Default

Other forces and developments move to harden the debate and to assure a resolution in the direction of what Donald Schön (1983) calls the Technical/Rationalist or empiricist model of thinking and acting.

The most stentorian note sounded in the blare of the debate has been the rise of professionalism to unprecedented hegemony in authoring social decisions. In our culture, professions have become the standard-bearers of science and its progeny, technology. The prevailing definition of the concept of profession would denote something like "... professional activity consists in instrumental problem-solving made vigorous by the application of scientific theory and technique" (Schön, 1983, p. 21). Ernest Greenwood (1957) in a most celebrated discourse on the nature of professions generally, and the social work profession in particular, argues that "To generate valid theory that will provide a solid base for professional techniques requires the application of the scientific method to the service-related problems of the profession" (p. 76). In essence, professionals are to become applied scientists.

Schön (1983) is highly critical of the Technical/Rationalist model because it distorts, if not denies altogether, the actuality of what most professionals know and do. It also comes tantalizingly close to confusing method with essence and tends to belittle other ways of knowing and doing as either soft-headed or subversive of rigor.

The professional as Technical/Rationalist becomes part of an elite, bureaucratic and entrepreneurial, that institutionalizes the positivist perspective (even though much of what passes for science and technology would fail any positivistic test of rigor and validity). No less a contributor to this hegemony, perhaps even a result of it—it is difficult to say—is the rampant individualizing or psychologizing of social misery. In our world, the idiom and world view of capitalism, and the language and judgment of the professions have become one. In a world where the marketplace rules, a blithe ignorance of the historical evolution and political/economic configurations that abet what we define as individual difficulties makes some sense. This "social amnesia" (Jacoby, 1975) has cast the professions adrift from social relevance so that some have evolved into a "jejune conglomeration of technical devices and methods" (Saleebey, 1987). So, for example, it is not politic to raise serious social, and economic, questions about why more women than men suffer depression. It is far more lucrative, and amenable to the extension of available technology, whether pill, placebo, or panacea, to treat each woman one by one as they troop through the office, consulting room, or clinic. We do postulate some notions about collective forces that may be involved but they usually are little more than multipliers of the single case. In social work, there has been notable effort to develop characterizations of the environment but even they may be somewhat debilitated by social amnesia. Germain (1987), in her review of developmental theory and the passing away of stage theories, gives a nod to the mutually interactive effect of individual-environment relationships, but speaks nary a word about the historical embeddedness of, or institutional pressures that drive, the course of individual development. Jacoby (1975) says it well in his critique of the individual psychologies that rule today's consciousness:

> The convergence from contrasting directions on the impor-
> tance of the subject as an emotional and psychic entity points
> to a real development of society; not as apologists would
> have it, that society has fulfilled basic material needs and is
> moving to the higher reaches of liberation, but the reverse:
> domination is reaching the inner depths of men and women.
> The last preserves of the autonomous individual are under
> seige. (p. 17)

The Technical/Rationalist model, funded by the individual-
ist bias, has swept (or is sweeping) other points of view, looney
and legitimate alike, under the rug. To its credit, social work
resists, but these forces are impressively powerful and culture is
shot through with them. We should not, as a profession, engage
in the debate over rigor versus relevance until we are clear about
our identity, until we firmly understand what we are about, and
thus, can asses the epistemological questions from a sound
ontological vantage point.

The Ontological Issues Denied

As I said above, broad cultural forces conspire to embolden
the advocates of a "scientific" world view. These forces work as
well to sap the identity of the profession of social work.

Christopher Lasch, in two books (1979; 1984) has drawn a
portrait of contemporary culture shot through with "narcissism", not the self-love of the overweening, strutting egoist, but
the self-doubt of an individual uncertain of the boundaries and
contours of the self, an individual who has trouble distinguishing between me and not-me, one who cannot comfortably
discern what is illusory and what is real about the self. Add to
this a miasma of disaster and threat permeating the culture—
"the threat of AIDS, the terrors of air flight, the looming of the
Big Earthquake", etc.—and you have individuals who must
travel light, avoid lengthy or profound personal commitments,
disavow emotional encumbrances, and ignore communal burdens and responsibilities. Such penetrating themes in our culture make the very notion of social welfare, of caritas, of
responsibility to others quaint, if not frankly annoying. Social
workers live in this culture, too, and it is not far-fetched to
imagine that such themes and strains can make us deaf to our
basic commitments and raisons d'etre.

The gradual decline of New Deal sensibilities and the weakening of the liberal agenda of the past few decades, and more
pointedly, over the last eight years, have also eroded the firm-
ness of our ontologic sense. Listen to Republicans and Democrats today talk about social welfare policy—if they do at all—
about the social good, and you might be listening to a cadre of
parvenus bat around stories about welfare "abusers." The error
here is to think, as some do, that the liberal quest has been
accomplished or to think, as others do, that it has abysmally
failed. But thinking either to be true, in a climate of political/

economic rationalism and restraint, dampens, in the profession and outside it, the central ontological business of social work, the pursuit of social justice. Recoiling, perhaps, from the excesses and failures of the 60s we find ourselves faced with a public morality that reflects, more often than not, the credos and prescriptions of the marketplace.

Not, then, simply the rise of the Technical/Rationalist conception of the professions has led us to this debate, but wider social and cultural trends compel us as well. Not only have they conspired to make us less certain than we might be about who we are, but they have suckered us into a debate which we cannot competently argue until we more firmly establish a professional identity.

The Ontology of Social Work

The word ontology promises more than I can deliver: all that is intended here is a survey of what I regard as the symbolic and existential infrastructure of our professional edifice. As you may discover, if we accept these notions, two effects follow: social work will never be, nor should it, like the other, more established professions; in the academy, we must spit out the positivist bit, and continue the search for a more thorough-going and humane inquiry.

It was John Romanyshyn (1971) who, years ago, through the power of his example, the clarity of his thinking, and the depth of his commitment best exemplified what might be the existential heart of this profession. We begin, he suggested, we are instructed and fueled by an *ethic* of *indignation* (Romanyshyn, 1972), not bloated self-righteousness, or mindless indignation, but a palpable sense of hurt and outrage at indignities afflicted—unjustly, unnecessarily, and often illegally—on people(s). It is a kind of rectitude, even resentment, over acts and attitudes which deny human dignity and thwart human possibility. It is a sense that, in all ways, we should strive for and support the triumphs of organism over machine, of home over institution, of learning over profit, of identity over celebrity, of the real over the illusory. This ethic requires that, in our small way, individually and collectively, we be stewards over the possibilities and requisites of humanness, and, as is needed, advocates for those who are oppressed, denied, misrepresented, and vulnerable.

Humane inquiry and understanding is part of the corpus of social work (Hampden-Turner, 1970; Romanyshyn, 1971; Reason and Rowan, 1981). We seek means of understanding that without violating its meaning, or distorting its nature, can bring us closer to the vagaries and mysteries of the human condition. Life is awash in ambiguity, change, paradox, contradiction, and the continuing tension between the possible and the thwarted, the tragic and the hopeful. We are reluctant to give up our own illusions and myths and to confront these sometimes discordant and frightening elements of the human condition. But we must. We do not want to lapse into the cheery bon mots of modern pop-psych, to pin on the "smile button" that obfuscates the genuine struggles and the real sadness that are the mortar of civilization's bricks (Saleebey, 1987). Neither do we want to wallow in a kind of European existential muck waiting for the Godot of unkind fate. And we may not want to distantiate ourselves from the objects of our interest and concern as the positivists urge. To be conversant with the tragic, to be aware of oppression is not to lose sight of the possibilities of liberation, the turning of the dross of mechanical detached labor, emotional numbness, and intellectual limit into the potential gold of eros—sensual, natural energy, and individual and collective empowerment. To accept the tragic is liberating because, no longer deluded, we can use our own powers of mind and body, our will, and our ethic to restrict the scope of ignorance, fear, prejudice, and oppression. Having confronted it, we can resolve to use the fruits of any inquiry in behalf of improving the human condition.

A second presumption of humane inquiry is that such inquiry is always participatory, a product of a mutual quest, dialogue, and joint learning. Just the opposite, of course, typifies the most elegant positivist mode of inquiry, the experiment. As Argyris (1975) says of this exquisite jewel in the empiricist crown:

> An experiment is a peculiar 'temporary' system. In order to obtain as unambiguous evidence about causation as possible and in order to control extraneous variables, the experimenter strives to gain as much control as possible over the design and execution of the experiment. (p. 474)

This is not a scenario in which one can easily discover the elements of human experience, although one might conceivably discover how people act when they are deceived, encouraged to obey, and not allowed to learn. More humane inquiry, however, rests on vastly different assumptions, and among these are that reality is, in significant degree as far as humans are concerned, constructed symbolically and through interpersonal negotiation; that discovery of lawlike constructs and the causal links are unlikely if not impossible goals, that research methodology is participatory and idiographic, and that all theories, methods, and questions for inquiry are enshrouded with values (Rodwell, 1987; Reason and Rowan, 1981).

A third ontological obligation of social work is *focused compassion and caring*, requiring of us a mimetic or empathic lens through which to see; a stance toward the world of human experience based on a profound appreciation of the root similarities of the human condition for all of us, a positive affective identification with others' humanness, a deep respect for others' uniqueness, and an active resolve to participate in the gathering of individual and group strengths, aspirations, and possibilities (Rifkin, 1983). The manifestation of such caring is dialogue, a peculiar sort of relationship between individuals based upon the mutual appreciation and respect of two (or more) people engaged in a joint project carried out in an affective matrix that is loving, humble, hopeful, trusting, and dedicated to a critical search for possibility, liberation, and empowerment within the surrounding environment (Freire, 1973).

> Dialogue is the only way, not only in vital questions of the political order, but in all expressions of our being. Only by virtue of faith, however, does dialogue have power and meaning; by faith in man (read: humanity) and [its] possibilities by the faith that I can only become truly myself when other [individuals] also become themselves. (Jaspers, in Freire, 1973, p. 45)

The last and most important element of our being is *the quest for social justice*, and although the most resonant, it is possibly the most difficult to pin down. Incapable of a philosophical treatise, I can only offer some of the threads that, with others, form the wholecloth of the social justice.

(a) Social resources are distributed on the principle of need with the clear understanding that such resources underlie the development of personal resources, with the proviso that entitlement to such resources is one of the gifts of citizenship.
(b) Opportunities for personal and social development are open to all with the understanding that those who have been unfairly hampered through no fault of their own will be appropriately compensated.
(c) The establishment, at all levels of society, of agenda, and policies that have human development and the enriching of human experience as their essential goal and are understood to take precedence over other agenda and policies is essential.
(d) The arbitrary exercise of social and political power is forsaken.
(e) Oppression as a means for establishing priorities, for developing social and natural resources and distributing them, and resolving social problems is forsworn.

These four cornerstones—indignation, inquiry, compassion, and justice—have at least two important corollaries. The first is that all human beings, even the most debilitated, defiled, and disenfranchised, have strengths and potential and some capacity to transform themselves. We do not give power to the people, we encourage them to discover and employ the powers of the self or of the people. Second, every human being exists in a web of relationships, institutions, and sociohistorical circumstances that are profoundly important in determining the possibilities of liberation, transformation, or development.

These first principles of our professional being, to the extent that you accept them, precede our participation in the great debate and suggest some of the terms of that debate.

(a) The personal is political: Even the most private problems of relationship and consciousness have political and social dimensions. In Jacoby's (1975) words: "... the isolation that damns the individual to scrape along in a private world derives from a public and social one" (p. 44).

(b) The politics of helping for social work centers on empowerment: We are committed to helping people discover and employ the resources (knowledge, experience, motivations, skills, relationships) that may have been suppressed by self-limiting ideologies and oppressive institutional arrangements. This requires that we focus on the strengths inherent within individuals, groups, neighborhoods and communities.

(c) Insight is, first and foremost, inspired by social critique: Transforming actions, strategies, and ideas are funded, in part, by a peoples' capacity to see beyond the conventional wisdom, and institutional ideologies and arrangements. The anorexic young female, for example, must be helped in understanding how her (and others) self-image, her very identity is obscured and manipulated by the marketplace and media, otherwise she remains at risk for other consequences of a distorted and abused identity (Saleebey, 1987).

(d) Closeness to the people is essential: If we desire to help give voice to the silent, advocate for the oppressed, we must approach them in communion, and cooperation through dialogue and not the implicitly required distance and detachment of esoteric technique.

(e) Theories for practice focus on the dialectical nature of human striving and interaction: The world of human experience is constructed of polarities, appositions, and tensions. The usual inclination of individuals is to control such tension through the suppression of one side of a dialectic that must be elevated to consciousness if action and movement is to be freed. For many males, as an example, one side of their potential for liberated action has been buried under the delicts of capitalism, commerce, and technology—the organic, sensual, caring part of their being has become alien. Males, to be empowered more fully, must confront both the instrumental and affective elements of their being.

Radicalism Redux

The preceding sounds suspiciously like an outworn radical agenda, now virtually forgotten or, perhaps, thoroughly discredited. Later radicalism waned as a significant social force because it forgot its history, wallowed in excess or because it failed to formulate an agenda for positive transformation. As a profession, we cannot foist off these beliefs and principles on the rest of society but we can, individually and collectively, pursue them as we engage in the daily round of practice and citizenship. If we fail to assert and follow them then we stand as one of the legion of guardians of the status quo, as one of the minions of social control or, perhaps more likely, as one of the corps of petty bureaucrats of therapeutic tinkerers.

If we hope to enter the current epistemological debate unfolding within the profession with vigor and resolution, our ontological awareness and commitments must be heightened and made formidable. To the extent that we do that, social justice will not be denied, and we will stand as advocates for relevance before rigor, and meaning before method.

References

Argyris, C. (1975). Dangers in applying results from experimental social psychology. *American Psychologist, 30,* 469–485.

Brekke, J.S. (1986). Scientific imperatives in social work research: Pluralism is not skepticism. *Social Service Review, 60,* 538–554.

Eccles, J.O. (1980). *The human psyche* NY: Springer-Verlag, 1–50.

Fischer, J. (1981). The social work revolution. *Social Work, 26,* 199–207.

———. (1984). Revolution: schmevolution: Is social work changing or not? *Social Work, 29,* 71–74.

Freire, P. (1973). *Education for critical consciousness.* NY: Seabury.

Gay, P. (1969). *The Enlightenment: An Interpretation.* V. II. NY: Alfred A. Knopf.

Germain, C.B. (1987). Human development in contemporary environments. *Social Service Review, 61,* 565–580.

Gordon, W.E. (1983). Social work: Revolution or evolution? *Social Work, 28,* 181–185.

———. (1984) Gordon replies: Making social work a science-based profession. *Social Work, 29,* 74–75.

Greenwood, E. (1957). Attributes of a profession. *Social Work, 2,* 45–55.

Hampden-Turner, C. (1970). *Radical man: The process of psychosocial development.* Cambridge, MA: Schenckman.

Heineman (Peiper), M. (1981). The obsolete scientific imperative in social work research. *Social Service Review, 55,* 171–97.

———. (1984). The future of social work research. *Social Work Research and Abstracts,* 20.

Hudson, W.W. (1982). Scientific imperatives in social work research and practice. *Social Service Review, 56,* 246–258.

Jacoby, R. (1975). *Social amnesia: A critique of conformist psychology from Adler to Laing.* Boston: Beach Press.

Karger, J. (1983). Science, research, and social work: Who controls the profession? *Social Work, 28,* 200–205.

Lasch, C. (1979). *The culture of narcissism.* NY: W.W. Norton.

———. (1984) *The minimal self: Psychic survival in troubled times.* NY: W.W. Norton.

Popper, K.R. (1982). *Quantum theory and the schism in physics.* NJ: Rowman and Littlefied; see esp. pp. 1–46.

Reason, P. & Rowan, J., (Eds.). (1981). *Human inquiry: Sourcebook of new paradigm research.* NY: Wiley.

Rodwell, M.K. (1987) Naturalistic inquiry: an alternative model for social work assessment. *Social Service Review, 61,* 231–246.

Romanyshyn, J.M. (1971). *Social welfare: Ch ʼity to justice.* NY: Random House.

Ruckdeschel, R. & Farris, B. (1981). Science: Critical faith or dogmatic ritual? *Social Casework, 62,* 413–419.

Saleebey, D. (1987). Insight as social critique: Prospects for a radical perspective in clinical practice. *California Sociologist.* (forthcoming).

Schon, D.A. (1983). *The reflective practitioner: How professionals think in action.* NY: Basic Books.

Weick, A. (1987). Reconceptualizing the philosophical perspective of social work. *Social Service Review, 61,* 218–230.

Welch, G.J. (1983). Will graduates use single-subject designs to evaluate their casework practice? *Journal of Education for Social Work, 19,* 42–47.

Emancipation and Reconstruction 1862-1879
Michael Perman

The other federal initiative which resulted from the Emancipation Proclamation was the creation by Congress of the Freedmen's Bureau in March 1865. The bureau was a major innovation in the role of the federal government in America. Through it, the government assumed responsibility, for the first time, for the social welfare of individuals. When the creation of a federal agency to oversee the transition from slavery to freedom was first considered, the notion of guardianship was proposed as a way of protecting the ex-slaves. But abolitionists and the three members of the government's American Freedmen's Inquiry Commission rejected this idea. Noting that the post-Emancipation experiment with apprenticeship in the British West Indies in the 1830s had failed abysmally, the commission's report concluded: "there is as much danger in doing too much as in doing too little. The risk is serious that, under the guise of guardianship, slavery, in a modified form, may be practically restored." Instead, "the freedman should be treated at once as any other free man." So the commissioners recommended that "we secure them the means of making their own way; that we give them, to use the familiar phrase, 'a fair chance.' " And it was this approach, not any kind of special protection, that shaped the Freedmen's Bureau Act in its final form.

The bureau's capacity to aid and protect the freedmen was actually further diminished by specific provisions in the law. The act stipulated that the agency's life was to be restricted to just one year after the war had ended; that its beneficiaries were no longer to be the freedmen alone but all who were in distress, regardless of race; and finally, that its responsibility was limited to only two concerns—the disposal of abandoned lands and the provision of relief to the destitute in the form of food and clothing. Evidently, Congress had decided that the problems arising from emancipation did not necessitate any significant expansion of the federal government's role, nor did the government need to take on any long-term or extensive responsibility for the former slaves. In general, this view of the proper role of government, particularly with regard to racial issues, would predominate in the postwar era.

Had the bureau, in its actual operation, adhered strictly to these guidelines, it would have offered only limited support to the freedmen. But, in fact, it took on responsibilities that went far beyond its specified mandate. The Bureau for Refugees, Freedmen and Abandoned Lands, as it was officially called, did of course dispense relief—more of it to whites than to blacks, as it turned out—and it did start to lease some of the 850,000 acres of confiscated and abandoned land that were in its control. Its most important functions, however, were assumed only after the agency went into operation. First, the bureau established special tribunals so that the freedmen could obtain the justice denied them by the southern civil courts. Then, it adjudicated labor contracts between landlords and their black employees. And finally, it set up and administered schools. None of these responsibilities had been assigned by the law, but, ironically, they became the bureau's main concern.

In its attempt to shield freedmen from injustice, the agency resorted to a number of expedients. Immediately after the war, southern courts discriminated against blacks and would not allow their testimony in cases where whites were involved. The bureau's response was to set up tribunals of its own to hear cases, though these were limited to minor offenses where blacks were in litigation with whites or where a fair trial had been denied by the civil courts. Meanwhile, pressure was applied on state legislators to grant blacks the right to testify against whites. In addition, bureau agents supported freedmen in complaints about unjust decisions handed down by the civil courts. But these efforts were frequently unsuccessful because the agency was understaffed, while its officials were insufficiently sympathetic to the blacks they represented and too worried about upsetting the whites in authority.

The bureau was similarly constrained when it assisted in the drawing up and enforcement of contracts between planters and plantation laborers. Outside the New Orleans district and the Delta, no official decision had been made about how the former slaves were to work and be remunerated. So, in each locality, the bureau agents found themselves involved in adjudicating the terms of labor. With no other model available to guide them, they invariably adopted Banks's annual contract as a way of guaranteeing that a worker would be available all year round. Simultaneously, they tried to ensure that black employees were fairly paid and treated and that they were able to negotiate without duress. Although the laborers were the bureau's clients, agents frequently seemed more concerned about getting contracts signed and ensuring that the plantations were supplied with labor and restored to working order than they were about protecting blacks from exploitation. Furthermore, when freedmen complained to them about the inadequacy of the terms or about a planter's failure to fulfill a contract, the bureau too often possessed neither the manpower nor the resources to conduct an investigation. Nevertheless, dissatisfied though blacks so frequently were at the bureau's feebleness and ambivalence, they knew that without it they would have been far worse off.

In its educational activity, the institution's effectiveness was, however, more evident. Under the leadership of its superintendent of education, Rev. John W. Alvord, a Congregationalist minister and former abolitionist from New England, it assumed responsibility for overseeing and expanding the schools for freedmen that were being established in the postwar South by northern missionary societies and by the coalition of secular agencies called the American Freedmen's Union Commission. By January 1866, the bureau reported 740 schools in the Confederate and Border states within its jurisdiction, involving 1,314 teachers and 90,589 students. Four years later, these numbers had increased dramatically to 2,677 schools, 3,300 teachers, and 149,581 students. Also, the training of black teachers was undertaken with the creation of about 60 normal schools and a number of black colleges, such as Howard and Fisk, both of which were named after bureau leaders, as well as Tougaloo, Claflin, and Atlanta.

The bureau did not, however, take over and run the schools set up by the freedmen's aid societies. The legislation of 1865 and 1866 that created the bureau and then extended its life and responsibilities had actually given it quite limited power. As a result, the financing of the schools and their day-to-day operation remained the duty of the societies and of interested local citizens. In time, however, as the philanthropists' zeal and money dwindled, agency officials were able to maneuver around the law and expand their role and contribution. Initially, they had merely set educational standards, provided coordination and structure to the loose network of missionary schools, and generally reinvigorated the existing teachers and officials. Over time, however, the bureau generated funds for the construction of school buildings as well as for their rental and repair; it paid a substantial portion of the teachers' salaries; and it worked actively to increase the number of teachers who were black, an effort that, by 1870, had raised the proportion to just over half.

The Freedmen's Bureau actually achieved considerable success. But it would do so only within a limited sphere. Although the bureau's role was expanding, it was still restricted either to assisting activities that were already under way or else to supplying temporary remedies until more permanent and satisfactory solutions could be found. Whether or not its scope could be increased depended, to a considerable extent, on the course that the federal government decided to take toward the defeated South as a whole—that is, its policy on Reconstruction. This would provide the context and determine the reach of Washington's involvement in the South.

Social Welfare: A History
of the American Response to Need
June Axinn
Herman Levin

Poverty and the Working Class

The Commission's report pointed out that during the period 1890−1912 personal wealth had increased 188 percent; but the aggregate income of wage earners in manufacturing, mining, and transportation had risen only 95 percent. The wage earner's share of the net product in manufacturing had actually declined. The Commission estimated that to achieve a minimum decency level, an average family of 5.6 members required an annual income of $700. Since 79 percent of the country's fathers earned less than $700 a year, earnings from other family members were necessary to sustain the family. And, indeed, the Census Bureau reported that 1,750,000 children between 10 and 15 years of age were gainfully employed in 1900; by 1910, this number had dropped to 1,600,000. In 1930, however, the figure still stood as high as 667,000.[12]

The report of the Commission on Industrial Relations concluded that, despite the labor of wives and children, and despite the widespread practice of taking in boarders and lodgers, 50 to 66 percent of working-class families were poor and that a third lived in "abject poverty." Other estimates confirmed the judgment of poverty and risk. Robert Hunter, a social worker, writing in 1904, estimated the poverty population at 10 million.[13] Father John A. Ryan, ethical theorist and economist, writing in 1906, found that the average family needed an annual income of at least $600 and that 60 percent of all wage earners received less.[14] Within the ranks of the working class, and, as the AFL succeeded in unionizing some crafts, dissatisfaction was further aggravated by the notable difference in payments to skilled and unskilled workers. Each recession (1910−1911, 1914−1915, 1920−1921) meant increased unemployment and lowered wages, especially for unskilled workers—largely ex-farmhands, blacks, and immigrants. Indeed, by 1928−1929 social welfare agencies were reporting increased caseloads. Between the newly rich, with their extreme wealth, and the working class, with its extreme poverty, lay the large middle class—a group with adequate income but little to spare, a group that was dissatisfied because it could not keep pace with the rapidly rising standard of living of those at the top.

Concomitant with labor unrest and with the dissatisfaction of the middle class was a developing farm crisis. The pre-World War I period was one of prosperity marked by rising farm income. The closing of the frontier, however, meant rising land prices. This, combined with rising costs of mechanization, made easy access to low-cost credit to buy land and machinery a major issue for most farmers. For the marginal farmer, land became more and more difficult to acquire. As the average size of farms started to grow, farm tenancy, already prevalent in the South, began to spread to the Midwest. In 1900, 35 percent of the nation's farms were tenant operated; by 1930 this had risen to 42 percent. For black farmers in the South, the figure reached 79 percent in 1930. The demands of World War I had led to an overextension of agriculture; and in 1920 an agricultural depression occurred, and it continued intermittently throughout the decade. Farm income, even for large-farm owners, did not rise as rapidly as corporate profits; for small-farm owners the crunch was intolerable. Between 1919 and 1929 the number of farms actually declined.[15]

Thus the lowest income classes—unskilled laborers and tenant farmers—fared poorly in the early years of the twentieth century, despite the general prosperity. Within this group, the black population particularly failed to share in the nation's economic growth. The expectation that Northern victory in the Civil War and that the conditions imposed upon the Southern states for return to the Union would bring about changed relations between Southern whites and blacks had been subverted. The advances begun by the programs of the Freedmen's Bureau, the political and civil protections guaranteed by the Thirteenth, Fourteenth, and Fifteenth Amendments to the Constitution, and the enforcement of black rights during the brief period of "radical reconstruction" had come formally to an end with the withdrawal of federal troops from the South by President Hayes in 1877. Through a series of legal and illegal acts and court decisions, the Southern black—now a freed person and a citizen—was abandoned to the "oppressions of those who had formerly exercised unlimited domination over him."[16]

The extent of the abandonment of blacks to white supremacists was not limited to the North's concession to the Southern states of complete control over domestic affairs and institutions or to Northern tolerance of the epidemic of lynchings and the outrageous activities of the Ku Klux Klan. Of equal significance was that process by which the North took on the Southern view of the black as "an alien, a menial, and a probable reprobate."[17] Collusion in the segregation and suppression of blacks was given judicial respectability by the Supreme Court's approval in 1896 of the "separate but equal" doctrine.[18] Northern rationalization of the necessity for segregation and suppression was epitomized by the widespread acceptance of D. W. Griffith's 1915 film, *Birth of a Nation*, in which freed blacks were stereotyped as cruel, vengeful rulers over starving, helpless whites and as "racially incapable of understanding, sharing, or contributing to Americanism."[19] In this atmosphere, Booker T. Washington's espousal of progress by separate evolution for his people found support among whites who gained comfort and conviction from the seeming acquiescence of the country's outstanding Negro leader—the founder of Tuskegee Institute—in policies of social segregation and political cooperation. Washington wrote:

> The wisest among my race understand that the agitation of questions of social equality is the extremest folly, and that progress in the enjoyment of all the privileges that will come to us must be the result of severe and constant struggle rather than of artificial forcing. No race that has anything to contribute to the markets of the world is long in any degree ostracized. It is important and right that all privileges of the law be ours, but it is vastly more important that we be prepared for the exercise of these privileges.[20]

Thus the Progressive Era was not one of progress as regards the economic, political, or social plight of blacks. Sunk in the tenancy-mortgage morass of the sharecropper and crop-lien systems and subjected to the lynchings and harassments of Klansmen, the black population began to migrate to urban areas, where they entered textile factories, steel mills, automobile plants, and packing houses. In 1900 there were only 2 million blacks living in cities. The largest single group was in Washington, D.C., and it totaled 86,702. Baltimore, New Orleans, Philadelphia, and New York each had more than 60,000 black residents.[21] Increasingly, the migration was to the North. Net migration of blacks to Northern states amounted to only 426,000 between 1910 and 1920, but it jumped to 713,000 during the next decade.[22]

The beginning of the flight from the South coincided with a period of dramatically increased labor productivity, as mass production techniques and assembly lines were introduced. From 1919 to 1929 manufacturing output increased by 53 percent, while the number of wage earners in manufacturing remained stable.[23] Annual real earnings rose and the length of the workweek fell, so that for those employed it was a prosperous period. But for blacks forced off the farms and trying to gain entry into the labor market, it was a difficult time. Although there were not enough black migrants in the cities for them to have political or economic clout, their numbers were sufficient to foster Northern hostility, both because of their competition with whites for jobs and because of their being used, along with immigrants, as strikebreakers in labor disputes. Discrimination dominated white-black relations, and blacks were successfully excluded from the ranks of both organized and unorganized labor. This pattern of exclusion allayed the fears of Southerners over the possible loss to Northern cities of a captive, cheap labor force for Southern farms and nascent textile industries.

The black population was generally unaffected by reform activities and the social welfare benefits that resulted from them. In an era marked by economic progress and social mobility, this group remained poor and powerless. More social legislation aiding and protecting the working class was passed during the Progressive Era than had been passed in any previous century. For the most part, however, legislation affecting the labor of women and children, workmen's compensation, regulation of hours and wages, and industrial safety all applied to industries in which black participation was minimal. This fact eluded social welfare reformers who tended to view the problems of all minorities as coextensive with the problems of immigrants. Despite periodic race riots, the relatively small number of blacks in the cities of the North (where most agitation for social reform was concentrated) and their segregation from the mainstream of economic, political, and social life made it possible to ignore their special problems.

Coalitions for Reform

The Progressive reform movement took shape as separate attacks upon political, economic, and social conditions. Reforms were demanded to protect against the excesses of big business and political machines. For the middle class, the base of support and the source of leadership for the movement, there was a reaction also to the more radical political and labor activities of the 1890s.

The industrial collapse of 1893 produced hardships for 4 million factory workers made jobless and for small businessmen, farmers, and investors. Many demanded a change in power relationships and the development of a more equitable system of distribution of wealth and income. The march of "General" Jacob Coxey's army of the unemployed on Washington, D.C., in 1894, the increased prevalence of strikes and industrial violence, the growth of union membership (particularly in the Western Federation of Miners and the United Mine Workers), and the strength of the Populist Movement were part of an agrarian/working-class coalition for reform.

In the early years of the twentieth century the reform movement shifted toward the center. The AFL, representing more highly paid craft workers than the older, industrial unions, became the dominant force in the labor movement. Writers and educators undertook an exposé of the "robber barons"; new political leadership took on the task of city and state reforms; social workers worked on behalf of the poor segregated into urban slums. Social protest became the property of intellectuals and professionals.

The economic changes of the early twentieth century involved a shift from an agrarian and commercial economy to an urban and industrial one. Along with that came a change in the style of living and in values—from the individualism of the nineteenth century to a recognition of collective interdependence. The era of small business firms engaged in competition had supported a model of individual achievement, but the emergence of large corporations or trusts engaged in monopolistic market control increasingly made this model appear unlikely. In a competitive, individualistic society the dominant social theorists had argued for social reform based on individual reformation; the corporate universe of the twentieth century seemed to require a reform of institutions. By 1900 laissez faire looked like an inappropriate social doctrine and a new social truth was proclaimed: social justice through legal regulation and protection. Research would provide knowledge of social and political problems; extension of democratic institutions in government would lead to enactment of the appropriate legislation. In retrospect it was a romantic and an optimistic belief in rational, peaceful, and democratic processes.

Characteristic of the reform activity of the Progressive Era was its emphasis upon opportunity for the underdog. Change in social conditions through the provision, improvement, or regulation of government programs and services was meant to facilitate the individual's chance for assimilation into the mainstream of society, as well as to enhance the potential for successful living. For immigrants this constituted an especially important opportunity to become like "us"—that is, like the dominant Anglo-Saxon members of the society. For immigrants and for blacks opportunity was to be the road to independence through the American self-help image. The focus on independence and the image of self-help constituted another, somewhat contradictory facet of this multidimensional reform movement—that is, the desire to return to a pre–big business era in which true competition flowed and success resulted from individual merit.

The reform activities of the Progressive Era were spearheaded by many groups, some working independently, some working cooperatively as particular issues warranted cooperation, some working for individual aggrandizement, and some working altruistically for the larger society. One group was composed of small businessmen who were anxious to control and stop the domination of trusts and banking establishments. They were joined by writers and social workers, as well as by lawyers and clergymen, two professional groups for whom the rise of big business had especially meant a loss of status. Lawyers had lost status by a shift from being independent professionals to employed representatives of *nouveau riche* industrialists; the clergy had lost status by the secular, impersonal thrust of the process of industrialization and the wholesale abandonment of the church by the working class. Farmers, in search of easy credit, also became a part of the struggle against the domination of "organized money."

The Socialist party joined the coalition too. Starting with a membership of less than 5,000 in 1900, it enrolled 118,000 members by 1912, including many of the nation's leading intellectuals—John Dewey, Stuart Chase, Paul Douglas, Jack London, Walter Lippmann, and Alexander Meikeljohn. Eugene Debs, running for president as the Socialist candidate, polled 6 percent of the popular vote in 1912. More important perhaps was the Socialists' success that same year in electing over 1,000 members to various public offices. Socialist doctrines were widely reviewed, discussed, and quoted. Socialists were sometimes allied in specific causes with other reform groups. The growth of the Socialist party and its increased visibility served as a threat and catalyst for more moderate reform groups seeking regulation of industry.[24]

In 1902 President Roosevelt instructed the attorney general to bring suit under the Sherman Antitrust Act against the Northern Securities Company, a consolidation of railways including the Northern Pacific, the Great Northern, and the Chicago, Burlington, and Quincy systems. The Supreme Court sustained the government's appeal and effectively frustrated the plan of E.H. Harriman to bring all the important railways in the country under his control. Regulation of big business was begun in 1906 with the passage of the Hepburn Act, which permitted the Interstate Commerce Commission (ICC) to fix the rates of railroads, of storage, refrigeration, and terminal facilities, and of sleeping car, express, and pipeline companies. In 1910 authority was extended to the ICC to regulate telephone and telegraph companies.

Economic and regulatory reforms took various shapes. As a result of Upton Sinclair's *The Jungle* and of other exposés of the food and pharmaceutical industries, editors of popular journals and the American Medical Association, among others, formed a coalition to secure passage of the Food and Drug Act in 1906. In 1909 the Sixteenth Amendment, which established a federal income tax, was introduced in Congress by Cordell Hull. By 1913 it had been ratified by the required number of states, and the income tax with its potential for redistribution of income was instituted. During this same year, Congress created the Federal Reserve System, bringing about major reforms in banking.

Labor's cause and the frequency with which the lower courts had found against that cause were increasingly arousing sympathy. 1914 saw the enactment of the Clayton Antitrust Act, representing a culmination of the struggle between labor and small business, on the one hand, and big business on the other. Passage of this act, then, was an indication of labor sympathy and strength and of the success of the reform coalition. The Supreme Court had already begun to reverse the antilabor decisions of lower courts. Now, by an act of Congress, a base was laid for further restricting corporate monopolies, while simultaneously exempting labor unions from much of the antitrust legislation. The Clayton Act was supplemented by the Federal Trade Commission Act, establishing a commission whose purpose was to bring to bear the knowledge and advice of a group of economic experts on "unfair" methods of competition and alleged infractions of antitrust laws.

The "democratic" thrust of the Progressive Era made political reform a partner to economic reform. Just as muckraking publications had reported lurid instances of fraud and graft and of monopolistic control in industry, in railroading, and in public utilities,[25] they detailed corruption in state and local governments, in the courts, and in the United States Senate.[26] A veritable avalanche of widely read, eagerly awaited exposés of the "shame of the cities," of "treason in the Senate" led the way to political change. The effort was twofold: to provide for greater citizen participation in political affairs and to increase governmental responsiveness and honesty. The first strengthened the movement for women's suffrage, the secret ballot, direct primaries, direct election of senators, the initiative, referendum, and recall, and municipal home rule. The second led to demands for civil service reform, the short ballot, regulation of campaign expenditures, accountability and leadership on the part of elected officials, and for the commission and city manager plans for municipal government. A few highlights suggest the thrust of the changes.

On the federal level, Congress in 1907 banned political contributions by corporations. In 1913 the Seventeenth Amendment to the Constitution provided for direct election of senators. In 1919 the Nineteenth Amendment, providing for women's suffrage, was passed. It was ratified by the required 36 states just one year later, bringing victory to this cause after almost 75 years of campaigning.

On a state and local level, 20 states introduced the initiative (making it possible for the citizenry to propose legislation) and the referendum (making it possible for voters to pass on measures introduced in legislative bodies). By 1915 direct primary and presidential preference laws were on the books of two-thirds of the states, thus giving a blow to the power of political bosses. The drive for efficiency, economy, and honesty in the administration of local governments began in Galveston, Texas, in 1900, when the entire political machinery of mayor, council, and bureaus was abolished and replaced by a board of commissioners. Thereafter, the commission form of government spread rapidly, especially in smaller cities, where its structure—generally five commissioners elected at large and each responsible for a particular department—was most appropriate. Starting with Dayton, Ohio, in 1914, the city manager type of government—a government run by an appointed expert in city administration—also found widespread acceptance.

In public welfare administration, change resulted in an initial shift of responsibility from local overseers of the poor to local or county departments of welfare. Kansas City, Missouri, established a city department of welfare in 1910, with authority to provide for the relief of the poor and the care of delinquents, the unemployed, and other needy groups. St. Joseph, Missouri, established a county-city department of public welfare and Chicago set up the Cook County Bureau of Public Welfare, both in 1913.

Nor did the country's entry into World War I completely stop local governmental restructuring. Westchester County, New York, established a department of welfare in 1916. In 1917 an important reorganization of the Illinois state government occurred with the passage of the Civil Administrative Code, which provided for the grouping of all state functions and activities into nine departments, each with its own director. Among the nine, was a Department of Welfare with its director of public welfare responsible for administering the state's assistance, services, and institutional programs. The Illinois code was emulated by other states and was the start of a new era in public administration. In many states, for example, public welfare services were consolidated into statewide systems administered by appointed heads of state departments of welfare. Both in the statewide scope of the organizations and in the removal of department executives "from current political responsibility, except through [the ultimate political responsibility of] the governor,"[27] the trend foreshadowed the requirements of the Social Security Act of 1935.

No reform activities were more representative of the Progressive Era than those that occurred in the arena of social welfare. The aura of justice, of social consciousness, of morality and ethics, most logically reposed here. The reform movement responded to and fostered the new profession of social work. Individual social workers through research, persistence, and expertise moved to the forefront of advocacy for social legislation. Theodore Roosevelt himself, acting on the commonly held conviction that all were personally responsible for the current state of affairs depicted so graphically in muckraking literature, called upon each citizen to contribute to "reform through social work."[28] Social work, acting on society's will for social change, carried that projection in two sometimes converging but basically different operations—the Charity Organization and Settlement House movements.

Those who labored for social reform were primarily concerned, as a matter of social justice, "to bring the power of the state and national governments into the economic struggle on the side of women, children, and other unprotected groups."[29] Whether prompted by the Charity Organization hope to sustain and strengthen individuals in their own efforts to cope, or by the Settlement House conviction that any intervention short of intrinsic societal restructuring must be considered only "a down payment toward justice,"[30] social workers could find common ground for the work that needed doing.

At the height of the reform movement, between 1905 and the beginning of World War I, leaders of the Charity Organization and Settlement House movements came together in behalf of social reform activity. The participation of Charity Organizations in reform was impelled by their changing view of the family. In 1900 Charles Faulkner's presidential address at the National Conference of Charities and Corrections had labeled the family "the unit of social order" and laid out a program of education in the home and in the school for the moral improvement of individuals. His Darwinian bent took him from a concern for the maintenance of "the blessings and protection of society through its family life" to call for avoiding "unrestrained conmingling of . . . defectives with the people. . . ."[31] By 1908, however, Mary Richmond was arguing for the protection of family life against the onslaughts of a hostile environment.[32]

Miss Richmond referred to the family as "the great social unit, the fundamental social fact." She demanded changes in agency practices, action in regard to child labor laws, industrial safety regulations, and protection of working women, as well as administrative changes in industrial operations to strengthen family life. She challenged the members of her social work audience to ask themselves: "Have we at least set plans in motion that will make the children better heads of families than their parents have been?" Miss Richmond's challenge was based on a new recognition of "the overwhelming force of heredity *plus* the environment that we inherit." Social workers and their allies strove for legislation to regulate tenement and factory construction; to prevent and compensate for industrial accidents and diseases; to prohibit child labor and provide for compulsory education; to improve sanitary and health conditions; to provide social insurance as security against unemployment, retirement, or death of the breadwinner; and to protect workers—especially women—in regard to minimum wages and working hours.

Improvement in housing conditions had been a concern of social workers at least since 1882, when the Boston Associated Charities appointed a Committee on Dwellings of the Poor. In the same year, the New York and Buffalo Charity Organization Societies combined to get a tenement housing bill through the state legislature. During the next decade, they allied themselves with settlement residents and others to investigate and publicize the housing conditions of the poor. The New York City Tenement House Law was passed in 1901. Aimed at preventing the construction of lightless, airless tenements, the law become a model to follow. Similar legislation was passed for Chicago in 1902; and by 1910 most large cities had inaugurated some housing reform.

Social Reform: Working Conditions

Child labor and women's working hours were matters of gravest concern. In 1900 nearly 2 million children aged 10 to 15 and almost 5 million women over 15 were in a labor force totaling about 29 million.[33] Twenty-eight states had already adopted some legal protections for children. By 1914, as a result of the continued assault by the National Child Labor Committee, the National Consumer's League, the General Federation of Women's Clubs, and others, almost all the states had laws covering hours and conditions of child labor in factories, mills, and workshops and setting minimum ages for leaving school.[34]

But the laws were weak and inadequate. Owen R. Lovejoy, secretary of the National Child Labor Committee and chairman of the Committee on Standards of Living and Labor of the National Conference of Charities and Corrections, reported the following:

> No state has made any adequate plan to protect its children to sixteen years from bare-handed contact with the red hot tools of our industrial competition. Nearly half the states have no effective way of protecting children even to the fourteenth birthday. Several permit their employment at twelve or even younger.[35]

Much of the problem occurred in industries engaged in interstate commerce and, therefore, federal intervention seemed necessary. The first formal attempts to bring child labor under federal control were made in 1906, when bills were introduced in Congress to prohibit the interstate shipment of articles produced in factories or mines employing children. The bills were not passed. A few years later, President Roosevelt directed the secretary of labor to investigate the situation. In 1912, the Children's Bureau was created to report, among other things, on "dangerous occupations, accidents and diseases of children, employment legislation affecting children."[36] The Bureau's investigations bolstered the report of the secretary of labor as to the need for child protections, and further efforts to obtain federal regulation of child welfare followed. The Keating-Owen bill was passed by Congress in 1916, but it was found unconstitutional two years later on the ground that it transcended "the authority delegated to Congress over commerce."[37] Subsequent improvements in child labor legislation remained with the states; and by 1930 all the states and the District of Columbia had taken legal measures to safeguard the employment and working conditions of children. In many instances old provisions had been strengthened.[38]

In the country as a whole, child labor had shown a steady decline, so that by 1930 less than 5 percent of the children between 10 and 15 years of age were employed, compared to 18 percent in 1900. Even in the South, which had lagged in regulatory legislation, the ratio of children employed in its newly developing textile industry was no higher than in its Northern counterpart. These advances were chronicled in the census of 1930. Despite within-industry equivalency, however, there were wide interindustry distinctions, reflecting geographic and racial differences. For example, only 3 percent of children between 10 and 15 were at work in industrial Rhode Island, whereas 24 percent were at work in Mississippi, where child welfare laws were loosely enforced and the cheap farm labor of black children was deemed necessary. Nor did the census takers secure information concerning the paid employment of children under 10.[39] One can only surmise what that meant for black children, especially in those Southern states where legislation provided minimal protection.

Efforts to effect child labor legislation were paralleled by efforts to regulate conditions and hours of female workers, who constituted 20 percent of the labor force. The coalition of groups working to obtain legislation for each was largely the same.

The Consumer's League, under the leadership of its executive, Florence Kelley, was particularly active in regard to legal protections for working women. Under the aegis of the League, Mrs. Kelley and Josephine Goldmark, a social worker, completed research that was successfully used by Louis Brandeis in arguing the constitutionality of Oregon's law limiting working hours for women to ten hours per day. When, in 1908, the Supreme Court upheld the constitutionality of the law, the right of states to protect women from excessive hours of labor was established, and virtually all the states moved to enact laws in this field. By 1912, the year in which the Committee on Standards of Living and Labor of the National Conference of Charities and Corrections made its report, the battle was for such specific protections as the eight-hour day and the six-day workweek. The Committee predicted: "the day will come—come tripping on the heels of social regulation—when our manufacturers and merchants will be able to distribute . . . [their products] without compelling the sacrifice of the health of our mothers or burning out the eyes of our little children who now bend over their work . . . at all hours of the night."

Success in obtaining protections for women from excessive work hours was achieved in the course of the larger struggle to attain a shorter workday. This particular fight began during the Jacksonian reform era as a ten-hour movement designed to provide leisure time during which workers could "give themselves to moral and mental improvement." In 1840 President Van Buren ordered a ten-hour day for all federal workers. Following this, the movement showed some success in state legislation, but legal loopholes made for very slow progress in attaining the goal on an industrywide basis.

The average work day at the close of the Civil War was still 11 hours,[41] and organized labor began to campaign for an eight-hour day. The eight-hour movement, such as it was, collapsed in 1886, when the violence and aftermath of Chicago's Haymarket Square riot proved disastrous to the Knights of Labor. In 1900, according to an estimate based on information of the Bureau of Labor Statistics, the average standard work week was still over 57 hours, having declined very little during the previous decade.[42] For industry as a whole, there was wide variation, so that unorganized workers, such as those in the blast furnaces of steel mills, normally worked a 12-hour day, 84-hour week, whereas organized workers in the building trades had achieved a 48-hour week, working eight hours a day, six days a week.[43]

After 1900 reduction in working hours might not have occurred without organization on the part of workers, who were panicked by the threat of unemployment posed by technological advance. The eight-hour day was seen, in effect, as "job making," a method of spreading available employment among the greatest number of workers. At the same time, the demand for fewer working hours coincided with higher labor-hour productivity and with increased sales from lowered prices. Differentials in work hours between unionized and nonunionized industries indicate the significance of unionization for reduced work hours. Average weekly hours in 1900 for unionized manufacturing industries were 53, compared to 62 for nonunion manufacturing. By 1920, unionized manufacturing hours had declined to 46 per week and nonunion manufacturing to 54. Unionized manufacturing had achieved the eight-hour day and nonunion manufacturing had made significant gains. The gap between organized and unorganized labor narrowed.[44]

Social Reform: Women, Work, and Suffrage

In 1900 the National American Woman's Suffrage Association, representing the joining of the two earlier rivals in the women's suffrage movement, was still unclear as to directions for achieving votes for women. The Association's flirtation with "educated suffrage," offering to counter the votes of lower-class blacks and immigrants with those of middle-class women, contributed to a separation of white women from black women, middle-class women from lower-class women, nonworking women from working women, and native-born women from immigrant women. There were seemingly irreparable divisions.

In the Progressive Era, racism and nativism, as integral parts of the suffrage movement, began to subside. Josephine Shaw Lowell's statement of 1888, pointing up the discrepancy between middle-class rhetoric and lower-class reality in the matter of working mothers signified a beginning shift in her own stance towards people in need.[45] The National American Woman's Suffrage Association moved away from a position which not only failed of success but which was generally untenable in the climate of the times. In addition, the limiting nature of a single-issue organization became apparent as other women's groups moved to the fore. These new organizations—for example, The National Consumers' League, The National Women's Trade Union League, and the Young Women's Christian Association—were at once concerned with matters affecting women as women and with the potential of the vote for righting wrongs. The National American Woman's Suffrage Association broadened its view. Its publication, *The Woman's Journal*, supported the garment workers' strike of 1909 and 1910 and reported the tragic Triangle Shirt-Waist Company fire of 1911 as demonstrating the need for women's votes to assured "more effective factory legislation and a larger number of [factory] inspectors."[46] This broadening of view resulted in increased membership. By 1910, the official numbers in NAWSA had risen to 100,000; in 1917, the membership stood at 2 million.

Part of the reality of the Progressive Era was the increasing participation of women in the labor force. In 1900, there were more than 5 million gainfully employed female workers. Most worked as unskilled factory hands or as domestics; most were foreign born or black; some were married. The number of female workers increased rapidly to meet the demands of this generally prosperous era, later the added demands of a Europe at war, and finally, in 1917, the demands of the United States itself as its own male workers, drafted to wartime service, had to be replaced. By 1910, the number of gainfully employed women had risen to 8 million. With the war over, labor force adjustments resulted from the return of soldiers to the work force and of many women to working solely in the home. Nevertheless, by 1920, the number of gainfully employed women had risen to more than 8½ million.[47] The formation of the National Women's Trade Union League and its activities in supporting existing unions of women wage earners and of assisting in the formation of new women's unions attest to the increase in the numbers of women workers, their beginning entrance in skilled positions, and their increasing political consciousness.

Progress toward the unionization of women was nevertheless slow and fraught with difficulty. Much of the history was characterized by spontaneous work stoppage and strikes against low wages and torturous working conditions. These strikes resulted in efforts to organize; but even when success in gaining demands followed, unionization tended to fall apart. In skilled industry the responsibility for this can be traced to the overall antagonism of male workers, who accused women of scabbing during strike actions on the part of male-dominated unions, of taking men's jobs, and of lowering wage rates. These antagonisms carried over in the half-hearted attempts by the American Federation of Labor, an organization of craft unions made up of skilled workers, to organize women's unions or to admit women into existing organizations. The Federation, like its constituents, was suspicious of women's commitment to work, of their staying power during strikes, and of their effect upon wages. The Federation's lack of interest was encouraged by the fact that by far the largest number of women continued to work in unskilled jobs—in textiles, in garments, shirt, and waist making, in laundries, in domestic service. Among these unskilled workers, foreign-born and black women predominated. Black women particularly suffered exclusion from unionizing efforts, even from the efforts of other unskilled workers.

The task of bringing together the work-related and suffrage-related concerns of women was not easy. Concern for their physical, moral, and emotional well-being welled out of the conviction that "the prime function of woman must ever be the perpetuating of the race . . . . The woman is worth more to society . . . as the mother of healthy children than as the swiftest labeler of cans."[48] The result was a great deal of effort to estimate "a living wage" for women and to clarify the special needs of women in regard to working hours and working conditions. Although similar concerns were being explored in connection with all workers, very special legislative protection was sought for the unique circumstances of women.[49] The culmination of these concerns for women, reflecting the additional burdens they had assumed during World War I, came with the establishment by Congress in 1920 of the Women's Bureau within the Department of Labor.

By the time of the armistice in 1918, women's groups had become accustomed to cooperation. This unity of action comprised a powerful political force. Under the direction of Carrie Chapman Catt, who had been reelected its president in 1915, the National American Woman's Suffrage Association was revitalized and led the final march toward victory. Mrs. Catt was able to gain President Wilson's support. Not the least of that support derived from the contribution of women and of women's organizations to the war efforts. The Nineteenth Amendment to the Constitution was approved by Congress on June 4, 1919. The amendment was ratified by the required number of states on August 26, 1920. The National American Woman's Suffrage Association went out of existence but was revived as the League of Women voters.

The end of World War I also brought success to another women led movement, the drive for prohibition. In fact, the strength of the National Woman's Christian Temperance Union combined with the government's wartime conservation efforts—i.e., the need to limit the use of grain for the production of liquors—to win Congressional approval for prohibition sooner than woman's suffrage. The Eighteenth Amendment to the Constitution prohibiting the manufacture, sale, and import or export of liquor was ratified in 1919. The disastrous results of attempts to enforce its provisions led to its being rescinded in 1933 by the Twenty-First Amendment.

With the passage of the Eighteenth and Nineteenth Amendments to the Constitution the women's movement went into an eclipse, a part of the decline in all reform activity suffered in the aftermath of World War I. The women's movement was not to revive until the 1960s.

Social Reform: Income Security

Social welfare legislation was additionally sought to protect against loss of income from the major hazards of the industrial society—accident, illness, death of the breadwinner, old age and retirement, and unemployment. Industrialization and urbanization required enormous change on the part of the family. Economic survival required mobility, freedom to move from farms to industrial sites where jobs existed. The mobile family was almost by definition a small family. Having moved to the cities the families were then trapped by low wages and a lack of resources, and by a lack of industrial skills. Most family members had to stand ready to work in order to meet the costs of urban living. The family became increasingly dependent for income on factory owners, who themselves felt no responsibility for their workers' welfare, and on non-family members for services previously performed internally—child care for working mothers, for example. The family of the Progressive Era was a unit caught in the stress of a period of social change, a unit socially and economically insecure in its day-to-day living and vulnerable to anxieties about an unknown future.

The changes forced upon the family by industrial society, coupled with the dependence upon others for the means of production and for money payments, led to a sharp decline in the economic independence of the family unit. Thus there was a need for safeguards to alleviate economic insecurity.

Workmen's compensation for injuries resulting from industrial accidents was first discussed at the American Sociological Conference of 1902. During this same year, when the National Conference of Charities and Corrections appointed a committee to investigate the topic, Maryland's Workmen's Compensation Act was declared illegal. The fact that no one could be found to appeal this decision of the lower court did not impede growing national enthusiasm for such a measure. Action was spurred by the realization that "the industries of our country every year claim an army of 15,000 men killed, and some half a million injured."[50] President Roosevelt's enthusiastic support of Senate action eventuated in the Federal Employee's Act of 1906.

In 1904 a Massachusetts commission and in 1907 an Illinois commission each recommended industrial insurance to their respective states. The recommendations went unheeded; nevertheless, agitation continued. Discussion of workmen's compensation occurred again at the annual meetings of the National Conference of Charities and Corrections in 1905 and 1906; and a National Conference on Workmen's Compensation was held in 1909. By 1910, the year of the second National Conference on Workmen's Compensation, a groundswell of support had developed. The American Association for Labor Legislation, the National Civic Federation, the American Federation of Labor, the American Economic Association, and, though reluctantly, the National Association of Manufacturers were all encouraging the enactment of industrial insurance. During 1911, the year regarded "as the beginning of an intelligent grappling with the problem," ten states enacted workmen's compensation laws.[51]

The issue of old age security was raised for discussion in the United States in the decade before World War I. The number of older people in the population had risen, and, at the same time, industrialization increased the likelihood of dependency in old age. The more advanced European industrial nations, France, Germany, and England, had already instituted old age support systems. Both the National Conference of Charities and Corrections and the Progressive party endorsed the principles of social insurance as a response to economic need from unemployment, illness, and old age, in

1912. Case studies documented the inability of individuals to save for their own old age, the inadequacy of private charity, and the inability or unwillingness of industry to provide private pensions. Nonetheless, attempts to provide income in old age either through public or private pensions failed. At the outbreak of World War I only Arizona and Alaska had even limited pension plans and less than 1 percent of American workers were covered by private insurance. The economic status of the elderly declined and their dependence on public welfare rose steadily.

In the years immediately following World War I, reform groups, especially the National Consumers' League, the American Association for Labor Legislation, and the Women's Trade Union League, gave health insurance their first priority, and the impetus toward old age pensions came to a standstill.

The old age pension movement began to gather support once more in the 1920s. But this time the research and leadership of social reformers, economists, and social scientists had a new political base of support. The Fraternal Order of Eagles, a broad-based popular group, began to organize community pension clubs and lobby for state pension bills. Three states— Montana, Nevada, and Pennsylvania—passed voluntary, limited pension bills in 1923. Most other states followed suit in the next few years. The first mandatory system was legislated in California in 1929. In every case the payments were too low and the coverage inadequate, but a major precedent of state responsibility for old age security had been set.[52]

Social Reform: Family Welfare

Legislation to regulate the working conditions of women and children and to insure against loss of income due to industrially caused illness and accident was the first part of a package that might loosely be identified with family welfare. Additional elements of the package were those that dealt with the development of juvenile courts and widows' pensions. The juvenile court movement was an expression of a growing consensus as to the importance of differentiating the needs of children. The first juvenile court law, An Act to Regulate the Treatment and Control of Dependent, Neglected, and Delinquent Children, had been enacted in 1899 by Illinois, where the Illinois State Conference of Charities had taken responsibility for having the act drafted. The law applied to children under 16 years of age and provided for a special juvenile courtroom and record-keeping system and for probation officers "to take charge of any child before and after trial as may be directed by the court."[53] Within ten years similar laws had been passed in 22 states. By 1919 all the states except Connecticut, Maine, and Wyoming had enacted juvenile court laws emphasizing the "principle of separate treatment of juvenile delinquents and. . . cure rather than punishment . . . ."[54] Once again Illinois set the character of juvenile probation services, when several agencies assigned social workers to the court in the hope of making the state's new juvenile court law operate effectively by providing casework services.

As professional services developed, social research became a tool for advancing social legislation. Social work's contribution to social reform during the Progressive Era was in large measure derived from its introduction of systematic social surveys to the study of social problems. This was best illustrated by the Pittsburgh Survey of 1907–1908, directed by Paul Kellogg, a social worker and assistant editor of *Charities and the Commons*, the national journal published under the auspices of the New York Charity Organization Society. An article in the March 1906 issue of *Charities and the*

Commons, "Neglected Neighborhoods in the Alleys, Shacks and Tenements of the National Capitol," led to the suggestion by the chief probation officer of the Allegheny County (Pennsylvania) Juvenile Court that a similar investigation be made in the Pittsburgh area. The suggestion was favorably received by the Publications Committee of the Charity Organization Society and an Advisory Committee was formed. Among the members of the committee, in addition to Kellogg, were William H. Matthews, head worker at Kingsley House in Pittsburgh; Robert A. Woods, another leading settlement house worker and former Pittsburgh resident; Florence Kelley, director of the National Consumers League; and John R. Commons, a well-known economist. Funding was secured from a number of sources but primarily from the Russell Sage Foundation, which used the survey as its initial large investment in social research.

The Pittsburgh Survey was "the first major attempt to survey in depth the entire life of a single community,"[55] and for this purpose Kellogg pulled together a study team of workers and students of social welfare and the social sciences. The findings, published serially in *Charities and the Commons* and later in book form, covered "wages, hours, conditions of labor, housing, schooling, health, taxation, fire and police protection, recreation [and] land values."[56] They became widely known not only through their publication in professional literature but also through their being brought to the public's attention in such popular periodicals as *Collier's Weekly*. The result was a factual base for use in social action.

Similarly, social research was a major weapon of the National Child Labor Committee, whose primary interest was child labor legislation. The officers of the National Child Labor Committee included persons who were active on the many fronts of the social reform movement. Edgar Gardner Murphy had seen to the formation of the Committee. Also on the Committee were Jane Addams, founder of Hull House; Florence Kelley; Felix Adler, of Columbia University and longtime crusader for tenement housing reform; Lilliam Wald, founder of the Henry Street Settlement House; and Edward T. Devine and Robert W. DeForest, executive and president, respectively, of the New York Charity Organization Society. An awareness of the value of coalitions for achieving social welfare goals was demonstrated when the Committee set up headquarters in Chicago's United Charities Building, which also sheltered the Association for the Improvement of the Conditions of the Poor, the Charity Organization Society, the Children's Aid Society, and the National Consumer's League.

As early as 1906 the National Child Labor Committee was able to have introduced in Congress a bill for the establishment of a children's bureau. As part of a campaign to have the bill passed, the Committee was successful in influencing President Roosevelt to call the 1909 White House Conference on Child Dependency. The President established the theme of the Conference by extolling the virtues of home life and by urging that children "not be deprived of it except for urgent and compelling reasons."[57] The Conference went on record as favoring home care for children—own home care, as well as foster home care—and recommended the creation of a publicly financed bureau to collect and disseminate information affecting the welfare of children and a national voluntary organization to establish and publicize standards of child care. The first, the Children's Bureau, was created in 1912; the Child Welfare League of America followed in 1921. Equally important was the establishment of the principle of federal interest in child welfare, a principle that has resulted in the reconvening of the Conference at ten-year intervals.

The federal government's interest in the well-being of children was demonstrated again in 1921 with the passage of the Act for the Promotion of the Welfare and Hygiene of Maternity and Infancy, better known as the Sheppard-Towner Act. The Act's major concern was with the health of rural children.

Annual appropriations for five years were made to states designating a state child hygiene or child welfare division to carry responsibility for the local administration of the Act's provisions. The general purpose of the Act was educational, and instruction in maternal and infant care was conducted by nurses and physicians either through itinerant conferences held in homes or at established health centers. Instruction in maternal and infant care was also offered to professionals involved in teaching or caring for mothers and young children. The life of the Sheppard-Towner Act was extended for two years in 1927, with the understanding that the Act would lapse after June 30, 1929. At the time of its expiration, 45 states and Hawaii were cooperating. The decision to continue the work begun was left with the states.

The recommendation of the White House Conference that children not be deprived of home care except for "urgent and compelling reasons" stimulated controversy. On one side were those social workers who supported the Conference's position that private—not public—funds be used to prevent the removal of children from their own homes. On the other were such prominent juvenile court judges as Ben Lindsey and Merritt Pinckney, whose daily practice required the institutionalization of children of poor (though competent) mothers. There was an underlying conflict, too, posed by the question of whether mothers should work at all. Before the enactment of the first mother's pension in 1911, while the possibility of such pensions was still being verbally explored, the question of balance between pension and earnings was major. A speaker at the National Conference of Charities and Corrections in 1910 stated the problem:

> The first question to consider, after regular relief on a pension basis has been decided upon, is whether it should be a full pension or whether the widow should be encouraged to earn. At a recent meeting of the Secretaries of the Boston Associated Charities . . . most . . . felt that a day or two of work a week outside was really better for the mother than to keep her always at home, for life can be too dull some times. . . .[58]

The first mother's pension law was passed by Missouri in April 1911. The law had been enacted at the behest of a single county and its provisions were permissive in that it left the decision to provide assistance to the individual counties. The first statewide mandatory law, the Funds to Parents Act, was passed by the General Assembly of the State of Illinois in June 1911. With the sudden adoption of laws providing public funds for the aid of dependent children in their own homes, the development of Mother's Aid as a public movement was a *fait accompli*. Leaving aside such Settlement House leaders as Lillian Wald, social workers were shocked. Mary Richmond's outcry that the Funds to Parents Act had been "drafted and passed without consulting a single social worker"[59] expressed the general view.

After the passage of the act, social workers did rally to help establish the program and to survey its operation. But Mary Richmond, for all her concern with the burdens that society placed on family life, maintained that families pensioned under the system were without the competent supervision of social workers to assure that "the children of the widow are in school, that they are morally protected, that their health is safeguarded, that they have a good chance to grow up right."[60] Frederic Almy, secretary of the Buffalo Charity Organization Society, was more willing to permit experiments in public relief giving. Nevertheless, he viewed private charity as safer. He warned that "to the imagination of the poor the public treasury is inexhaustible and their right, and that they drop upon it without thrift, as they dare not do on private charity."[61] Almy stresssed the importance of professional casework help in investigating the need for relief and for redeeming recipient families. And since such help was not characteristic of public relief giving, he favored having public relief funds administered by voluntary agencies. He objected to relief's being dispensed without professional help, for "like undoctored drugs, untrained relief is poisonous to the poor. . . . Poor charity is worse than none."[62]

The number of states with Mother's Assistance programs increased rapidly. Within two years of the passage of the Illinois Funds to Parents Act, 20 states had provided cash relief programs for widows with children, and within ten years, 40 states had done the same.[63] The Children's Bureau's study of Mother's Assistance, conducted in ten representative localities during the period October 1923 to April 1924, reported that "the principle of home care for dependent children as a public function is generally accepted in this country."[64] The Bureau also reported generally good relationships between voluntary agencies and the public agencies studied and, of most importance, that families were functioning with the help of Mother's Assistance "on a par with . . . self-supporting families."[65] Thus, in the Mother's Assistance or Widow's Pension Movement, a movement basically concerned with help for children, the changing nature of social welfare was demonstrated. A beginning change of relationships between voluntary and public welfare agencies and a beginning recognition of governmental responsibility for family welfare were shown.

The policy intent that mothers were not to be expected to work was clear, but the reality was that the policy was being undermined by inadequate funding of budgets. Emma O. Lundberg, director of the Children's Bureau, and C. C. Carstens, executive of the Child Welfare League of America, made this clear when they addressed the national conference in 1921. Carstens said this:

> The granting of this aid [Mother's Pensions] was intended to meet the needs of the budget. . . . In theory this was a clearly established policy . . . but in practice . . . in many of the states the mother is expected to earn a very large share of the budget and much more than it is best that she should earn in view of her own needs and those of her children.[66]

A Children's Bureau report of a study of the administration of mother's pensions suggests the latent intent of inadequate budgets.

> It was the testimony of the workers in the field and of the executives that the aid did not tend to develop a spirit of dependency but on the contrary developed self-confidence, initiative, and generally a desire for economic independence as at early a date as possible.[67]

The example of someone in the family working was important. To be expected then was the failure of another intent of the various state mother's and widow's pensions—that is, the education of women, particularly immigrant women, for American motherhood:

> The degree to which mothers receiving aid were encouraged to join clubs and classes of an educational character varied greatly. . . . In some communities the grants were too small to permit the mothers to give their time to anything more than housekeeping and gainful employment.[68]

The inability of the Mother's Pension Movement to fulfill its intent because of inherent conflicting values need not detract from its contribution to publicizing the plight of women in the American economic structure. Despite reform efforts, however, it was not until the Great Depression that there were any federal programs to maintain female-headed families. After World War I federal programs were restricted to insuring federal employees against a loss of income due to retirement or disability and to insuring the families of veterans against the loss of the breadwinner's life. Insurance programs operated or required by the states were few, scattered, and inadequate. In the private sector—notably in the railroad industry—pension systems were started and then collapsed.[69] For the most part, then, the responsibility for resolving family economic problems continued to fall on local public welfare departments or on private agencies. The sparcity of the public effort is shown in the data on public welfare expenditures at federal, state, and local levels. In 1913 they totaled only $57 million—1 percent of total government expenditures and only 0.1 percent of the gross national product.[70]

Social Work and the Black Population

Neither the public nor the private sector was responsive to the needs of black families. The overall indifference of white social welfare workers to black problems was demonstrated by the thrust of interests of the Charity Organization and Settlement House Movements, those movements that had taken the lead in social welfare. In 1905, the year in which W.E.B. Du Bois and his followers met at Niagara Falls to consider legal solutions to Negro problems, an entire issue of *Charities and the Commons* was devoted to "The Negroes in the Cities of the North."[71] In 1909 and in 1910 *The Survey* gave the news of the first and second national Negro conferences, at which the National Association for the Advancement of Colored People was organized.[72] In 1913 *The Survey* carried a special collection of articles on the status of negroes.[73]

The primary interest of Charity Organizations, however, was not in blacks, not in their deprivation or segregation as factors requiring broad social reform. Nonetheless, their emphasis on character reform might have helped fuel public discussions of the black's ability to function in a civilized society. In the 1905 examination of blacks in the cities of the North, for example, the famous anthropologist Franz Boas said:

> There is every reason to believe that the Negro when given facility and opportunity will be perfectly able to fill the duties of citizenship as well as his white neighbor. It may be that he will not produce as many great men as the white race and that his average achievement will not quite reach the level of the average achievement of the white race, but there will be endless numbers who will be able to outrun their white competitors, and who will do better than the defectives whom we permit to drag down and to retard the healthy children of our public schools.[74]

Such interest in the plight of blacks as might have developed from direct contact was stifled by the relatively few blacks in the caseloads of Charity Organization Societies. Again, the small number of blacks in the North was partially responsible. In Chicago in 1900, for example, blacks numbered 108,000 in a total population of 1,698,000. They ranked tenth among the city's ethnic groups.[75] The black population did, of course, have major social welfare problems, and in 1910 the National Urban League was established to help with those problems, as well as to promote interracial cooperation.

Settlement house workers were more geared to social change. But they, too, tended to lump the problems of blacks with those of immigrant groups and then to expend their energies on the latter. Among the leaders and allies of the Settlement House Movement, however, were those who recognized the problem as a prohibition of common rights to a particular group of Americans. Louise de Koven Bowen, Sophenisba Breckenridge, and others spoke out in opposition to discrimination and prejudice that held minorities responsible for the economic and social inferiority to which they had been condemned. Florence Kelley and Lillian H. Wald were among those who gathered for the first meeting of the National Committee on the Negro held in New York on May 31, 1909. Jane Addams was among a group of distinguished white reformers who joined Du Bois and the Niagara group in founding the National Association for the Advancement of Colored People. When antiblack discrimination surfaced at the Progressive party's presidential convention of 1912, Miss Addams debated leaving. Her decision to remain suggests again the tenor of the times. The party's nominee, Theodore Roosevelt, eventually lost the election, partly perhaps because his having entertained Booker T. Washington at the White House dashed all hope of gaining votes in the solid South.

The sparcity of governmental programs for blacks and for whites and the overall absence of a sense of responsibility for helping families meet the risks of industrial living demonstrate how little acceptance there was of societal causation of family problems. Indeed, in official circles the nineteenth-century belief still held. Family problems were indicative of the deviant family, the family that was unable and unwilling to make use of its own potential for taking advantage of opportunities offered so abundantly by society. Unquestionably, a great deal had been accomplished as America's attention shifted to the war in Europe. Nevertheless, the amount of reform activity should not obscure the fact that basic inequities remained intact and basic needs unmet.

The End of Reform

The end of World War I did not see a return to reform activity. The years between the close of the war and the depression of the 1930s were a time of peace during which many Americans achieved individual prosperity. They found it through credit and installment buying and through participation in the glittering promises of speculation. They did not concern themselves with the problems of those brushed aside by society's advances or with the obvious abuse of power and influence by those who led the way in speculative activity. Despite the recession of 1921, urban standards of living moved up. Booming profits, high levels of employment, and rising real wages meant that Americans felt able to purchase and enjoy a flood of new products—cars, radios, home electricity, motion pictures, silk stockings. There was new life in the doctrine of laissez faire and a renewed belief that what was good for business was good for the nation. The solution to poverty did not lie in corporate regulation, minimum wages, social insurance, or public welfare, but rather in providing an atmosphere that was encouraging to business.

Americans were determined to believe assurances offered by President Hoover in his inaugural address:

> We in America today are nearer to the final triumph over poverty than ever before in the history of any land. The poorhouse is vanishing among us. We have not yet reached the goal, but given a chance . . . we shall soon with the help of God be in sight of the day when poverty will be banished from this nation.[76]

At the close of the war, it became clear that the era of the reform coalition had come to an end and that a new era of professionalization of social work had begun. The change seems attributable to a number of factors. The war itself had wrought havoc among social work leaders who, prior to the events leading to the country's involvement, had in the main counted themselves pacifists. Jane Addams was a leader in pacifist causes. Her membership on the Platform Committee of the Progressive party in 1912 was an effort to further specific social goals despite her disagreement with the party's stand in regard to war and defense.[77] World War I of necessity split those who could not abandon a lifetime's philosophical stance from those who supported the war and saw this support as serving their country in a time of crisis. The Russian Revolution effected a further split in the reform spirit of social workers; some moved closer to revolutionary positions, some moved further away from an interest in social action. All were subject to the threatening atmosphere created by the investigations and raids of U.S. Attorney General Mitchell Palmer. The wartime and postwar fear of subversive activity, sparking a demand for law and order, led to severe political repression, to expulsion of radical aliens, and, in turn, to hostility toward expressions of need for political change or political redress. Emphasis shifted to personality reform, as psychoanalysis—the work of Sigmund Freud—offered a new professional direction for social workers and social work education.

The push for social reform was further dissipated by the stemming of the flow of immigrants. The increase in immigration during the early years of the twentieth century, with masses of immigrants coming from Eastern Europe at a time of anarchy and revolution there and of labor unrest and wartime preparation here, had stimulated efforts for social reform and socialization. Severe legal restrictions caused the numbers to drop dramatically and almost disappear during the late 1920s. This cessation of immigration and of the needs associated with immigrants now lessened the priority of efforts for social reform.

The prosperity of the 1920s—with its surge of economic growth and affluence accompanied by the hope for the imminent disappearance of poverty—came on top of the seeming achievement of many of the goals of the reform movement and decreased the pressure for further social legislation. In actuality, the reform spirit of the agencies regulating business was often reversed by administrative practices; new political bosses arose to negotiate the ballot reforms, and much of the social legislation passed by the states was thrown out by the courts. The moral fervor, the Social Gospelism, that pervaded the Progressive Movement shifted to the drive against alcoholic beverages. The success of Prohibition became a crowning moral victory.

With social reform abandoned, character reform was revived as an orientation toward people in need. Emil Frankel's *Poor Relief in Pennsylvania*, a statewide survey published in 1925, demonstrated renewed suspicion of public relief and of relief recipients. In a report that generally attacked historic fears of public welfare, Frankel supported the significance of professional social work service, if only to allay the fear that public aid would be considered a right. Frankel wrote:

> Outdoor relief without constructive service can lead only to increasing dependency because while a certain portion of the families receiving relief may pull themselves out of a rut with the aid of the grants, a good many will not. . . .
> A good many have the feeling that inasmuch as the poor fund is raised through public taxation they have a right to demand relief and are entitled to it

as a matter of course. And a good many families feel that although they may not be in need of relief they can see no reason why they should not get it when other families do.[78]

Public and voluntary orientations toward relief giving—especially toward public relief—seemed to have changed little since the inception of the Charity Organization in 1877. The views and foreboding of Frankel, a public official, were not unlike those of Josephine Shaw Lowell, who had argued in 1890 that public relief should be given only in cases of extreme distress, "when starvation is imminent." The refuge from pauperism, according to Mrs. Lowell, was self-support or help provided by private sources.[79] The similarity in their views is probably not surprising when one considers the 1918 appeal of Francis McLean, director of the American Association for Organizing Charities, that member agencies aid "in the socialization [i.e., professionalization] of both staff and methods of work of . . . public family social work agencies."[80] Not until 1921 was membership in the Association extended to public agencies, and their joining was indicative of a common voluntary/public social welfare viewpoint.

The Social Welfare of Veterans

As in past periods, veterans escaped the overall diminution of social welfare entitlements and benefits. Armed forces participants in World War II numbered 4,744,000.[81] Prior to the outbreak of war in 1914, the chief benefits being received by veterans and their families were pensions, which were being paid at an annual rate of $174 million. The war brought about an enormous expansion of benefits and services, first to attract enlistees, later to compensate veterans and their families for services rendered.

On September 2, 1914, only one month after the declaration of war in Europe, Congress passed the War Risk Insurance Act, insuring enlistees in the merchant marines against the hazards of submarine warfare. In 1917 President Wilson appointed a Council of National Defense to review and make recommendations in regard to veterans' benefits. The Council's report, incorporated shortly after into law, introduced a new concept: the offer of readjustment and rehabilitation services, along with monetary benefits. The new package of benefits and services included:

1. Compulsory allotments and allowances to families of soldiers, paid for by the soldiers themselves and by the government.
2. A system of voluntary insurance against death and total disability.
3. Medical and surgical hospital treatment, as well as prosthetic appliances for those injured in the line of duty.
4. Vocational rehabilitation services for injured veterans who could not resume prewar occupations.

The close of the war, on November 11, 1918, compelled further consideration of veterans' benefits. Not only had an enormous number of Americans served in the armed forces, but a large number—116,000—had died and an even greater number—204,000—had been wounded. By mid-1920 the Public Health Service had increased its total available beds to 11,639 in 52 hospitals. A year later the use of available beds in army and navy hospitals and in National Homes for Disabled Volunteer Soldiers was also authorized. The necessarily rapid expansion of in-hospital services to meet the needs of wounded veterans helped clarify the returning veterans' need for outpatient and nonmedical services. The urgency of the need also pointed up the extent to which veterans' benefits were fragmented by the historical delegation of responsibility for benefits among the Bureau of War Risk Insurance, the Rehabilitation Division of the Federal Board for Vocational Education, the Public Health Service, and the armed services themselves.

Early in 1921 President Harding appointed the Dawes Commission to devise a program for the immediate and future needs of ex-servicemen "to the end that the intention of Congress to give the full measure of justice to ex-servicemen may be adequately, promptly, and generously met." The Commission's report concluded that "no emergency of war itself is greater than is the emergency which confronts the Nation in its duty to care for those disabled in its service and now neglected."

The new Congress, which convened on April 11, 1921, took up consideration of the Commission's report and incorporated most of its recommendations in Public Law No. 47, passed on August 9, 1921. The Commission's most important recommendation, the creation of a single entity to administer veterans' affairs, resulted in the establishment of the Veterans' Bureau. The Bureau brought together most veterans' benefits,* including medical care, insurance payments, and vocational rehabilitation services.

A still further expansion of benefits for veterans occurred in 1924, when Congress made hospital services available for honorably discharged veterans with non-service-connected disabilities. The recommendation for this particular benefit had been submitted jointly by the director of the Veterans' Bureau, the American Legion, the Disabled American Veterans, and the Veterans of Foreign Wars to the House Committee on World War Veterans' Legislation. The enactment of this law highlighted the continuing, enlarging interest that Congress and the American people had in providing special consideration for the needs of veterans. Additionally, the 1924 enactment demonstrated the strength of the constituencies organized to advance and to protect the social welfare rights of this particularly "worthy" group of Americans.

The Professionalization of Social Work

No such constituencies as supported veterans' rights—neither the Charity Organization nor the Settlement House Movement—stood ready to support public relief giving as a major requirement for the maintenance of family welfare. In voluntary social welfare as well as in corporate management the 1920s were years of bureaucratization and professionalization. For Charity Organization Societies and for Settlements, "scientific philanthropy" had led to internal organizational changes paralleling the managerial changes of corporate enterprise. The developing of supervision, of supervisors accountable for the successful operation of professional workers, was a further example of internal adherence to structural authority. Beyond that, Charity Organization Societies were largely responsible for the formation of Councils of Social Agencies accountable for social welfare planning and of Federated Funds that undertook "effective economy" in funding the social welfare establishment.[82]

The definition of "scientific philanthropy" was broadened to encompass developments in helping methodology. The failure of friendly visiting, the hiring of paid agents, and, finally, the emergence of social workers were sequential steps in the search for techniques to deal with the variety of situations uncovered by individualized investigations of families. The body of techniques that were codified in Mary Richmond's *Social Diagnosis*, pub-

*Not including pensions of the pre—World War I veterans.

lished in 1917, further explicated in *What Is Social Casework?*, published in 1922, and enriched by the newly discovered psychological theories of Freud, established casework as a major methodology of social work. Casework represented a therapeutic model of professional service. In addition, the development of casework from friendly visiting, at a time when these Charity Organization societies were relinquishing responsibility for social reform, not only reawakened an old image of the rich helping the poor but also strengthened the view of individual and family responsibility for social and economic problems.

The overriding interest of Charity Organizations in relief, their longtime charity organizing purposes, and their slowness in moving toward an explicit family welfare stance are demonstrated in the successive names given the Societies' national association:

1911: National Association of Societies for Organizing Charity
1912: American Association of Societies for Organizing Charity
1917: American Association for Organizing Charity
1919: American Association for Organizing Family Social Work
1930: Family Welfare Association of America
1946: Family Service Association of America

Not until 1919, when the era of professionalization had begun to take hold, did the Association's name include the word "family": American Association for Organizing Family Social Work. Not until 1930, with the adoption of Family Welfare Association of America as its name, did the title suggest an aggressive force for the welfare of families. This slow evolution of purpose from charity organization to social work organization to family welfare can be traced through a relatively cursory perusal of the *Proceedings of the National Conference of Charities and Corrections* (1880–1929) for the contributions of Charity Organization leaders. Particularly striking in the *Proceedings* is the extreme fragmentation of topics discussed. There is limited concern with the family as a unit or with the interaction between family life and social institutions.

The Settlement Movement shifted to its own brand of professionalism. Social reform activity diminished as an area of functional responsibility and "social group work," a methodological approach to helping through recreational and educational activities, became the core of Settlement House programming. The extent of the shift was indicated by George Bellamy of Cleveland's Hiram House in 1914, when he addressed the National Conference on the use of recreational programs by neighborhood centers to help neighborhood residents maintain community control and strengthen family life. "It is far better," he said, "for the city to throw the responsibility of self-support and self-improvement upon the people themselves than to hire at great expense . . . others to entertain the community. We need a recreation by the people, not, for the people."[83] In 1926 Mary K. Simkhovitch addressed the National Federation of Settlements on Settlement goals for the "next third of a century." She argued that Settlements had "turned the social welfare corner" and were "launched on the larger task of social education" in an effort to democratize and civilize industrial society by popularizing art and developing the creative instinct.[84] A far cry from social reform!

1. Herbert Hoover, *The New Day* (Stanford, Calif.: Stanford University Press, 1928), p. 16.
2. S. E. Forman, *The Rise of American Commerce and Industry* (New York: Century, 1927), p. 369.

3. U.S. Department of Commerce, Bureau of the Census, *Historical Statistics of the United States: Colonial Times to 1957* (Washington, D.C.: Government Printing Office, 1960), p. 414 (hereafter cited as *Historical Statistics*).

4. Forman, op. cit., p. 442.

5. *Historical Statistics*, p. 139.

6. Ibid., p. 14.

7. U.S., Bureau of the Census, *Fourteenth Census of the United States: 1920*, vol. 3, p. 15, and *Fifteenth Census of the United States: 1930*, vol. 2, p. 27.

8. Forman, op. cit., p. 439.

9. *Historical Statistics*, p. 14.

10. An excellent survey and analysis of the growth of concentration in American industry may be found in Arthur R. Burns, *The Decline of Competition* (New York: McGraw-Hill, 1936).

11. U.S. Commission on Industrial Relations, *Final Report* (Washington, D.C.: Government Printing Office, 1915), p. 8.

12. U.S. Bureau of the Census, *Sixteenth Census of the United States: 1940, Comparative Occupation Statistics for the United States, 1870 to 1940*, p. 93.

13. Robert Hunter, *Poverty* (New York: Grossett & Dunlap, 1904), pp. 2–7, 56–65, 76–88, 96–97, 350–351. Reprinted in Roy Lubove, ed., *Poverty and Social Welfare in the United States* (New York: Holt, Rinehart & Winston, 1972), pp. 7–18.

14. John A. Ryan, *A Living Wage: Its Ethical and Economic Aspects* (New York: Macmillan, 1910), pp. 123–177. Father Ryan estimated the minimum "living wage" at over $900 for the large Eastern cities.

15. *Historical Statistics*, p. 278.

16. Justice Miller, Supreme Court Decision, 16 Wallace 36, 1873.

17. G. W. Cable, "The Freedman's Case in Equity," *The Century Magazine*, January 1885. Quoted in Samuel Eliot Morrison and Henry Steele Commanger, *The Growth of the American Republic* (New York: Oxford University Press, 1962), p. 90.

18. *Plessy* v. *Ferguson*, 163 U.S. 537 (1896).

19. Imperial Wizard Hiram W. Evans, "The Klan of Tomorrow." Quoted in William Miller, *A New History of the United States* (New York: Braziller, 1958), pp. 355–356.

20. Booker T. Washington, "The Atlanta Cotton Exposition Address of 1895." Quoted in *Up From Slavery*, in *The Booker T. Washington Papers*, ed. Louis R. Harlan (Urbana: University of Illinois Press, 1972) 1:333.

21. Lillian Brandt, "The Make-up of Negro City Groups," *Charities and the Commons* 15 (October 7, 1905): 7.

22. *Historical Statistics*, p. 46. New York, Pennsylvania, Ohio, Illinois, and Michigan accounted for 78 percent of this.

23. Ibid., pp. 409, 73.

24. Sidney Lens, *Poverty: America's Enduring Paradox* (New York: Thomas Y. Crowell, 1969), pp. 209–210.

25. See, for example, Ida M. Tarbell, *The History of the Standard Oil Company* (New York: McClure, Phillips, 1904); Ray Stannard Baker, "The Right to Work," *McClure's Magazine*, 20 (January 1903): 323–326; Samuel Hopkins Adams, "Fraud Medicines Own Up," *Collier's* 48 (January 20, 1912).

26. See, for example, Lincoln Steffens, *The Shame of the Cities* (New York: McClure, Phillips, 1904); David Graham Phillips, "The Treason of the Senate," *Cosmopolitan* 40 (March 1906): 603–610.

27. Arthur P. Miles, *An Introduction to Public Welfare* (Washington, D.C.: Heath, 1947), p. 124.

28. Theodore Roosevelt, "Reform Through Social Work," *McClure's Magazine* 26 (March 1901): 448–454.

29. Arthur S. Link, *American Epoch: A History of the United States Since the 1890's* (New York: Knopf, 1955), p. 68.

30. Lens, op. cit., p. 212.

31. Charles Faulkner, "Twentieth Century Alignments for the Promotion of Social Order," *Proceedings, NCCC: 1900*, pp. 2–6.

32. Mary E. Richmond, "The Family and the Social Worker," *Proceedings, NCCC: 1908*, pp. 76–79.

33. *Sixteenth Census: 1940*, pp. 93, 100.

34. *The Child Labor Bulletin*, vol. 3, no. 1, May 1914 (New York: National Child Labor Committee).

35. Owen R. Lovejoy, "Report of the Committee on Standards of Living and Labor," *Proceedings, NCCC: 1912*, p. 386.

36. U.S. 37 stat. 79. The Act establishing the Children's Bureau, approved April 7, 1912.

37. *Hammer* v. *Dagenhart* 247 U.S. Reports 251, 268 (June 1918). To be found in Grace Abbott, *The Child and the State* (Chicago: University of Chicago Press, 1938), pp. 495–506.

38. "State Child-Labor Standards, January 1, 1930," a chart prepared by the U.S. Department of Labor, Children's Bureau, and reprinted by permission of the Federal Board for Vocational Education (Washington, D.C.: Government Printing Office, 1930), chart no. 2.

39. *Fifteenth Census: 1930*, vol. 2, pp. 1180–1196.

40. Lovejoy, op. cit., p. 383.

41. Edward C. Kirkland, *A History of American Economic Life* (New York: Appleton-Century-Crofts, 1969), p. 409.

42. Paul H. Douglas, *Real Wages in the United States, 1890–1926* (Boston: Houghton Mifflin, 1930), p. 208.

43. George Soule, *American Economic History* (New York: Dryden Press, 1957), p. 277.

44. Douglas, op. cit., pp. 112, 114.

45. "Discussion on Charity Organization," *Proceedings, NCCC: 1888*, p. 420.

46. Alice Stone Blackwell, "Editorial," *The Woman's Journal*, April 11, 1911.

47. U.S. Department of Labor, Women's Bureau, *Handbook on Women Workers*, Bulletin No. 294, (Washington D.C.: Government Printing Office, 1969); and *Historical Statistics*, op. cit., pp. 132–133.

48. Annie Marion Mac Lean, *Wage-Earning Women* (New York: Macmillan, 1919), p. 178.

49. Even a small number of references to the literature of the Progressive Era confirm the nature of special concern for women. See John A. Ryan, "A Minimum Wage and Minimum Wage Boards: With Special Reference to Immigrant Labor and Woman Labor," *Proceedings, NCCC: 1910*, pp. 457–475; Ann Garton Spencer, "What Machine Dominated Industry Means in Relation to Woman's Work: The Need for New Training and Apprenticeship for Girls," *Proceedings, NCCC: 1910*, pp. 202–211; Florence Kelley, "The Family and the Woman's Wage," *Proceedings, NCCC: 1909*, pp. 118–121; Mary Anderson, "Women's Work and Wages: The Women's Bureau and Standards of Work," *Proceedings, NCCC: 1921*, pp. 285–287.

50. Douglas, op. cit., p. 384.

51. Ibid.

52. An excellent review of this history may be found in Clarke A. Chambers, *Seedtime of Reform* (Minneapolis: University of Minnesota Press, 1963), pp. 151–182.

53. Abbott, op. cit., 2:395.

54. Ibid., 2:332.

55. Clarke A. Chambers, *Paul U. Kellogg and the Survey* (Minneapolis: University of Minnesota Press, 1971), p. 36.

56. Ibid.

57. Special message by the president of the United States to the Senate and House of Representatives at the conclusion of the White House Conference Meeting of 1909. Reprinted in *Dependent and Neglected Children*, Report of the Committee on Socially Handicapped—Dependency and Neglect—of the White House Conference on Child Health and Protection (New York: Appleton-Century, 1933), p. 56.

58. Alice Higgins, "Helping Widows To Bring Up Citizens," *Proceedings, NCCC: 1910*, p. 140.

59. Mary E. Richmond, "Public Pensions to Widows—Discussion," *Proceedings, NCCC: 1912*, pp. 492–493.

60. Ibid.

61. Frederic Almy, "Public Pensions to Widows: Experiences and Observations Which Lead Me to Oppose Such a Law," *Proceedings, NCCC: 1912*, p. 482.

62. Ibid.

63. Abbott, op. cit., 2:229.

64. U.S. Department of Labor, Children's Bureau, *Administration of Mother's Aid in Ten Localities,* prepared by Mary F. Bogue in Children's Bureau Publication No. 184 (Washington, D.C.: Government Printing Office, 1928), p. 4.

65. Ibid., pp. 25–26.

66. C. C. Carstens, "Discussion" of Emma O. Lundberg's "The Present Status of Mother's Pension Administration," *Proceedings, NCSW: 1921,* pp. 230–240. Mr. Carsten's remarks are to be found on p. 240.

67. Mary F. Bogue, *Administration of Mother's Aid in Ten Localities: With Special Reference to Health, Housing, Education and Recreation.* Children's Bureau Publication No. 184, (Washington, D.C.: Government Printing Office, 1928), p. 5.

68. Ibid., p. 20.

69. J. S. Parker, *Social Security Reserves* (Washington, D.C.: American Council on Public Affairs, 1942).

70. *Historical Statistics,* pp. 139, 723.

71. "The Negroes in the Cities of the North," *Charities and the Commons* 15 (October 7, 1905).

72. W. E. Burghardt Du Bois, "National Committee on the Negro," *The Survey* 22 (June 12, 1909): 407–408, and "National Negro Conference," *The Survey,* 24 (April 23, 1910): 124.

73. *The Survey* 29 (February 1, 1913): 567–581.

74. Franz Boas, "The Negro and the Demands of Modern Life: Ethnic and Anatomical Considerations," *Charities and the Commons* 15 (October 7, 1905): 2.

75. Steven Diner, "Chicago Social Workers and Blacks in the Progressive Era," *Social Service Review* 44 (December 1970): 393–410.

76. Herbert Hoover, op. cit., p. 16.

77. Jane Addams, *The Second Twenty Years at Hull House* (New York: Macmillan, 1930), pp. 10–48.

78. Emil Frankel, *Poor Relief in Pennsylvania: A State-Wide Survey of Pennsylvania* (Commonwealth of Pennsylvania: By the Public Board of Welfare, 1925), pp. 65–66.

79. Josephine Shaw Lowell, "The Economic and Moral Effects of Public Outdoor Relief," *Proceedings, NCCC: 1890,* p. 82.

80. Margaret E. Rich, *A Belief in People: A History of Family Social Work* (New York: Family Service Association of America, 1956), p. 74.

81. All material dealing with the expansion of benefits to veterans in the Progressive and predepression eras is based on information to be found in U.S. Congress, House Committee Print No. 4. *Medical Care of Veterans,* 90th Cong., 1st sess., April 17, 1967. Printed for the use of the Committee on Veterans' Affairs.

82. Roy Lubove, *The Professional Altruist: The Emergence of Social Work as a Career, 1880–1930* (New York: Atheneum, 1969).

83. George A. Bellamy, "The Culture of the Family from the Standpoint of Recreation," *Proceedings, NCCC: 1914,* pp. 104–105.

84. Arthur Kennedy, ed., *Settlement Goals for the Next Third of a Century: A Symposium* (Boston: National Federation of Settlements, 1926), p. 45.

85. Porter R. Lee, "Social Work: Cause and Function," *Proceedings, NCSW: 1929,* p. 20.

From Charity to Enterprise:
The Development of American Social Work in a Market Economy
Stanley Wenocur
Michael Reisch

The Earliest Definitions of the Social Work Commodity

INTRODUCTION

The economic crisis of the 1890s stimulated a reappraisal of prevailing attitudes toward the "Social Question." By traditional standards, a large number of the new poor were undeserving: the products of mental instability, environmental conditions, or racial and ethnic inheritance. Old-style charity was designed to reinforce the work ethic, but how could it affect this population? Ironically, those who sought to preserve the status quo and those who sought to reform it both searched for means to harness the forces of "progress." Given the climate in which this search occurred, it was not surprising that defenders and critics of American society embraced technology "as a principle of order and preserver of union, [as] the harbinger of peace and guardian of prosperity" (Kasson, 1976: 186).

While corporate and political leaders applied technology to strengthen their control over the direction of society, social workers compensated for their lack of scientific theory by creating a new technology based on a generation of practical experience and the theoretical formulations of the other professions with whom they came into regular contact. This integration of a "technological approach" into what had been viewed as a practical field moved social work into the economic and political mainstream in terms of the problems it addressed, the clients it served, and the institutional forms it created. In other words, the definition of the service commodity as "social treatment" made social work more attractive to potential sponsors, and, ultimately, to the larger pool of potential consumers. While the economic and political forces that shaped these developments were already in place by the early 1890s, the emergence of casework as the primary form of social work practice and the professional dominance of its East Coast practitioners were by no means foregone conclusions.

The antecedents of social casework were the friendly visiting and scientific charity practiced by the Charity Organization Societies (COS). Friendly visiting—a peculiar synthesis of evangelical community service, positivism, Social Darwinism, and social control—reflected the views of social philosophers like William Graham Sumner and corporate leaders like Andrew Carnegie. Scientific charity helped shape the evolution of the social work profession by defining social work in the language of science, order, and efficiency which was compatible with parallel organizational efforts by U.S. industry.

The COS flourished because they claimed to offer solutions to previously intractable individual and social problems, couched in terms of the ideology of the dominant classes they sought as sponsors (Boyer, 1978). By emphasizing science and secularism, the COS broke in significant ways from the tradition of U.S. charitable provision as practiced earlier by church-affiliated charities, urban missions, and especially the Association for the Improvement of the Condition of the Poor, or AICP.[1] COS leaders, therefore, attempted to fuse the traditional American emphasis on individualism and individual responsibility with the application of the scientific method and a business-oriented philosophy. This fusion had the "latent function of further individualizing the stigma of poverty" through the primary utilization of the casework approach (Waxman, 1977: 83).

In a speech to the business community of Philadelphia in 1899, Mary Richmond (then secretary of the Philadelphia Society for Organizing Charity) tried to "sell" the COS definition of social work to potential sponsors by validating the business community's view of the poor: "I know that there are a great many people born lazy who will never do one stroke more of the world's work than direct necessity forces them to." [Charitable expenditures are] "hopelessly wasted . . . encourage idleness, vice, crime and disease. . . . Heretofore, we have encouraged the lowest and worst [characteristics of man], let us now try to arouse the better instincts of his nature: Teach him industry, sewing, cleanliness, self-control" (Richmond, 1899a: 17).

Firm in the belief that the scientific organization of charitable work represented an enlightened mode of social intervention which would benefit both the poor and their benefactors, the COS developed as their guiding principles the enhancement of the productivity of the individual and the refusal "to support any except those it [could] control" (Lowell, 1889: 68). They implemented these principles by restricting access to services and by giving clients no voice in the determination of the outcome goals of service (Archives of New York COS; Bolin, 1973: 6).

Many supporters of the COS movement also felt that organized charity represented "the real answer to the Socialistic and Communistic theories now being energetically taught to the people"

(Kellogg, 1880). It is significant, therefore, for the development of the social work profession that it was largely through the COS that organized social work first began the self-conscious process of professionalization.

Who Were the Earliest Social Workers?

Both the men and women of the COS came from roughly similar urban, upper-class backgrounds and possessed comparable educational credentials. Although well educated, some male COS volunteers were "leisured," i.e., gracefully unemployed; most were lawyers or retired businessmen. Paid agents tended to be former teachers or ministers. Most were over 30 and married, although a higher proportion of men were single than in other professions. Their primary motivation for engaging in social work activities appears to have been a sense of noblesse oblige, in a few instances stemming from their family's history of community service (Becker, 1968; Rauch, 1975).

In their early years, these men dominated the COS as board members, directors, supervisors, and paid agents, while women comprised virtually the entire corps of "friendly visitors" and unpaid office staff (Rauch, 1976). Although they earned less than male professionals in other fields, male COS employees were paid the highest salaries within social work (Rauch, 1975). Recent evidence also suggests that the paternalistic and often punitive approach of the COS was also the product of male domination and class bias (Cumbler, 1980; Rauch, 1976; Vaile, "The Denver Bureau of Public Welfare," n.d.). While many women in the COS deeply resented their subordinate role and actively fought to overcome persistent male dominance (Rauch, 1975), other women leaders regretted the lack of more such men. Josephine Shaw Lowell, for example, remarked, "What we need are more men of leisure with the tradition of public service like so many of the nobility and gentry of England. Our young men, those that we catch, are very good, but usually too busy" (Stewart, 1911: 129).

Women COS volunteers tended to come from what we now term "two-career" families, in which their fathers often held political office and their mothers were unpaid community or social activists. Such families not only encouraged their daughters to seek a college education, but instilled in them the value of education directed at a social purpose and the importance of the woman's role beyond that of wife and mother (Blumberg, 1966; Conway, 1969; Goldmark, 1953; Huggins, 1971; Levine, 1971; Linn, 1935; Wise, 1935). In addition, these families tended to be more strongly influenced by religious values, particularly those associated with British Christian Socialism and the Social Gospel movement in the United States. Women in the COS, therefore, embraced both the "mission" aspect of social work and its growing emphasis on scientific philanthropy and innovation. For them, social work was simultaneously cause and career (Becker, 1968; Clark, 1970).

Most women, however, were not drawn to charitable activities by radical social impulses. They were motivated more by a desire to protect families, children, and themselves from the hazards of industrial society than by a wish to carve out a new role for women in that society. Many agreed with Jane Addams that women possessed a unique combination of rationality and intuition which made them especially suited for what she termed a "civilizing mission" (Hymowitz and Weissman, 1978). Even awareness of their own exploitation within organizations like the COS did not "radicalize" such women.

Consequently, the COS reinforced prevailing sexual stereotypes by recruiting men for executive positions, paying them far higher salaries than women in comparable roles, and firing married women as bad examples to their peers (Archives of NY COS; Archives, Philadelphia Society for Organizing Charity). Only after considerable struggle within the COS and other social work agencies did women begin to occupy a larger share of administrative and supervisory jobs (C. Chambers, 1986; Rauch, 1976; Archives of the National Federation of Settlements; Kessler-Harris, 1982; Hymowitz & Weissman, 1978; Becker, 1968). In order to do so, women had to break the pattern of traditional role behavior and imitate the practices of men, including their social prejudices. At least one woman leader in the COS movement, Zilpha Smith, joined male colleagues like Joseph Lee and Jeffrey Brackett in supporting the openly anti-Semitic work of the Immigrant Restriction League (Becker, 1968; Leiby, 1962).

Early social work leaders retained such views because they seldom consulted with representatives of the populations for whom services were created, and because their professional lives were every bit as insulated as their personal lives. Their ranks were largely homogeneous, with few non-Protestants and virtually no members of racial minority groups admitted. The few outsiders admitted to leadership circles tended to represent sectarian agencies which attempted to apply COS principles and philosophy in their own communities.

It is not surprising, therefore, that many poor Jews, Catholics, and blacks regarded the services which these agencies developed as alien and threatening and turned instead to self-help organizations such as the Irish Emigrant Society, *Die Deutsche Gesellschaft*, the Hebrew Benevolent Society, and the White Rose Home for Girls (Handlin, 1959; Becker, 1968; Boroff, 1975; O'Grady, 1931; Karp, 1976; Hymowitz & Weissman, 1978). Through the 1870s, in fact, most of the social services provided to new immigrants were delivered by voluntary sectarian and self-help organizations, serving as many as 50% of new immigrants immediately upon their arrival (Riis, 1890). Their provision, unfortunately, was hampered by the limited resources available even to the well-off members of ethnic communities and by the distrust, fear, and mutual strangeness which existed between "old" and "new" immigrant groups. This problem was especially pronounced among the small, urban black elite who founded organizations like the Urban League early in the twentieth century (Carlton, 1982).

Unlike the COS, self-help organizations provided concrete services such as employment counseling, material relief (especially to newcomers, widows, and orphans), education, social supports, and burial funds. They also served as institutional means to resist the explicit and subtle attacks on immigrant culture and tradition by the public schools and organized churches. Many immigrants soon recognized that the price of "Americanization" was the loss of their unique heritage, their language and customs (Letters to *New York Jewish World*, 1901–12). Self-help organizations strengthened ethnic cohesion through recreational, educational, and social activities. They provided a foundation for the development of ethnically based trade unions, business associations, and political parties. In short, they served as an anchor, providing a modicum of material and psychological security in the dangerous and unpredictable environment in which the immigrants were attempting to survive and prosper. Their presence made the creation of a cohesive social work enterprise more difficult for the COS.

PROFESSIONAL VERSUS VOLUNTARY WORK

Another persistent problem in the field of organized charities was the role differentiation between paid staff and volunteers. A continuing tension existed between the ideology of charitable agencies, which exalted volunteer status, and the reality of service delivery, which required education and expertise particularly in the areas of administration and supervision. Shortly after the Civil War, as paid workers became more conscious of their own professional aspirations, such tensions heightened, and the boards of charitable agencies reacted defensively to the demands of paid workers for salary increases and sanction of their superiority over volunteer staff (AICP, Minutes, Board of Managers, June 9, 1866). Nevertheless, the increase in social distress in the 1870s compelled charitable organizations to rehire paid workers, who soon reestablished their dominance of the agencies' relief distribution activities (deForest, 1904; Becker, 1961; Schuyler, 1915).

As the COS replaced "old-style" charitable agencies, paid staff—usually the district agents—were restricted to administrative functions, fundraising, and recruitment, and were regarded as the "handmaidens" of the friendly visitors who made the final decisions about cases. The primary standard by which paid staff were measured was "whether [they] increase[ed] or diminish[ed] the amount of fruitful volunteer work in the community" (Devine, 1898; Rauch, 1975.) In the aftermath of the depression of the 1890s, however, COS leaders realized that volunteer friendly visitors could not adequately cope with the extensive intellectual demands of their work or the charitable organizations' growing need for efficiency in operation, and they increased their professional staff by as much as one-third (Kusmer, 1973; Levin, 1969). At the same time, other socioeconomic and cultural changes further diminished the pool of potential volunteers. This strengthened the position of paid workers within the COS, weakened the position of other organizations in the charitable field, especially those which were church-sponsored and relied exclusively on volunteers, and enhanced the attractiveness of public welfare activities in which all staff were salaried (Richmond, 1896e; C. J. Davis, 1901b).

Within a few years, the importance of volunteers in social work, especially friendly visitors, rapidly declined (Gutridge, 1903; Folks, 1893a; Richmond, Davis, op.cit.). By 1907, more than 50% of the major COS had abandoned the use of friendly visitors entirely (Jones and Herrick, 1976). Soon volunteers were restricted to carefully defined and supervised activities and, in many cities, did little more than routine office work. By 1917, their number declined to 25% of that of the peak years of voluntary activity (Kusmer, 1973; Becker, 1964).

Once the dominant position of paid workers was secured, the issue of wages became a real concern. Data on social workers' salaries at this time are sparse and widely varied due to the indistinct definition of the boundaries of the social work enterprise and, perhaps above all, because social-work wage scales reflected the disparity in wages which existed throughout the U.S. As the COS and other large social service organizations spread to small and midsize cities and into rural areas, workers were paid according to prevailing rates for the region. These rates were uniformly lower for women. Many workers had caseloads of unmanageable size; virtually all were terribly underpaid, starting as low as $6–8/week. A part-time paid visitor, for example, earned as little as $180/year in some communities, while the annual salary for the (male) Superintendent of Inspection of the New York State Board of Charities ranged from $1,800 to $2,500 (NY Civil Service Records, 1899; letter of Charles S. Fowler, Chief Civil Service Examiner, to Homer Folks, November 25, 1899; unsigned article in *Charities*, April 20, 1901; Robert Treat Paine, 1901; letter of John S. Newbold to H. LaBarre Jayne, July 8, 1902). An inspector for the New York State Board received a starting salary of $1,200/year for men and $900/year for women. This compared favorably to similar posts in other states and to the salaries of paid workers in COS at the time (letter of Meigs V. Crouse, Supt. of Children's Home in Cincinnati, to Folks, July 30, 1903).

The transition of social work from a largely volunteer enterprise to one dominated by paid staff with specialized expertise was by no means smooth. Paid social workers bemoaned the lack of well-trained colleagues and began to push hard for programs which would swell their ranks with better-educated and more-skilled staff. Yet, they recognized the difficulty of recruiting young people because of the low salaries, lack of clear lines of authority within social agencies, and the absence of a clear definition of the purpose and methods of social work (Folks Archives, letters, November 1895—May 1896).

Ironically, many potential sponsors of social work resisted efforts to make charity work more scientific and financially rewarding out of concern that a transformed charitable enterprise would lose the moral attributes of the old charity. In a sense, these tensions indicate the transitional nature of the environment in which social work emerged as a professional enterprise. The efforts social work leaders made in the generation before World War I to define the social work commodity and to recruit new producers and sponsors embody, to a significant degree, an attempt to reconcile these tensions in a manner satisfactory to all parties concerned, just as the social reforms of the Progressive Era "first emerged as a more-or-less conscious effort . . . to stabilize American society" (Ehrenreich, 1985:19).

THE SETTLEMENTS

The other major branch of the social work enterprise in the late nineteenth century was the settlement house movement and its affiliates in such social service agencies as the YMCA and the Salvation Army. Settlement houses practiced a more democratic conception of social work, emphasizing community participation and the link between social services and broader social themes like democracy, equality, and social justice. Settlement work had the quality of a social movement, which was its greatest attraction, especially to young people and social reformers. It was also the source of the settlements' difficulty in establishing credentials as a legitimate branch of professional social work.

Settlement "residences" opened in the late 1880s and early 1890s in urban slums like New York's lower East Side and Chicago's South Side, exhibiting many of the characteristics of secular missions. Early settlements were staffed largely by women from the same class background as their COS counterparts, with similar personal needs, social biases, moral codes, and social goals. Settlement women, however, tended to be better educated than their COS counterparts and less likely to be married (C. Chambers, 1986). To some observers, like Josephine Shaw Lowell, settlement house residents and friendly visitors differed only in the settings in which they labored. Mary Richmond argued, however, that the daily contact of settlement workers with the poor, labor unions, and a broad assortment of domestic radicals, along with their greater receptivity to some of the newer currents in social thought (particularly those which looked to environmental conditions as the source of social problems), transformed their orientation into one with dangerous implications for the field of social work (Boyer, 1978; C. Chambers, 1963).

Influenced by the women who provided the movement's early leadership, particularly Jane Addams, the founder of Hull House in Chicago, settlements created an institutionalized form of self-help for the new urban poor, attempting to meet concrete needs and to socialize the poor into the new industrial order. At the same time, other influential leaders like Florence Kelley, a close friend of Addams, director of the National Consumers League, and the first translator of Friedrich Engels into English, pushed the movement strongly in the direction of institutional change. Kelley recognized that concrete assistance to the immigrant poor needed to be augmented by efforts to alter the physical and social environment which produced so many of their problems (Blumberg, 1966; Conway, 1969; Goldmark, 1953; Levine, 1971; Linn, 1935; Lynd, 1961; Wise, 1935).

Although women like Addams were involved in both aspects of settlement work—for example, she and Lillian Wald, director of the Henry Street Settlement in New York City, were instrumental in creating the Women's Trade Union League in 1903—their conception of the role of settlements as agents for social change was limited by their desire to reduce the level of social conflict and to seek solutions satisfactory to all classes (Addams, 1895; Wald, 1915). Thus, both contemporary and modern commentators have criticized settlements as simplistic undertakings which reflected many of the prejudices of their age (Riis, 1890; Woods & Kennedy, 1910: 430–31; Kessner, 1977: 135–39; Gans, 1964). Nevertheless, the settlements' recognition of the interconnection between the well-being of individuals and the betterment of society, coupled with their advocacy of programs to serve poor and working-class women and children, laid the foundations for the policies of the New Deal and the Great Society (National Association of Social Workers, 1977; Skocpol and Ikenberry, 1982).

In addition, despite Victorian attitudes about sexuality (Addams, 1912a: 22), many settlement leaders shared a deep commitment to feminist causes, such as the promotion of women's suffrage, a viewpoint radical for its day which set them apart from the political mainstream and their more conservative counterparts in social work. This "social feminism" (O'Neill, 1971) provided the basis for cooperation between "liberal" and "radical" settlement workers on such women-centered issues as public health, temperance, pornography, prostitution, and white slavery. Through social feminism, settlement workers became involved in the wider cause of social justice. In fact, for some, "social justice activities became the principal justification for feminism" (O'Neill, 1971: 135).

These cooperative efforts also facilitated the growth of female support networks linking settlement leaders like Addams, Kelley, and Wald to each other and to radicals outside of social work such as Crystal Eastman and Emma Goldman (Cook, 1979). Such networks enabled settlement workers to strengthen their ties with working-class women and to overcome, in part, the social distance created by their disparate class and educational backgrounds (cf. Addams, 1893b). In New York, for example, working-class women enlisted the help and support of Lillian Wald in their union-building drives in order to "lend respectability to a venture otherwise viewed as disreputable" (Banner, 1979).

The feminist orientation of many early social workers strengthened the public's perception of the field as a "women's profession," yet one dominated by women who defied traditional social and cultural norms. This negative impression surfaced during World War I when reform efforts sponsored by women social workers came to national attention and approached enactment into law.[2] To a considerable extent, the conscious professionalizing efforts of social work, especially in its early years, included an attempt to correct this impression in the public mind.

By the early twentieth century, over 100 settlement houses had been established throughout the East and Midwest, 32 in New York State alone. Their work and philosophy challenged many of the basic assumptions of the COS about the political economy and the social environment it had created. The research of Robert Hunter (1904) and Edith Abbott, for example, questioned the prevailing view of poverty as linked to individual behavior and morality and developed the concept of the "public economy" in which government intervention was the ultimate solution to people's social and economic distress (Weisz-Buck, 1982: 5–6, 12).

Few members of the settlement movement, however, had consciously radical or revolutionary intent in their work. Most viewed the consequences of monopoly as *administrative* problems which could be resolved without drastic institutional change. Nevertheless, their work went counter to the complacent view of the United States as a land of boundless opportunity. Old-style charities, in their view, further divided society into classes, increased the number of poor, and made their condition more static (Tucker, 1903). The goals of the new movement would be, instead, "justice, not charity" (deForest, 1901). It was in the potential implications of that quest for justice, if not in its actual achievements, that the settlement house movement represented a threat to the established order.

Settlement Methods

Although settlements borrowed as much as the COS from emerging corporate techniques, fundamental distinctions in focus and methodology appeared early in their development. Mary Richmond noted that settlement workers were more receptive to the progressive social currents of the era, such as the work of Lester Ward and John Dewey in sociology and education, which provided the basis for a synthesis of religious and secular thought (Hofstadter, 1955). Ward's assertions that "class distinctions depend entirely upon environmental conditions and are in no sense due to differences in native capacity" provided a guide for both the service and reform aspects of settlement work (Ward, 1974). Dewey's emphasis on the ability of applied intelligence to transform society and on the social responsibility of intellectuals to apply themselves to that transformation served as an intellectual justification for the moral compulsion many settlement residents felt to do good works (Dewey, 1916; Hofstadter, 1959; J. Chambers, 1980).

By combining the scientific method's emphasis on explanation and prediction with the corporate enterprise's focus on efficiency, settlements "launched a search for systems through which to manage change in an orderly manner" (C. Chambers, 1963; A. Davis, 1967; J. Chambers, 1980: 110–12). This aspect of settlement work was the clearest in its goals and its implementation. What proved far more difficult was the translation of these goals into a comprehensive, unified *method of practice* which would legitimate settlement work as a sphere of activity within the U.S. political economy and enable settlement workers to attract the resources and sponsorship they needed to sustain themselves as a professional enterprise (Powers, 1895: 591).

At first, the eclectic methods of the settlements were a definite asset. By adopting the roles of good neighbor and good citizen (rather than those of philanthropist and reformer), and by promoting these roles in others, settlements exercised considerable influence on the communities in which they were established. This influence ranged from electing good government candidates, to forging ties with organized labor, to educating the middle and upper classes about the nature of urban social problems (Woods, 1901).

Yet the settlements also experienced a variety of early problems, such as a shortage of qualified residents (and concomitant morale difficulties), instability caused by frequent leadership changes, and conflicts with local authorities over issues such as housing codes (Addams, 1910; Wald, 1915). Moreover, the dual role which settlements professed—to broaden the educational and cultural opportunities of the poor and to promote a broader conception of democracy throughout society—did not lend itself easily to a distinct, unique service commodity or a distinct organizational form. In fact, settlement workers viewed "social work"—one of four aspects of their work along with reform efforts, work in rural communities, and visiting nursing—largely in terms of organized clubs and classes offered to the immigrant populations of the neighborhoods in which they were located (Wallach, 1903).

Another major barrier to professional influence was the lack of clarity as to what constituted a "settlement." The term was applied to a range of diverse organizations—university settlements, college settlements, church settlements, and social settlements (Hoy, 1904)—whose objectives ranged from the training of college graduates for social service work, to the delivery of specific services, to attempts "to bring men and women of education into closer relations with the laboring classes in [the] city for their mutual benefit" (Wallach, 1903: 10). In addition, some churches appropriated settlement names to their missions, thereby adding to the confusion (letter of Henry Moskowitz of Downtown Ethical Society in New York *Evening Post*, September 23, 1908).

Shortly after its emergence, therefore, the settlement movement abounded in contradictions. It attempted to provide service *and* to reform existing institutions, to respond to the peculiar cultural currents of a community *and* to promote its own nonsectarian gospel. The movement tried to overcome ethnic and class barriers while holding onto class-based ideals and prejudices. Finally, it strove to establish an alternative sense of justice and democracy through the acquisition of support and sponsorship from the very classes who benefited most from retaining a foothold in the status quo. The consequences of this latter contradiction were, perhaps, the most profound for the movement's future.

Settlement workers even disagreed over what their clarion for justice signified. Robert deForest argued that justice involved some redistribution of resources to combat inequality (1901: 431), with the specific goal of expanding the opportunities of the poor, while Robert Woods stated rather vaguely that settlement work attempted "to get suggestions to bear on procuring a better life in the nation" (quoted in *New York Times*, 1916 n.d.). Although some settlement workers professed socialist sympathies, most favored redistributive efforts which would be made possible by increasing the overall wealth of the country (Tucker), prefiguring modern Keynesian policies.

Nor was there consensus as to what should constitute the practical program and methods of settlement work. Some people defined the settlements' function in terms of "social uplift," including such specific reforms as improved housing, coordination of social service efforts between public and private agencies, expansion of public welfare services, especially in areas of prevention, and the establishment of a broad range of educational, cultural, and recreational activities (Hoy, 1904). Others believed that settlements should focus on shaping public opinion, developing a better general understanding of the social environment, and promoting cooperation between social classes. George Herbert Mead (1907: 110) considered the primary purpose of the settlements not to "fight . . . evils, but [to] determine . . . what evils [exist]; not [to] enforce preferred moral judgments, but [to] form . . . new moral judgments."

Implicit in both views of settlement work was the belief that the implementation of settlement goals would serve the interests of all classes in American society and would create Whitman's "city of friends" (Barnett, 1906: 186–89). In other words, a "community of interest" would exist in which all classes would benefit from the achievement of social justice. Not surprisingly, this community of interest contained many of the major ingredients of the prevailing social philosophy of the age: the importance of education as the basis for expanding economic opportunity, the focus on individual achievement and the role of self-help, and even the identification of social uplift in terms of the Americanization of immigrant groups (Tucker, 1903; Wallach, 1903; deForest, 1901). The latter was precisely how William Alexander Hoy (1904: 4) proposed settlements should "sell" their goals to the general public: "[The Settlement] is the work of America for all who long to become Americans. It is the work of Americans for America. It is an affair of high sentiment. It is equally an affair of conservative, matter-of-fact business."

Thus three approaches appeared within the settlements. One emphasized the delivery of concrete services as a temporary solution to social problems that economic growth would eventually correct (Ward, 1974; Commager, 1967). A second approach expanded the notion of concrete services to include advocacy on behalf of poor women, children, and their families (Addams, 1902; 1908). And a third and most radical approach viewed the social settlement as a vehicle for radical reform of U.S. society and, in some instances, the implementation of revolutionary social goals (Kelley).

By the second decade of the twentieth century, settlement houses also began to move into the cultural arena and to focus increased attention on the development of recreational alternatives to popular attractions of mass culture like the movies and vaudeville (Addams, 1910). This development, which soon transformed the character of settlement work, emerged out of three conflicting motivations. One was a moral reaction, rooted in the values of the Protestant middle and upper classes, to both the substance and form of popular culture. Rather than propose censorship, the Progressive strain within the settlements favored the promotion of more suitable activities for the physical and intellectual betterment of the working classes (whose available leisure hours had increased by 25% between 1900 and 1920) (Addams, 1912b).

A second, contradictory motive was the encouragement of "cultural pluralism" as an alternative to the cultural homogeneity being stressed in public schools and the popular press. The influence of John Dewey and progressive education on the settlements, particularly on Jane Addams, was decisive in this area, especially in the settlements' emphasis on workshops and other "learning by doing" experiences (which also were adopted by social work educators with their early and continuing emphasis on field work).

A final motive stemmed from the efforts of the broad-ranging settlement movement to define a distinct service commodity which it delivered and for which it could obtain the support of economic and political sponsors. As described above, the early years of the settlement movement produced a plethora of activities, ranging from hands-on services to public education to aggressive social reform efforts. None of these activities was distinct enough or attractive enough to powerful sponsors to emerge as a clearly defined area of expertise for settlement workers and, thereby, give them a foothold on the ladder of occupational specialization and control. The growth of organized recreation offered settlements the opportunity to "sell" their services in the marketplace in a manner which was politically acceptable and consistent with the established interest of the settlements in the promotion of education and culture.

By the outbreak of World War I, as Mary Simkhovitch (1926) later noted, settlements were well on their way to entering the social work mainstream by becoming involved in the larger task of social education—a task which was not only popular but also far more conducive to the overall professionalizing efforts of social work (Boyer, 1978: 160ff.).

The Hull-House Tradition and the Contemporary Social Worker: Was Jane Addams Really a Social Worker?

Donald Brieland

JANE ADDAMS' Hull-House, the first settlement house in the Midwest, was founded on September 18, 1889, on Chicago's Near West Side. The Hull mansion, where it all started, was located on the edge of a tenement district and now is surrounded by the campus of the University of Illinois at Chicago. The mansion and the residents' dining hall have become a museum.

"Museum" might suggest that the Hull-House centennial celebration, which began last year and continues until June 1990, is a memorial to the artistic legacy of Jane Addams. Not so. Her contribution was to improve the lives of people primarily through changing social policies and institutions. The centennial observance explicates the Hull-House tradition and promotes rededication to those elements of the tradition that can improve contemporary society. In this article, the author examines the tradition in the light of recent developments in social work and poses the question, Was Jane Addams really a social worker?

"Social work" is an ambiguous term at best. Every few years, students at the Jane Addams College of Social Work, University of Illinois at Chicago, have surveyed their friends and people on the street to find out what the lay public considers the core role of a social worker. The modal answer is no surprise; over the years, it has not changed: A social worker gives money to the poor. Yet no professional social worker would accept that definition.

Modern social workers might define social work in terms of their own focus: a social worker is a caseworker, a group worker, or a community worker. Or perhaps a social worker is one who practices in a specialization such as child welfare; mental health; aging; or hospital, school, or occupational social work.

What does the literature say? A mission and purpose statement for the profession was developed by a task group of social work leaders (Conceptual Frameworks II, 1981):

> The purpose of social work is to promote or restore a mutually beneficial interaction between individuals and society in order to improve the quality of life for everyone. (p. 6)

The statement included six objectives as follows:

1. Help people enlarge their competence and increase their problem-solving and coping abilities.
2. Help people obtain resources.
3. Make organizations responsive to people.
4. Facilitate interaction between individuals and others in their environment.
5. Influence interactions between organizations and institutions.
6. Influence social and environmental policy. (p. 6)

How does the Jane Addams–Hull-House tradition square with that formulation?

The Hull-House Charter

Illinois requires that each not-for-profit organization file an official statement of purpose with the secretary of state. The legal model on which the Hull-House tradition was built included three purposes: (1) to provide a center for higher civic and social life, (2) to institute and maintain educational and philanthropic enterprises, and (3) to improve conditions in the industrial districts of Chicago (Addams, 1910, p. 88).

Elements of the Tradition

Neighborhood Identification

Settling. Commitment to the neighborhood was the core value implied in "settling"—to be both in and of the neighborhood, not nine to five or Monday through Friday or for a 2-year demonstration project. The commitment was to settle amid the people who were one's concern. The goal was to reduce the distance between the social classes. Jane Addams had seen this concept at work at Toynbee Hall in London, the model on which Hull-House was based. She quotes its founder, Canon Samuel A. Barnett: "The things which make men alike are fine and better than the things that keep them apart" (Addams, 1910, pp. 111–112).

Toynbee Hall opened in 1884. Its philosophy was to give male Oxford University students a few months' residence to serve the poor. In contrast, the women of Hull-House stayed, often for a lifetime. Living there and working there were essential, but remaining there conveyed authenticity, especially for the Hull-House residents—women who had never known poverty personally.

Incidentally, Jane Addams chose the unassuming title "head resident." She identified herself in *Who's Who in America* (1935) as a settlement worker.

Esthetics. As part of neighborhood identification, the Jane Addams tradition began with a welcoming spirit and a home that included personal furniture and art. Hull-House soon also provided the means to develop skills in art, music, and drama. Its residents included teachers and group leaders who provided an antidote to drab living and engaged the creative energy of adults and children in the community.

Personal Acquaintance. People trust the people they know. Hull-House residents knew their constituents and perceived them as neighbors. In the middle years of Hull-House, photographer

Wallace Kirkland knew nearly everyone in the neighborhood. He served as leader of the Hull-House Boy's Club, and he took many pictures of the people of the West Side, which have been published in one volume for the Hull-House centennial (Johnson, 1989). Kirkland did fine work because his subjects trusted him and could relax in his presence.

No Moral Means Test. Social work historians contrast the settlement house with another tradition, the friendly visitor—the well-off volunteer coming in from a better neighborhood to assist the poor under the auspices of the Charity Organization Society (COS). The visitor's main role was not as a helper but rather as a welfare gatekeeper to determine who deserved assistance and who did not. The visitor's charge was to reject the sturdy beggar who was too lazy to work, as well as the drunk, the womanizer, and the prostitute.

The COS and friendly visitors are considered to be the forerunners of modern casework. Franklin (1986) has described their methods as follows:

The Charity Organization Society emerged from a concern for making almsgiving scientific, efficient, and preventative. For the COS, poverty was to be cured not by the distribution of relief but by the personal rehabilitation of the poor. The guiding philosophy was that pauperism could be eliminated through investigating and studying the character of those seeking help and by educating and developing the poor. Case conferences and "friendly visiting" made vivid the problems, the needs for, and the responsibilities of rehabilitation.

Friendly visitors ran into hostility and indifference, however. They came from different neighborhoods in cities that were segregated by social class and ethnicity. The original idea of districting had presupposed local acquaintance and made more sense in communities where the rich and the poor grew up together. (p. 508)

Addams (1902) commented on charity visitors:

Let us take a neighborhood of poor people, and test their ethical standards by those of the charity visitor, who comes with the best desire in the world to help them out of their distress. A most striking incongruity, at once apparent, is the difference between the emotional kindness with which relief is given by one poor neighbor to another poor neighbor, and the guarded care with which relief is given by a charity visitor to a charity

recipient. The neighborhood mind is at once confronted not only by the difference of method; but by an absolute clashing of two ethical standards. (pp. 19–20)

Mary Richmond, representing the COS view, had expressed her opinion earlier. To her, the settlements were old-fashioned missions "doing harm by their cheap, sprinkling sort of charity" (*Proceedings of the Conference on Charities and Corrections,* 1897, p. 473).

Jane Addams probably avoided the designation social worker (except in quotation marks) to dissociate herself from the COS model. Welfare was not Hull-House's main business, and it did not have to impose a moral means test. It could emphasize neighbor-to-neighbor helping and at the same time show respect for the heritage that each person brought to a new world.

The elements of the Hull-House tradition—settling, beauty, and personal acquaintance—are now hard to find in low-income urban neighborhood. Public agencies' first and foremost concern might be the means test. Today the typical social agency office is hardly homelike, and the office interview has replaced the home visit. Out of concern for their safety, social workers have come to fear many of the neighborhoods where their clients live. In authoritative interventions including alleged abuse of children, a spouse, or elderly people, the social worker is increasingly likely to have a police escort, or the police may come alone to determine the facts. Union contracts covering social work personnel often set limits on home visiting to protect the workers.

Environment

Social work has adopted the formulation that behavior is the product of a person interacting with an environment. Concern with the environment has been the distinguishing characteristic of social work. Housing as a fundamental choice determines most other aspects of one's environment: schools, parks, churches and synagogues, and access to employment. Jane Addams addressed the problems of housing and sanitation. The physical structures that had the greatest negative effect on life on the West Side of Chicago were deteriorating wooden cottages, brick tenements, and factories. Hull-House dealt with landlords and lawmakers to improve housing and to help

individual families find better quarters within or outside the neighborhood.

Housing is still a central problem. Prices have skyrocketed. For many families, shelter requires at least half of total income. In Jane Addams' time, the proportion was less than one-fourth. The late Mayor Richard J. Daley admitted to sociologists that high-rise public housing was Chicago's greatest mistake. More recently, rather than producing affordable housing units, the Reagan Administration succeeded best in providing handsome consultant fees for political associates. The social work profession has not been able to deal successfully with housing the poor. It often settles for accommodation to grossly inadequate housing rather than participating in aggressive efforts for change.

Jane Addams probably never used the word "ecology," but she knew about garbage. Her only term on the public payroll came as a garbage inspector for the Nineteenth Ward in 1895. Today, garbage and other solid waste again pose big problems that threaten the well-being of our cities. Community workers are needed not only to develop and promote recycling and clean water and air but also to mobilize citizens to oppose expedient decisions made by commercial interests.

Use of Research

Neighborhood Surveys. Both COS and Hull-House staff members developed and promoted neighborhood-based research. Although Hull-House did not have to conduct investigations of the living habits of its constituents to obtain relief for them or to provide social diagnosis, it did gather information to promote change, including detailed maps showing characteristics of housing and wage levels (Residents of Hull-House, 1895). The top wage category adopted for the survey was $20 per week, indicating neighborhood income standards. Residents became technical experts on their neighborhood, and survey data were used with the city council and the state legislature to back up demands for change. Hull-House conducted investigations into factory conditions, housing conditions, truancy, sanitation, typhoid fever, tuberculosis, cocaine distribution, midwifery, children's reading, infant mortality, newsboys, and social value of the saloon.

Accessible Multiple Services

Noncategorical Multiple Services. The neighborhood location made Hull-House accessible. It was not necessary to travel very far to participate. Hull-House offered many services in one complex under a single authority. It came to constitute a network of services and soon gained the power and prestige to make effective referrals for the services that it did not provide.

More recent multiservice centers have failed because of hardening of the categories. The centers have included no adequate overarching authority to facilitate cooperation.

Emerging Female Leadership

The settlement house provided a career outlet, especially for bright college-educated women without distractions from parents or spouses or domestic demands. Hull-House generated its own family life, but with respect for autonomy of the residents. Net income was small, but the life hardly could be called cultured poverty. The model provided both security and opportunity.

As with most altruistic endeavors, gaining personal fulfillment was part of the motivation to serve. The vast literature on Hull-House suggests no maudlin sense of self-sacrifice among the residents. Clearly, the residents found their roles satisfying. The same philosophy that guided provisions for resident staff guided the development of the Jane Club, which provided accommodations for working women. When Florence Kelley, the leader in factory reform, left Chicago for New York after 8 years at Hull-House, she moved into the Henry Street Settlement to continue the same life-style for 27 more years.

The Hull-House setting was also conducive to innovation. Significant Hull-House firsts included social settlement in Chicago, social settlement with men and women residents, public baths in Chicago, a public playground in Chicago, a gymnasium for the public in Chicago, little theater in the United States, citizenship preparation classes, a public kitchen in Chicago, college extension courses in Chicago, a group work school, a painting loan program in Chicago, a free air school in Chicago, a public swimming pool in Chicago, and a Boy Scout troop in Chicago.

Unlike the people of the Hull-House neighborhood, the members of the major national social welfare conference did not accept female leadership readily. The National Conference on Charities and Corrections first met in 1874, but it was not until 1910 that Jane Addams was elected its first female president. On that occasion, she addressed the conference on "charity and social justice." By that time, throughout the country three-fourths of the residents of settlement houses were women.

Hull-House Functions

How did Hull-House residents work? To what extent was their program oriented to social service? Three functions were fundamental to the operation of Hull-House: direct service, urban education and recreation, and social reform.

Direct Service

To many people, social work consists of direct helping. Hull-House responded to personal needs, including thousands of emergencies. Examples selected for publication often were chosen to show the attitudes of the neighborhood more than the helping process. One such example recounts Jane Addams and Julia Lathrop delivering a baby:

> When Hull House was only a few months old, a young woman rushed through the door saying that a girl in her tenement house was having a baby all by herself and "hollering something fierce." None of the neighbor ladies would touch "the likes of her" because she was not married, and none would call a doctor for fear of being stuck with the bill. No relatives were available, so while one of the residents called a doctor, Julia Lathrop and Jane Addams set out to help. The doctor arrived only after several hours, by which time he found the young mother lying quietly in a clean bed with a healthy young boy, to be named Julius John after his deliverers, by her side. (Levine, 1971, p. 44)

Jane Addams' nephew, James Weber Linn (1935), author of the most personal biography, showed her lack of fear:

> According to the police, the house was in a "bad" section. But Jane Addams even in those earliest days would go anywhere, quite alone, if she was summoned, at three o'clock in the morning, "just as if she was a doctor." She had all her life many doubts, but no fears. On two occasions, it is recorded, she woke to find a burglar in her room. The first time her small nephew was asleep in the next room, and she thought only of not awakening him. "Don't make a noise," she said to the burglar. Startled, he leaped for the window by which he had entered. "You'll be hurt if you go that way," she said. "Go down by the stairs and let yourself out." He did. On the second occasion, addressing the housebreaker, without embarrassment, she succeeded in removing his own. Discovering that he was not a professional, but an amateur out of employment, she told him to go away and come back at nine the next morning, when she would see what she could do about getting him a job. He came, and she got him work. (pp. 113–114)

In *Twenty Years at Hull-House*, Addams (1910) described mediation with other organizations:

> We early found ourselves spending many hours in efforts to secure support for deserted women, insurance for bewildered widows, damages for injured operators, furniture from the clutches of the installment store. The Settlement is valuable as an information and interpretation bureau. It constantly acts between the various institutions of the city and the people for whose benefit these institutions were erected. The hospitals, the county agencies, and State asylums are often but vague rumors to the people who need them most. Another function of the Settlement to its neighborhood resembles that of the big brother whose mere presence on the playground protects the little one from bullies. (p. 167)

Direct services were usually short-term, based on a concept of health rather than pathology. Value judgments were avoided, and service from the residents included developing competence for self-help. Clinical social work was to come years later.

The Addams personnel model relied on staff with a liberal-arts perspective rather than promoting the social work training that became available after the turn of the century. However, Hull-House did include Edith Abbott and Sophonisba Breckenridge, who were to establish professional social work education at the University of Chicago. Although Jane Addams declined to join the faculty, their focus on social policy and social change as dominant curriculum elements was consistent with the Hull-House philosophy.

Urban Education and Recreation

What later would be called group work was the core of the Hull-House neighborhood program. First came the kindergarten, and then a variety of activities to make up for deficits in the public schools (Addams, 1910):

> The dozens of younger children who from the first came to Hull-House were organized into groups which were not quite classes and not quite clubs. The value of these groups consisted almost entirely in arousing a higher imagination and in giving the children the opportunity which they could not have in the crowded schools, for initiative and for independent social relationships. (p. 105)

Jane Addams (1910) added:

> We were very insistent that the settlement should not be primarily for the children. It was absurd to suppose that grown people would not respond to opportunities for education and social life . . . If it is natural to feed the hungry and care for the sick, it is certainly natural to give pleasure to the young, comfort to the aged, and to minister to the deep-seated craving for social intercourse that all men feel. (p. 107)

Group education also encompassed recreation. The gymnasium and the public playground were major resources. Public baths facilitated personal hygiene. Alice Hamilton extended those concerns to the water and milk supplies and to industrial medicine.

In the emerging social work profession, the status of group work became controversial. Social work tended to be defined as what social workers themselves do. Group activities were carried out mainly by people who were not social workers. Caseworkers therefore saw group workers as nonprofessional and disparaged them as merely playing with children, or teaching arts and crafts.

The American Association of Social Workers was established in 1921, but group workers were not admitted for 16 years. The first group work courses in a school of social work were offered at Western Reserve in 1927, and after a decade, 10 other schools had followed suit.

Group work gradually earned its place in social work, but its acceptance was greatly enhanced after World War II, when newly developed clinical treatment groups required professional leadership (Brieland, 1987). Both casework and therapeutic group work education and experience are now offered to master's degree candidates.

Group work of the Hull-House type has survived in settlements—often renamed community centers. There still is ambivalence about these activities. Many social workers hold that to qualify as social work, group work must at least include socialization based on an assessment of the needs of each group member.

The Hull-House programs were dispersed in 1963 and now are offered in seven sites. Eleven of the 13 original Hull-House buildings were demolished to make way for the new university campus. One model of urban education had replaced another.

Social Reform

The causes for social reform provide the drama of the Hull-House tradition. Two priorities from the initial years of operation—labor reform and juvenile justice—are of special interest.

The most serious problem in the work realm was "sweating," the highly competitive system of piecework in the garment trades that put industry into the tenements and devastating pressure on the family. Labor reforms included factory inspection, legislation for working hours, and the development of unions. Legislation brought new protections, especially for women and children. Here the prime mover was Hull-House's Florence Kelley, who was appointed the first factory inspector in Illinois because she had the support of Governor John Peters Altgeld.

Four labor unions were organized at Hull-House: the Women Shirt Makers, the Women Cloak Makers, the Dorcas Federal Labor Union, and the Chicago Women's Trade Union League. Chambers (1980) described the role of women in labor reform:

> Settlement leaders opened their halls to the organizing efforts of working women, they walked the picket lines to demonstrate solidarity, they testified before civic groups as to the needs and rights of working women, and they helped raise strike funds. Settlement efforts led to protective legislation; they also led toward the enablement and empowerment of working women. (p. 13)

Although labor activities generated opposition, the creation of the juvenile court was widely accepted. The court established in Chicago in 1889 was developed under the leadership of Julia

Lathrop of Hull-House. It separated juvenile justice from adult corrections. Social studies of the accused considered the offender's environment and reduced the tendency to blame the victim. The court was located next to Hull-House and a "psychopathic" facility to provide services to youth. The juvenile court model eventually was exported to the rest of Illinois and to every other state.

The success of local innovations energized the later and larger causes, including support of Theodore Roosevelt and the Progressive party, women's suffrage, and world peace. Hull-House became prominent in national coalition building. Jane Addams had direct access to several presidents, and her followers contributed the major provisions of the Progressive platform.

Although they could not vote, the women were credited with delivery of at least a million votes for Theodore Roosevelt. The quaint pictures of the suffragettes do not do justice to their power in finally getting the franchise. Levine (1971) summarizes Addams' view of "women suffrage":

> Well-to-do women should vote as a matter of right. Poor women should vote for the same reason that poor men should vote— they needed the franchise for their own protection. All women needed the franchise in order to bring their natural human sympathies more effectively to bear on the problems of industrial America. For after all, were not most of these problems in fact simply extensions of the primordial female task of protecting her children? (p. 171)

Jane Addams' primary goal and her most troubling experiences came around World War I from her leadership on behalf of world peace, which included opposition to American involvement in the war. Addams asserted that war could not make the world safe for democracy. After the war, she found blockades of the defeated nations, which denied them food, to be unconscionable. Her views were much better accepted by 1931, when she was awarded the Nobel Peace Prize.

Contemporary Reform

How do the reforms so briefly recounted here accord with our contemporary social action goals? The more modest term "advocacy" has replaced "social reform" in social workers' vocabulary. Has social work abandoned social reform and substituted modest efforts at advocacy—mostly for the needs of one client at a time?

Is reform stymied, at least in part, both because the president of the United States does not embody social work values and because social workers do not have access to him? During his campaign, President Bush perverted the term "liberal." Now, when he talks about the war on drugs, he still sounds as if he were running for sheriff. In foreign relations, the nation still relies on costly weapon systems for traditional defense against a traditional enemy. Sadly, the opposition party provides neither a coherent set of policies nor manifest strength.

In its early years, the National Association of Social Workers (NASW) focused on poverty and racism, but recently it has chosen a different priority each year. Poverty and racism still require strong advocacy efforts, but perhaps the terms are too general and timeworn to stimulate meaningful strategies. NASW regards abortion as a key women's issue, but it gives much less attention to the economic status of women and such basic innovations as comparable-worth legislation. (Remember that NASW chooses priorities for social action in a predominantly female profession.)

Social workers' energies for advocacy lately seem to be targeted on health and mental health, emphasizing high-priority issues (third-party payments and vendorship) that are necessarily self-serving.

Social workers' relative passivity on large social issues is, no doubt, an accommodation to legal and political realities. Public employees consider themselves legally restricted from political action, and the private sector must maintain delicate relationships with funding sources. Also, no social worker has the access to the president that Jane Addams had to Roosevelt and Wilson. The White House staff protects the president from most advocates, and the media do not take social workers' efforts very seriously.

Who Is a Social Worker?

The model of committed people fulfilling themselves by living amid the poor is outdated, but how can social workers demonstrate their essential commitment in the next century? How do service providers ensure that they identify with their clients and thus reduce the barriers that separate them from mainstream society? How and where do social workers expend their efforts for advocacy, even for social reform?

Perhaps Jane Addams, at an earlier time and in a simpler context, embodied the true social worker better than the inheritors of the helping process. Social workers today might profit from asking themselves the following questions:

1. Are they neighbors as well as professionals?
2. Do they educate for fulfillment as well as treat for pathology?
3. Do they put enough of their energy into the truly great causes?
4. Should they be social workers in the Jane Addams tradition?
5. Is she one of them; are they enough like her?

References

Addams, J. (1902). *Democracy and social ethics.* New York: Macmillan.

Addams, J. (1910). *Twenty years at Hull-House.* New York: New American Library.

Brieland, D. (1987). History and evolution of social work practice. In A. Minahan (Ed.-in-Chief), *Encyclopedia of social work* (18th ed., Vol. 1, pp. 739–754). Silver Spring, MD: National Association of Social Workers.

Chambers, C. A. (1980). *Seedtime of reform: American social service and social action 1918–1933.* Westport, CT: Greenwood Press.

Franklin, D. L. (1986). Mary Richmond and Jane Addams: From moral certainty to national inquiry in social work practice. *Social Service Review, 60,* 504–525.

Johnson, M. A. (1989). *The many faces of Hull-House, the photographs of Wallace Kirkland.* Urbana: University of Illinois Press.

Levine, D. (1971). *Jane Addams and the liberal tradition.* Madison: State Historical Society of Wisconsin.

Linn, J. W. (1935). *Jane Addams: A biography.* New York: D. Appleton-Century.

Minahan, A. (Ed.). (1981). Conceptual Frameworks II [Special issue]. *Social Work, 26,* 5–96.

Proceedings of the Conference on Charities and Corrections. (1897).

Residents of Hull-House. (1895). *Hull-House maps and papers.* New York: Thomas Y. Crowell.

Who's who in America. (1935). Chicago: A. N. Marquis.

Donald Brieland, PhD, ACSW, is Professor and Dean, Jane Addams College of Social Work, University of Illinois at Chicago, P.O. Box 4348, Chicago, IL, 60680. This article is adapted from a paper presented at the inaugural centennial seminar at Hull-House Museum in Chicago, Illinois, on October 5, 1989.

Establishing an Updated Standard of Need for AFDC Recipients

Charles L. Skoro and David A. Johnson

Aid to Families with Dependent Children (AFDC) was established in 1935 through authorizing legislation of the Social Security Act, Title IVA. The AFDC program was an expansion of the widow's pension fund established by many states in the early 1920s and of social legislation contained in the Sheppard-Tower Act of 1921 (Trattner, 1979). AFDC's purpose is to provide financial assistance that will enable parents and relatives serving as guardians to provide care for their dependent children in their own homes.

AFDC is the major program in the United States providing such assistance. Federal and state governments spent $16.6 billion for AFDC in 1987 (Plotnick, 1989). States determine eligibility and the level of benefits and decide how the program is administered. These criteria are presented by the states to the U.S. Secretary of Health and Human Services for approval (U.S. Department of Health and Human Services, 1987).

State policymakers need to examine the criteria that define who should be helped by AFDC and to what degree. States are required to establish a "statewide standard, expressed in money amounts" that can be used to determine benefit eligibility and amount (U.S. Department of Health and Human Services, 1987, p. 12). Although federal law allows states numerous ways to avoid paying the full amount of the standard and to avoid making all those whose incomes fall below the specified amount eligible for payment, once established, the standard serves as a yardstick against which actual eligibility and payment policies may be judged.

In reviewing the wide variation on the dollar values states place on need level (Table 1), the authors found no consistency among states in either need or payment levels (U.S. Department of Health and Human Services, 1987). It is doubtful that much of the disparity between Oregon's $395 per month standard and Washington's $941 per month is accounted for by differences in the cost of living between those neighboring states. Nor was any consistency found between those levels and the official poverty line of the United States, which in 1988 was about $971 per month for a family of four for all states except Alaska and Hawaii. Alaska's need level was $1,213 per month and Hawaii's was $1,117 (U.S. Department of Health and Human Services, 1988).

Should a state standard of need be correlated with the federal poverty line? What should states evaluate in formulating a standard of need? Should there be consistency among states in how a standard is developed? What are the political implications in the development of a standard? The social work literature's silence regarding how standards of need are determined and the reluctance or inability of some state officials to provide detailed information on the formula that determines standard of need both point to the critical nature of this research. This article discusses how such a standard can be constructed and shares insights gained in the process of developing an empirically defensible standard of need.

DEFINING NEED AT THE STATE LEVEL

A 1980 Social Security Administration study identified five methods used or proposed for use by states seeking to develop a standard of need (U.S. Department of Health and Human Services, 1980): (1) the market-basket approach, in which an agreed-on set of items necessary for a minimum decent standard of living is priced; (2) low-income family expenditure surveys, in which low-income families' buying patterns are used to determine the amount necessary for a minimum decent standard of living; (3) the Bureau of Labor Statistics (BLS) lower level budget, which involves use of the lower living standard calculated by the BLS; (4) the Orshansky Multiplier, a method that uses a combination of the market-basket and expenditure-pattern approaches; and (5) official poverty guidelines, which originally were based on the Orshansky methods but for many years have simply been updates using the consumer price index of a standard computed many years ago. Each method, in one way or another, rejects the idea that a family's needs can be defined in a purely biological way and seeks to reflect a social rather than a physical minimum standard of living. Although decision makers generally do not explicitly develop policy based on a relative view of poverty, there is a tacit acceptance among policymakers that a standard of need is shaped by the social context in which an individual or family lives (Zimbalist, 1977).

The market-basket approach has several advantages over the alternatives. This approach forces policymakers to directly confront the issue of how much food, clothing, and shelter a household requires. This method also allows particular characteristics of an area to be considered such as climate, which affects home heating costs, and availability of public transportation, which affects transportation costs. These factors can substantially influence a standard of need. In addition, price differences for food, clothing, and other necessary items are easily calculated for different geographic areas.

A STATE STRATEGY FOR DEVELOPING A STANDARD OF NEED

In 1988, the Idaho administrative agency for AFDC sought to update its 1969

TABLE 1. Need Standard and Payment of Aid to Families with Dependent Children to Family Composed of One Adult and Three Children

States, Terntories, and Possessions	Need Standard (Monthly) ($)	Payment (Monthly) ($)	Need Standard (Annual) ($)	Payment (Annual) ($)	Payment as Percent of Need
Alabama	480	147	5,760	1,764	31
Alaska	823	823	9,876	9,876	100
Arizona	748	353	8,976	4,236	47
Arkansas	273	224	3,276	2,688	82
California	734	734	8,808	8,808	100
Colorado	510	420	6,120	5,040	82
Connecticut	593	593	7,116	7,116	100
Delaware	363	363	4,356	4,356	100
District of Columbia	870	444	10,440	5,328	51
Florida	468	298	5,616	3,576	64
Georgia	432	302	5,184	3,624	70
Guam[a]	210	210	2,520	2,520	100
Hawaii	546	546	6,552	6,552	100
Idaho	627	345	7,524	4,140	55
Illinois	768	385	9,216	4,620	50
Indiana	363	316	4,356	3,792	87
Iowa	578	443	6,936	5,316	77
Kansas	436	436	5,232	5,232	100
Kentucky	246	246	2,952	2,952	100
Louisiana	738	234	8,856	2,808	32
Maine	674	489	8,088	5,868	73
Maryland	574	415	6,888	4,980	72
Massachusetts	556	556	6,672	6,672	100
Michigan	643	536	7,716	6,432	83
Minnesota	621	621	7,452	7,452	100
Mississippi	443	144	5,316	1,728	33
Missouri	365	327	4,380	3,924	90
Montana	514	426	6,168	5,112	83
Nebraska	420	420	5,040	5,040	100
Nevada	341	341	4,092	4,092	100
New Hampshire	451	451	5,412	5,412	100
New Jersey	465	465	5,580	5,580	100
New Mexico	313	313	3,756	3,756	100
New York	596	596	7,152	7,152	100
North Carolina	538	269	6,456	3,228	50
North Dakota	454	454	5,448	5,448	100
Ohio	834	374	10,008	4,488	45
Oklahoma	583	361	6,996	4,332	62
Oregon	395	395	4,740	4,740	100
Pennsylvania	724	451	8,688	5,412	62
Puerto Rico	208	104	2,496	1,248	50
Rhode Island	503	503	6,036	6,036	100
South Carolina	458	240	5,496	2,880	52
South Dakota	408	408	4,896	4,896	100
Tennessee	421	189	5,052	2,268	45
Texas	691	221	8,292	2,652	32
Utah	809	439	9,708	5,268	54
Vermont	963	642	11,556	7,704	67
Virginia	386	347	4,632	4,164	90
Virgin Islands	263	215	3,156	2,580	82
Washington	941	578	11,292	6,936	61
West Virginia	623	312	7,476	3,744	50
Wisconsin	764	649	9,168	7,788	85
Wyoming	390	390	4,680	4,680	100

NOTE: Standards and payments are as of October 1, 1986.

SOURCE: U.S. Department of Health and Human Services, Family Support Administration, Office of Family Assistance. (1987). *Characteristics of state plans for aid to families with dependent children.* Washington, DC: U.S. Government Printing Office.

[a]Guam includes no amount for shelter and utilities, which are treated as a special need.

standard of need. Recognizing the political nature of updating such a standard and the substantial political overtones (Orshansky, 1965), the state agency contracted with personnel at a university to conduct the study. The parameters placed on the study required first that it use a market-basket approach and second that it consolidate a number of needs identified in the 1969 Idaho standard. Federal statute requires that when a state decides to consolidate a need standard, the process "may not result in a reduction of the content of the standard" (U.S. Department of Health and Human Services, 1987, p. 12). This requirement shaped decision making on some of the items to be included in the market basket.

Initial Steps

An important first step was to organize a committee to oversee the creation of an updated standard and to provide input on value judgments inherent in establishing a market basket of goods and services (Bradshaw, Mitchell, & Morgan, 1987; Plachaud, 1987). State legislators, members of an advocacy group, key personnel from the state's department of health and welfare (the agency administering the AFDC program), and representatives from the governor's office and one or two other key agencies were invited to participate. Any market basket used is subject to criticism from a variety of perspectives; diversity on the committee is essential to establishing broad-based support for a new standard. If the most likely critics have a chance to participate in the process, problems can be resolved as they arise.

One major criterion the committee developed for the market basket was that it should allow for full social participation of AFDC clients rather than for mere maintenance. Full social participation, although not operationally defined initially by the committee, developed into a guiding principle: A family's living standard should be such that its members can be in full contact with the broader society. Family members should have the transportation, communication, and other resources necessary to participate in society, including being able to search for employment. For instance, the committee decided that children should be able to attend school functions and participate in activities even if their parents have to pay for transportation and activity tickets. A second decision was that the standard should meet long-term needs and, therefore, should include provisions for durable goods.

Defining the Market Basket

The next step was selecting items for the market basket. The researchers from the university provided the oversight committee with a model market basket gathered from a variety of sources (Dean & Tomlinson, 1982). The market basket that ultimately emerged included the categories listed in Table 2. Food and clothing standards were established for a variety of age and gender groups. The final total dollar amount was adjusted to reflect the cost of meeting the standard for a person from each of the age and gender groups and the percentage of the AFDC caseload each group constituted (Davidson, Skoro, & Higgins, 1988).

Fearing that inclusion of such costs could jeopardize federal acceptance of them, the department of health and welfare asked that medical and dental care be omitted from the standard. This exclusion is significant in light of the total resources required by a family to meet a minimum standard of need. In 1986, average Medicaid expenditures amounted to $521 per AFDC child and

$952 per AFDC adult recipient (Plotnick, 1989). A family of four required more than $200 per month to meet medical expenses.

The general philosophy the authors followed in generating the standard was that the standard include needs except for health care regardless of program availability. For instance, a portion of food costs for an AFDC family is typically met through food stamps. Some committee members argued that the dollar amount of food costs in the standard be reduced to reflect the impact of food stamps. That reasoning was rejected by the full committee, which sought to formulate a standard reflecting what it costs a family to live. It then would be up to state legislators and other policymakers to design a package including food stamps, housing subsidies, and other elements that would meet those needs.

METHODOLOGICAL ISSUES AND FINDINGS

Pricing the Market Basket

After selecting goods and services that constitute the standard of living for an AFDC family, the committee determined the money amounts that correspond to items in the market basket. Ideally, a statistically valid sample of vendors offer-

ing each of the goods and services would be selected, and a statistically valid study that results in exact price measures would be conducted. But in most research this is not possible; compromises are made to complete information gathering. The committee faced some major issues in pricing each of the categories and devising strategies to price items while maintaining reasonable research costs.

Food. It is not possible simply to send a designated shopper to a store with a list of food items that would appear on the AFDC family's shopping list. Pickles, for example, are dill or sweet, sliced or whole, packaged in large or small jars, and of a national or a store brand. Thus, to conduct any kind of a price study, a shopping list must include the type, size, and brand of each item.

Personnel from a national grocery store chain provided the sizes, types, and brands most commonly purchased for each of the items on the authors' list, allowing the authors to assemble a shopping form that listed a type and size for each item as well as the best-selling nationally available brand. The instructions that accompanied the list directed the shopper to price a local or store brand of each item whenever one was available and to price the national brand only when necessary.

To avoid high research costs in train-

TABLE 2. Monthly Cost Based on Family Size

Expense	Monthly Cost ($) by Family Size						
	1 Person	2 People	3 People	4 People	5 People	6 People	7 People
Food	83.41	166.82	250.23	333.64	417.05	500.46	583.87
Clothing	25.76	51.52	77.28	103.04	128.80	154.56	180.32
Personal care items	15.07	30.14	45.21	60.28	75.35	90.42	105.49
Newspaper	3.25	3.25	3.25	3.25	3.25	3.25	3.25
Laundromat and dry cleaning	8.76	17.52	26.28	35.04	43.80	52.56	61.32
Housewares	3.79	7.58	11.37	15.16	18.95	22.74	26.53
Household supplies	7.74	15.48	23.22	30.96	38.70	46.44	54.18
Haircuts	3.54	7.08	10.62	14.16	17.70	21.24	24.78
Recreation	3.00	6.00	9.00	12.00	15.00	18.00	21.00
Telephone	14.76	14.76	14.76	14.76	14.76	14.76	14.76
Transportation	24.86	24.86	24.86	24.86	24.86	24.86	24.86
School fees	0.31	0.62	0.93	1.24	1.55	1.86	2.17
School supplies	0.81	1.62	2.43	3.24	4.05	4.86	5.67
Toys, games, and books	1.09	2.18	3.27	4.36	5.45	6.54	7.63
Rent	263.80	286.97	286.97	353.19	353.19	390.11	390.11
Utilities	73.65	87.83	87.83	102.36	102.36	117.24	117.24
Total minus rent and utilities	196.14	349.43	502.71	655.99	809.27	962.55	1,115.83
Total including rent and utilities	533.59	724.23	877.51	1,111.54	1,264.82	1,469.90	1,623.18
Total sales tax (5 percent)	6.88	13.77	20.65	27.53	34.42	41.30	48.18
Total with 5 percent sales tax	540.47	738.00	898.16	1,139.07	1,299.24	1,511.20	1,671.36

SOURCE: Davidson, S. M., Skoro, C. L., & Higgins, N. G. (1988). *Idaho AFDC standard of need study: 1988 update.* Boise, ID: Boise State University.

ing shoppers and to provide transportation across the state, the authors subcontracted with the Agricultural Statistics Service of the U.S. Department of Agriculture, which maintains a statewide corps of part-time enumerators who work during crop seasons to gather data from farms. These enumerators were able to gather the data inexpensively and quickly with few erroneous, late, or unusable data forms.

The grocery sample was based on stores participating in the Special Supplemental Food Program for Women, Infants, and Children, with the elimination of convenience stores, which tended to have higher prices. Food price data were checked for the previous winter to evaluate seasonal variations. The total price did not vary with the season.

The final calculation of a statewide average cost for food was weighted to incorporate the average for each region by the percentage of AFDC recipients in that region. Prices in areas with high proportions of AFDC clients received a larger proportional weight in figuring the average than prices from other areas. The calculation of the nutritious monthly food budget of $334 for a four-person family reflected approximately 30 percent of the total need standard.

Clothing. The task of developing a standard list of clothing was laborious and fraught with value judgments. The 1969 standards used as a starting point assumed that girls wore dresses nearly all the time, that women wore bloomers, and that men wore garters and "braces" (suspenders). They also implied that everyone maintained several sets of long underwear but bought only two new pairs of underpants a year. The oversight committee was instrumental in developing a clothing list for each age and gender group.

Lidman (1981), in developing a standard of need for Washington State, recommended pricing the second-lowest-priced clothing items at the K-Mart chain because they met signficiantly higher quality standards than the lowest priced items but were lower in price than clothing purchased at other outlets. Moreover, K-Mart stores tend to be located in areas available to low-income shoppers. Lidman also pointed out that used clothing was a viable option and that about one-third of clothing needs could be met this way at a savings of about one-half the store prices (Lidman, 1981). K-Mart has stores in all regions of Idaho, and their

cooperation was secured in pricing clothing. Clothing costs for a four-person household added $103 to the monthly standard and constituted approximately 9 percent of the total.

Personal care and medicine chest items, household supplies, housewares, and school supplies were generally available in grocery stores or K-Marts. These items were priced along with the food and clothing surveys. Supplies and personal care items totaled $110 for a four-person household. The combined food, clothing, supplies, and personal care costs reflected about one-half of a families' monetary needs in this standard.

Housing and Utilities. The largest portion of the total need of an AFDC family is the cost of housing and utilities. Therefore, it is important to develop an accurate housing cost. The authors identified three sources of data for calculating rental costs: (1) the federally published fair market rents (U.S. Department of Housing and Urban Development, 1988), (2) surveys by other private or public organizations such as realtors and community action agencies, and (3) newspaper rental ads. The overwhelming majority of states use the federal fair market rents to reflect housing costs. But researchers and oversight committee members believed the federal figures to be much higher than actual Idaho rents.

The Idaho Housing Agency, which administers the state's federal housing subsidies, provided an alternative measure of costs. The agency maintains records of the full rental price (tenant portion plus subsidy) charged for each house or apartment occupied by one of its clients. Federal statutes require an inspection of each unit to ensure compliance with minimal construction and maintenance standards. These data showed uniformly lower rental costs than the fair market rents and more closely fit the personal experience of those on the committee. Another set of rental data was collected by selecting a sample of newspapers' classified advertisements serving the 10 counties with the largest AFDC populations. Rent prices were ranked, and the lowest 20 percent were used to estimate housing costs. The mean rent price provided the lowest estimates by unit size of housing costs.

With three sets of dollar amounts, all justifiable from a research standpoint, which data set should be used? The oversight committee decided to reject the classified advertising data because there

was considerable doubt about whether the housing advertised at those prices would meet minimum standards. The committee directed the researchers to use the rents provided by the agency administering the federal housing subsidies. This agency also provided data on utility costs by housing unit size, data the agency maintained in administering a variety of federal subsidy programs to pay utility costs for low-income clients. Housing and utility costs totaled $456 per month, or 40 percent of the total standard for a household of four.

Transportation. Because public transportation is minimally available in only two or three cities in Idaho, the automobile was chosen as the basis for establishing transportation costs. Most of the costs of owning and operating a car are fixed; they are incurred whether the car is driven or not. The choice of how many miles of travel to allocate to the family makes little practical difference to the dollar total in the standard. To estimate travel costs, cost data were collected for such fees as vehicle registration, driver's licenses, and liability insurance. Other costs were estimated based on data from studies performed in other states allocating miles per family. In addition, data were used from the Motor Vehicle Manufacturers Association of the United States (1987). The annual depreciation on a car was reduced to reflect the 10-year-old automobile an AFDC recipient was assumed to own if he or she owned a car. Finance charges, based on the assumption that the driver was buying a new car, were also reduced. These considerations are reflected in the very low monthly transportation cost derived of $25 per household.

Other Items. Other items presented numerous problems. For some items (for instance, telephone service and hair cuts), it was possible to obtain lists of service providers by county from the public utilities commission or state licensing boards. For other items, such as newspaper service, statewide industry associations maintained lists of members. The state education department provided a list that was used to sample school districts on their student fees. In a few cases, telephone directories were resorted to for the selection of samples of stores or service providers. The items in this category totaled $85 per month, or approximately 7 percent of the total standard for a four-person household.

DISCUSSION

Several compromises were involved in the development of the final standard. In the first formulation, furniture replacement, automobile depreciation, and use of the federal fair market rents resulted in an amount that left policymakers aghast. After they pointed out that several agency secretaries were single parents who earned less than the amount specified in the standards, they asked the authors to develop alternative standards that would reflect lower costs. In the next formulation, the lowest alternative budget was developed by using rental figures from newspaper ads and clothing and other allotments reduced to 1969 levels. Finally, an intermediate budget was prepared that reflected a short-term need standard that therefore eliminated durable goods, furniture replacement, and automobile depreciation, but the rental figures from the agency administering housing subsidies were used and other additions were left intact. In reviewing the three alternative standards, the oversight committee chose the intermediate budget with a few modifications. (Full implementation of the standard awaits resolution of an unrelated problem.)

The final monetary standard (Table 2) is based on a market basket composed of items to meet short-term basic needs with the important exception of health care, which would add a substantial amount to the cost. A review of the items reveals how spartan a life-style the market basket implies (Davidson, Skoro, & Higgins, 1988), but, nonetheless, it does allow for some social participation. The amount "required" for a family of four in 1988 was $1,139 per month. The significance of this finding is its comparison to the federal poverty line, which in 1988 was $971 for a family of four. One definition of poverty is having less than an objectively defined absolute minimum (Hagenaars & de Vos, 1988). The standard of need defined in the present study is an objectively defined absolute minimum.

The present study is based in a rural northwestern state (Idaho) with a lower cost of living than larger, more metropolitan states. The standard developed, however, is higher than that of all other states (Table 1) and is 17 percent higher than the federal poverty line prevailing at the time. This raises an important question: Is the standard developed in the present study a biased overestimate of what is needed to meet minimum need levels? The authors believe it is not. In fact, there is cause to believe that it is too low on the basis of the alternatives reviewed and agreed to by the oversight committee.

The question that remains is why the proposed standard is higher than others. This standard is higher because it is based on a market-basket approach; others are developed using less satisfactory methods. Flawed methods are widely used because of ambivalent public opinion toward people living in poverty (Roff & Klemmack, 1983) rather than lack of technical capabilities among researchers and policymakers. The ambivalence is based on the view that children are worthy of help, but their parents (guardians) are unworthy. A standard of need is therefore likely to reflect this negative view.

Benefit levels are often set below the poverty line. Only 20 states plus Guam provide a benefit level equal to their defined standard of need. Similarly, minimum wage standards are grossly inadequate to meet basic needs. An adult supporting two children by working eight hours a day for five days a week every week of the year requires a wage of more than $5 per hour to provide basic necessities.

CONCLUSION

This research was conducted under the assumption that a standard of need could be established that truly reflected the cost of a minimal socially acceptable living standard. The standard was developed using principles of empirical investigation to ensure accuracy and an oversight committee to ensure objectivity. The following conclusions emerged:

• A careful, systematic analysis of living costs generates a dollar figure at least as high as those cited here. In states in which rents and utility costs are higher than in Idaho, the standard of need should be higher.

• There is little agreement from state to state on either how a standard should be developed or what a standard is.

• An underclass exists in U.S. society that must survive on much less than an objectively defined absolute minimum.

• The federal poverty line is the criterion used to estimate the number of people living in poverty. The findings reported here suggest that this criterion underestimates the poor population.

Additional research is needed to bring clarity to the issue of poverty and to inform the public debate about a realistic minimum standard of need. Accurate information is important for policymakers to design programs to adequately address the needs of poor and vulnerable people.

REFERENCES

Bradshaw, J., Mitchell, D., & Morgan, J. (1987). Evaluating adequacy: The potential of budget standards. *Journal of Social Policy, 16,* 165–181.

Davidson, S. M., Skoro, C. L., & Higgins, N. G. (1988). *Idaho AFDC standard of need study: 1988 update.* Boise, ID: Boise State University.

Dean, A. C., & Tomlinson, P. S. (1982, July). *A guide to conducting a cost-of-living study.* Chicago: Clearinghouse of Legal Services.

Hagenaars, A., & de Vos, K. (1988). The definition and measurement of poverty. *Journal of Human Resources, 23*(2), 211–221.

Lidman, R. M. (1981). *Cost of living in 1980 for low-income families in Washington State.* Olympia, WA: Office of Research, Analysis & Information Services Division, Department of Social and Health Services.

Motor Vehicle Manufacturers Association of the United States. (1987). *The Motor Vehicle Manufacturers Association's facts and figures.* Detroit: Author.

Orshansky, M. (1965). Counting the poor: Another look at the poverty profile. *Social Security Bulletin, 28,* 17–21.

Plachaud, D. (1987). Problems in the definition and measurement of poverty. *Journal of Social Policy, 16,* 147–164.

Plotnick, R. D. (1989). Directions for reducing child poverty. *Social Work, 34,* 523–530.

Roff, L., & Klemmack, D. (1983). Attitudes toward public welfare and welfare workers. *Social Work Research & Abstracts, 19*(3), 29–30.

Social Security Act of 1935, IV A U.S.C. §401.

Trattner, W. I. (1979). *From poor law to welfare state* (2nd ed.). New York: Free Press.

U.S. Department of Health and Human Services, Family Support Administration, Office of Family Assistance. (1987). *Characteristics of state plans for aid to families with dependent children.* Washington, DC: U.S. Government Printing Office.

U.S. Department of Health and Human Services, Social Security Administration. (1988). *Social security bulletin: Annual statistical supplement 1988.* Washington, DC: U.S. Government Printing Office.

U.S. Department of Health and Human Services, Social Security Administration, Office of Policy, Office of Research and Statistics. (1980). *AFDC standards of need: An evaluation of current practices, alternative approaches, and policy options.* (SSA Publication No. 13-11741). Washington, DC: U.S. Government Printing Office

U.S. Department of Housing and Urban Development, Office of the Assistant Secretary for Housing–Federal Housing Commissioner. (1988). Section 8 housing assistance payments program. *Federal Register, 53*(71), 12278-12356.

Zimbalist, S. (1977). Replacing our obsolete poverty line. *Public Welfare, 35*(4), 36–41.

Charles L. Skoro, PhD, is Professor, Economics Department, and David A. Johnson, MSW, is Professor and Chair, Social Work Department, Boise State University, 1910 University Drive, Boise, ID 83725.
This study was funded in part by the Idaho Department of Health and Welfare.

Historical Perspectives on Contemporary Social Work
David M. Austin

The Winter 1985 Special Issue included a wide ranging series of commentaries, not only on the current status of social work, but also on the historical roots of social work. There are a number of comments which might be made on the assessments of the status of social work in 1985, but my comments will be directed to the historical analyses which underlie several of the articles.

Many social work commentators use social work history to support already arrived at conclusions which are at the center of their commentary. This use of history is often highly selective, or it reflects a cultural belief system that was part of an early socialization into the profession. Before dealing with some of the specific historical issues raised in the several articles, which do not reflect the full complexity of the development of social work, there are two general issues that need a brief comment.

There is an interesting diversity of conceptual frameworks reflected in the several articles, but there is one framework which is generally missing — the interactive or transactional framework which emphasizes the interactive role of *both* social environment and individual behavior. One conceptual framework which is used, for example, in Gratton's article, is that of historical, and environmental determinism. Everything in American history, in particular in the development of social welfare, can be accounted for by the economic requirements of capitalism. Similarly, in Warshawsky's article it is capital formation which drives the welfare state. (No matter that capital formation is a powerful economic process in all industrial societies, socialist and capitalist.) In this conceptual framework there are no individual historical actors; there is no significant diversity of motive. Both reactionary conservatives and humanistic liberals are pawns of the "hidden hand" of economic forces. On the other hand, social workers are simultaneously admonished in the article by Frumkin and O'Connor to pursue the social work "commitment to alter the societal conditions that influence clients' lives." Such an approach must argue for human free will, and for a process of interaction between individuals and environment, and for the possibility of human initiatives shaping human history regardless of the economic system.

The concept of free will also appears in an interesting version which can best be described as the "autonomous institution of social work." The theme of the Special Issue, as well as that of several of the articles, is built around the concept of a unitary, self-acting, flesh and blood institutional entity named "social work." There are no individual social workers, with different interests and perspectives. There are no individual organizational leaders or opinion makers; there is only "social work" which has abandoned its "heritage." There is no suggestion that the development of social work as an organized profession may have, at least in part, been shaped by events in the larger society, in particular changes in the pattern of employment opportunities for social workers.

There is, in the analysis of the behavior of "social work," no clue as to how the institution of social work is, in fact, being defined; whether "the profession" is assumed to be a representation of an average of the attitudes and behaviors of every person in a job position labelled social work, the attitudes and behaviors of the members of the professional associations, the actions of the offices and staff of NASW, or of the Council on Social Work Education, the attitudes and behaviors of social work faculty, the sum of all opinions expressed in the major social work journals, or an analysis of commentary in the public media about the profession of social work. Even if there were a precise definition offered of "social work," it is still impossible for the institution of social work — a symbolic representation of a complex association of several tens of thousands of particular individuals — to "abandon" anything, or to "go" anywhere.

Several specific historical truisms are reflected in these articles which comment on the behavior of "social work." One of them is that social workers originally were linked together by a highly unified relief system and social commitment that today have been lost. A second is that social work as an organized profession was developed solely around the provision of financial assistance to families in poverty. A third truism is that at some time in the past every individual social worker was overwhelmingly involved in social change efforts. The fourth is that in the process of working together to establish the institutional structures of an organized profession social workers chose to abandon their commitment to poverty-striken individuals and families.

The initial development of social work as an organized profession reflected a highly diverse, and contentious, process in which there was as much disagreement about the essence of social work as there was agreement. The arguments between the earliest social workers in medical and psychiatric settings and those in charity organizations and settlements were at least as acute as the current debates over the legitimacy of "private practice." While social workers were employed in positions dealing with problems of poverty, often replacing volunteers, this included many different groups: orphans abandoned on city streets — unemployed homeless men ("tramps"), fatherless families — as a result of disease, industrial accidents, imprisonment, or abandonment, unemployed workmen and their families, juvenile delinquents, and shell-shocked veterans (whose psychological problems were quite similar to those of some of the Vietnam veterans) to name only a few. The work with World War I veterans was one of the initial forms of mental health practice in social work, which at least since the 1950s has been the single largest sector of practice among social workers with a graduate professional degree.

This pattern of initial social work employment reflected the pervasive existance of poverty in an early industrial society with frequent economic crises. Every social problem was linked to poverty. However, social workers, then, as well as now, dealt day-to-day with individuals, not the paradigm of the economic system. This was not an avoidance of social action, but a natural response considering that is is individual human beings who experience crisis. Societies and cities do **not have** "human" problems; people have human problems. And the original social workers dealt with the individuals who were in immediate need of help, even when they were also working on more far-reaching social policy issues.

While Gratton traces the beginnings of the "social work apparatus" back to the pre-Civil War relief investigator, and makes it clear that he believes that now, as then, social workers involved in financial assistance, (and by implication all social workers,) are tools of capitalist oppression, other authors imply that social workers were at some point in history the cutting edge of social reform in the United States. This ignores the fact that organized social welfare, and the institutional aspects of professional social work, developed primarily as part of a middle-of-the-road, progressive reform tradition in the United States that took the free-market, capitalist economic system as a given. Much of the motivation for such efforts was to push social reform as an alternative to socialist political initiatives.

Much of the attention of social workers was not on income assistance, or on issues of redistribution or economic justice. They were particularly concerned with problems of mothers and children, often oppressed as much by their working class husbands as by the economic system. One of the primary concerns of Mary Richmond during her years as a charity organization executive in Philadelphia was with the survival problems of "deserted wives."

In some of the more far-reaching social reform efforts, such as the effort to pass a constitutional amendment outlawing child labor, and the effort to pass the Prohibition Amendment, social workers were only a small part of a much larger coalition. Perhaps most noticeable was the limited connection between social worker leaders and the suffragette movement, which was the most militant reform effort at that time (with the exception of the often bloody effort to organize unions in major industries).

Many social workers were involved in social reform efforts during the Progressive Era. Some of these efforts involved reforms which today appear to have been quite oppressive, strengthening middle-class oriented social controls over immigrant families. Others are key elements in social welfare provisions in current society. But most of the leadership in these social reform efforts did not come from individuals employed as social work professionals. It came from civic leaders involved in other sectors of society, from university faculty members, from board members of social welfare organizations, particularly the Charity Organization Societies, and from individuals, like Jane Addams, who were career social workers by our definition, but who did not think of themselves as a "professional social worker." Indeed by the time of the First World War Jane Addams was active as a leader in an international pacifist movement, which had little connection with organized social welfare, bringing criticism from social workers who supported the War.

Many suggest that social workers were in the forefront of social reform efforts during the 1960s. However, the increased interest in community organization among social work students was essentially an increase from 5% of the student body to 15%. Many social workers did work in community action agencies, and many community action agencies had significant impact on local communities, particularly in the early mobilization of black political movements in industrial cities. However, the concept of the community action agency as a federally-funded, "social movement" organization, controlled and operated solely by the residents of low-income central city neighborhoods (an interpretation of history which appears quite widely in social work literature) was never an operational reality in any community. The effective protests during those years against "the establishment" involved some social workers, but the leadership came primarily from a variety of local residents, primarily in black residential neighborhoods and black organizational and political leaders.

The visibility of social action among social workers has varied from time-to-time. It has never been the dominant day-to-day activity of most social workers. And there is little evidence that social work social action is any less developed in the 1980s, than in the 1960s, although the issues may be different. Many of the efforts today address older citizens and persons with disabilities rather than the problems of unemployed workers and their families. Some of the efforts address issues affecting women, regardless of income. One interesting characteristic of these issues is that they do not fit neatly into a traditional class conflict theory of social problems. However, most social workers help individual persons, individual families, individual organizations. Just as in the days of Mary Richmond that individual involvement may from time to time produce information about social problems which becomes important in broader social reform efforts.

The political economy environment within which social workers practice their profession has clearly changed; the batting average on social action has slumped. But this is not the consequence of an overnight "abandonment" by social workers of a social conscience. Nor is there a sudden abandonment of "public welfare" as Dobelstein suggests. Again there is a misreading of history. The early charity organization social workers were not primarily involved in financial assistance. In fact, one of the key concepts of the COS movement was opposition to "outdoor relief" administered by local governments. In the late 1800s social welfare leaders succeeded in getting outdoor relief programs eliminated in a number of cities. Mary Richmond strongly supported the concept that the COS should not, itself, administer financial assistance, although when an economic crisis occurred in 1907, she changed her opinion and the Philadelphia Society for Organizing Charity organized an emergency fundraising effort to meet the needs of newly unemployed families.

The key responsibility of the charity organization social worker was the analysis of the total family situation using a "social systems" framework, the mobilization of all possible resources available to the family, and the direct provision of charitable assistance only as a "residual" last resort. Some social workers were involved in the efforts to promote social insurance plans during the 1920s, but the leadership came primarily from economists.

Social workers never dominated the administration of the federal-state public assistance programs established in the 1930s and 40s. From the beginning there was a decision at the federal level that the administration of the Social Security insurance system was not a social work function. Although a number of social workers, particularly in large cities, were recruited as administrators and supervisors in the initial AFDC and Old Age Assistance programs set up by the states, and social workers were active in the formation of the American Public Welfare Association, it became clear by the early 1950s that income assistance eligibility determination was not viewed as a specialized social work function in most state agencies, regardless of the job titles used. While in part that reflected the movement among social workers towards a psychological model of personal counseling and the failure of schools of social work to give priority attention to public assistance social work (it was NIMH and its mandate to develop mental health practitioners that provided financial support for the expansion of graduate social work), it also reflected the attitude of public assistance administrators.

While the Charlotte Towle publication, *Common Human Needs*, was written with federal funding as a training guide for public assistance workers, it was also clear by the time it was published that neither federal officials, nor state administrators were prepared to support a model of AFDC which emphasized the use of professionally educated social workers providing intensive, individualized assessment and treatment for each AFDC household. Bachelor's degree persons, some with and many without, social work training, became the backbone of the AFDC staff. The more successful effort to build state child welfare components using graduate social workers had little impact on public assistance administration across the country.

The further effort to strengthen the role of social workers in AFDC in the 1960s with federal funding for "social services" had limited impact. Many states were reluctant to add graduate social workers to their permanent staff, fearing that Congress might change its mind and remove the funding. By 1968, by Congressional definition "social services" were primarily day care, family planning, and job training. Social casework counseling for AFDC families, which, in reality, had never been very extensive, diminished steadily, in part as a result of research studies which questioned its effectiveness in moving families out of poverty. By the time that "separation" was mandated, in the early 1970s, the role of social workers with formal professional training as front-line workers in public assistance was already on the decline. Under Title XX casework counseling was relatively low on the list of "social services" funded by the states, with day care at the top of the list. It is at least as reasonable to suggest that public assistance administrators "rejected" social work, as that social workers "deserted" public assistance.

A final issue has to do with "professionalization," the object of much critical comment in the Special Issue. There are suggestions on one hand that organized social work should be defined as an association of organizational employees, perhaps as a nationwide occupational labor union. In the current scene it is not clear what advantages there are for anyone in such a model. Unions, at the moment, are no more active, nor successful, in the public policy arena than professional associations. The other suggested alternative is that organized social work should be a pure social movement organization. Actually there are social movement segments of social work which have maintained such a pattern successfully over a long period of time. The most visible example is the Salvation Army. However, social movements are built on personal commitments, not on occupational roles. Many social workers are participants in social movements, concerned with many different types of social issues, but their employment is not equal to their social movement involvement and the social movements they are involved in are not limited to social workers.

Much of the criticism of professionalization is an attack on an orientation to personal career and income opportunities on the part of social workers. But it is these concerns which were central to the original development of social work as an organized profession of *women*. The professionalization of social work in the early part of this century was primarily an effort by college educated women to gain status recognition from other professions, including university faculty, that were dominated by men, and to achieve a level of pay that would support them as independent persons. Indeed, it was shared problems of public recognition and economic status that brought together the diverse group of women, and men, who worked in very different settings performing very different tasks. Without these common concerns there might never have been a distinctive occupation of social work. The organizational development of social work was, in a way, a forerunner of the "comparable pay" campaign of the 1980s.

One essential element in the campaign for professional recognition was the establishment of boundaries around the concept of professional social worker. This did lead to the long battles over graduate vs. undergraduate education, status distinctions between "psychiatric" social workers and other social workers, and such recent developments as ACSW and the Clinical Register. There have been, indeed, a variety of consequences over the years from the strong push for recognition as an organized profession. The alternative, 75 years ago, was for women social workers to have settled for the same type of subordinate social position of elementary school teachers and nurses.

Whatever assessment one makes of the current status of social work it is essential that the historical background which is being used as a basis for contrast be thoroughly analyzed. It might also be relevant to look for assessments of the current position of social work from social worker practitioners, particularly women, rather than relying exclusively on the opinions of male university faculty members, including this author, who have chosen to pursue very seriously elite academic status without abandoning their commitment to social causes.

Public Professions and the Private Model of Professionalism
Elizabeth Howe

SOCIAL WORK is an interesting field in the way it has tried to lay claim to professional status. Since its origins in the late nineteenth century, social work has been trying to make the case that it should be accepted as a regular, legitimate profession. Somehow it does not seem to feel that it has been really accepted, or, apparently, that it really merits such acceptance.

The argument of this article is that this feeling of a lack of acceptance and of professional inadequacy may have less to do with the nature of social work per se and more to do with the inappropriateness to the field of the dominant model of professionalism that social workers have been trying to achieve. All professions, including social work, can be divided into two groups—the public and the private. The currently accepted model of professionalism is appropriate only to the private ones, and, increasingly, not even to them.

This article develops the concepts of "publicness" and "privateness" in professional life and examines the implications for social work as compared with a variety of other fields, including medicine, law, urban planning, public administration, and university teaching. The key issue is how autonomous professionals are in relation to the people they serve. All these professions aspire to the kind of socially granted, legitimate autonomy characteristic of a traditional profession like medicine, but such autonomy is most easily achieved when a profession is private, that is, when its members are primarily responsible to individual clients. However, a number of professions, including social work, urban planning, and public administration, provide collective services and involve economic externalities that affect the public at large. This makes them public professions in which control is retained by the public, and they are unlikely to achieve significant autonomy.

Although the public or private nature of a profession can only be inferred from the overall pattern of the services it provides and the behavior of its members, one indicator of how a profession views itself and wishes the public to see it is its code of ethics. Thus, this article examines the codes of ethics of various professions to determine how they have dealt with the dilemmas arising out of their public or private orientations.

SEARCH FOR ACCEPTANCE

As a profession, social work grew out of work with the poor—out of the settlement houses, the Charity Organization Societies, and the friendly visitors of the late nineteenth century. At that time it performed three functions: (1) redistributing income, which was primarily done through private charity, (2) encouraging the assimilation of the immigrant poor into the broader culture and the resocialization of the "idle" poor to the work ethic, and (3) campaigning for social reforms, such as housing and labor legislation, that would help the poor.[1]

Right from the start, the field had built into it a conflict of responsibility or loyalty between its clientele, the poor, and the society at large. There was a sympathy and identification with the poor, perhaps found more characteristically in the social reform wing of the field. But social workers also shared values of the wider society and felt a responsibility to it, holding the poor responsible for their poverty, carefully regulating and coordinating the giving of alms through Charity Organization Societies so that there would be no waste and no "welfare cheaters," and trying to change the attitudes and values of the poor through education, recreation, and friendly visiting.

As social work moved from being a volunteer or amateur activity to being a full-time paid one, it began to aspire to professional status. The only models of professionalism available to it were the traditional professions such as medicine and law, and social workers took the former as their primary model. The two obvious characteristics of the medical profession were its knowledge base or expertise, with the requirements for training that went with it, and the profession's service to individual clients.

In social work the development of a claim to expertise went hand in hand with service to individual clients.[2] During the period before World War I, specialties were developing, and their proponents were searching for expertise that would both distinguish social work from other professions and define their unique functions in the organizations where they worked, primarily hospitals and schools. Building on the early casework methods of the Charity Organization Societies and on the idea of diagnosis in medicine, Richmond wrote the definitive work on what she called "social diagnosis."[3] It was a method that focused on analyzing the relationship between the individual and his or her social environment and that thus cut across the various specialties. The advent of Freudian psychology in the 1920s provided social work with a more elaborate underlying theory for its casework method and a more solid claim to professional status.

The adoption of Freudian theory also

led to a greater focus on the individual client. Social casework, following the medical model, had always been primarily concerned with individuals in their social setting. The Freudian approach shifted the focus of a large number of social workers, as it did also for psychiatrists, from the social environment of the client to purely mental or psychological processes.[4]

This shift toward a highly individualistic and psychological model of casework coincided with the public takeover in the 1930s of social work's major function, the redistribution of income through private charity. Since professionals tend to take on the status of their clients, identification with the poor had been a problem.[5] The public assumption of welfare enabled social workers not only to break free from the poor, but also gave them a good reason to look for a new role, one more oriented to the new psychiatric model and to a new constituency.

By the 1930s the field was pluralistic. The social reform thrust from the Progressive era continued, but was isolated within the field. A major group, using the Freudian model of casework, increasingly served a middle-class clientele. Others continued to work with the poor in what became public welfare, although, increasingly, trained social workers employed by public agencies served only in supervisory positions.

The highest status in social work went to caseworkers, especially psychiatric caseworkers, with group work and community organization running a poor second. Psychiatric social work came closest to achieving the medical model of professionalism. Although only about 10 percent of all social workers are in individual fee-for-service practice, they have the knowledge base and the confidential, trust-based relationship with individual clients that doctors have.[6] In such middle-class, psychiatric practice the early conflict between loyalty to the client and responsibility to the society at large for social control is resolved in favor of the client.

Social work has never lost its historical identification with the poor. In practice that is concerned with the poor, whether in planning, administration, or direct service, the incompatible functions of helping and of resocializing

or controlling have remained, blocking the clear achievement of professional status as measured against the medical model, so the conflicts and professional insecurities remain.

In this pattern, however, social work is not unique. It exhibits, in a more conflict-ridden and intractable form, issues that trouble other professions as well. Urban planning, for example, although thought by some social workers to be well established, suffers from much the same kind of aspirations and uncertainties. In a different vein, traditionally accepted professions such as medicine and law have recently been subject to much criticism and to considerable loss of trust from the public. Both these trends are aspects of the same problem: the inappropriate nature of the traditional model of professionalism to much of current professional practice.

Understanding how this model is inappropriate does not neatly solve the problem of professionalism in social work, but it indicates which efforts and expectations have been inappropriate and unrealistic. It also suggests some new directions for structuring a new sense of professionalism.

AUTONOMY

The distinctive characteristics of a profession are generally thought to be prolonged specialized training in a body of abstract knowledge, with admission to the field only after examination by members of the profession, and a service orientation, which is usually spelled out in a code of ethics enforced by members of the profession and which protects clients who are not in a position to evaluate the technical quality of the services they receive.[7] Freidson, however, makes a distinction between the institutions of a profession—such as its knowledge base and training requirements, its code of ethics, and its licensing and regulatory arrangements—and its more fundamental attributes. He argues that the central attribute of a profession is legitimate, organized autonomy or control over its own work, such that the people in the field are subject to evaluation only by other professionals in the same field. Any group aspiring to professional status can establish most or all of the institutions, but it is far

more difficult for a group to achieve legitimate autonomy.[8]

Autonomy does not arise out of the nature of a profession's work. It is not the result of practical difficulties in evaluation, such as isolation from observation. Doctors in hospitals could be evaluated by nondoctors, but are not. Many so-called street-level bureaucrats—policemen, ward attendants in mental hospitals, and teachers, for example—are difficult to evaluate, but are not thereby given any formal grant of autonomy.[9] Nor does autonomy seem to be related to the need to make discretionary technical judgments, since many groups that make such decisions do not have autonomy; social workers and planners are good examples.

Autonomy is basically a grant of power or status made by the society, often by governmental action.[10] To gain autonomy, the profession must argue convincingly that its expertise is so specialized and esoteric that laymen cannot evaluate the quality of the service and that the members of the profession are motivated by a service ethic to act in the best interests of their clients and the public. Indeed, it is the major function of a code of ethics to lay out the profession's service ethic, pledging not to take advantage of the clients' lack of technical knowledge and specifying the duties and responsibilities of the professional in relation to clients, colleagues, and the public.[11] These arguments need not be empirically true, but the profession must be perceived as meriting trust.

Thus, autonomy is desired partly for intrinsic reasons—work is less alienating if its nature, pace, and outcome are controlled by the worker. But the most desirable quality of autonomy is the power and status it provides both in the work setting and in general social life. It is a sign of the public's belief in the importance and worth of the profession's activity and in the trustworthiness of its practitioners.

As a practical matter, autonomy can only be a relative thing.[12] It is given only if society judges that the professional will protect the interests of those he or she serves in situations where they may not be able to do it for themselves. This is a kind of indirect responsibility and implies, as is always the case, that there is someone for the professional to serve, to work on or with or for. The differences in the prepositions indicate how much the degree of independence can be.

Professionals have two kinds of groups they can be responsible to: individual clients and the public at large. Logically this leads to three possible patterns of responsibility, one to each of the groups alone and one to both clients and the public. Generally, professions argue that they are responsible both to clients and to the public. But this dual loyalty can be full of conflicts, and in practice, professionals may try to reduce these conflicts by owing primary loyalty to only one group. Moreover, because of the status and power that result from autonomy, there is an obvious incentive to try to convert direct responsibility to the client or the public to indirect responsibility to the client through professional regulation.

For any given profession, the pattern of whether it serves primarily individual clients, the public, or both groups equally is determined in large part by the nature of the service it provides and by whether its beneficiaries are individuals or larger groups. When the beneficiary is an individual client, the service would be what an economist would call a private good; if the service benefits some collectivity, it would be a collective or public good.

In the case of individual or private goods, the benefit accrues only to the person being served. The treatment of a noncontagious disease is a good example. Collective goods are more complex. Not only are they provided to groups of people; in their pure form, they have the characteristic that if the good or service is provided to one individual, it is automatically provided to everyone in the group because it would be impossible or economically inefficient to exclude anyone from consuming it.

There are few purely public goods. National defense is the usual example, since in today's world of nuclear weapons, protecting one person generally means protecting all. However, many services have some collective qualities, whereby providing the service to one person also benefits others as well. These benefits to people other than the initial recipient are called "externalities" by economists, since they are external to the initial, individual transaction.[13] Thus an inoculation for a contagious disease such as measles or polio not only protects the individual inoculated, but also others who are thereby less likely to catch the disease.

The treatment of noncontagious disease is a good example of a private good, and medicine has generally been the best example of a profession dedicated primarily to the welfare of individual clients. As the inoculation example indicates, medicine has a public side, but it is limited to the separate subfield of public health. Medicine's general approach was accurately characterized by Halberstam: "In the long run, the social obligation of the physician is to ignore society."[14]

At the other extreme are the professions that provide collective goods to the public. Planning and public policy-making are largely collective goods. Laws and plans treat all similarly circumstanced people alike, and one person's compliance with or "consumption" of them often does not reduce anyone else's. For some laws or plans to be effective, everyone must consume. This means that physical and social planners, city managers, and other public administrators are primarily responsible to the public at large, usually through elected representatives.

Most complex of all the professions, however, are those such as law, university teaching, and social work whose services have both private and collective dimensions. Lawyers, academics, and social workers all serve individual clients, but these services are also associated with the larger social benefits of justice, the increase of knowledge, and the assimilation of people into the wider culture or the mitigation of the effects of economic dislocation.

Thus, following the distinction between public and private goods, the kinds of services provided by the various professions suggest that the professions be divided into those that are predominantly private, such as medicine; those that are predominantly public, such as urban planning and public administration; and those that are mixed, including law, university teaching, and social work. However, the nature of these services provided is not the only determinant of professional behavior. The attempt to reduce conflicts in loyalty, especially among professions whose services involve a mixture of public and private benefits, and the attempt to achieve autonomy produce variations in this basic pattern.

AUTONOMY AND RESPONSIBILITY

Status has traditionally been associated with a professional's autonomy from direct control by clients or the public. It would seem likely that if a profession were responsible both to the public and to individual clients, it would try to reduce its dependence on one. Similarly, professions with only one loyalty would be expected to try to create as large a sphere of independence from that group as possible. For a variety of reasons, significant autonomy has been and is likely to be achieved only by the private professions. The public professions, in trying to achieve similar independence, have set an inappropriate and often unachievable goal for themselves.

Autonomy from individual clients is easier to achieve than independence from the public. Individuals are at a significant disadvantage with professionals in terms of knowledge. They are also likely to have been socialized to look up to and to trust professionals. In contrast, the public, either as a mass or as represented by elected officials, does not seem to feel itself so uniformly at a disadvantage; nor does it stand so much in awe of public professionals, with the probable exception of judges. No one would call a doctor a "servant," but the term "public servant" is not only a fairly common usage, it is an expression of praise.

More significantly, public professions are not independent of public control because of the collective aspects of the services they provide. Collective goods would generally not be provided at all or their quality would suffer if they had to be provided by the private market. Therefore, they are financed collectively by taxes or quasi-voluntary contributions and are provided by the public or voluntary sectors of the economy.[15]

This, in turn, places the professional in a bureaucratic setting where supervision and control are much easier than they are in the individual practice of the private professional. The public goals of the profession or the service are then embodied by the organization, and they may or may not be fully shared by the professionals in it. In mixed professions such as social work, conflicts between the individual service goals of the professionals and their direct clients and the public goals of the agency are not uncommon.

Thus, if status comes from autonomy, it is apparent that there are systematic reasons why the private professions can attain it and why the public ones cannot. This has led to a division between the autonomous, accepted professions and the public ones that casts the latter in the role of aspiring preprofessions, with all the mixed feelings of inadequacy and aspiration that go with not having made it yet.[16] If the public professions are not likely to achieve autonomy and if the model they aspire to is inappropriate, the feelings of being second rate can become a chronic problem with no useful solution.

Medicine is the only profession in which the autonomous model has generally been appropriate, but, as indicated earlier, even medicine has traditionally had its own exception in the field of public health, in which significant externalities lead to the public sector's providing these services. This has been a minor and easily separated aspect of the profession, however. In recent years, the adequacy of the traditional model of medicine, that of curing illness, has come into question, and there has been a concomitant questioning of the autonomous, individual fee-for-service model of organization and regulation. If health, a far more diffuse and collective goal, were to become the dominant concern of the medical profession, independence, both from patients and from the public, might have to be reconsidered.

Among the mixed fields, academics seem to have developed a fairly workable, if sometimes uncomfortable, adaptation to their public status, one that allows for a clear and strong sense of professionalism. In large, prestigious universities at least, the conflict between serving students and doing research has commonly been resolved in favor of research, which is a collective good. Pressure from students for more emphasis on teaching is neutralized by the bureaucratic incentive system and by the informal pressures from colleagues that naturally occur in the university.

Some mixed fields have tried to enhance their status by following the private, client-oriented model, thereby negating much of their public responsibility. Law has been most successful at this strategy. It has gained autonomy for individual lawyers, although not for judges, by emphasizing the individual lawyer-client relationship and by playing down the possible conflicts between that relationship and the lawyer's commitment to justice. This is done by relying on the adversary model of justice in which, it is argued, the diligent efforts of each lawyer for his or her client best serve to bring out facts and resolve disputes justly. However, the possibility that this model can be used to justify lying for a client and the frequent and obvious inequities in the adversary process have resulted in considerable public skepticism that the maximum defense of one's client's interests and justice are always compatible.

Social work has tried much the same strategy but with less success. In psychological counseling, social work has developed a client-oriented model that can be achieved in many voluntary agencies and in individual fee-for-service practice, but practice with the poor in public agencies remains an important part of the field. In such practice, conflict between the interests of individual clients and the demands of the agency are common, and several studies have described how orientation toward the agency comes to dominate over loyalty to the client.[17]

In public fields that lack individual clients, professionals have tried to create a sphere of autonomy in the bureaucratic setting by emphasizing the technical expertise involved in their work. They resort to the role of the value-free technician to separate them from the more public or political aspects of their jobs. This strategy has been characteristic of public administrators, such as city managers, and of urban planners; it may also be adopted by the newly developing field of social planning.

The private model is not simply impractical for public professions; it is inappropriate, because it provides an incentive for professionals to neglect the key aspect of their fields. Collective goods cannot be effectively achieved by individual action. Changes in the distribution of income will not be made if the poor are held individually responsible for their poverty. Control of air pollution cannot be achieved by individual effort. Justice is only possible in the context of a carefully impartial, public judicial system that is backed up by legal requirements for due process. Health, in a large social sense, is not likely to be achieved simply by focusing on the illnesses of individual patients.

More fundamentally, autonomy, whether that of the physician in private practice or of the value-neutral, technically expert planner, may run counter to the very idea of the service ethic, which is supposed to distinguish the professions from mere commerce.[18] Self-regulation in private professions is generally ineffective, and it leaves dissatisfied consumers distrustful and with little recourse. Public professionals, even radical ones, often deplore the unprofessional constraints of the bureaucratic organizations they work for.[19] Controls are sometimes excessive, and professionals do not always accept unquestioningly their agency's definition of the public interest. There are, however, advantages to the scrutiny and the accountability that the bureaucratic setting allows for.

CODES OF ETHICS

Codes of ethics, which lay out a profession's responsibilities to clients, colleagues, and the public, provide some evidence of the tension between responsibilities to these various groups. Since the codes are also, and sometimes primarily, symbolic documents that try to shape the public's view of the profession, they provide a good indication of the way a profession has tried to resolve the tension and lay claim to professional status.

The author compared the codes of ethics from all the professions discussed earlier.[20] The provisions of each code are initially classified into four categories: (1) those concerned with the individual characteristics of an ethical professional, (2) those concerned with business affairs or etiquette toward other professionals,

(cont. on p. 206)

The NASW Code of Ethics

PREAMBLE

This code is intended to serve as a guide to the everyday conduct of members of the social work profession and as a basis for the adjudication of issues in ethics when the conduct of social workers is alleged to deviate from the standards expressed or implied in this code. It represents standards of ethical behavior for social workers in professional relationships with those served, with colleagues, with employers, with other individuals and professions, and with the community and society as a whole. It also embodies standards of ethical behavior governing individual conduct to the extent that such conduct is associated with an individual's status and identity as a social worker.

This code is based on the fundamental values of the social work profession that include the worth, dignity, and uniqueness of all persons as well as their rights and opportunities. It is also based on the nature of social work, which fosters conditions that promote these values.

In subscribing to and abiding by this code, the social worker is expected to view ethical responsibility in as inclusive a context as each situation demands and within which ethical judgment is required. The social worker is expected to take into consideration all the principles in this code that have a bearing upon any situation in which ethical intervention or conduct is planned. The course of action that the social worker chooses is expected to be consistent with the spirit as well as the letter of this code.

In itself, this code does not represent a set of rules that will prescribe all the behaviors of social workers in all the complexities of professional life. Rather, it offers general principles to guide conduct, and the judicious appraisal of conduct, in situations that have ethical implications. It provides the basis for making judgments about ethical actions before and after they occur. Frequently, the particular situation determines the ethical principles that apply and the manner of their application. In such cases, not only the particular ethical principles are taken into immediate consideration, but also the entire code and its spirit. Specific applications of ethical principles must be judged within the context in which they are being considered. Ethical behavior in a given situation must satisfy not only the judgment of the individual social worker, but also the judgment of an unbiased jury of professional peers.

This code should not be used as an instrument to deprive any social worker of the opportunity or freedom to practice with complete professional integrity; nor should any disciplinary action be taken on the basis of this code without maximum provision for safeguarding the rights of the social worker affected.

The ethical behavior of social workers results not from edict, but from a personal commitment of the individual. This code is offered to affirm the will and zeal of all social workers to be ethical and to act ethically in all that they do as social workers.

The following codified ethical principles should guide social workers in the various roles and relationships and at the various levels of responsibility in which they function professionally. These principles also serve as a basis for the adjudication by the National Association of Social Workers of issues in ethics.

In subscribing to this code, social workers are required to cooperate in its implementation and abide by any disciplinary rulings based on it. They should also take adequate measures to discourage, prevent, expose, and correct the unethical conduct of colleagues. Finally, social workers should be equally ready to defend and assist colleagues unjustly charged with unethical conduct.

I. THE SOCIAL WORKER'S CONDUCT AND COMPORTMENT AS A SOCIAL WORKER

A. Propriety—The social worker should maintain high standards of personal conduct in the capacity or identity as social worker.

1. The private conduct of the social worker is a personal matter to the same degree as is any other person's, except when such conduct compromises the fulfillment of professional responsibilities.

2. The social worker should not participate in, condone, or be associated with dishonesty, fraud, deceit, or misrepresentation.

3. The social worker should distinguish clearly between statements and actions made as a private individual and as a representative of the social work profession or an organization or group.

B. Competence and Professional Development—The social worker should strive to become and remain proficient in professional practice and the performance of professional functions.

1. The social worker should accept responsibility or employment only on the basis of existing competence or the intention to acquire the necessary competence.

2. The social worker should not misrepresent professional qualifications, education, experience, or affiliations.

C. Service—The social worker should regard as

primary the service obligation of the social work profession.

1. The social worker should retain ultimate responsibility for the quality and extent of the service which that individual assumes, assigns, or performs.

2. The social worker should act to prevent practices that are inhumane or discriminatory against any person or group of persons.

D. Integrity—The social worker should act in accordance with the highest standards of professional integrity and impartiality.

1. The social worker should be alert to and resist the influences and pressures that interfere with the exercise of professional discretion and impartial judgment required for the performance of professional functions.

2. The social worker should not exploit professional relationships for personal gain.

E. Scholarship and Research—The social worker engaged in study and research should be guided by the conventions of scholarly inquiry.

1. The social worker engaged in research should consider carefully its possible consequences for human beings.

2. The social worker engaged in research should ascertain that the consent of participants in the research is voluntary and informed, without any implied deprivation or penalty for refusal to participate, and with due regard for participants' privacy and dignity.

3. The social worker engaged in research should protect participants from unwarranted physical or mental discomfort, distress, harm, danger, or deprivation.

4. The social worker who engages in the evaluation of services or cases should discuss them only for professional purposes and only with persons directly and professionally concerned with them.

5. Information obtained about participants in research should be treated as confidential.

6. The social worker should take credit only for work actually done in connection with scholarly and research endeavors and credit contributions made by others.

II. THE SOCIAL WORKER'S ETHICAL RESPONSIBILITY TO CLIENTS

F. Primacy of Clients' Interests—The social worker's primary responsibility is to clients.

1. The social worker should serve clients with devotion, loyalty, determination, and the maximum application of professional skill and competence.

2. The social worker should not exploit relationships with clients for personal advantage, or solicit the clients of one's agency for private practice.

3. The social worker should not practice, condone, facilitate, or collaborate with any form of discrimination on the basis of race, color, sex, sexual orientation, age, religion, national origin, marital status, political belief, mental or physical handicap, or any other preference or personal characteristic, condition, or status.

4. The social worker should avoid relationships or commitments that conflict with the interests of clients.

5. The social worker should under no circumstances engage in sexual activities with clients.

6. The social worker should provide clients with accurate and complete information regarding the extent and nature of the services available to them.

7. The social worker should apprise clients of their risks, rights, opportunities, and obligations associated with social service to them.

8. The social worker should seek advice and counsel of colleagues and supervisors whenever such consultation is in the best interest of clients.

9. The social worker should terminate service to clients, and professional relationships with them, when such service and relationships are no longer required or no longer serve the clients' needs or interests.

10. The social worker should withdraw services precipitously only under unusual circumstances, giving careful consideration to all factors in the situation and taking care to minimize possible adverse effects.

11. The social worker who anticipates the termination or interruption of service to clients should notify clients promptly and seek the transfer, referral, or continuation of service in relation to the clients' needs and preferences.

G. Rights and Prerogatives of Clients—the social worker should make every effort to foster maximum self-determination on the part of clients.

1. When the social worker must act on behalf of a client who has been adjudged legally incompetent, the social worker should safeguard the interests and rights of that client.

2. When another individual has been legally authorized to act in behalf of a client, the social worker should deal with that person always with the client's best interest in mind.

3. The social worker should not engage in any action that violates or diminishes the civil or legal rights of clients.

H. Confidentiality and Privacy—The social worker should respect the privacy of clients and hold in confidence all information obtained in the course of professional service.

1. The social worker should share with others confidences revealed by clients without their consent only for compelling professional reasons.

2. The social worker should inform clients fully about the limits of confidentiality in a given situation, the purposes for which information is obtained, and how it may be used.

3. The social worker should afford clients reasonable access to any official social work records

concerning them.

4. When providing clients with access to records, the social worker should take due care to protect the confidences of others contained in those records.

5. The social worker should obtain informed consent of clients before taping, recording, or permitting third-party observation of their activities.

I. Fees—When setting fees, the social worker should ensure that they are fair, reasonable, considerate and commensurate with the service performed and with due regard for the clients' ability to pay.

1. The social worker should not divide a fee or accept or give anything of value for receiving or making a referral.

III. THE SOCIAL WORKER'S ETHICAL RESPONSIBILITY TO COLLEAGUES

J. Respect, Fairness, and Courtesy—The social worker should treat colleagues with respect, courtesy, fairness, and good faith.

1. The social worker should cooperate with colleagues to promote professional interests and concerns.

2. The social worker should respect confidences shared by colleagues in the course of their professional relationships and transactions.

3. The social worker should create and maintain conditions of practice that facilitate ethical and competent professional performance by colleagues.

4. The social worker should treat with respect, and represent accurately and fairly, the qualifications, views, and findings of colleagues and use appropriate channels to express judgements on these matters.

5. The social worker who replaces or is replaced by a colleague in professional practice should act with consideration for the interest, character, and reputation of that colleague.

6. The social worker should not exploit a dispute between a colleague and employers to obtain a position or otherwise advance the social worker's interest.

7. The social worker should seek arbitration or mediation when conflicts with colleagues require resolution for compelling professional reasons.

8. The social worker should extend to colleagues of other professions the same respect and cooperation that is extended to social work colleagues.

9. The social worker who serves as an employer, supervisor, or mentor to colleagues should make orderly and explicit arrangements regarding the conditions of their continuing professional relationship.

10. The social worker who has the responsibility for employing and evaluating the performance of other staff members should fulfill such responsibility in a fair, considerate, and equitable manner, on the basis of clearly enunciated criteria.

11. The social worker who has the responsibility for evaluating the performance of employees, supervisees, or students should share evaluations with them.

K. Dealing with Colleagues' Clients—The social worker has the responsibility to relate to the clients of colleagues with full professional consideration.

1. The social worker should not solicit the clients of colleagues.

2. The social worker should not assume professional responsibility for the clients of another agency or a colleague without appropriate communication with that agency or colleague.

3. The social worker who serves the clients of colleagues during a temporary absence or emergency should serve those clients with the same consideration as that afforded any client.

IV. THE SOCIAL WORKER'S ETHICAL RESPONSIBILITY TO EMPLOYERS AND EMPLOYING ORGANIZATIONS

L. Commitment to Employing Organization—The social worker should adhere to commitments made to the employing organization.

1. The social worker should work to improve the employing agency's policies and procedures, and the efficiency and effectiveness of its services.

2. The social worker should not accept employment or arrange student field placements in an organization which is currently under public sanction by NASW for violating personnel standards or imposing limitations on or penalties for professional actions on behalf of clients.

3. The social worker should act to prevent and eliminate discrimination in the employing organization's work assignments and in its employment policies and practices.

4. The social worker should use with scrupulous regard, and only for the purpose for which they are intended, the resources of the employing organization.

V. THE SOCIAL WORKER'S ETHICAL RESPONSIBILITY TO THE SOCIAL WORK PROFESSION

M. Maintaining the Integrity of the Profession—The social worker should uphold and advance the values, ethics, knowledge, and mission of the profession.

1. The social worker should protect and enhance the dignity and integrity of the profession and should be responsible and vigorous in discussion and criticism of the profession.

2. The social worker should take action through appropriate channels against unethical conduct by any other member of the profession.

3. The social worker should act to prevent the unauthorized and unqualified practice of social work.

4. The social worker should make no misrepresentation in advertising as to qualifications, competence, service, or results to be achieved.

N. Community Service—The social worker should assist the profession in making social services available to the general public.

1. The social worker should contribute time and professional expertise to activities that promote respect for the utility, the integrity, and the competence of the social work profession.

2. The social worker should support the formulation, development, enactment and implementation of social policies of concern to the profession.

O. Development of Knowledge—The social worker should take responsibility for identifying, developing, and fully utilizing knowledge for professional practice.

1. The social worker should base practice upon recognized knowledge relevant to social work.

2. The social worker should critically examine, and keep current with, emerging knowledge relevant to social work.

3. The social worker should contribute to the knowledge base of social work and share research knowledge and practice wisdom with colleagues.

VI. THE SOCIAL WORKER'S ETHICAL RESPONSIBILITY TO SOCIETY

P. Promoting the General Welfare—The social worker should promote the general welfare of society.

1. The social worker should act to prevent and eliminate discrimination against any person or group on the basis of race, color, sex, sexual orientation, age, religion, national origin, marital status, political belief, mental or physical handicap, or any other preference or personal characteristic, condition, or status.

2. The social worker should act to ensure that all persons have access to the resources, services, and opportunities which they require.

3. The social worker should act to expand choice and opportunity for all persons, with special regard for disadvantaged or oppressed groups or persons.

4. The social worker should promote conditions that encourage respect for the diversity of cultures which constitute American society.

5. The social worker should provide appropriate professional services in public emergencies.

6. The social worker should advocate changes in policy and legislation to improve social conditions and to promote social justice.

7. The social worker should encourage informed participation by the public in shaping social policies and institutions.

Summary of Major Principles

I. THE SOCIAL WORKER'S CONDUCT AND COMPORTMENT AS A SOCIAL WORKER

A. *Propriety*. The social worker should maintain high standards of personal conduct in the capacity or identity as social worker.

B. *Competence and Professional Development*. The social worker should strive to become and remain proficient in professional practice and the performance of professional functions.

C. *Service*. The social worker should regard as primary the service obligation of the social work profession.

D. *Integrity*. The social worker should act in accordance with the highest standards of professional integrity.

E. *Scholarship and Research*. The social worker engaged in study and research should be guided by the conventions of scholarly inquiry.

II. THE SOCIAL WORKER'S ETHICAL RESPONSIBILITY TO CLIENTS

F. *Primacy of Clients' Interests*. The social worker's primary responsibility is to clients.

G. *Rights and Prerogatives of Clients*. The social worker should make every effort to foster maximum self-determination on the part of clients.

H. *Confidentiality and Privacy*. The social worker should respect the privacy of clients and hold in confidence all information obtained in the course of professional service.

I. *Fees*. When setting fees, the social worker should ensure that they are fair, reasonable, considerate, and commensurate with the service performed and with due regard for the clients' ability to pay.

III. THE SOCIAL WORKER'S ETHICAL RESPONSIBILITY TO COLLEAGUES

J. *Respect, Fairness, and Courtesy*. The social worker should treat colleagues with respect, courtesy, fairness, and good faith.

K. *Dealing with Colleagues' Clients*. The social worker has the responsibility to relate to the clients of colleagues with full professional consideration.

IV. THE SOCIAL WORKER'S ETHICAL RESPONSIBILITY TO EMPLOYERS AND EMPLOYING ORGANIZATIONS

L. *Commitments to Employing Organizations*. The social worker should adhere to commitments made to the employing organizations.

V. THE SOCIAL WORKER'S ETHICAL RESPONSIBILITY TO THE SOCIAL WORK PROFESSION

M. *Maintaining the Integrity of the Profession*. The social worker should uphold and advance the values, ethics, knowledge, and mission of the profession.

N. *Community Service*. The social worker should assist the profession in making social services available to the general public.

O. *Development of Knowledge*. The social worker should take responsibility for identifying, developing, and fully utilizing knowledge for professional practice.

VI. THE SOCIAL WORKER'S ETHICAL RESPONSIBILITY TO SOCIETY

P. *Promoting the General Welfare*. The social worker should promote the general welfare of society.

TABLE 1. FREQUENCY OF ETIQUETTE AND COMMON-GOOD PROVISIONS IN CODE OF ETHICS

Organization	Common Good			Etiquette		
	Fre-quency	Percent-age	Rank	Fre-quency	Percent-age	Rank
Public Administration, U.S. Government Service	5	41.7	1	0	0.0	1–2
National Association of Social Workers (1967)	4	26.7	2	3	20.0	7
American Bar Association (1969)	43	23.9	3	15	8.3	4
International City Managers' Association (1962)	5	20.0	4	0	0.0	1–2
American Association of University Professors	3	16.7	5	4	22.0	8
International City Managers' Association (1924)	3	15.0	6	1	5.0	3
American Institute of Planners	3	13.0	7	4	17.4	5
American Bar Association (1908)	8	11.1	8	25	34.7	9
National Association of Social Workers (1979)	7	9.9	9	14	19.7	6
American Medical Association	8	4.5	10	90	50.3	10

(3) those concerned with how the individual professional should behave in various substantive situations, and (4) those concerned with the responsibility of the individual practitioner or the profession as a whole to the common good.[21]

In addition, the author counted the number of times each code used words denoting the public compared to the number of times it used words denoting individual clients. References to the latter were generally to "clients" or "patients" or, in public professions, to "employers." The words denoting the public were more varied. Besides obvious terms such as "the public," "the community," or "mankind," the count included terms that denoted the public aspect of each profession—"the court" and "the law" for lawyers, "health" for doctors, and "knowledge" or "academic freedom" for college professors. Context was considered for some words. The word "law" in the American Bar Association codes of ethics did not always denote the entire body of law, but only when it did mean that was it counted. Similarly, "health" could refer to the illness of an individual patient and was counted only when it meant something collective. The difference between the two counts was that the classification of provisions dealt with entire ethical statements or principles and the word count simply counted words.

The various codes were then ranked according to their publicness as indicated by these two measures. Tables 1 and 2 show the results. Provisions related to etiquette are concerned with responsibilities to other members of the profession and with business practices and are a sign of autonomy. They tend to be negatively correlated with provisions relating to the public good. In part, this reflects the tendency of the short codes of aspiring or public professions to be symbolic statements; day-to-day regulation of these professions is done by employing organizations. The codes of self-regulating professions are considerably longer and reflect the long-term accretion of provisions that are concerned with etiquette toward colleagues or financial and business affairs.

In both tables, the extremes are clear and correspond to the distinction between purely public and private professions. Medicine is clearly the most private by both measures. It is interesting to note that in the code of the American Medical Association the word "health," used in a sense that could be seen as collective good rather than the illness of an individual patient, occurred only 17 times out of the 346 words counted as indicating public or private orientation. Furthermore, 60 percent of these references were in the section on the profession's traditional public health responsibilities. At the other extreme, public administration is clearly the most public profession. The rest of the pattern, however, is mixed because of the tension in many fields between being public and trying to appear private.

There is considerable variation, for example, between the various codes of ethics in the two professions characterized here as purely public—public administration and planning. The code of the American Institute of Planners, for example, plays down that profession's responsibilities to the common good. The code is designed in part to deal with the problems of private consultants rather than publicly employed planners, and in the style of codes for the private professions, it stresses responsibilities to clients, to other planners, and to expertise.

In all the codes of the purely public fields, references to "clients" do not really mean individual clients. City managers and all public and many consulting planners are employed by elected officials of government and are

TABLE 2. FREQUENCY OF WORDS DENOTING "PUBLIC" IN CODES OF ETHICS

Organization	Frequency of word denoting "public"	Percentage of all words counted	Rank	Adjusted rank from Table 1[a]
International City Managers' Association (1962)	30	85.7	1	3
American Association of University Professors	9	60.0	2	4
National Association of Social Workers (1967)	4	57.1	3	1
International City Managers' Association (1924)	12	54.5	4	5
American Institute of Planners	13	43.5	5	6
American Bar Association (1969)	175	41.3	6	2
American Bar Association (1908)	56	39.2	7	7
National Association of Social Workers (1979)	14	23.7	8	8
American Medical Association	76	21.9	9	9

[a] The U.S. Government Service's Code of Ethics is left out of this table because 100 percent of the words denoting public and client would refer to the public.

clearly responsible, through them, to the public. The percentage of words denoting public in the American Institute of Planners code and the two International City Managers' Association codes would be close to 100 percent if the client references in their codes were construed as referring to the public.

The codes of ethics in the mixed fields clearly indicate the conflicts of loyalty in these professions. Academics tend to emphasize their collective responsibility. The code of the American Association of University Professors gives almost equal space to research and to students, but the provision on research comes first, and overall there are more references to knowledge, truth, academic freedom, and the public—all aspects of the public side of the field—than there are to students. In the legal profession, the recent revision of the American Bar Association code contains considerably more provisions related to the public good than the old code did, but still about 60 percent of the words counted in both codes were references to clients.

Social work is clearly the most interesting of the fields, both in its conflict and in the way the profession has tried to deal with it. The Code of Ethics has been something of an issue in the field. A 1977 proposed revision, similar to the original 1967 code, was not adopted by the Delegate Assembly; but a more thoroughgoing revision was proposed and adopted in 1979.[22]

The original 1967 code shows clearly the conflict between public and private orientations. It had close to a fifty-fifty split between public and private references and was second only to the U.S. Government Service code in the number of provisions related to the public good. However, it offered little guidance for situations in which public and private loyalties conflict. The dilemma created is epitomized by the first provision of the code, "I regard as my primary obligation the welfare of the individual or group served, which includes action for improving social conditions." At least two and possibly three responsibilities are stated here as the field's "primary" obligation.

The earlier discussion of the development of social work as a profession indicates that it is pluralistic. The conflicting ethical provisions in the 1967 code may have represented a political solution to the problem of how to write a code of ethics in which no single group would be dominant. Even if this explained the conflict, however, the provision still remained as evidence of the underlying strains in the field.

The 1979 revision of the Code of Ethics (reprinted on pp. 184–188), however, is quite another story. Whereas the American Bar Association has moved in the direction of a more public code, NASW has clearly moved toward a more private one—so much so that the new code ranks only just above the American Medical Association code in both the proportion of common-good provisions and in words denoting the public. While the 1967 code set no priorities between conflicting sources of accountability, the new one states clearly that "the social worker's primary responsibility is to clients." (§II, ¶F)

The choice of the client-oriented medical model seems to be a response to social work's particularly difficult dilemma. In a public or mixed field, status based on public responsibility is more likely to be achieved if the collective benefit provided by the field is attractive both to professionals and to the public. Justice and the increase of knowledge are attractive goals, and even planning, which has been anathema to most Americans in the past, seems now to be gaining greater acceptance. Social work's predominant collective benefit—"regulating the poor," to use Cloward and Piven's highly critical term—is not one that either the public or the profession like to be too open or blunt about.[23]

How realistic this choice of a private model of professionalism is remains to be seen. Responsibilities to employing organizations are clearly viewed as separate from responsibilities to clients, with the former apparently subordinate to the latter. Nevertheless, as long as public money funds services provided by social work, the employing organization is still likely to have more power in the social worker's professional life than the clients, especially in the public sector. Several provisions dealing with the lack of the absolute confidentiality found in the private model seem to be trying implicitly to deal with this reality. However, the primary provision governing responsibilities to the employer states only, "The social worker should adhere to commitments made to the employing organization." (§IV, ¶L) Most of the subprovisions in this section are concerned with responsibilities for changing the employing organization, again perhaps implicitly recognizing the possibility of conflicts.

Overall, however, the new NASW code is a great improvement over the old one. It is longer and provides more detailed guidance, having sixty-nine provisions compared with fifteen before. The greater detail has not increased the proportion of provisions dealing only with etiquette among professionals, and these are now balanced with substantive provisions dealing with the responsibilities of supervisors to employees. Most important, the new code is explicitly organized according to different areas of responsibility—to clients, colleagues, employing organizations, the profession, and society at large. The built-in conflicts of the 1967 code are sorted out and priorities are set.

The choice to give priority to clients will be a step backward for the profession if it is the result of an attempt simply to resolve the public-client tension by returning to the private medical-type model, heralding a new era of "disengagement from the poor."[24] However, the expansion of the sections dealing with the public responsibilities of the profession suggests that this is not the case. These sections stress availability of services, equal access for all, expansion of choices, particularly for the disadvantaged, concern with social justice, and respect for cultural diversity. If the priority given to clients in the new code is seen more as an attempt to even up the balance of power between clients and the public, then the implications are somewhat different.

For such a strategy to work it is necessary to bring more to the balance than a new code of ethics. Organization by clients is one possible force in such a balance, but one that may be insufficient, given the experience of the 1960s and especially of the welfare rights movement.[25] Another alternative is Richan's idea of a "new professionalism."[26] He sees social workers as working for a change toward a more client-oriented social welfare system at both direct service and policy levels. Social workers would continue to work in public bureaucracies, which would be the primary regulators of their everyday behavior. But the organized backing of the profession would enable them to challenge an agency practice or policy that seemed harmful or demeaning to clients.

Under such a model, the NASW Code of Ethics would be an alternate guide, not generally in conflict with agency rules, but available to help individual practitioners evaluate the legitimacy not only of their actions, but of agency regulations as well. As such, it can be effective as a counterforce, both for individuals bringing up cases under its guidelines and in policy debates, only if the profession is willing to enforce it.

Notes and References

1. Roy Lubove, *The Professional Altruist: The Emergence of Social Work as a Career, 1890–1930* (Cambridge, Mass.: Harvard University Press, 1965), chaps. 1 and 2; and Harriett M. Bartlett, "Early Trends," in Neil Gilbert and Harry Specht, eds., *The Emergence of Social Welfare and Social Work* (Itasca, Ill.: F. E. Peacock Publishers, 1976), pp. 287–302.

2. For background to this section, *see* Lubove, op. cit.

3. Mary Richmond, *Social Diagnosis* (New York: Russell Sage Foundation, 1917).

4. Lubove, op. cit., chap. 4.

5. Richard Cloward and Irwin Epstein, "Private Social Welfare's Disengagement from the Poor: The Case of Family Adjustment Agencies," in George Brager and Francis Purcell, eds., *Community Action against Poverty* (New Haven, Conn.: College & University Press, 1967), p. 46; and Jerome Carlin, *Lawyer's Ethics* (New York: Russell Sage Foundation, 1966), pp. 22–27 and 176–178.

6. Willard C. Richan and Allan R. Mendelsohn, *Social Work: The Unloved Profession* (New York: Franklin Watts, New Viewpoints, 1973), chap. 2.

7. Frances Alan Bennion, *The Consultant Professions and Their Code* (London, England: K. C. Knight, 1969), pp. 15–16; and William J. Goode, "Encroachment, Charlatanism, and the Emerging Profession: Psychology, Medicine and Sociology," *American Sociological Review*, 25 (December 1960), pp. 902–914.

8. Eliot Freidson, *Profession of Medicine: A Study of the Sociology of Applied Knowledge* (New York: Dodd, Mead & Co., 1973), chap. 4.

9. Dorothy Smith, "Front-Line Organization of the State Mental Hospital," *Administrative Science Quarterly*, 10 (December 1965), pp. 381–399; and Michael Lipsky, "Toward a Theory of Street Level Bureaucracy," in W. D. Hawley and M. Lipsky, eds., *Theoretical Perspectives on Urban Politics* (Englewood Cliffs, N.J.: Prentice-Hall, 1976), pp. 196–213.

10. Corinne Gilb, *Hidden Hierarchies: The Professions and Government* (New York: Harper & Row, 1966).

11. Charles Levy, "On the Development of a Code of Ethics," *Social Work*, 19 (March 1974), pp. 207–216.

12. For a discussion of the distinction between consulting professions that serve clients and are client dependent, and scholarly professions that deal with symbols and are colleague dependent, *see* Freidson, op. cit., pp. 73–75.

13. For an introduction to the idea of public goods, *see* Francis Bator, "Government and the Sovereign Consumer," in Edmund Phelps, ed., *Private Wants and Public Needs* (New York: W. W. Norton & Co., 1965), pp. 118–133. For more thorough treatments of this subject, *see* Francis Bator, "The Anatomy of Market Failure," *The Quarterly Journal of Economics*, 72 (August 1958), pp. 351–379; and Paul Samuelson, "Diagrammatic Exposition of a Pure Theory of Public Expenditures," *Review of Economics and Statistics*, 37 (November 1955), pp. 350–356.

14. Michael Halberstam, "Professionalism and Health Care," in Lawrence Tancredi, ed., *Ethics of Health Care* (Washington, D.C.: National Academy of Sciences, 1974), p. 250.

15. For the relationship and similarities between the public and the voluntary sectors, *see* Burton Weisbrod, "Toward a Theory of the Voluntary Non-Profit Sector in a Three-Sector Economy," in Edmund Phelps, ed., *Altruism, Morality and Economic Theory* (New York: Russell Sage Foundation, 1975), pp. 171–195.

16. For discussions of distinctions between accepted or full professions and paraprofessions and between full professions and the category that this article terms "aspiring" and that Etzioni calls "semiprofessions," which includes social work, *see* Freidson, op. cit., pp. 75–77; Amitai Etzioni, *Modern Organizations* (Englewood Cliffs, N.J.: Prentice-Hall, 1964), pp. 87–89; and Etzioni, ed., *The Semi-Professions and Their Organization: Teachers, Nurses and Social Workers* (New York: Free Press, 1969).

17. Peter Blau, "Orientation toward Clients in a Public Welfare Agency," *Administrative Science Quarterly*, 5 (December 1960), pp. 341–361; and Andrew Billingsley, "Bureaucratic and Professional Orientation Patterns in Social Casework," *Social Service Review*, 38 (December 1964), pp. 400–407.

18. Bennion, op. cit., p. 7.

19. Richan and Mendelsohn, op. cit., pp. 98–102; and Earl Finkler, *Dissent and Independent Initiative in Planning Offices*, Report 269 (Chicago: American Society of Planning Officials, May 1971), pp. 11 and 57–59.

20. *Policy Documents and Reports* (Washington, D.C.: American Association of University Professors, 1973); *Canons of Professional Ethics* and *Code of Professional Responsibility* (Chicago: American Bar Association, 1908 and 1969, respectively); *Code of Professional Responsibility* (Washington, D.C.: American Institute of Planners, 1962); *Opinions and Reports of the Judicial Council* (Chicago: American Medical Association, 1969); *A Suggested Code of Ethics for Municipal Officials and Employees* and *The City Manager's Code of Ethics* (Chicago: International City Managers' Association, 1962 and 1924, respectively); *Code of Ethics* (Washington, D.C.: National Association of Social Workers, 1967); "The NASW Code of Ethics," *NASW News*, 25 (January 1980), pp. 4–25, and reprinted in this article; and U.S. Congress, *A Code of Ethics for Government Service*, H.R. Cong. Res. 175, 85th Cong., 2nd sess., 1958.

21. Albert Jonsen and Andre Hellegers, "Conceptual Foundations for an Ethics of Medical Care," in Tancredi, op. cit., p. 4.

22. *See* Task Force on Ethics of the National Association of Social Workers, "Proposed Revised Code of Ethics," *NASW News*, 22 (March 1977), pp. 16–17.

23. Richard Cloward and Frances Fox Piven, *Regulating the Poor* (New York: Pantheon Books, 1971).

24. Cloward and Epstein, op. cit.

25. Richard Cloward and Frances Fox Piven, "Weight of the Poor: A Strategy to End Poverty," *Nation*, May 2, 1966, pp. 510–517; and Larry Jackson and William Johnson, *Protest by the Poor: The Welfare Rights Movement in New York City* (New York: New York City Rand Institute, 1973).

26. Willard C. Richan, chaps. 6 and 7 and appendix, in Richan and Mendelsohn, op. cit.

Elizabeth Howe, Ph.D., is Assistant Professor, Department of Urban and Regional Planning, University of Wisconsin–Madison.

The Welfare Marketplace
Arthur Schiff

To understand the current welfare mess, you have to understand people like Rose Johnson. Rose (her name has been changed) loves training programs. A mother of two boys, four and six years old, Rose has been on public assistance five out of the last seven years. This is the fourth time she has trained for a career as a word processor. Rose is no fool. She knows training programs can be a lot better than most jobs, and with the two kids to take care of, she has more than a day's work at home. Besides, Rose has money problems. Unexpectedly, she had to go to North Carolina to visit her ailing mother. She was unable to pay the rent that month, so to keep her from being evicted, the welfare department paid it and is now recouping it from her welfare check; money is tight.

As a veteran of training programs, Rose is a smart consumer. Most training programs will pay stipends for transportation, lunch, child care, and even give a one-time grant for new clothes. The one Rose has just joined is a gold-plater. She has arranged child care for her boys with a neighbor whose kids she sometimes baby-sits in the evening. The welfare department will pay for the baby-sitting services; as part of her deal with Rose, the neighbor will split the child-care payments. Rose is bringing lunch from home and keeping the lunch money. She used the clothing grant for necessities and has managed to convince the department that she lives two fares away from the training site, although she actually walks one of the bus routes. When she finishes the program, she will go back to staying home with the kids.

Since the advent of the Great Society in the Sixties, America has experimented with a variety of programs to help the poor, from food stamps and expanded welfare benefits to job training. After almost 30 years both the taxpayers who fund these programs and the poor who use them are unhappy with the results. After more than 20 years of observing poverty programs up close, including nearly a decade as a player inside New York City's welfare bureaucracy, I have slowly come to the conclusion that there is something fundamentally wrong with the way we think about helping the poor.

All of our diverse social service programs have one thing in common: They are based on a particular idea of what poor people are like: passive, helpless, dependent, and easily manipulated. This view of the poor is wrong, as is the usual portrait of the poor passively shuffling off to welfare centers to be signed up for the dole. Rather, most lower-income people are, like Rose Johnson, resourceful, practiced consumers of welfare and other social services. Like most consumers, the poor assess welfare "products" based on how they fit their own lives and goals. They perform "cost-benefit" analyses, exploring the benefits and requirements of assistance programs, deciding to use or reject various "products" according to their personal circumstances.

In the course of many years, first as a manager of one of these behemoth programs and then as a close observer of them, I have seen these consumer dynamics at work. Some people will not fill out a food-stamp application to get $200 per month in benefits; others will go to legal aid to fight for 10 dollars' worth. Some people in dire straits will beg or borrow to avoid welfare; others, with a regular income, will hide it to continue getting Medicaid. I remember one older woman applying for food stamps. The interview was going well when the worker asked: "Do you have any money in a bank account?" "Goodbye," said the woman, getting up and stalking out.

For those truly interested in the welfare of the poor, this is good news, because it suggests that the poor are inclined to run their own lives and are mostly capable of doing so. The bad news is that social service programs elaborately designed to make the poor behave in certain ways, don't. They simply become part of a stream of family income, a package poor people put together to live on.

The packages range from the unlikely strategy of living only on public assistance and food stamps, to the far more common strategy of combining income from as many sources—including work—as possible. Poor people, of course, break the rules and fudge the answers they put down on the forms. In this, lower-income people mirror the rest of society, which completes loan applications, mortgage forms, and job résumés with the same kind of creativity.

This is an important point, often overlooked by policy analysts. Government welfare policy fails in part because it is,

inevitably, based on information furnished to the welfare system by the clients. Because poor people are not dumb, the information they give to inquiring welfare bureaucracies is hardly reliable. To get welfare you must tell the worst story about your life, about how you have no other money, no support from family or friends, no money from a part-time job, no income from unreportable sources. In this picture, welfare recipients really do look like passive, virtually helpless dependents, even "patients," whose lives can be micromanaged by benevolent bureaucracies for their own and for society's greater good.

A recent, and very rare, in-depth study of the income and expenditures of 25 welfare mothers published in the journal *The American Prospect* painted quite a different and far more realistic picture. The study, by Christopher Jencks and Kathryn Edin, found that nearly all the mothers supplemented their welfare checks with income from other sources, including work: "None reported all her extra income to the welfare department, and only two reported any of it." National studies of the expenditures of welfare families, which turn out to be far higher than their supposed income, confirm this finding. So does common sense: Few mothers could support their families on welfare alone.

As this study suggests, the welfare system's beneficiaries are not automatons or pawns; they are playing their own game. Thus, one of the most important and long-standing issues in the welfare debate—how we can get clients off welfare and back to work—is not a question about the real world. In the real world many or most welfare mothers are already working, though usually part-time or off-the-books, and less productively than if they did not have to conceal their income. They are on welfare because they want more cash and other benefits than they can get by working alone.

The official title of the basic welfare program is Aid to Families with Dependent Children. But for years the dominant theme of the welfare debate has been the misbehavior of *parents* and how to correct it. Welfare policy became preoccupied with such ambitious and complicated tasks as distinguishing the deserving from the undeserving poor and designing a system that would support those who could not work, without tempting those who could, balancing a decent provision for the poor against the lure of dependency. The system has affected the way the poor behave, but it has not directed them in the way social service professionals hoped. But because real poor people do not fit into these neat categories, the result was always a system that infantilized, demeaned, and corrupted the people receiving benefits.

The welfare system is a horrid, dispiriting failure for the same reason that Eastern European economies are horrid, dispiriting failures: Central economic planning does not work. Managing an entire economy and the lives of the people in it is just too complex a task for a central bureaucracy.

Poor people operate in their own special economy. Like all economies this one has its own rules; in this case, rules largely made by the social service bureaucracy. Welfare, food stamps, Medicaid, job training, school lunch, for that matter the public schools themselves, are closed-ended systems, worlds unto themselves, gulags if you will. Central planning replaces choice, forced work replaces jobs, waiting rooms replace motion, forms replace substance. Most importantly, unlike the rest of the American economy, the planned poverty economy is not accountable to its consumers.

There is a way to tear the iron curtain between welfare public policy and reality. This does not require "getting the government out of welfare" or abandoning our collective responsibility to the poor. The government, after all, has a very large role to play in the regular economy. Rather, the way out of the welfare mess begins by recognizing that the poor are customers. The demand for welfare and other services is a market. We must let that market work.

Businesses plan too. Businesses, like social service bureaucracies, must evaluate their clients' needs and offer goods and services to satisfy them. But unlike central planners, businessmen never forget, because the market reminds them, that their customers are free to use their products or to find alternatives. In the real economy, businessmen cannot develop marketing strategies with the theoretical beauty and completeness of social science. Instead, they use a less elegant and ambitious, but far more successful method: market research. Market research may be as simple as watching which items move out of the inventory and which do not, but it is always driven by the humble realization that businesses must take the needs, desires, and goals of consumers into account.

The trouble with welfare is not that policymakers do not try to find out whether or how welfare programs "work." They do.

Congress, state legislatures, welfare administrators, and all the experts who design social service programs rely heavily on social science research to tell them about the behavior of the poor and to design programs to modify that behavior. The problem is that social science research does not gather information as accurately or efficiently as a market.

Social science experiments are conducted on human subjects, a poor choice for laboratory tests. The vagaries of the human will are a variable for which no regression-analysis can control. Rose Johnson, our student of training programs, took part in an experiment to see if training would make her independent of welfare. It will not, not because the training program was objectively good or bad, well or inadequately funded, but because her goals are very different from those the job-training experts assume she has.

In the "laboratory," Rose Johnson wants to work and only lacks the panoply of supportive services (child care, counseling, role playing, group meetings, aptitude testing, basic education, health education, etc.), financial supports, training, and job placement services to achieve economic independence. These premises are wrong. What Rose wants is to stay home with her young children. The training program meets her needs for diversion and investment in the future, but she is not, in her own mind, in the market for a job. Experiments test hypotheses. But Rose Johnson confounds such experiments because she has her own agenda that defies the hypothesis.

Rose Johnson is in the program, essentially, because she was paid to enter it. But by paying her to enter the program, we deprive ourselves of the answer to one crucial question: If Rose really wanted a job, is this the sort of training program she would have entered and completed? If we had offered Rose no extra benefits, but charged her $10, would she have signed up?

Here the difference between social science research and market research is obvious. Market researchers would never bribe Rose to buy a product, because they want to know if Rose wants the product itself. But under the current approach to social services, we leave no stone unturned, no carrot withheld or stick unused, no rule unwritten, in an attempt to redirect the lives of the poor. Inevitably, though inadvertently, the system encourages clients to play games, as Rose did.

All of the successive waves of welfare reform—from programs to pay people to train, to programs to force them to work—amount to little more than failed attempts to do the hardest thing in the world: transform people's hearts and minds to make them behave "better." The goals of market research, on the other hand, are more modest: to observe how people behave and to find ways to accommodate that behavior. Small wonder it is easier to sell a car than turn a criminal into a law-abiding citizen. The Rose Johnson scenario suggests we ought to keep it simple.

That was the conclusion of a recent $12 million evaluation of four work-training programs. All but one failed to achieve its goals. According to Mathematica, Inc., a leading public-policy research firm, the one that did succeed did so by jettisoning all the services and extra cash and simply offering skill training tailored to jobs available in the area. The time between entry into the training program and starting the job was therefore shortened; the trainees quickly learned the

chore in order to get to
work and to get the paycheck. The government paid for the training, which the employers might well have done.

Much expert opinion casts aspersions on such programs: The client was trained for a particular job, but not given the attitudes and background to fit him for advancement, or for other jobs; the client could just as easily have been trained to pick crops; when the job goes, the client will be back on welfare. Perhaps. But if we designed training programs on the basis of what people want, they would probably look a lot more like the one that worked than the ones that did not. The people we are trying to reach would say that classrooms are places of failure and frustration and what they want is a job. We would not spend time and money on Rose Johnson, or she on the program.

What about creating "the whole person," equipped to handle an uncertain future? Is that not a worthy goal? Actually it is not a "goal" at all. It is a social science paradigm. It does not make any sense to regard something as a policy goal if we have no idea how to achieve it, especially when the poor are able to frustrate any strategy for reaching it that we might devise. Distinguishing between the good we can do and the good we can only imagine is the difference between a training program designed by market researchers and one designed by social scientists. It is the difference, not only between two sets of values, and two assumptions about the nature of poor people, but far more importantly, if you care about such things, the difference between a program that works and one that does not.

In this and other cities around the country, professional advocates for the poor are a powerful force in designing and lobbying for social service programs. They are dedicated and generous people who work in social service agencies, public and private, and in more explicitly activist groups, such as the Children's Defense Fund and the Community Service Society, whose primary mission is to lobby for expanded social programs. To change the system, these people, well-intentioned as they are, must change as well.

Advocates for the poor are rarely elected or hired by the people on whose behalf they speak. They hardly ever consult their poor clients while negotiating on their behalf and never submit those deals to clients for ratification. These advocates loathe and despise the same programs they fight to expand and impose upon lower-income people: They denounce food stamps as demeaning, but denounce even more loudly their underutilization; they decry welfare as a "bureaucratic nightmare," but want more people to enroll. Theirs is a difficult position to maintain. I know, I have been there myself.

It would dawn on my colleagues and me only dimly, when we were cutting deals for clients, that maybe they did not want a school breakfast program compared to, say, longer library hours. When an organization I was with fought for expanded emergency assistance to Supplemental Security Income (SSI) beneficiaries, we never consulted a single potential beneficiary. When we won, we celebrated our victory, not theirs.

There is considerable evidence that the programs we fought for so vigorously are not those the clients wanted. Or at least they did not want them in the way they were marketed, or with the elaborate, often discouraging strings that came attached. Major programs, such as food stamps, SSI, school breakfast, even welfare itself, are significantly undersubscribed. Simple programs like food pantries, often run by local churches, are besieged, while more ambitious universal assistance programs must advertise to attract recipients. Advocates blame bureaucratic obstacles as the cause of underenrollment, but thousands manage to use the programs even as thousands of others ignore them.

There is a market for loans, a market for mortgages, a market for insurance, a market for farm subsidies, and a market for labor. There is a market for food stamps, a market for unemployment compensation, a market for income transfers, a market for Social Security, and a market for school lunch. These markets have more in common than they do differences, if one has the minimal decency to credit all people—rich and poor, young and old—with the ability to make decisions about their own lives. Ignoring the information that markets can provide is a way to guarantee that programs will fail.

We want consumers—the poor—to run their own lives and do it better. And we want the system to offer services that might actually help the poor to do this, and to shut down programs that do not work. To accomplish this we must do two things. First, we must summon the political and moral humility to acknowledge that we cannot direct the lives of the poor in any elaborately detailed way. The poor need extra income, and we should provide it. But we must strip income supports of the detailed rules and bureaucratic oversight that inevitably encourage the poor to behave in ways that will keep them poor.

Secondly, we must design social service programs that respond to the market—to the people who use them. The great advantage businesses have over bureaucracies is information. If they guess wrongly about a product, the market soon corrects them. Welfare programs and those who run them need the same sort of feedback. We must build into social service "products" tests that will show whether the market is buying them. And we must shut down programs that do not prove themselves in the market, programs that fail to attract customers.

To shift from a bureaucratic model of welfare and social services to a market and consumer-oriented model would require a major change in the way the social service system and the academic community evaluate programs. Newly proposed programs should be pre-tested using market research techniques, such as consumer surveys, test marketing, and focus groups. Once programs are under way they must be made to face the acid test: If they attract only a small portion of their potential "market" because the clients do not show up, the programs must be allowed to die. For some programs, such as job training, we might even establish small fees to test the depth of customers' commitment to the product.

Even better would be to build market accountability directly into the programs, so that failed programs would die automatically, without the bureaucracy having to intervene. Currently, many social services are provided by private contractors, including private charitable groups and churches. Right now most of the work is done on contract. Wherever possible we should shift to a system in which the contractors must "sell" their services to the clients. Under such a system for, say, job-training programs, clients would receive from the government a voucher worth a certain amount of money, which the clients, with a modest copayment, could use to pay "tuition" at the job-training program of their choice. Of course, there would have to be safeguards against abuse, but the biggest safeguard is the market itself, the consumer preferences of the poor: Popular, effective programs would collect lots of vouchers, others would not attract enough clients to stay in business. Under such a system, the market research is "live," and the penalty for failure is bankruptcy.

Such tactics work best for service rather than welfare programs, which primarily provide income. Income programs also need a radical reform.

Our current welfare system is an unfixable failure. The only way out is to drop the requirement that people stay poor and dependent in order to get assistance. This will mean a huge philosophical change in the way we approach welfare. In fact, it will mean abolishing the welfare program as we have known it.

We can design income-support programs that give poor people the money they need, without managing their lives in detail or encouraging dependency. We can design programs that actively encourage work, not by rules and regulations around which huge enforcement bureaucracies must grow, but by built-in incentives that leave the details up to the people getting the benefits.

The principal task is to eliminate welfare and replace it with a national income-support system. The most obvious way to do this is to greatly expand the existing earned-income tax credit. The earned-income tax credit rewards poor people for having earned income, not for lacking it. It boosts their paycheck with a government bonus at tax time. An expanded version would say to potential recipients: As long as you demonstrate the basic initiative and social skills necessary to get a job and keep it, we will make sure you have enough money to live on. It does not have to be a good job, it can be any job. Just do that much, just do your fair share according to your abilities, and we'll help you out. Instead of penalizing people for productivity, the way the current means-tested welfare program does, this program would reward people for productivity. As income rises, the benefits of the expanded earned-income tax credit would be gradually taxed away, creating a program that would tailor benefits to need, without discouraging work.

Inevitably, the program would end up giving some money to some people who by some definition do not need it. So does AFDC, even with tens of thousands of bureaucrats guarding the till. The advantage of the earned-income tax credit is that it eliminates the need for bureaucratic oversight.

Any government program has to have some sort of system of accountability, some way of knowing whether the program is working. But if we replaced welfare with tax credits, or even more direct wage supplements, we would not need bureaucratic accountability: The clients would be accountable not to the welfare bureaucracies trying to manage their lives, but to the real world, the real economy, as represented by their employers. No caseworker would have to check up on whether they were following through with their training programs, whether they had the right clothes for a job interview, whether they were developing the life skills they need for future independence. We could safely assume that their employers were requiring employees to do those things insofar as they were appropriate, and doing so in a less demeaning way than the social service system. The real market, not the poverty market, would provide all the enforcement the program would need.

The earned-income tax credit program would work with, rather than against, the market in other ways as well. Hundreds of thousands of jobs will materialize from the hidden economy when off-the-books jobs can no longer be used to complement welfare, and on-the-books jobs trigger tax credits. Even in the midst of a recession, low-wage industries are facing a labor shortage, because the wages they can afford to pay are not enough to lure people into work. If those wages were supplemented by tax credits, those jobs would become much more attractive. Of course, to keep the faith with job seekers in a world without welfare, the government would have to ensure that jobs are available if the private sector fails to provide them.

Some poor people, however, cannot or should not work. Of course, support programs for the disabled would continue. Some other nonwelfare programs, such as unemployment insurance, should also continue, as should a streamlined food-stamp program, stripped of dysfunctional work and household-composition rules.

Most importantly, however, once we get rid of welfare we will need a new program to help parents of young children. So to supplement the earned-income tax credit, the U.S. should also begin to do what many European countries do: pay parents, all parents regardless of need, child allowances to help with the costs of child-rearing.

Coming up with the right formula for a child allowance is a bit tricky. The program must be universal, because we do not want to require parents to stay poor in order to qualify. Equity, however, suggests that the government should not be supporting the children of the rich or upper-middle class, so the benefits (probably distributed through the social security system, to avoid establishing another bureaucracy) would also be gradually taxed away as incomes rise.

These reforms shift responsibility from economic planners to individuals. Because the child allowances and tax credits are not based on need, no means-testing bureaucracy and telephone directory-sized books of regulations will be necessary to manage them, and they should not encourage dependency. The allowance and the tax credit will replace not just the welfare grant, but the welfare client as well. The incentive to stay poor will disappear with the welfare program.

It is not hard to envision the outrage invoked by any attempt to deal with lower-income people as if they were ordinary human beings. Millions of benevolent Americans are more comfortable with the image of poor people as victims, or sick people needing counseling and care, or subjects for research, or objects for all the pathos, compassion, and religious concern they can muster. Others, less compassionate, see the poor as a body of people separated from the larger population by sloth, indifference, immorality, and self-destructive behavior.

What is needed is a third view of low-income people, which acknowledges their keen instinct for survival and their well-developed sense of self-interest. If we wish poor people to join the mainstream economy, we must allow them to play by the same rules that govern the mainstream economy. If we want to design programs that work, we must take advantage of the feedback mechanisms that make the mainstream economy work.

Poor people are no better or worse than the rest of the population—only ill-served as consumers in a nation that otherwise leads the world in its attention to consumer demand. To really reduce poverty we need to free the poor within our borders.

Arthur Schiff is a research consultant in social policy and recently participated in an evaluation of several manpower training programs for the State of New York. The research for this article was funded by the Klingenstein Foundation.

The New Deal and Relief
Frances Fox Piven
Richard A. Cloward

While the organizational shells of the various relief movements survived until late in the depression, they had really been destroyed much earlier by such measures as social security, by labor legislation, by the Wealth Tax Act, by massive work relief, and by partial economic recovery. Although it was not recognized at the time, the election of 1936 had sounded the death knell for those who believed that anything was possible in America. The signs were there to be read in the election returns: taken together, the extremist parties polled only 2.9 percent of the vote, down from 3.1 percent in 1932. Although the insurgent organizations persisted for a time, the underlying popular unrest upon which insurgency draws had been quelled. The little the poor had gotten was enough. Indeed, it was apparently more than enough, for with political stability restored by the great election victory in 1936, the Administration rapidly reduced concessions to the poor, not least by slashing emergency relief measures and by restoring the traditional practices by which relief systems help to maintain the marginal labor pool—all in the name of "reform."

THE "REFORM" OF RELIEF

Harry Hopkins, writing in 1936, had high hopes for the Works Progress Administration and what it signaled for the American future. The communities of America, he maintained, having experienced the benefits of new WPA parks, roads, schools, and hospitals, and WPA programs for hot school lunches, free theater, and public health services, would never again settle for the shabbiness of public life before WPA. And the American government, having once lifted millions of the poor out of destitution, would not allow them to sink back:

> Communities now find themselves in possession of improvements which even in 1929 they would have thought themselves presumptuous to dream of . . . [but] everywhere there had been an overhauling of the word *presumptuous*. We are beginning to wonder if it is not presumptuous to take for granted that some people should have much, and some should have nothing; that some people are less important than others and should die earlier; that the children of the comfortable should be taller and fatter, as a matter of right, than the children of the poor.

Harry Hopkins was wrong. It was WPA that was presumptuous, for it ran against the grain, it violated the American way. Once Main Street began to feel that things were better, it wanted to return to that Way. The communities of America had never really accepted WPA, and they settled readily for its withdrawal. The poor settled as well.

By late 1936, WPA rolls were being reduced; early in 1937, it was announced that half of the remaining workers would be discharged. When the President's budget request of January 1937 allocated only 650 million dollars to WPA, there was considerable agitation across the country, but to little avail. During the peak month of March 1936, some 2.9 million

1936 2.9 million workers had been employed

1937 1.5 million were still on WPA rolls.

workers had been employed; by September 1937 only 1.5 million persons were still on the WPA rolls. With the new recession of 1938, WPA appropriations were increased to 1.25 billion dollars, and for a brief period the rolls again rose to 3 million. But they were rapidly reduced the following year, when Congress stipulated that those who had been in the program for more than eighteen continuous months should be removed—a measure presumably intended to force project workers to seek private employment. Just how these workers fared is suggested in a report issued by the WPA in January 1940:

> In July and August more than 775,000 WPA project workers were dropped from their jobs in accordance with the 18-months' provision of the 1939 Relief Act. A survey covering more than 138,000 of these workers, in 23 large and representative cities, disclosed that 3 to 4 weeks after their lay-off 7.6 percent were employed in private jobs. In November, a second interview with the same group showed that 2 to 3 months after dismissal 12.7 percent, or fewer than 100,000 of the 775,000 workers, were employed in private industry. In industrial centers like Buffalo, Cleveland, Cincinnati, Detroit, and Birmingham, the proportion with jobs was about one in six; in eight of the 23 cities it was about one in ten.

With the onset of World War II, the work relief program was even more sharply reduced and then terminated altogether.

What programs then remained to sustain the poor of America? There were, to be sure, the new insurance plans for aged and unemployed workers passed under the Social Security Act. Both of these insurance provisions, however, covered only certain classes of workers in preferred occupations. Such low wage industries as agriculture and domestic service were exempted. Moreover, as noted earlier, the insurance benefits for the aged became payable only in 1942. As for unemployment insurance, the implementation was left to the states which were free to adopt any level of benefits they wished, to set any waiting periods, and to fix the maximum period of benefit. In any case, both insurance plans applied only to workers who established their eligibility by their sustained participation in the workforce, and then became eligible for aid only by virtue of age or job retrenchments.

only covered people in preferred professions

insurance benefits payable in 1942

unemployment insurance left to states to decide what to do what benefits waiting period fix maximum period of benefit.

The relief program that remained was the provision for the aged, the blind, and the orphaned also contained in the Social Security Act of 1935. Control over relief-giving was substantially returned to the states and localities, with the difference that federal grants-in-aid would be available to supplement their expenditures. And although these measures did not receive much public attention at the time, overshadowed as they were by the provisions of the Act providing unemployment insurance and old-age pensions, they laid the foundations for the contemporary public welfare system.

× control of relief giving was given to the states & localities

But federal grants-in-aid would be available to supplement their expenditures

The new relief legislation did, however, receive considerable attention from some members of Congress, who eliminated various alternative proposals before settling on the final wording. That process suggests some of the concerns that shaped our contemporary public assistance program. For example, an Advisory Committee on Public Employment and Relief (appointed by Frances Perkins, the Secretary of Labor, and composed mainly of social workers) had strongly opposed "categorical" assistance—that is, assistance only to those categories of the poor who were aged, blind, or orphaned—and had called upon the federal government to retain substantial authority over state programs. Similarly, an early draft of the public assistance provisions prepared by the FERA staff had defined "dependent children" broadly, intending the legislation to cover all children who were in severe need, not just those who lacked a parent.

The measures enacted by the Congress were substantially different, however. The simple absence of money was not deemed sufficient to justify coverage, and so the absence of a parent was imposed as a condition for the aid of children, more or less duplicating the old Mothers Aid program; wording to the effect that the aged should receive a grant "compatible with decency and health" was eliminated; the federal administering agency was given little authority over the states, which reflected a growing concern with restoring local options in relief-giving, particularly the option to set grant levels.

aid of children needed absence of a parent

Not surprisingly, the main push for narrow coverage and local autonomy in administering these narrow programs came from Southern Congressmen, who were already irritated by what they considered the high-handed practices of the Federal Emergency Relief program. Their concerns were twofold: that the grant levels, if set by the federal government, would undermine the low wage structure in the South; and that a federal super-visory agency, if vested with great authority, would curtail local prerog-atives to say who should get relief, thus opening the rolls to blacks and undermining the caste economy of the South. The original wording of the bill reported to the House said that relief could not be denied to a citizen if qualifications regarding age and need were met; the final wording provided only that no citizenship requirement could be used to exclude applicants, thus allowing the state to discriminate against blacks. Finally, there was no provision at all for federal aid to those who had neither blindness nor age nor orphanhood to justify their poverty. The modified and amended provisions were submitted for a vote as part of the Social Security package, which, as noted earlier, passed overwhelmingly and was hailed widely as a major reform.

Between the years 1935 and 1939 most of the states enacted legislation to make use of the categorical grants-in-aid. In the main, the legislation enacted was modeled after the state mothers' aid programs and pension programs for the aged that had existed prior to the passage of the Social Security Act, since most of the traditional "poor relief" restrictions which had been the hallmark of these earlier relief programs were reintroduced. The states exercised their prerogative to establish grant levels by setting them very low. Some states set them much lower than others. In December 1939, for example, Arkansas gave an average of $8.10 a month to families with dependent children and Massachusetts gave such families $61.07. Nationally, levels of aid under categorical assistance averaged about half what employables were earning on federal work relief projects.

Most important, few got any aid at all. Just how few is vividly demon-strated by the future course of the categorical assistance program for depen-dent children (AFDC). For one thing, many states were slow to implement this program; some had not done so as late as 1940. By December 1940, as a consequence, only 360,000 families had been admitted to the nation's AFDC rolls. Nine states, five of them in the South, still had fewer than 1,000 families on their rolls; Texas, for example, had a caseload of 85 fam-ilies, and Mississippi a caseload of 104.

The sluggish growth of the program was reversed by World War II; between December 1940 and December 1945, the rolls dropped by 25 percent. But with the end of the war, the upward trend resumed; between December 1945 and December 1950, the rolls rose 132 percent. Even so, only 635,000 families were obtaining AFDC payments in 1950. At this level, caseloads stabilized, rising only 17 percent between 1950 and 1960 (despite sharply mounting unemployment in both agriculture and in the cities).

The cycle was complete. Turbulence had produced a massive federal direct relief program; direct relief had been converted into work relief; then work relief was cut back and the unemployed were thrown upon state and local agencies, which reduced aid to the able-bodied in most places and eventually eliminated it in many. What remained were the categorical-assistance programs for the impotent poor—the old, the blind, and the orphaned. For the able-bodied poor who would not be able to find employment or secure local relief in the days, months, and years to come, the federal government had made no provision. Nor are there statistics that describe their fate.

The New Deal and Social Welfare
Robert H. Bremner

ROOSEVELT'S ATTITUDES TOWARD SOCIAL WELFARE

In August 1931, at a time when President Hoover was seeking to assist the unemployed by mobilizing and coordinating the charitable resources of the nation, Governor Franklin Roosevelt told a special session of the New York state legislature that "aid must be extended [to the unemployed] by Government, not as a matter of charity but as a matter of social duty." Roosevelt acknowledged that in normal times and under ordinary conditions relief of the poor was a function of local government and private agencies. He emphasized that the $20 million he proposed to take from state funds for apportionment among counties and cities was to supplement amounts raised locally. As if to reiterate the extraordinary circumstances that made state action necessary, he proposed the name "Temporary Emergency Relief Administration" for the commission responsible for distributing the fund. Roosevelt made clear his own preference for work relief as opposed to "the dole" and recommended that if local officials were unable to find or provide work for public service, relief should take the form of food, clothing, and shelter. "Under no circumstances," he declared, "shall any actual money be paid in the form of a dole . . . by the local welfare officer to any unemployed [man] or his family."

Early in 1932 Roosevelt commended Senator Robert Wagner for his efforts to get federal appropriations for relief. Federal aid was justified and sorely needed in the present crisis, said Roosevelt, "although it should not be regarded as a permanent Government policy." Roosevelt's speech accepting the Democratic nomination for President had little to say on the subject of relief except that "while now, as ever" primary responsibility rested with localities, the federal government "has always had, and still has a continuing responsibility for broader public welfare." During the closing weeks of the campaign he declared that when states and communities were unable to provide necessary relief "it then becomes the positive duty of the Federal Government to step in to help." This was, in fact, the course reluctantly adopted by the Hoover Administration in the summer of 1932 when the Reconstruction Finance Corporation began to make loans to states for relief and public works. In his inaugural address of March 4, 1933, Roosevelt indicated he was willing to go substantially further, including "direct recruiting" of the unemployed by the federal government for work on "projects to stimulate and reorganize the use of our natural resources."

Scarcely a month after taking office, President Roosevelt signed the executive order establishing the Civilian Conservation Corps (CCC), the first and longest-lived New Deal unemployment relief agency. Within three months the CCC had enrolled 250,000 young unemployed men, 25,000 World War I veterans, and 25,000 experienced woodsmen and put them to work on reforestation, soil conservation, and similar projects in parks and forests at more than 1,400 camps across the nation. In Roosevelt's words, "It was the most rapid large-scale mobilization in our history." Enrollees received $30 a month (of which all but a small allowance was ordinarily sent home to their families), plus food, shelter, clothing, transportation, medical and dental attention, and, after the program had been in operation for some time, the opportunity for general educational and vocational training. During the life of the program enrollees sent a total of $670 million in allotments to their families. After 1937 family need was given less consideration in selection of enrollees and, in 1939, the director of the Corps announced, "The CCC as a monetary relief and job-giving agency has been replaced by the CCC as a work-training agency." When the program came to an end in June 1942 more than 2.5 million youths had served in the CCC; enrollment hit a peak of 500,000 in August 1935 and a low point of 240,000 in March 1937. As late as 1940, more boys entered the Corps each year than entered colleges and universities as freshmen.

In the message to Congress proposing the CCC, Roosevelt also pointed out the need for grants to the states for relief and recommended establishment of an office of Federal Relief Administration "to scan requests for grants and to check the efficiency and wisdom of their use." The Federal Emergency Relief Act, adopted on May 12, 1933 in response to Roosevelt's request, was a landmark in the development of federal-state cooperation in the relief of distress. It authorized outright grants, instead of loans, to the states; transferred administration of the grants from the Reconstruction Finance Corporation to a new social agency, the Federal Emergency Relief Administration (FERA) and, by giving the agency authority to make or withhold grants, allowed the federal government to exert some influence over the kind and quality of relief offered in the states. Roosevelt's remarks on signing the measure emphasized that localities and states must do their utmost to relieve the needy before the federal government would make funds available. In fact, the need for immediate assistance was so well recognized that Harry L. Hopkins, former director of the New York State Relief Commission, approved grants to seven states on the day he took office as head of FERA.

Under Hopkins' leadership, and partly because there were few precedents to follow, the FERA proved one of the most resourceful and innovative of all New Deal executive agencies. In theory it simply supplemented the work of local and state governments, by providing funds dispensed by local officials with a minimum of federal direction. One of the FERA mandates was that its funds should be spent only through public agencies, a requirement that strengthened public agencies and, in some communities, brought them into existence. In addition to making funds available (or withholding them and thereby stimulating laggard states to bestir themselves), the FERA maintained programs for transients, distributed surplus commodities supplied by the Agricultural Adjustment Administration to people on relief, instituted a rural rehabilitation program for the needy in rural areas, and granted funds to colleges and universities for the employment of students on part-time work projects.

Both Roosevelt and Hopkins vastly preferred work relief to direct cash relief, which Roosevelt often referred to, always slightingly, as "the dole." Hopkins recognized that direct relief might tide the unemployed over a period of a few months or even a year, but he believed that when people were out of jobs for a long time, worklessness was as destructive as physical

Trattner

Articles from manual

1. The New Deal and Relief by Frances Fox Piven
   and Richard A. Cloward (pp. 219-222)

2. The New Deal and Social Welfare by Robert H.
   Bremner (pp. 223-221)

3. Ideology and Opportunity in Social Work
   during the New Deal years by Norma
   Kolko Philips. (pp. 242)

4. Kennedy, Johnson, and the Great Society
   by John H. Ehrenreich (pp. 296-297)

5. The Objectives of the Reagan Administration's
   Social Welfare Policy by Martin Anderson
   (pp. 301-306)

6. The Conservative Program Is a Women's Issue
   by Mimi Abramovitz (pp. 307-321).

Books

7. Reagonomics and the Welfare State by Mimi
   Abramovitz & Tom Hopkins (pp. 72-81).

comp. & analysis of the

political, economic & social

programs of the

An analysis of the Social welfare System.

want. Hopkins also distinguished between work relief of the leaf-raking or snow-shoveling kind, favored by some local governments, and employment on a federally financed work project. "To the man on relief," Hopkins observed, "the difference is very real." He went on to note:

> On work relief, although he gets the disciplinary rewards of keeping fit, and of making a return for what he gets, his need is still determined by a social worker, and he feels himself to be something of a public ward, with small freedom of choice. When he gets a job on a work program, it is very different. He is paid wages and the social worker drops out of the picture. His wages may not cover much more ground than his former relief budget but they are his to spend as he likes.

In November 1933 Roosevelt announced the establishment of the Civil Works Administration (CWA), a branch of the FERA, which was intended to take 4 million persons off relief rolls and convert them, for the winter of 1933–34, into "self-sustaining employees" on small public works projects. During the four and a half months that the CWA operated, Hopkins and his lieutenants devised 180,000 work projects which, at their peak in mid-January 1934, employed slightly more than 4 million persons. Most of the jobs were in construction projects but the CWA also set up projects for teachers, engineers, architects, artists, nurses, and other white-collar workers. The total cost of the CWA was just under $1 billion, nearly 80 percent of which went for wages.

Both during and after the CWA experiment with federally controlled work projects, FERA continued to make grants to states for direct relief of persons who could not be employed on the work projects. After the dissolution of the CWA in the spring of 1934, the FERA supported an Emergency Works Relief Program, transferring to it a number of CWA projects and employees. The FERA continued efforts begun under the CWA to adapt work relief to the occupational skills and backgrounds of people from all walks of life.

In the State of the Union message of January 1935, Roosevelt distinquished between the 1.5 million relief recipients who, for reasons of age or physical or mental incapacity, were unable to maintain themselves independently, and the 3.5 million employable persons then on relief rolls who were victims "of a nationwide depression caused by conditions which were not local but national." Care of the former group, "the unemployables," had traditionally been a local responsibility. In declaring that "the Federal Government must and shall quit this business of relief," Roosevelt signified his intention to return responsibility for their care to local and state officials, justifying the decision by "the dictates of sound administration." "The dictates of sound policy," strongly influenced by the President's reverence for "the moral and spiritual values of work," determined his prescription for the employables: "Work must be found for able-bodied but destitute workers," he declared. "We must preserve not only the bodies of the unemployed from destitution but also their self-respect, their self-reliance and courage and determination."

The Emergency Relief Appropriation Act of 1935, passed at Roosevelt's recommendation, authorized a massive federal works program with an initial appropriation of nearly $5 billion. The Works Progress (after 1939 Projects) Administration, headed by Harry Hopkins, replaced the FERA as the key agency in the fight against unemployment. Over the next eight years the WPA received a total of $11.4 billion in appropriations and gave work and wages to 8.5 million people. WPA employment rolls varied from month to month and year to year in accordance with the availability of funds and the administration's not always accurate prediction of economic conditions. In September and October 1937, when a deep recession was commencing, the number of WPA workers fell below 1.5 million; during the latter half of 1938, when the recession was easing, there were more than 3 million WPA workers.

One of the WPA's tasks was to coordinate and report on the progress of the forty other federal agencies, including the CCC, the Public Works Administration, and the National Youth Administration (NYA), a subsidiary of the WPA, all of which participated in the works program. The NYA, for example, gave employment on work projects to 2.5 million out-of-school youth aged 16 to 25, and funded part-time work projects that allowed 2 million young people to remain in school. The WPA approved and supervised "small useful projects"—mainly in the fields of construction, reclamation, rehabilitation, and conservation—sponsored by state and local governments, which paid for most of the nonlabor costs. The 1935 Appropriation Act included "assistance for educational, professional, and clerical persons" among the projects authorized for support by the WPA. Drawing upon the experience of both the FERA and the CWA, Hopkins funded projects capable of using the labor or talent of people in fields as diverse as equipment operating, acting, dancing, painting, music, and historical research. WPA projects enhanced the quality of life in countless communities, not only in tangible, brick-and-mortar ways, but by supporting educational, cultural, and recreational opportunities and amenities. The projects promoted literacy programs, surveyed and preserved historical and architectural records, and fostered awareness and respect for the diversity and richness of American culture. In 1943, when Roosevelt awarded the WPA an "honorable discharge," he saluted its record in rendering "almost immeasurable kinds and quantities of service," and "reaching a creative hand into every county" of the nation. "It has added to the national wealth," he said, "has repaired the wastage of depression, and has strengthened the country to bear the burden of war."

The contributions of New Deal work projects to the morale of workers employed on them is harder to measure than the physical and social results of the programs. It is important to keep in mind that their purpose was not to rehabilitate the unemployed but to rescue them from idleness and to foster a sense of self-respect among people not deemed responsible for their misfortune. The distinction Roosevelt and the New Deal made between the unemployed and chronic dependents, and the special status accorded the "employables," made for a more favorable public attitude toward, and a better self-image among, the unemployed. But, as the years passed and the Depression dragged on, the difference between the "new poor" and the "old" became less apparent. The distinction between employables and unemployables, always sharper in principle than in application, became thoroughly blurred before the end of the 1930s.

A *Fortune* survey of unemployment and relief, made in 1937 under the mistaken impression that the Depression was over, concluded "the despised WPA" had worked, even if expensively. Most of the countless criticisms of the works program alleged waste, extravagance, and inefficiency on the part of project management and loafing on the part of employees. Hopkins, however, in a book appropriately entitled *Spending to Save* (1936), maintained that the most telling and truthful criticism was "We have never given adequate relief." In 1934–35 under FERA, the average *monthly* grant paid to an unemployed worker and his family (less than $30) was about the same as the average *weekly* wage of an industrial worker before the

Depression. WPA workers received a "security wage," higher than direct relief under the FERA but less than the prevailing wage in the community for a comparable job in private industry. In 1941 WPA monthly earnings for the country as a whole averaged $60, somewhat less than the total benefits (cash allowance, clothing, shelter, subsistence, and medical care) received by CCC enrollees, which amounted to $67 a month.

Hopkins once acknowledged that the Roosevelt Administration, in its eagerness to win acceptance for the federal works program, "overemphasized the undesirability of relief." Roosevelt's 1935 State of the Union message denounced relief as "a narcotic, a subtle destroyer of the human spirit." Later in 1935, he admitted "a dole would be more economical than work relief," but added, "Most Americans want to give something for what they get. That something, in this case honest work, is the saving barrier between them and moral disintegration. We propose to build that barrier high." The WPA's official *Workers' Handbook* (1936), distributed to new employees, asked and answered a loaded question:

> What happens to us when we are on the dole? We lose our self-respect. We lose our skill. We have family rows. We loaf on street corners. Finally, we lose hope.

Such attacks on direct relief were unfortunate, as Hopkins conceded, "inasmuch as we have not been able to remove from hundreds of thousands of people the inescapability of accepting it." "Seeking" would have been a better word than "accepting" because New Deal work projects, despite their number, variety, and the large appropriations supporting them, were never adequate to care for all of the needy unemployed. There was always a pool of employable persons, certified to be in need and eligible for assignment to federal work projects or special youth programs, who were not added to the rolls because funds were not available for their employment. At various times after 1935, the number of these unfortunates ranged from 600,000 to 1.3 million a month.

After 1935, except for subsistence grants to poverty-stricken farmers, distribution of surplus commodities, and grants-in-aid for groups covered by the Social Security Act, the federal government left relief of the poor (often called general assistance) entirely to local communities, with such assistance as the states chose to provide. With federal aid withdrawn and with either no state funds or inadequate ones, local authorities faced, but seldom met, the need for helping both the unemployables and many of the employables. The federal relief administration no longer, as under the FERA, had any leverage for inducing or compelling states to bolster local efforts. Had Roosevelt and Hopkins chosen to do so, they might have diverted some funds from work relief to direct relief since all the emergency relief appropriation acts from 1935 through 1939 stated that the appropriated funds might be used for "relief" as well as "work relief." Their refusal to do so, despite clear need for such action, shows how strongly committed a supposedly pragmatic administration was to certain moral assumptions and to traditional assignments of responsibility for poor relief.

SOCIAL SECURITY

In 1928, while campaigning for the governorship of New York, Roosevelt endorsed his party's platform pledge for a study of old-age pensions, a subject then as radical and socialistic, he joked, as factory inspection and workmen's compensation had seemed twenty years earlier. After the election a commission jointly appointed by legislative leaders and Governor

Roosevelt studied the problem, issued a report, and early in 1930 the chairman of the commission introduced an old-age pension bill in the legislature. Roosevelt was disappointed in the report and unenthusiastic about the bill which, instead of providing for a contributory system with uniform application throughout the state, made old-age pensions an extension of the poor laws and allowed local authorities wide discretion in administering them. "Our American aged do not want charity," Roosevelt asserted, "but rather old-age comforts to which they are rightfully entitled by their own thrift and foresight in the form of insurance." Despite his objections he accepted the measure as a stopgap and a possible beginning toward something better: "We can only hope that this will be a forerunner of a proper system of security against old-age want in the years to come."

In accepting the Democratic nomination in 1932, Roosevelt cited "work and security" as the goals toward which he and the party should strive. After a little more than a year in the presidency, he declared that the first objective of the administration was security for individuals and families and announced his intention of furthering the objective through social insurance. In June 1934, Roosevelt told Congress that he was looking "for a sound means which I can recommend to provide at once security against several of the great disturbing factors in life—especially those which related to unemployment and old age." Roosevelt made it clear that he believed the funds necessary to provide the insurance should be raised by contributions of workers and employers rather than by general taxation, and that the insurance system should be national in scope. To study the matter further and recommend a "sound means," he appointed a Committee on Economic Security, which he directed to report its findings and recommendations no later than December 1, 1934.

The committee consisted of the secretaries of the Departments of Labor (chairman), Treasury, and Agriculture, the Attorney General, the Federal Emergency Relief Administrator, an advisory council composed of representatives of industry, labor, and social welfare, a technical board made up of officials from interested federal agencies, and a staff directed by Edwin E. Witte, an expert on social legislation and chairman of the Department of Economics at the University of Wisconsin. The members and staff of the committee worked under the pressure of time; against the background of agitation for proposals such as the Townsend Plan and Huey Long's Share-Our-Wealth Plan,* which the President considered unsound and too radical to be considered; in receipt of contradictory testimony from expert witnesses; and amidst uncertainty whether the Supreme Court would recognize the constitutionality of any national system of social insurance. Committee members were divided in their opinions about the relative importance of unemployment and old-age insurance. Those who thought unemployment insurance was the most urgent issue were further divided between supporters of a national system under federal control and a federal-state system permitting the states greater freedom for experiment and innovation. The President's views, possible congressional reaction, and questions of administrative feasibility all had to be taken into consideration in weighing alternatives. As a result, a key member of the group, Arthur J. Altermeyer, recalled, "the committee did not arrive at its final recommendations without considerable travail." The legislative program recommended by the committee included:

*The Townsend Plan proposed paying a pension of $200 per month to everyone over the age of sixty who promised to spend the sum within a month. Long's Share-Our-Wealth plan advocated the liquidation of private fortunes so that the government could distribute enough money for each family to buy a home, a car, and a radio.

1. a federal-state system of unemployment insurance;
2. a compulsory, federally administered old-age insurance system, financed by contributions from employees and employers, with benefits payable to insured workers at age 65; and
3. federal grants-in-aid to the states for old-age pensions (for people too old to benefit from the old-age insurance system), for the support of dependent children, for an expanded public health program, and to finance maternal and child health and welfare programs.

In January 1935, Roosevelt transmitted the committee's report to Congress with a message that strongly endorsed the proposed Economic Security Act and warned against discrediting "the sound and necessary policy of Federal legislation for economic security" by applying it, at the outset, on too ambitious a scale. He specifically noted that the measure he recommended for adoption did not include health insurance. During congressional consideration of the economic security bill, witnesses referred to it as the "social security bill" and it was the Social Security Act that finally received the approval of Congress and, on August 14, 1935, Roosevelt's signature. Social security, a more inclusive term than economic security, covered the three areas or kinds of programs provided for in the act: protection against some of the "hazards and vicissitudes of life" by social insurance; provision of public assistance for certain categories of the needy; and extension of public services to promote public health, child and maternal health and welfare, and rehabilitation of the handicapped. The act created a new federal agency, the Social Security Board, to keep the records and make payments to the millions of workers to be covered by the old-age insurance program, to exercise general responsibility for the federally subsidized (but state-administered) unemployment insurance plans, and to supervise the program of grants-in-aid to states for old-age assistance, aid to dependent children, and aid to the blind.

Roosevelt's statement on signing the Social Security Act sounded a note between pride in its enactment and modesty in recognition of its limitations. The measure, in his words, would give "at least some measure of protection" to an estimated 30 million persons who would benefit from unemployment compensation, the public assistance programs, and services for children and public health. It would give "some measure of protection to the average citizen and to his family against the loss of a job and against poverty-ridden old age." Most important, in the President's view, the law represented "a cornerstone in a structure which is being built but is by no means complete."

Knowledgeable contemporary observers mixed criticism of shortcomings of the act with recognition of its significance and optimism about possibilities of improving it. The economist Paul Douglas, a long-time advocate of social insurance, called it "a worthy effort to protect better the lives of wage-earners and salaried employees," but "full of weaknesses" and "merely a first step which must soon be followed by others." Edith Abbott, a noted social-work educator, criticized the act's failure to provide grants-in-aid for general relief, for low benefits, gaps in coverage, and absence of a health insurance program. On balance, however, she concluded: "We can also count great gains. In the first place, and of tremendous significance, the responsibility of government and industry to insure security will be recognized for the first time. The system can and will be improved in the light of experience."

In contrast to the CCC, the FERA, and the WPA, the Social Security Act was intended to launch a permanent, rather than a temporary, program. Appropriations to carry out its provisions were the first—with the exception of the Railroad Retirement Act of 1934, which was declared unconstitutional in 1935—in the area of relief and public welfare without the prefix "emergency." Adoption of the act inaugurated a lasting commitment, as well as a significant involvement, on the part of the federal government in social welfare. Supreme Court decisions in 1937 made possible continuance and further development of the federal government's activity in programs for protection against economic insecurity. In *Steward Machine Co. v. Davis*, a case involving the unemployment insurance titles of the act, Justice Benjamin Cardozo, noting the billions of dollars spent on unemployment relief between 1933 and 1936, declared "the parens patriae [the state as parent and protector] has many reasons—fiscal and economic as well as social and moral—for planning to mitigate disasters that bring these burdens in their train." In *Helvering et al. v. Davis*, Justice Cardozo, again speaking for the majority of the Supreme Court, unequivocally endorsed the constitutionality of the old-age insurance titles: "The problem [old-age poverty] is plainly national in area and dimensions. Moreover, laws of the separate states cannot deal with it effectively.... Only a power that is national can serve the interest of all."

On the same day the Supreme Court sustained the Social Security Act, the President sent a special message to Congress stating, "The time has arrived for us"—meaning the three branches of the federal government—"to extend the frontiers of social progress, by adopting a minimum wage law." Roosevelt presented the measure, which revived some of the wage, hours, and child-labor provisions of the NRA codes, overthrown by the Supreme Court in 1935, as essential to economic recovery. Its objectives were "to reduce the lag in purchasing power of industrial workers and to strengthen and stabilize the markets for the farmers' products." In calling for a floor under wages and a ceiling over hours, he appealed to the nation's sense of fairness but not to pity: "A self-supporting and self-respecting democracy can plead no justification for the existence of child labor, no economic reason for chiseling workers' wages or stretching workers' hours."

In the year that elapsed, and during the three sessions of Congress that met while the wage-hour bill was under consideration, opponents offered numerous amendments and the House Rules Committee attempted to prevent a vote on the measure. Most of the seventy-two amendments sought to weaken the act by broadening the industries and occupations exempted and by narrowing the coverage of workers to whom it applied. Roosevelt vigorously supported the bill, always emphasizing economic rather than humanitarian arguments for its passage. In January 1938, referring to underpaid industrial workers, he said, "Aside from the undoubted fact that they thereby suffer great human hardship,"—and apparently of equal or greater import in Roosevelt's view—"they are unable to buy adequate food and shelter, to maintain health or to buy their share of manufactured goods." His approach may have been influenced by the sharp economic recession of 1937–38, but it was consistent with his general tendency to look at social problems from what he called "the practical, dollars-and-cents point of view" and to justify social legislation on the grounds of common sense and fair play.

As finally adopted in June 1938, the Fair Labor Standards Act provided, at the start—in those industries and occupations not exempted from its provisions—for a minimum wage of 25 cents an hour to go into effect at once and gradually to be increased to 40 cents; a maximum workweek of 44 hours (to be reduced within three years to 40 hours) with time-and-a-half pay for overtime work; a prohibition of the shipment in interstate commerce of goods produced by children under 16 years of age (18 in hazardous industries); and the establishment of a Wage and Hour Division in the Department of Labor to supervise application and enforcement of the Act.

Like the Social Security Act, the Fair Labor Standards Act represented only a modest beginning toward realization of its objectives. Roosevelt recognized that the rudimentary standards established by the Act fell far short of the ideal. "Backward labor conditions and relatively progressive labor conditions," he explained, "cannot be completely assimilated and made uniform at one fell swoop without creating economic dislocations." For constitutional reasons, the Act applied only to employees in manufacturing establishments that shipped their products in interstate commerce, and for political and/or expedient reasons it exempted agricultural workers, employees in intrastate retail and servicing establishments, seamen, fishermen, and employees in a number of other industries. Of the approximately 850,000 children under 16 years of age who were gainfully employed in 1938, only about 50,000 came within the purview of the act. Children in agriculture, the street trades (selling newspapers or other merchandise in the streets), messenger and delivery service, stores, hotels, restaurants, bowling alleys, filling stations, and similar intrastate enterprises were not subject to the law. As in the case of the Social Security Act, a favorable decision by the Supreme Court on the constitutionality of the Fair Labor Standards Act—*United States v. Darby Lumber Co.* (1941) in which the court endorsed a broad interpretation of the powers of Congress under the interstate commerce clause—permitted subsequent broadening of coverage and elevation of standards.

In 1939 Congress passed the first of a series of amendments to the Social Security Act, which extended its coverage to more workers and improved benefits to the insured and their dependents. The 1939 amendments incorporated recommendations developed over a period of two years by the President, the Advisory Council on Social Security, and the Social Security Board, which was given the task, in the 1935 Act, of conducting studies and making recommendations for legislation and policies to improve economic security through social insurance. The most important of the numerous changes made by the 1939 amendments converted old-age insurance into Old Age and Survivors' Insurance (OASI) by making wives and young children of insured workers eligible for monthly benefit payments in the event of the worker's death either before or after retirement. OASI thus became a system offering protection both to individual workers and their families. The amendments also improved benefits under the public assistance program for Aid to Dependent Children by increasing the federal matching ratio from one-third to one-half of the aid granted. The amendments also provided for larger federal contributions to federal-state programs in public health, maternal and child health, child welfare services, care of crippled children, and vocational rehabilitation.

Almost a decade earlier, disappointed in the New York State old-age pension law, Roosevelt admitted "progress comes slowly." He could point to the 1939 amendments with some pride as a further advance toward the "kind of old-age insurance . . . our most progressive thought demands" and as evidence that progress is possible, even if slow.

of the economic system rather than individual moral failure, voluntarism represented a significant shift from the earlier thinking. Along with this new understanding of the causes of poverty came a broader view of the responsibilities of the society to provide opportunities for people (Hoover, 1922). Although the Federal government was in no way seen as a provider of income or social services, it was seen as the protector of citizens and to this end government intervened by encouraging the development of cooperative institutions, including trade associations, professional societies, and organizations of farmers and laborers (Hawley, 1974; 117-118; Burner, 1979). The 1920s also saw the development of welfare capitalism in America, another form of voluntarism, based on the premise of mutuality of interests between labor and management (Brandes, 1970: 26-28).

Hoover's applications of voluntarism as a solution to massive suffering linked social work and government during the early years of the Great Depression. He maintained that if self-reliance and self-respect were to survive, private charity and local government rather than the Federal government must assume responsibility for funding and administering social welfare programs. At this point in history the Federal government and the society as a whole turned to social work agencies to take on responsibility for distributing relief funds. By 1931, as mass need increased, more and more people were turning to social workers in family agencies for financial help.

STRUGGLES WITHIN SOCIAL WORK DURING THE EARLY YEARS OF THE DEPRESSION

The first winter of the Great Depression saw social work sharing with many other groups the belief that the economy would soon improve (Bruno, 1957: 300-301).[2] In spite of the increase in unemployment that began with the economic disaster of 1929, it was not until 1931 that the Proceedings of the National Conference on Charities and Corrections reflect the concern of social workers about widespread unemployment. During the early 1930s, as the severity of the economic and social conditions was becoming apparent to more and more social workers, the process of re-establishing the historical connection between the social work profession and the task of relieving poverty began.

Consequently, two major conflicts arose within the profession. First, in response to public pressure, social work reluctantly downgraded the importance of the counseling function which had been highly valued by family agencies during the 1920s and began the shift to assuming the function of relieving poverty once again. In addition, the profession struggled with the question of Federal government responsibility for relief. In the early Depression years, only some social workers supported federal grants to states for unemployment relief. Others continued to see local government and local charities as the appropriate sources for relief.[3] As economic conditions continued to worsen, social work became more unified in its position, supporting federal responsibility for providing relief and advocating more strongly for work relief. In an article in the Survey in April 1931, Mary van Kleeck, of the Department of Industrial Studies of the Russell Sage Foundation and an outspoken social work leader, criticized President Hoover's veto of the Wagner bill, which called for a national employment service. At its annual meeting that year, the American Association of Social Workers (AASW) appointed a Committee on Unemployment to collect information on unemployment from local chapters and publicize it, to consider unemployment insurance and more adequate funding of relief, and to further consider federal funding of relief.[4]

Although more and more social workers supported Federal government intervention in social welfare policy and programs, it was by no means the dominant attitude within the profession and it was not until 1932, three years into the Depression, that AASW gave its support to the Costigan-LaFollette bill providing for federal grants to the states for unemployment relief, thereby officially endorsing the principle of federal responsibility for this program (Fisher, 1980: 39-40).[5]

A group of radical social workers organized what became known as the Rank-and-File movement in 1931. They believed the Depression was the result of a breakdown in the old economic order and that only the replacement of the old social order with one based on public ownership of resources of the nation, and a planned and rational use of these resources would bring it to an end. The movement opposed the political position of the social work establishment which, it claimed, was committed to the preservation of the status quo and was deferential to the conservative views of businessmen who assumed positions of leadership in social work agencies. Although most people in the movement were not Communist Party members, their disillusionment with Hoover's policies and with the ability of social work leaders to propose plans to meet the needs of the unemployed, led to what Jacob Fisher referred to as a "fascination" with Communist thinking. In addition to discussions of social problems and participation in political activities, the Rank-and-File movement sponsored a journal, Social Work Today, which provided a forum for voices of reform thought during the critical years of 1932-1942 (see Fisher, 1980: 91-100).

SOCIAL WORK AND THE PROMISE OF RECOVERY AT
THE PRICE OF REFORM

In February 1934, a year after Franklin D. Roosevelt took office, the first AASW Delegate Conference, also referred to as the Conference on Governmental Objectives for Social Work, met for the purpose of integrating the work of government on all levels with that of social work.[6] Both the AASW establishment and the radical faction were heard, the former advocating recovery of the economy and the latter urging reform of capitalism.[7]

Speaking at the 1934 meeting was Harry Hopkins, who headed the New Deal Federal Emergency Relief Administration (FERA) and who previously had headed Roosevelt's Temporary Emergency Relief Administration in New York State. Also a social worker, Hopkins appealed to AASW to support current governmental actions. Hopkins identified Roosevelt's goals with those of social work, focusing on the President's interest in increasing the degree of planning in the economy and his desire to create a structure to provide security for the unemployed, the elderly, and handicapped.[8]

At the same conference, Harry Lurie, of the Bureau of Jewish Social Research, represented the radical social work position that the intention of the New Deal was not change but recovery--"restoration of our present industrial and agricultural system so that it might function again as it did in the reign of Mr. Roosevelt's predecessors." He interpreted Roosevelt's cuts of the emergency welfare programs of the New Deal as surrendering to the pressures from industry which feared that permanent programs would challenge the private ownership system. Lurie encouraged social workers to take a stand in opposition to the President and to urge the formation of programs designed to alter the distribution of wealth (Delegate Conference, 1934: 240-253).

Although the recommendations of the 1934 Delegate Conference were aimed at influencing federal policy in the direction of more substantial relief programs, they did not support the major policy revisions urged by Harry Lurie. For example, the Conference endorsed the Wagner-Lewis bill, which would have established state systems of unemployment insurance providing seven dollars a week for a maximum of ten weeks, rather than the more liberal Lundeen bill, which would have provided compensation to the unemployed on a level equal to the average local wage for similar work. The Conference's recommendation was that minimum benefits and the period of compensation under the Wagner-Lewis bill be increased.

In her address, "Our Illusions Regarding Government," delivered at the 1934 National Conference of Social Work, Mary van Kleeck criticized the 1934 Delegate Conference, saying that the social work pro-

fessional association "had committed itself to identification with the present administration, to
endorsement of . . . its principles." Van Kleeck
urged social workers to surrender their "illusions
regarding government" as representing all the people
and to recognize that "government tends to protect
property rights rather than human rights." She
claimed that by failing to approach poverty as a consequence of the economic system, the government
avoided making basic changes in the economic system.
She encouraged social workers to give up their nonpartisan position, pointing out that failure to make commitments to principles can result in a defense of the
status quo. Van Kleeck suggested that social workers
refuse positions in public social welfare agencies if
the positions required that they serve as apologists
of the government (Proceedings, 1934: 474-484).[9]

FERA'S OPPORTUNITIES FOR SOCIAL WORK EXPANSION

In spite of this warning, by 1934 social work was
already heavily involved in the new government relief
programs. FERA's decision that public funds should be
administered by nonpartisan public officials marked
the start of the expansion of the public sector of
social work, bringing with it a vast enlargement in
the jurisdiction of the profession. FERA was able to
spend large sums of money to employ as many social
workers as could be found. Social workers were hired
to work on all levels, ranging from investigators to
administrators of FERA's Social Service Division,
implementing the government's programs and interpret-
ing them to the community. Hopkins had said, "'I want
at least one competent social worker in every district
office in America'" (Kurzman, 1974: 174-176). Paul
Kurzman has stated of this remark, "and thus in one
sentence, the die surely had been cast. All over the
country, where there never had been a sign of a social
worker before, social workers suddenly appeared"
(Kurzman, 1974: 174). The demand created a growth
spurt for social work education as well, and early in
1934, Hopkins earmarked funds from FERA for states to
send their relief workers to accredited graduate
schools of social work, strengthening the professional
base of social work. Between 1930 and 1940 the
number of professional social workers almost doubled
(Kurzman, 1974: 175).[10]

Although futile in its efforts to retain FERA,
the profession did speak out in unison against
Roosevelt's announcement in his State-of-the-Union
address that "the Federal Government must and shall
quit this business of relief" in the beginning of
1935. FERA was to be terminated and the Works
Progress Administration (WPA) created as an alternative work relief program. It was anticipated by the
Roosevelt administration that the categorical aid program of the proposed Social Security bill would meet

the needs of the aged, the blind, and of dependent children needing relief, and Roosevelt proposed that total responsibility for relief for those not covered by WPA or the social security programs be returned to states and localities. Although AASW welcomed the categorical aid programs, it feared that some states would not have sufficient resources, administrative tools, or in some cases even the necessary legislation to take on responsibility for the needy who fell between WPA and the categorical assistance provisions of the proposed social security program. AASW considered it essential that a general relief or general assistance title be added to the proposed social security bill to provide for families who fell between WPA and the categorical assistance programs.[11] At stake, as well, were the self-interests of the profession, which had benefited from its involvement in the administration of FERA (Compass, 1935: 3-6; see Fisher, 1980: 58-59).

In many chapters of AASW, protest meetings were held and telegrams sent to President Roosevelt opposing the termination of federal grants for public assistance. The executive secretary of AASW, Walter West, sent a telegram to Roosevelt urging the continuation of federal grants to states. The Division on Governmeent and Social Work of AASW suggested, and the executive committee of the association accepted, the recommendation to adopt a resolution calling on the Federal government to resume its responsibility for providing grants to states for general assistance. According to this recommendation, such a plan would be administered by the newly appointed Social Security Board (Fisher, 1980: 62).

FAILURE TO CHALLENGE THE PROVISIONS OF THE SOCIAL SECURITY ACT

Although two social workers, Frances Perkins and Harry Hopkins, were highly influential in formulating the Social Security Act, their activities cannot be viewed as representative of the participation of the social work profession in the accomplishment of that legislation.[12] To the contrary, the profession was both distracted and torn by various factions and was unable to function effectively as a pressure group to influence it.[13] In addition, social work was absorbed by the issue of the withdrawal of FERA funds during 1935 and consequently debate within the profession about the Social Security Act, both in its planning stages and after its passage in August 1935, was scarce (see a non-evaluative article, Bond, 1935: 7-10).

During that year, the _Compass_ emphasized professional issues related to the introduction of the public sector in social work, such as the establishment of professional standards, analyses of membership in AASW, education for social work, and the question of the relationship of public relief workers to the profession. Even before the Social Security Act was passed the radical group of social workers also had turned its interests towards professional issues rather than issues of social welfare policy. Few articles appeared in Social Work Today challenging the various controversial aspects of the Social Security bill.[14] Both journals featured articles concerning the professional standing of public relief workers and the role of social work in public welfare programs. In addition, Social Work Today addressed the issue of labor unions for social workers--a movement which the radical group initiated.

The AASW Delegate Conference in 1935 was devoted to the various controversial aspects of the Economic Security program, later renamed the Social Security Act. Opinions of the members in this group varied widely. Most of the speakers at the Conference prefaced their suggestions for change with recognition and admiration for the advances the bill symbolized. Others were clear in their support for the President's program and declined to suggest changes (Delegate Conference, 1935: 149-50, 235-236). Radical social workers, including Mary van Kleeck, took a position in support of the provisions of the Lundeen bill as the preferred plan for unemployment insurance. Linton Swift of the Family Welfare Association of America advocated putting pressure on the Federal government for change. He warned that if an economic system cannot meet the test of providing an adequate working income to all classes of the population, then "we must develop a different system. It becomes a question in the minds of many of us as to when you apply that test" (Delegate Conference, 1935: 19-20).

The Conference could not resolve differences and no recommendations for changes in the Economic Security bill were made (Delegate Conference, 1935: 22-23). Bertha Reynolds commented on this lack of participation in her article, "Whom do Social Workers Serve?" which appeared in Social Work Today in May 1935. Reynolds said:

> For a social worker to deny that there is a class struggle today is to confess to an ignorance of what is going on so appalling that it amounts to a confession of unwillingness to know. As the opportunities to know beat more insistently upon our ears each day, such unwillingness comes more and more to mean participation on the side of maintaining privilege and exploitation, with all its frightful toll of human life (1935: 5-7,34).

EXPANDED OPPORTUNITIES FOR SOCIAL WORK

In its final form, the Social Security Act of 1935 was a legislative compromise responsive to the complexities of the economic and political conditions of the Great Depression. As with most compromises, it was the result of pressures from special interest groups representing conflicting values. A fundamental objective was the restoration of confidence in the Roosevelt administration and in the existing economic and social system.

Legitimized by the Supreme Court in May 1937 through the Helvering v. Davis decision, the Social Security Act signified the Federal government's commitment to responsibility for the general welfare (Helvering v. Davis, 1937). With this decision, the Court established a legal basis for the ideology of the welfare state. This critical decision has been described as altering "the future course of social welfare in the United States" (Pumphrey and Pumphrey, 1961: 433).

From the point of view of social work, the social insurances and the public assistance and child welfare titles of the new legislation provided additional opportunities for professional growth by expanding the area of influence of the profession and making permanent the new job opportunities and demands for increased education. The 1930 census counted 31,000 "social welfare workers" while there were 70,000 in 1940. The increase of 117% was greater than that of any other professional group during this period.[15] It is estimated, however, that there were actually 150,000 people employed in social work in 1939 in either a professional or semiprofessional capacity.[16] With this rapid expansion of employment opportunities and lack of qualified people to fill the new positions, seventeen new schools of social work were established during the decade, bringing the total to forty (Fisher, 1980: 235).

Changes were required in social work as well as the government as both joined in common tasks. In addition to the need to further define the social work-government relationship, social work was presented with complex tasks, such as redefining the function of private agencies, coordinating the roles of public and private agencies, assimilating public welfare agencies and their social work staffs into the profession, determining the extent of the involvement of the profession in the public sector of social welfare, and clarifying the role that the profession would officially assume in social action. Conflicts and opportunities emerged as social workers debated these issues (see for example Swift, 1936: 282-283, 350; Swift, 1937: 10; Hodson, 1938: 33; Belsley, 1936: 9-10; Klein, 1936: 5-7).[17]

During the years following passage of the Social Security Act, social work continued its concern with federal legislation. AASW made recommendations for expansion of a federal work program and a non-categorical public assistance program, and the radical social work group as well continued to pressure for liberalization of the Social Security Act.

However, within a few years attention turned from ideology to optimizing opportunities for social work. By 1940, AASW had abandoned its demand for a general assistance title under the Social Security Act or for the alternative plan of a comprehensive public assistance title for all needy people and gave wholehearted support to the administration's social welfare programs. <u>Social Work Today</u> became increasingly involved in discussion of unionism for social workers at the expense of working towards legislative changes. The American Public Welfare Association, which in 1936 had advocated that a general assistance title be included in the Social Security Act, also went along with the administration. The organization's director, Frank Bane, was selected to be executive director of the Social Security Board, and that organization and the Federal government became "partners in a common enterprise" (Fisher, 1980: 179-180). For the mainstream of the profession the struggle--the cause--was over and it addressed itself instead to the details of the new problems centering around implementation and professionalization that were introduced by the passage of the Social Security Act. Social work reconciled itself to the social welfare programs of the administration, supported them, and accepted the opportunities it was offered.

CONCLUSIONS: CONFLICT AND COMPROMISE IN SOCIAL WORK IDEOLOGY

The Social Security Act of 1935, signifying the movement from voluntarism to the introduction of the welfare state in this country, marks that point of qualitative change when, finally, there could be no retreat from the assumption of federal responsibility for "the general welfare." By the time the Act was passed the Depression was into its sixth year. The pervasiveness and severity of the Depression extended beyond previous economic crises. The severity and extent of social distress disputed the viability of privatism and voluntarism; it both required and enabled approaches towards resolution that were beyond the scope of what previously had been done in the area of social welfare in this country. With the passage of the Social Security Act and its hearings in the Supreme Court, the new conception of government's responsibility for the general welfare was broadened, legitimized, and made permanent, paving the way for additional legislation and further development toward the welfare state.

Growing out of its own history, social work was a natural "partner" with government as these changes occurred. This growing involvement of social work with government dovetailed with the process of professionalization. As the institution of social welfare gained complexity, so did the tasks of the social work profession. Herbert Hoover had linked social work and government during the early years of the Great Depression in his request that social workers assume the task of raising and distributing charitable funds. This assignment of relief-giving functions was carried on by Roosevelt. In this latter period, as the profession became involved in the public as well as the private sector of social welfare, these functions became institutionalized.

Social workers were firmly entrenched in the public relief system by the time the Social Security Act was proposed, and continued to work in the administration and delivery of the public assistance titles of the new legislation. The question of how to satisfy both the occupational and the professional aspects of the profession arose for social work in the 1930s and has continued until today.

When the New Deal programs began, social work was well on its way to achieving the status of a profession including a commitment to community interest and an ethical system. It functioned as both a political interest and pressure group, and insofar as it aimed to improve its own status, it also met the criteria of an occupational interest and pressure group. Armand Mauss has pointed out that political and occupational interests may overlap (1975: 12-15). Conflicts arose within the social work profession in the 1930s as the functions of pressuring for political change and striving to expand professional jurisdiction at times worked against each other. It was at this juncture that a price had to be paid by the social work profession, either in ideology or in opportunity.

The choice was determined by the needs of the profession for sanction. M. S. Larson has pointed out that a profession's values and goals will be acceptable and sanctioned by society only if they appeal to the values of the dominant ideology. The quest for sanction and power, which ultimately derives from a profession's connections with government, precludes persistent and serious challenges to government policies (1977: 157-158,226).

Conflict arises for a profession-occupation which, insofar as it is a profession, is responsible to act in the interest of clients, including political action, and insofar as it is an occupation, needs to protect occupational self interests, including advancement of status. The moderate position that AASW assumed in relation to government policy and legislation during the New Deal years best fits the model of the occupational interest group.

The concept of feedback as a professional function, as discussed by Louis Levitt, bridges the functions of the social work profession and the institution of social welfare:

> The two concepts are reciprocal, each intertwined with the other in a constantly interacting relationship, each influencing the

other. The institution's constant unfolding
of newly legitimated social needs evokes new
services as the profession feeds back to
society its continuing discovery of the pat-
terning of social hurt emanating from its
practice experience. (1980: 637)

Viewing the function of feedback as a cornerstone
to the relationship between the social work profession and the institution of social welfare also
introduces balance between the preservation of occupational interests and the maximization of professional
objectives.

As social work grew in numbers and influence, it
became a critical force in advancing social welfare
activities involving government interest and funding.
As an organized entity the profession did not advocate
radical reform but both social work and government
accommodated to each other. This stance has required
an integration of the concepts of cause and function
in the profession. Harold Lewis has suggested that it
is the dynamic relationship between cause and function
that shapes service. He defines service "as the
evolving form and substance of the unity and conflict
of cause in function, necessitating the constant
addressing of both sides of this conflict if positive
social change is to be achieved" (1977: 24).

The recent challenges to social welfare programs
in this country reflect renewed and increased conflict
between the values of the dominant society and social
work. Attitudes in the society and the social work
profession are shifting and roles are redefined as
voluntarism and privatism are reawakened. We can
reflect back to Bertha Reynolds, writing in 1936,
"There will never be money enough for relief while the
richest country in the world places the burden of
taxation so disproportionately, not where there is
ability to pay but where there is inability to protest" (1936: 12). Once again the profession must
confront the obsolete ideologies of privatism and
voluntarism as they again are called upon by the
Reagan administration. Now, too, the profession must
determine how it will move to sustain permanent
Federal government involvement in promotion of the
general welfare.

NOTES

[1]Theodorson and Theodorson have stated that when
the term "ideology" was introduced at the beginning of
the 19th century, it referred to the study of ideas.
However, it soon took on its present meaning of "a set
of ideas justifying particular interests" (1969: 195).

[2]Samuel Eliot Morison wrote of the 1929 crash,
"No nation ever faced a business decline more optimistically than America did this one. Nobody highly
placed in government or finance admitted the existence

of a depression for six months or more after the crash" (The Oxford History of the American People, Vol. 3, 1972: 291).

[3]However, later in 1930, statements were made by the Executive Committee of the American Association of Social Workers to the effect that the resources of government and industry, rather than philanthropy and voluntarism, would be necessary to cope with the national emergency (see Fisher, 1980: 34-35). During the same year, Linton Swift, Executive Secretary of the Family Welfare Association, urged that a greater proportion of relief should be publicly funded (Chambers, 1963: 192).

[4]For example, the settlement workers, who favored federal aid to state and local governments for relief, took initiative by stimulating and guiding social protest and moved toward direct political action. In 1931, the Unemployed Committee of the National Federation of Settlements published the widely-read Case Studies of Unemployment, describing 150 cases in which unemployment was seen as a result of industrial rather than individual causes, and which stressed the human cost of unemployment. Around the same time, articles urging social workers to look more closely at the social insurances began to appear in the Compass. Unemployment insurance in the U.S., which was in the form of the dole, was contrasted to the social insurances provided in Europe (Fisher, 1980: 35, 39-40).

[5]Concerning work relief, the Association for Improving the Conditions of the Poor sponsored a privately supported work relief project as early as 1930 (Chambers, pp. 194-195). The American Association of Public Welfare Officials refused to take a stand on the issue of federal grants to states for unemployment relief (Fisher, 1980: 42-43).

[6]The "Proceedings" of the American Association of Social Workers referred to in this paper are located in the Library of the National Association of Social Workers in Washington, D.C.

[7]Shortly after the 1934 AASW Delegate Conference, Social Service Review reported of the Conference:

> In its early days there was danger that the Association might be too much like a narrow kind of trade union. . . . The Washington meeting, in many ways, constitutes a landmark in our professional history. In a time of national crisis, the delegates of the Association accepted their responsibility in regard to national planning and the necessity of formulating clearly the govern-

mental objectives in social welfare. There
is assurance that clear thinking to formulate policies that are in the interests of
the poor clients whose case and cause we
represent and courage to defend those policies should be a part of the new tradition
that is in the making. (1934: 145-146)

[8]President Roosevelt was quoted in 1934 as
saying, "Social workers and I have the same objectives
in common--social justice for everyone" (Compass,
1934: 6).

[9]Arthur Schlesinger, Jr., in his book, The Age
Roosevelt: The Politics of Upheaval reported a spec-
tator at van Kleeck's address at the 1934 National
Conference as saying, "'Never in a long experience of
conferences has this observer witnessed such a prolonged ovation'" (1960: 194).

[10]The efforts of Sophonisba Breckinridge, the
president of the American Association of Schools of
Social Work, ensured that the training of personnel
for FERA was carried out in accredited professional
schools with aid from federally funded scholarships,
rather than in brief training courses for emergency
relief workers. Edith Abbott, then dean of the School
of Social Service Administration at the University of
Chicago, noted that not only were standards maintained, but because of publicity of the new opportunities in public welfare, of which college graduates
had not been previously well informed, and because of
lack of other employment opportunities, requirements
for admission were actually raised (Costin, 1983:
227-228).

[11]Social work reformers were concerned that WPA
assistance, unemployment compensation, and old age
pension were all tied to work, with no federal aid for
the millions of able-bodied unemployed who were also
dependent on relief (Bremer, 1984: 166-167).

[12]Hopkins and Perkins both made important and
controversial recommendations to the President during
the process of formulating the Social Security
program. Hopkins suggested to Roosevelt that social
security and relief be combined so that relief would
be given as a matter of right. Roosevelt rejected the
proposal, maintaining that although the relief system
and the social insurance system often applied to the
same people, the two systems should be kept separate.
A relief program, Roosevelt believed, should be temporary and should end as soon as business and employment
opportunities revived, while he envisioned employment
insurance and old age insurance as permanent parts of
the economy (Schlesinger, Jr., 1953: 303-304).
Concerning Hopkins' attempt to include relief as a

part of the institutional social welfare system, Frances Perkins reported that Roosevelt "saw that this would be the very thing he had been saying he was against for years -- the dole" (Perkins, 1946: 284-285).

Another of the many controversial issues around the Social Security program had to do with the decision to fund social security insurances through employee contributions. Frances Perkins was amongst the many who raised objection to this, preferring that it be paid out of general tax revenues. With amazing foresight, Roosevelt saw this as a political decision rather than an economic one. He believed that public insurance should be a self-supporting system financed out of contributions and special taxes instead of general revenues. Years later, in response to a complaint about employee contributions, Roosevelt said:

> I guess you're right on the economics, but those taxes were never a problem of economics. They are politics all the way through. We put those payroll contributions there so as to give the contributors a legal, moral, and political right to collect their pensions and their unemployment benefits. With those taxes in there, no damn politician can ever scrap my social security program. (Quoted in Schlesinger, Jr., 1958: 308-309).

[13]William Bremer maintains that except for Mary van Kleeck and Harry Lurie, the group of New York influential social workers supported the conservative tone of the New Deal's social programs (Bremer, 1984: 173).

[14]See for example the challenging article by Dorothy Douglas in Social Work Today, "Unemployment Insurance -- For Whom?" in which she concluded that the Lundeen bill was far superior to the Social Security bill. Of the latter, she said:

> At every step the supposed object of the Bill has increasingly been ignored. At every step each real safeguard for the 'security' of the workers had cynically been thrust aside, at every step increasing concern has been shown for each new device for the employers' immediate interests, at every step there has been more effective insistence upon saving the wealthy taxpayer at all costs (Douglas, 1935: 9-12, 34).

A similar point of view was taken in an unsigned article, "New Deal Security" (Social Work Today, 1935: 3-4).

[15]These figures excluded nonprofessional employees of social agencies, such as case aides and

others who conducted initial interviews with applicants for relief or assisted with forms needed to determine eligibility (Fisher, 1980: 235).

[16]This number included newly recruited and untrained people working in the new or expanded local public welfare departments, and professional social workers who worked in FERA and its state and local divisions, in WPA and local work-relief programs in the Bureau of Public Assistance after the creation of the Social Security Board in 1935, and with the federal Children's Bureau, which was enlarged and strengthened (from Marion Hathaway, Trade Union Organization for Professional Workers, United Office and Professional Workers of America, CIO, 1939, in Fisher, 1980: 235).

[17]During 1936, a plea for social action was made by Harry Lurie:

> Whether the Democrats or the Republicans achieve political power at the next election, the new Administration will be reinforced in the desire to quit the 'relief business.' There is nothing to prevent such a step except an aroused and organized movement of all elements who are in sympathy with the unemployed and who adhere to economic theories which will not make economic recovery dependent upon reduction of wages, standards, workers' insecurity and destruction of relief provisions (Lurie, 1936: 5-8).

REFERENCES

Belsley, J. Lyle
    1936   "The merit system in social work administration." Compass 17: 9-10.

Bond, Elsie
    1935   "Summary of the provisions of the Economic Security Bill." Compass 16: 7-10.

Brandes, Stuart
    1970   American Welfare Capitalism, 1880-1940. Chicago: University of Chicago Press.

Bremer, William
    1984   Depression Winters: New York Social Workers and the New Deal. Philadelphia: Temple University Press.

Bruno, Frank
    1957   Trends in Social Work. New York: Columbia University Press.

Burner, David
    1979   Herbert Hoover: A Public Life. New York: Knopf.

Chambers, Clarke
    1963   Seedtime of Reform. Minneapolis: University of Minnesota Press.

Compass

1934   "The conference on governmental objectives for social work." No author. 15: 1-6.

Compass
1935   "National relief policies." No author. 16: 3-6.

Costin, Lela
1983   Two Sisters for Social Justice. Urbana, ILL: University of Illinois Press.

Douglas, Dorothy
1935   "Unemployment insurance - for whom?" Social Work Today 2: 9-12, 34.

Fisher, Jacob
1980   The Response of Social Work to the Depression. Cambridge, MA: Schenkman.

Hawley, Ellis
1974   "Herbert Hoover, the Commerce Secretariat and the vision of an 'Associative State,' 1921-1928." Journal of American History 6: 116-140.

Helvering v. Davis
1937   301 U.S. 671, 57 Sup. Ct. 792, 81 L. Ed. 1336 (1937).

Hodson, William
1938   Proceedings of American Association of Social Workers Delegate Conference: 33.

Hoover, Herbert
1922   American Individualism. New York: Doubleday, Page and Co.

Klein, Philip
1936   "The future of the private agency." Social Work Today 4: 5-7.

Kurzman, Paul
1974   Harry Hopkins and the New Deal. Fair Lawn, NJ: R.E. Burdick.

Larson, Magali Sarfatti
1977   The Rise of Professionalism. Berkeley: University of California Press.

Levitt, Louis
1980   "Social work and social welfare: A conceptual matrix." Journal of Sociology and Social Welfare 7: 636-647.

Lewis, Harold
1977   "The cause in function." Journal of the Otto Rank Association 11: 18-25.

Lurie, Harry
1934   Proceedings of American Association of Social Workers Delegate Conference: 240-253.

Lurie, Harry
1936   "Quitting the relief business." Social Work Today 3: 5-8.

McMillan, Wayne
1937   Proceedings of American Association of Social Workers Delegate Conference: 191-224.

Mauss, Armand
    1975   Social Problems as Social Movements. Philadelphia: Lippincott.

Morison, Samuel Eliot
    1972   The Oxford History of the American People, Vol. 3. New York: Mentor.

Olds, Victoria
    1963   "The Freedmen's Bureau: A 19th century federal welfare agency." Social Casework 44: 247-254.

Perkins, Frances
    1946   The Roosevelt I Knew. New York: Viking.

Pumphrey, Ralph and Muriel Pumphrey
    1961   The Heritage of American Social Work. New York: Columbia University Press.

Reynolds, Bertha
    1935   "Whom do social workers serve?" Social Work Today 2: 5-7, 34.

Reynolds, Bertha
    1936   "Education for public social work." Social Work Today 3: 10-12.

Schlesinger, Arthur, Jr.
    1958   The Age of Roosevelt: The Coming of the New Deal. Boston: Houghton Mifflin.

Schlesinger, Arthur, Jr.
    1960   The Age of Roosevelt: The Politics of Upheaval. Boston: Houghton Mifflin.

Social Service Review
    1934   "The Washington meeting." 8: 145-146.

Social Work Today
    1935   "New deal security." No author. 3:3-4.

Swift, Linton
    1935   Proceedings of American Association of Social Workers Delegate Conference: 12-20.

Swift Linton
    1936   Proceedings of American Association of Social Workers Delegate Conference: 279-294.

Swift, Linton
    1937   Proceedings of American Association of Social Workers Delegate Conference: 1-12.

Theodorson, George and Achilles Theodorson
    1969   Modern Dictionary of Sociology. New York: Thomas Crowell.

van Kleeck, Mary
    1934   "Our illusions regarding government." Proceedings of National Conference of Social Work. Chicago: University of Chicago Press: 473-485.

With Charity for All: Welfare and Society, Ancient Times to the Present
Merritt Ierley

Former President Harry Truman stood a little uneasily, leaning heavily on his cane. His voice faltered now and then. To an observer, he looked all of his 81 years—more than just a mite older than when he used to "give 'em hell"—though his grin was as broad and unmistakable as ever.

"We're gonna do it boys," said Truman, quoting himself, as he spoke of one of his great ambitions as president. He was talking to a visitor in the Harry S. Truman Library in Independence, Missouri.

"Well, Mr. Truman," said the visitor, of the reason for being there that day, "it is twenty years ago that you started this."

"Yes," replied the former President, "I remember that I mentioned it in my State of the Union Message."

Even within his own administration there was some doubt he could do it, Truman recalled, but he told them, "We're gonna do it boys, we're gonna do it. *We* may not make it, but someday . . . "

"Someday" was this day, Friday, July 30, 1965. The visitor was Lyndon Johnson, Truman's successor twice removed. What Truman was gonna do and what Johnson did do, there in the Truman Library, was sign into law a bill of more sweeping social significance than anything since social security: medicare

When Truman proposed medicare in 1945, not only for the elderly but for all ages, the time was not right. In 1965, it was. And now that a bill had cleared Congress and was ready for signing, Johnson had flown to Independence to put his signature on it in Truman's presence. There, in the company of the vice-president, 12 senators, 19 representatives, 1 cabinet member, 1 governor, and other guests, Johnson (using 72 pens for distribution to the faithful)* signed the 133-page bill into law and then paid tribute to its progenitor: "It all started with the man from Independence," said Johnson, "so it is fitting we have come back to his home to complete what he began."

Medical care and full employment were central to Truman's postwar domestic plan. Truman had been president for five months, and the war had been over for three weeks, when, on September 6, 1945, he outlined domestic goals that included a full-employment law, expanded unemployment benefits, an increase in the minimum wage, and an extensive housing program. On November 19th of the same year he made his medicare proposal.

---

*The 72 pens Johnson used to sign the medicare bill cost the federal treasury $79.92, or $1.11 each. Three weeks later, to sign antipoverty legislation, Johnson switched to a pen costing 17 cents.

Truman's unemployment compensation proposal was for an extension of the program to states not yet covered and for a nationwide standard of $25 per week for up to 26 weeks. That, however, figured out to 63 cents an hour for a 40-hour week, which would mean more money for being idle than for working, since the minimum wage was 40 cents an hour. The House Ways and Means Committee shelved the bill.

The full-employment proposal would have pledged the federal government to seeing to a job for any adult willing and able to work. It, too, was set aside. Instead, Congress passed the Employment Act of 1946, which established the Council of Economic Advisers to recommend ways of maintaining maximum employment and to help steer the nation clear of future depressions. Subsequent to that, Truman proposed his medical care program and civil rights legislation, both of which Congress deferred to another day.

Truman's domestic program — his Fair Deal — was clearly secondary in impact to his record in foreign affairs. Relatively few of Truman's domestic proposals were enacted; and those that were enacted largely constituted an extension of existing programs. An increasingly hostile Congress (including defectors within his own party) and the Korean War both kept new social legislation to a minimum. Nevertheless, there were these programs enacted:

- Housing legislation, in 1946, providing $600 million in federal assistance, primarily to help returning veterans buy homes; and the Housing Act of 1949, which facilitated slum clearance
- An increase in the minimum wage to 75 cents an hour
- The Social Security Act of 1950, which extended benefits to an additional 10 million persons
- Legislation making permanent the National School Lunch Program. The federal government had begun subsidizing school lunches, on a year-to-year basis, in 1935, under the old Federal Surplus Commodity Corporation. In making the program permanent in 1946, Congress appropriated $75 million to provide nutritious lunches for 8 million pupils in 46,000 public and non-profit private schools

President Dwight D. Eisenhower was more preoccupied with the Cold War than with domestic matters. Indeed, the Cold War, with its heightened concern about communism, increased suspicion of anything smacking of socialism, and hence of any radical departure in social legislation. Furthermore, high expenditures for defense inhibited increases in domestic spending.

There were, however, amendments to the Social Security Act in 1954 and 1956, notably the latter year, when disability insurance was added to take care of those workers who became premature retirees by virtue of disablement or illness. The Eisenhower Administration also produced HEW, the Department of Health, Education and Welfare, that monster-sized member of the cabinet that had been hatching since Harding's 1920 campaign. It was finally born in April 1953 as an embodiment of such diverse agencies as the Social Security Administration, Public Health Service, Office of Education, Food and Drug Administration, Children's Bureau, Office of Vocational Rehabilitation, and Bureau of Federal Credit Unions. As secretary, Republican Eisenhower named Democrat Oveta Culp Hobby, the second woman to become a cabinet officer.

The administration of President John F. Kennedy marked a return to social activism — the New Frontier. Although such legislation faced an obstacle in the same coalition of Republicans and southern Democrats that had countered much of Truman's Fair Deal, the Kennedy administration saw passage of some significant social legislation. Notable were these:

- Legislation, in 1961, expanding Aid to Dependent Children (ADC) into Aid to Families with Dependent Children (AFDC), which would permit aid to families with an unemployed father rather than only to families with a deceased or absent father, thus seeking to counter the tendency for fathers in such families to desert as a means of generating public assistance
- The Manpower Development and Training Act, of 1962, to help retrain the unemployed
- The Area Redevelopment Act, of 1961, providing loans to depressed areas for the purpose of encouraging new businesses
- The Accelerated Public Works Act, of 1962, establishing grants-in-aid for public works in depressed areas

Kennedy also revived Truman's proposal for medicare, also without success. Unlike Truman, he sought only medical care of the aged as a start.

DECLARING WAR ON POVERTY

Less than two months after the assassination of John F. Kennedy, it fell upon the former vice-president to declare what kind of administration his would be, even for the one year remaining of the term. Thus, early in January 1964 did Lyndon B. Johnson give the Congress "Information of the State of the Union," that which the Constitution required even on such short notice.

Such information took the new president six weeks and 24 different speech writers and rewriters (Mrs. Johnson included) to prepare. The speech came to 3,059 words. Kennedy's State of the Union messages had run 6,000 words; Truman's, in 1946, 25,000.

Speaking in his slow, ambling Texas drawl as he addressed Congress on January 8, 1964, Johnson made it a long speech after all. On the text in front of him were notations to "Pause," "Look Left," "Look Right." He knew how to stir an audience, and this one, in particular. He was still one of them: the many-termed congressman, the strong-armed majority leader of the Senate. He paused frequently, looked left frequently, looked right frequently, making the most of every expressive turn of phrase; and 79 times — once every 39 words — his old colleagues rewarded him with applause.

Johnson set his administration to continuing Kennedy's legislative program, but in particular he would press for cuts in government spending, a reduction in atomic weaponry, broad new civil rights legislation, and

This Administration today, here and now, declares unconditional war on poverty in America, and I urge this Congress and all Americans to join with me in that effort. It will not be a short or easy struggle, no single weapon or strategy will suffice, but we shall not rest until that war is won.

What victory over poverty would be like was explained a few months later. Speaking in Ann Arbor, May 22, 1964, at the University of Michigan commencement exercises, Johnson revealed a vision that could be summed up in two words. They were headlined next day by the Washington *Post* at the top of page 1:

MICHIGAN U. CLASS
TOLD OF AIM FOR
A 'GREAT SOCIETY'

"In your time," Johnson proclaimed to the graduates and their families and friends, "we have the opportunity to move not only toward the rich society and the powerful society, but upward to the Great Society. The Great Society rests on abundance and liberty for all."

The first major step in securing abundance for all, Johnson had already proposed in March: a $1 billion package of antipoverty measures to begin the War on Poverty. The Economic Opportunity Act of 1964, with an appropriation eventually set at $947.5 million, provided for:

- a Job Corps, through which young men and women might receive remedial education and medical care as well as job training at residential centers
- a Neighborhood Youth Corps, to keep young people from dropping out of high school by giving them part-time work while living at home
- VISTA (Volunteers in Service to America), a domestic Peace Corps, providing service in poverty areas as well as to the community generally
- the Community Action Program, locally administered by federally approved community agencies, with "maximum feasible participation" on the part of the community, making use of federal funding to carry out a wide variety of projects
- a Work-Study Program to provide needy college students with part-time jobs
- loans to farmers and small businessmen

The Economic Opportunity Act cleared the Senate by a two-to-one margin in July 1964 but ran into stiff opposition in the House. The leadership made a head count and found there weren't enough votes to bring the bill to a vote. What saved it was some strenuous arm-twisting. House Speaker John McCormack called Democrats into his office, one by one, to inquire of each his interest in federally funded projects back home in his district. Presidential aides roamed the Capitol and the House Office Buildings, making it look, said one Democrat, like Engine House No. 5 when the four-alarm bell sounds. Johnson himself got on the phone and called reluctant legislators; some, he invited to the White House to pose with him for election year photographs.

The result was that the War on Poverty bill, when it came to a vote early in August, passed by a comfortable margin. On the 20th, on the steps overlooking the White House rose garden, Johnson made it the law of the land. Squinting into the intense sun of a bright summer morning, he beheld a "new day of opportunity" for the nation's needy and declared that "the days of the dole in our country are numbered."

Kennedy had already begun drafting a policy on poverty, although it was not as broad as the Economic Opportunity Act. It was a start for Johnson. What stirred up support for the far-reaching War on Poverty was virtual war itself: the convulsive summer of 1964.

It began in Harlem on July 18th, five days before the Senate's vote on the antipoverty bill. A black boy was shot by a white police officer. The boy, who had reportedly menaced the officer with a knife, died. Four days of violence followed. One rioter was killed, 121 persons were injured and 185 were arrested. Mobs smashed store windows, looted, and hurled debris at police. As the long, hot summer continued, the rioting continued: in Brooklyn's mostly black Bedford-Stuyvesant; in Rochester, New York; Jersey City, Paterson, and Elizabeth, New Jersey; the Chicago suburb of Dixmoor, and, at summer's end, Philadelphia. At the time Johnson was squinting into the sun to sign the Economic Opportunity Act on August 20, the smoke of racial violence was darkening the sky across the land.

Johnson's election to a term of his own in November 1964—by a landslide victory, with a two-to-one Democratic Congress at his side—generated a new and larger Great Society program for Congress to work on, one providing for even more extensive machinery of government and assuming a still greater role in the lives of the nation's citizens.

Fresh from his huge victory at the polls, LBJ was riding tall in 1965. Like a ranch foreman at roundup time, he kept his congressional ranch hands in their saddles, and, when necessary, also used cajolery, flattery, calls to patriotism and party loyalty, reminders of favors past and hints of favors future, or plain old arm-twisting to get what he wanted out of the 89th Congress. What he got, by the time the first session ended in October 1965, included:

- Medicare, administered through social security, to persons over 65, covering the cost of hospital and nursing home care as well as home nursing services. A supplementary plan (optional at $3 a month) was made available to cover medical costs and doctors' bills. Eligible beneficiaries at the start were estimated at 19 million.
- Medicaid, for persons on public assistance, and, at state option, for the medically indigent generally. Medicaid was included in the medicare act.
- A $1.1 billion program of aid to the depressed 11-state Appalachia region, most of the money going for new highways that would mean temporary construction jobs and bring in new industry for permanent jobs.
- A $7.8 billion housing program providing for public housing, urban renewal, and college campus housing, plus a new cabinet department, Housing and Urban Development, to administer this and existing programs.
- A $1.8 billion extension of the War on Poverty.
- A $3.2 billion program of public works grants to create jobs in depressed areas.
- A $1.3 billion program of aid to all but the wealthiest school districts in the nation.
- Voting rights, medical research, highway beautification, and farm and immigration legislation.

• Public funding of legal aid for the poor through the Office of Economic Opportunity.

All in all, Congress in 1965 appropriated $119.3 billion (an amount to that time exceeded only during World War II) and filled 33,250 pages of the *Congressional Record*, itself a congressional record.

But problems were brewing. The War on Poverty was beginning to get some bad press. At Camp Breckinridge, Kentucky, in August 1965, some 400 trainees at a Job Corps center brawled over the food they were served, making headlines. At Fort Custer, Michigan, early in November, Job Corps trainees fought with local youths and the police after a dance at a local junior high school, making more headlines. The Job Corps, in its first ten months, was reported to have spent $96 million on 12,371 youths at 59 training centers, making more headlines. At $7,760 per youth, the same amount of money could have sent the same number to college for four years.

Elsewhere, there was good news. Project Head Start, launched in July 1965, was off to a start worthy of its name. It was initially intended as a summer-only program but was made year-round by popular demand.

In their scope and diversity, these programs represented an unprecedented involvement of the federal government in the lives of its people. "The nation is witnessing a social revolution," observed Washington columnist Michael O'Neill of the New York *Daily News*. O'Neill was talking basically of the Community Action Program (CAP). Never before had the federal government worked directly with the community (and often that "community" was no more than a neighborhood) in the implementation of federal programs. It had always worked through the state capital, which in turn worked with the municipality. But the Economic Opportunity Act of 1964 had mandated "maximum feasible participation" on the part of the local community.

All too often the result was maximum feasible confusion. Once a community action program got started, those who were not among the original participants often demanded a role, and, in city after city, the more aggressive and more militant frequently pushed aside those who were already taking part. In some cases the Office of Economic Opportunity (OEO) sponsored elections so that "poverty representatives" might be chosen for CAP boards of directors. The OEO even paid the expenses of campaigning in many cases. The average voter turnout was 2 to 5 percent of those poor who were eligible to vote.

Despite the diversity of these various programs, there was a serious question as to how well they were reaching their intended beneficiaries, the hard-core poor. In mid-August 1965, Los Angeles *Times* staff writer Paul Weeks, examining the antipoverty program now that it had been in operation for a year, wrote that one could see the light burning late into the night at the Office of Economic Opportunity in Washington, and yet walk a few blocks away, amid the stark slums of the nation's capital, and seek in vain a single poor person who had even heard of the War on Poverty.

Weeks' story was on page 2. It might have made page 1 except for another story. In the Watts district of Los Angeles people were running through the streets yelling, "Burn, baby, burn." And Watts was burning. Towers of thick smoke stretched upward. Sirens cut through the streets, drowning out rifle shots and the moans of the hurt and dying. Looters chanced the jagged remnants of broken store windows to steal television sets or grab, at random, armloads of shoes that wouldn't even fit. Small children took ice cream. "They've gone crazy," said a black businessman; "you can't talk to them. Even Negroes can't talk to them." What talked was the National Guard (California's 40th Armored Division and its 15,000 troops). What talked were 800 heavily armed, steel-helmeted lawmen. Roadblocks and machine guns talked. The madness stopped, and then the rioters could see what they had done—to their neighborhood, their homes, their stores—like the insane who sometimes mutilate their own bodies: 32 dead, 874 injured, and 737 structures damaged or destroyed.

The worst day of the Watts riot was August 14th. A continent away next morning, some 3,000 of New York City's elderly, members of the Golden Ring Council of Senior Citizens, clambered aboard buses for a pilgrimage up the Hudson River. At their destination they stood in a soft, summer breeze, under the maples and pines of Hyde Park, to help commemorate the signing of the Social Security Act on another August 14th, exactly 30 years past.

On August 20, 1965, as Watts' embers were turning to ash, the Senate approved a $1.65 billion extension of the War on Poverty. But would it be enough? A week later President Johnson warned that "the clock is ticking, time is moving," and Watts could happen again.

A BOX DIVIDED

In 1966 the loyal 89th Congress continued to give the president most of what he wanted, including:

- another $1 billion for the War on Poverty
- a $1.3 billion Demonstration Cities program for renewal of blighted neighborhoods
- an increase in the minimum wage from $1.25 to $1.40 (effective in 1967) and to $1.60 (1968), and, for the first time, extension of the minimum wage to agricultural workers
- rent supplements for low-income families as an alternative to direct subsidization of housing, the supplement representing the difference between 25 percent of an eligible family's income and the amount to be paid for rent

Meanwhile, medicare had gone into effect (it was in January 1966 Johnson gave Truman his medicare card) and by the end of the year, medicaid as well. The Department of Health, Education and Welfare in November gave approval to the first five medicaid systems among the states: those in Maine, Michigan, New Mexico, New York, and Vermont. In New York City, medicaid was slow in attracting interest. The city expected 1 million to apply, but after two months counted only 18,500 indigent poor who had done so, over and above the 575,000 welfare clients who were automatically registered. The city undertook a campaign to attract medicaid clients, at first through radio and television announcements and later through a door-to-door canvass.

The War on Poverty itself was not going smoothly. To a large extent, it was inevitable. So much money was available that there was bound to be squabbling over it: over what programs to carry out, over who made the decisions, over who got how much, over the authority of locally elected government as against the authority of antipoverty agencies. In Newark, for example, the United Community Corporation, the antipoverty agency serving the city, had an 87-member board of directors, only two of whom were city officials.

Since money is power, federal funds by the millions were cleaving the local power structure in Newark and around the country. Elected mayors and councils were being rivaled by nonelected boards and agencies purporting to be carrying out the mandate of maximum feasible participation by the poor. Oftentimes, antipoverty officials drew salaries far in excess of what elected public officials were paid. A New Jersey CAP director divulged his salary as more than $100,000 per year, plus expenses. But the difficulties went beyond this. As more federal money became available and more programs were devised, CAP agencies demanded even more authority.

In Syracuse, New York, in January 1966, there was a two-day "People's Convention for Total Participation of the Poor," sponsored by the Syracuse People's War Council Against Poverty. The convention adopted a resolution calling for outright control of the War on Poverty by the poor. When the Citizens' Crusade Against Poverty, principally funded by the United Auto Workers and chaired by Walter Reuther, assembled in Washington to defend community action programs against their critics, radicals among the delegates so booed OEO Director Sargent Shriver that he had to leave the hall.

In the mid-term election of 1966, Republicans gained 47 seats in the House, narrowing the Democrats' majority to 248 to 187. That majority, however, included southern Democrats who could not be counted on to vote for Great Society legislation, and Johnson was riding a little lower in the saddle.

Riots again swept the country in the summers of 1966 and 1967. Helping to fuel the violence was an influx of unemployed blacks from the South, many of them formerly agricultural workers. When the law was changed in 1966 to extend the minimum wage to agriculture, farmers began laying off men and turned more and more to mechanization.

The riots of 1967 were perhaps the most frightening of all, taking on the ugliness of guerrilla warfare throughout the land. Newark's Springfield Avenue looked like a scene out of World War II. Detroit alone counted 27 dead and damage at more than $200 million. Johnson sent in federal troops only after repeated requests from Governor George Romney, and then only after going on television to observe that Romney, a potential rival for the presidency in 1968, had been unable to bring the situation under control. Newspapers denounced the president for playing politics with people's lives.

Congress now was cooling to ever-larger War on Poverty appropriations. What many thought, Rep. George H. Mahon, chairman of the House Appropriations Committee, said in so many words: "The more we have appropriated for these programs, the more violence we have." Congress, nevertheless, appropriated $1.8 billion for the War on Poverty in 1967—an increase, but less than the administration had asked.

Helping to build public uncertainty were well-publicized examples of waste, mismanagement, and inequity in the poverty program. In Kansas City, enrollees in a summer youth program for the poor included a young man who drove around in an expensive new Thunderbird. In Detroit, a jobless auto worker, who had been taking home $104 a week when he worked, found he could make $160 a week tax-free in a job-training program. In Johnston, Rhode Island, 73 parents of children in a poverty program owned, among them, 58 homes and 113 cars. A congressional survey disclosed that there was one supergrade ($15,000 +) official for every 18 employees in the Office of Economic Opportunity; in the Department of Agriculture it was one for every 500, and in the Department of Defense one for every 1,000.

For varied reasons, but particularly the Vietnam War and the riots, there was a rising sense of alarm sweeping the land. In August 1967, Senate Foreign Relations Chairman J. William Fulbright declared: "The Great Society is a sick society.".

The war in Vietnam had become the most divisive issue in memory. Johnson, in the election campaign of 1964, posed as the peace candidate, declaring he wouldn't send American boys to fight a war "that Asian boys ought to fight," even as he was mapping then-secret plans for bombing North Vietnam. Three years later there were more than 1 million American boys in the Vietnam theater of operations. There had been 16,000 when Johnson took office. In August 1967, when the Johnson administration had been at war for one month longer than all of World War II, the president was still insisting the nation could fight the war in Asia and the one at home—the war on poverty—at the same time. But the cost was steep. Federal spending had already gone up by 50 percent during the Johnson years, and now the president was asking for an income tax surcharge of 10 percent. Fulbright, declaring a "sick society," argued that both wars were going badly. But the problem, he said, was not so much a matter of financial feasibility as the "psychological incompatibility" of trying to do both at the same time.

Lyndon Johnson, in mid-1965, had been as powerful a man as ever occupied the White House. Now, two years later, his war in Vietnam quagmired and his war on poverty floundering, he was a president in deep political trouble. His rating in the polls was at an all-time low of 32 percent. He seemed no longer to have the nation's trust. He was being further and further demoted from president to mere politician by each successive appearance on the nightly news. The war the "Asian boys" were supposed to fight: Would it go on forever, taking the lives of countless American boys? And the war on poverty: Was it holding out more promise than it could deliver, further sagging the hopes of an increasingly disillusioned age? Even the bubbly Hubert Humphrey, that eternal optimist, wondered. Speaking of Model Cities in the summer of 1967, the vice-president said it was like having a hundred kids to a party where there was only one box of Crackerjacks. "By the time we divide up the box," observed Humphrey, "each kid will get just one Crackerjack, and you know that's not going to be anywhere near enough."

In January 1968 the Office of Economic Opportunity began a cutback in the antipoverty program, the result of Congress appropriating less money for the fiscal year and, moreover, transferring some funds to other agencies. A further sign of the shift away from massive government spending was an announcement in May, by the Department of Labor, of a pledge by private industry to create at least 100,000 new jobs for the unemployed, the government paying the cost of training.

Meanwhile, Johnson on March 31st announced, to an astonished nation, that he would not seek another term as president. He would not be a candidate in the 1968 election. That concluded his presidency, for all practical purposes, leaving a nation divided by its incompatible wars and unfulfilled of the vast hopes that had been raised—perhaps less a Great Society than what had to seem, to many, a grated one.

Kennedy, Johnson, and the War on Poverty
Carl M. Brauer

When President Lyndon B. Johnson declared metaphorical war on poverty in 1964, he set in motion an important, complex, and controversial phase in the history of reform in the United States, whose shockwaves were still being felt in the early 1980s, a time of counterreformation. Although poverty reform in the 1960s influenced the historical profession no less than some others—in the rise of social history, for example—historians concentrated their research efforts on the more distant past. Analysis of the history, workings, consequences, and lessons of the War on Poverty remained largely the business of social scientists, who turned it into a sizable industry. The passage of time and the growing availability of primary sources now invite historical investigation, which has no more apposite starting point than the War on Poverty's genesis.

Social scientists explain the War on Poverty's creation in essentially three different ways. Daniel P. Moynihan in his *Maximum Feasible Misunderstanding* does not treat motive systematically or explicitly, but he builds a powerful implicit argument that the War on Poverty grew out of the rising influence of social science itself. In particular, Moynihan attributes the Community Action Program, which became central to the War on Poverty, to reform-minded, though unscientific, sociologists. A second school of thought emphasizes interest groups and political calculation. Among those who take this approach, Frances Fox Piven and Richard Cloward have probably been most widely read. President John F. Kennedy and President Johnson, they argue, launched the War on Poverty in order to attract a high percentage of black votes in the 1964 election. Third, the War on Poverty's birth has been explained through the cyclical theory of reform. After a period of dormancy, James Sundquist maintains, the reform impulse once again swept through the American political system, bringing with it a national effort to eradicate poverty.[1]

These treatments have value, particularly in describing the intellectual and institutional backgrounds of specific programs associated with the War on Poverty and in providing eyewitness accounts. Separately from his analytical chapters, it should be noted, Sundquist presents an accurate, though incomplete, narrative of events. In light of documentary and oral evidence now available, however, none of these treatments provides a satisfactory explanation of the War on Poverty's beginnings. Historical research leads to a different picture of them than social scientists have thus far painted.

The War on Poverty most definitely had political motives, but not the particular ones that Piven and Cloward claim. It also had intellectual motives and did reflect the rising influence of social science, yet Moynihan emphasizes sociology when economics figured far more significantly. Political and intellectual motives were intertwined, though in flux, throughout the War on Poverty's gestation. At some moments, political calculation was narrow; at others, broad. Likewise the ideas involved varied widely in terms of complexity, implication, and ideology. The very slogan ''War on Poverty'' represented the marriage of political self-interest to political culture. Although a cycle of reform may be observed in American politics, its existence alone fails to explain why poverty was singled out for attention.

Most accounts of the War on Poverty's birth make it seem inevitable, but historical research highlights the roles of chance—the assassination of President Kennedy—and of circumstance—the succession of President Johnson. Indeed, discussions of its birth sometimes pay too little attention to an obvious, but critical, fact: the War on Poverty was called into being by a president. Government policies sought to reduce poverty long before then; they continued to do so well after the rallying cry, War on Poverty, faded into memory. An examination of why President Kennedy considered making the elimination of poverty a centerpiece of his program in 1964 and why President Johnson did so proves instructive about the problem of origins while simultaneously illuminating the role of the presidency in recent American history.

From its rediscovery in the 1950s, poverty was a partisan issue, pushed by Democrats, usually liberal Democrats, and resisted by Republicans. Campaigning for reelection in 1954, Senator Paul H. Douglas of Illinois a liberal and a professional economist, made the economic depression that gripped the southern part of his state an effective issue. When he was returned to office, he sponsored legislation to aid depressed areas, through which the federal government would underwrite public works projects, job retraining, and business expansion in high unemployment areas. President Dwight D. Eisenhower and a majority of Republicans would only go along with a much smaller program than Douglas and a majority of Democrats sought; so the legislation stalled. The long struggle, however, popularized the notion that "pockets of poverty" existed in different parts of the country. Similarly, Senator Hubert H. Humphrey of Minnesota, another liberal Democrat, proposed a Youth Conservation Corps, modeled after the New Deal's Civilian Conservation Corps (CCC), to put 150,000 unemployed young people to work on conservation projects. This proposal also languished in Congress but helped publicize high rates of unemployment among youth and accompanying increases in juvenile delinquency, both of which were particularly associated with the poor.[2]

Prominent Democrats outside Congress also began to raise the poverty issue in the mid-1950s. Governor Averell Harriman asked the New York legislature in 1956 for funds to study the causes of poverty and to establish pilot projects to raise the earning capacity of low-income families. The program received publicity disproportionate to its extremely modest scope. Later that year, in a campaign speech in Oklahoma, Adlai E. Stevenson, the Democratic presidential nominee, recounted his party's efforts to push back poverty and pointed out that a sizable number of Americans lived on excessively low incomes. Without proposing a program to remedy the problem, Stevenson declared his faith "that we can abolish poverty."[3]

Liberal writers likewise called attention to the endurance of poverty. Economist John Kenneth Galbraith's best-selling book, *The Affluent Society*, did not have as much impact as Henry George's enormously popular *Progress and Poverty* of the previous century, but it made a similar observation: that poverty existed alongside plenty. Poverty, Galbraith wrote, "can no longer be presented as a universal or massive affliction. It is more nearly an afterthought." To Galbraith, poverty was a national disgrace, but he saw widespread affluence as the more notable phenomenon of the time. By featuring it in his title he struck a responsive public chord. Where George had proposed taxing away the unearned increment on land as the solution to poverty, Galbraith recommended increased social investment in the poor and in their communities. Using higher income floors, writers to the left of Galbraith, such as Michael Harrington, estimated that as many as a third of the nation's population had substandard incomes.[4]

While some liberals and Democrats were rediscovering poverty and questioning the extent and moral worth of affluence, many conservatives and Republicans were celebrating prosperity and the wondrous benefits of the free enterprise system. The Advertising Council, for example, hailed the arrival of "people's capitalism" for creating prosperity and making workers stockholders. The Eisenhower administration expanded some of the broad-based social programs of the New Deal, such as Social Security, but resisted special assistance to the poor. Campaigning for president in West Virginia in 1960, the Republican nominee, Richard M. Nixon, castigated his Democratic opponent's assertion that seventeen million people went to bed hungry every night. That only provided "grist for the Communist propaganda mill," Nixon charged. He recounted Eisenhower's response: "Now look, I go to bed hungry every night, but that's because I'm on a diet. The doctor won't let me eat any more."[5]

Although international threats in the 1940s and early 1950s had served to discourage critical examination of America's internal shortcomings, the growing perception of renewed dangers from abroad in the late 1950s had the opposite effect. The Soviet Union's successful launching of Sputnik, the first artificial earth satellite, galvanized American fears of Soviet technical, educational, and military prowess and precipitated a wide-ranging questioning of America's ability and resolve to meet the communist challenge. Democratic politicians both led and exploited this questioning process. The theme of Kennedy's presidential campaign in 1960, as set out for his speechwriters, was "to summon every segment of our society . . . to restore America's relative strength as a free nation . . . to regain our security and leadership in a fast changing world menaced by communism."[6]

Kennedy called attention to weaknesses in the American economy, in particular its sluggish rate of economic growth. Too many of America's workers were unemployed, he insisted, too much of its industrial capacity idle. He criticized Republicans for opposing legislation to aid the nation's economically depressed areas. In the important West Virginia primary election, he made the poverty, unemployment, and hunger he witnessed in that state major themes of his winning effort. During the general election campaign, he occasionally singled out poverty. Commemorating the anniversary of the Social Security Act, he called that legislation an "opening battle" while declaring that the "war against poverty and degradation is not yet over."[7]

In his eloquent inaugural address, Kennedy several times mentioned the fight against poverty; but characteristic both of the speech and his early administration, he referred to poverty as a foreign or international problem, not a domestic one. American poverty did not become a focal point of debate or policy during his first two years in office. Kennedy signed area redevelopment and manpower development and training legislation. He created a Committee on Juvenile Delinquency and Youth Crime, which he placed under the direction of his brother, Robert, the attorney general. At his behest, Congress emphasized the rehabilitation of welfare clients. Each represented a discrete response to discrete social or economic problems, which were not collectively identified as poverty.[8]

Sluggish economic growth, slack demand, and unacceptably high rates of unemployment, not poverty, captured Kennedy's attention in his first two years as president. After his first approaches to these interrelated problems failed to stimulate the economic expansion he desired or, in the case of expenditures, were ruled out by congressional opposition, he gradually, in 1962, came to adopt the solution put forth by professional economists on the Council of Economic Advisers (CEA), across-the-board tax reduction for individuals and corporations. Although a significant part of the economics profession and some influential businessmen welcomed this proposal, it encountered opposition from those who believed in balanced budgets, from those who worried greatly about inflation, and from certain liberals who preferred tax reform to tax reduction and increases in social expenditures to a potential diminution of government's capacity to spend on worthy causes. Hence the tax cut made slow progress through Congress.[9]

The tax cut left President Kennedy open to criticism that he was indifferent to poverty. Prior to appearing on a year-end interview show in 1962, Kennedy asked Walter Heller, chairman of the CEA, for an analysis of assertions by Harrington and Leon Keyserling that poverty was much more widespread than commonly assumed. Harrington, a journalist, socialist, and social activist, estimated that 50 million Americans were poor. Keyserling, once chairman of Harry S. Truman's CEA and an acerbic critic of the tax cut, put the number at thirty-eight million and said an additonal 39 million lived above the poverty line though still in deprivation. In responding to President Kennedy's request, Heller noted that "there was controversy about past and future progress against the scourge of poverty" but insisted that under "any *absolute* poverty line, we have reduced the share of the population in poverty during all periods of prosperity." "Contemporary poverty," he observed, though, "to the extent it is peculiarly associated with nonwhite color, widowhood, old age, etc.— may be harder to overcome than the more generalized poverty of earlier generations."[10]

No one, in fact, asked Kennedy about poverty on the show, but in February a television documentary narrated by Howard K. Smith stimulated about one hundred letters to the president, most of them, it appeared, from Democrats who were neither poor nor southern. The writers wanted the president "to adopt a mood either of sympathy for the poor (like Eleanor Roosevelt) or of vigorous demands for action (like FDR)," according to a summary prepared for the White House. Frequently the letters referred to phrases from Kennedy's own campaign or from his inaugural address. Many proposed public works projects, training programs, and increased social services, but few mentioned "the tax cut as a way to alleviate or prevent poverty." Indeed, more correspondents singled it out for opposition than any other policy.[11]

Although poverty was not producing a groundswell of public interest or an outbreak of public protest, it was attracting more attention in 1962 and early 1963 than at any time since the 1930s. Dwight MacDonald's long review essay in *The New Yorker* in January 1963 undoubtedly was more widely read than the books it discussed, including Harrington's *The Other America*, which, it should be noted, did not become a best seller until after the War on Poverty was declared the following year. President Kennedy read MacDonald's essay and Harrington's book. Born to wealth and privilege himself, Kennedy had been brought up with a firm sense of noblesse oblige. He believed in government's duty and ability to solve social and economic problems. In addition, he was sensitive to the intellectual currents of his times and to any suggestion that he was not meeting the country's problems. So it is not surprising that he asked Heller to look into the poverty issue in greater depth.[12]

Heller welcomed the assignment. Although he had been instrumental in selling Kennedy on the tax cut, stressing growth and efficiency objectives, he had been trained in the economics department of the University of Wisconsin, which, since the days of John R. Commons, had been concerned with distributional objectives, with social justice and economic equity. Heller thus combined the techniques of modern post-Keynesian economics with the moral ideals of Wisconsin progressivism. In Heller's view, the elimination of poverty was not only to be sought on moral grounds but on efficiency ones, for poverty bred disease, ignorance, and crime and therefore reduced productivity. Like his mentor, Harold Groves, and other Wisconsin economists, such as Edwin Witte or Commons himself, Heller operated comfortably in the world of politics, which meant living with small, incremental steps on the road to the ideal.[13]

Heller turned to Robert J. Lampman for assistance. Lampman, a fellow student of Groves and a leading expert on wealth and income distribution, had come to the CEA as a consultant in 1961 and as a full-time staff member in 1962. He now updated an earlier study he had done for the Joint Economic Committee of Congress. He found that the impressive rate of reduction in income-poverty, which he had previously documented for the ten years, 1947 to 1956, had slowed down. Between 1947 and 1956, the percentage of families with less than $3,000 of total money income (in 1961) declined from 33 percent to 23 percent; in the five years since 1956, though, it dropped only 2 percent more. The findings distressed Heller. "They offer one more demonstration of the costs of economic slack," he wrote President Kennedy, "and they, therefore, also provide another dimension of what's at stake in the proposed tax cut."[14]

In Heller's view, economic growth historically held the key to reducing poverty, and the tax cut held the key to economic growth. Yet several things in the spring of 1963 caused Heller to focus on the poverty problem itself. The new data from Lampman indicated a worse picture than one might have expected from his earlier study. Sensitive to politics, Heller worried about the tax cut's liabilities, for its greatest immediate benefits would go to those with middle or upper incomes. It might simply be politically prudent, he reasoned, for the president to have something specifically aimed at helping the poor. Heller was impressed when Kenneth O'Donnell, a political aide to the president whose judgment Heller respected, told him to "stop worrying about the tax cut." "It will pass and pass big," O'Donnell optimistically forecast; "worry about something else." Heller has also recalled learning from a newspaper story that a Republican presidential aspirant was considering an antipoverty program of his own. It was folly, Heller believed, to allow a

Republican to steal a march on a naturally Democratic issue. A search of Heller's papers and clippings files at the Kennedy Library failed to turn up the particular story; so it is possible that Heller's memory was faulty. Accurate or not, however, the recollection reveals that Heller viewed poverty not only as an economic or moral problem but also as a political one.[15]

Dramatic events in the spring and summer of 1963 gave the poverty issue an additional allure to this administration. During that time the racial issue was reaching a boil in the South. Kennedy made an important shift in his own civil rights policy when he advocated sweeping civil rights legislation and thereby risked a break with the southern wing of his own party. Since the 1930s the racial issue had been dividing Democrats roughly along the Mason-Dixon line. Although not always united across regional lines on economic issues, southern and northern Democrats found more to agree on economically than on civil rights matters. For both intellectual and political reasons, President Kennedy often framed civil rights issues in economic terms. Even in proposing his civil rights legislation in 1963, he renewed requests he had earlier made of Congress for educational and training programs which would, of course, benefit people of all races. Southern members of Congress could be expected to oppose civil rights legislation in force, but some of them, the president and Heller hoped, would welcome efforts to reduce poverty because their region had a disproportionately large share of it.[16]

President Kennedy at this point worried far more about how southern whites would vote in 1964 than he did about how blacks would vote nationwide. In fact he had little concern about where he stood with black voters. He was not taking their votes for granted exactly, for his success in politics had been predicated on vigorously pursuing all voting blocs he might have a chance of winning. Yet his close identification with the civil rights cause and then his championing of it in June 1963 precluded the need for doing anything fundamentally new, like proposing an attack on poverty. Furthermore, he and Heller viewed poverty either as more of a white problem than a black one or as one that superseded race. When Heller informed Kennedy on June 20 that he was having Lampman "consider what might go into an Administration 'assault on poverty' program in 1964," he observed that "the civil rights message covers a lot of the ground, but there may well be room for a broader program not limited to race." At a cabinet-level meeting in the fall, Heller noted how "disadvantaged groups other than Negroes now deserve our attention." When the president considered dramatizing the poverty problem in the fall, he contemplated a trip to Appalachia, which was populated predominantly by whites.[17]

Heller asked Lampman on June 3 for his ideas on "a possible Kennedy offensive against poverty." He wanted to know how much of the poverty problem would "yield to a successful tax cut, full employment, and faster growth." "What specific measures aimed at the victims and the sources of poverty are needed," Heller wondered, and what had the federal government done and left undone? He requested recommendations for a "practical, Kennedy antipoverty program in 1964."[18]

A week later Lampman responded at length. Full employment and long-term growth could certainly reduce poverty significantly, he maintained, just as it had in the ten years beginning in 1947. In that period, however, three groups generally proved immune to the benefits of economic growth: the elderly, the disabled, and families headed by women. Numerous federal programs, such as medical care for the aged and job retraining, were either under way or had been proposed to help these groups and others. Practically speaking, Lampman proposed that they think in terms of "opening the exits out of poverty (particularly for young people) and preventing retreats into poverty." He would open exits by "aggressive expansionist full employment fiscal policy, by antidiscrimination efforts, by better school and public facilities for low income children." He would "supplement retraining programs by relocation allowances" and "improve environments of the poor by community development and public housing." Finally, Lampman would "prevent retreats by stronger programs against extended unemployment, prolonged disability, and loss of savings," and through "higher transfers to families of disabled and women without husbands."[19]

Lampman wanted an annual accounting of "exits and retreats into poverty" that would "concentrate upon the inter-generational transmission of poverty." Though he did not explicitly say so, such an accounting would have tested a key element in the popular theory of a culture of poverty, put forth by Harrington, the anthropologist Oscar Lewis, and others, according to which poverty was handed down from generation to generation, trapping the young in an interminable cycle of deprivation. In this culture or cycle, the young supposedly acquired defeatist attitudes and a variety of bad social habits that only impeded their chances of ever escaping poverty. If valid, the culture of poverty implied the need for extensive new rehabilitative and educational services, aimed particularly at the young. Because poverty was presumably "deep" and inbred, mere cash assistance could not be expected to cure the underlying problem.[20]

Although some sociological evidence suggested that poverty was being passed down from generation to generation—a sample of welfare recipients, for example, found that over 40 percent of their parents had been raised in homes where some public assistance had been received—Lampman knew that no one had shown how far back in time this phenomenon went, how statistically significant it was, or whether it was increasing or decreasing. Six months later, however, when the CEA included a chapter on poverty in its annual report, it facilely embraced culture-of-poverty theory.[21]

If the jury was still out on the intergenerational transmission of poverty, the verdict seemed clearer to Lampman and other economists on the salutary role of education. Human-capital theory, which maintained that education was critical in raising productivity and therefore in reducing poverty, had swept the economics profession in the late 1950s and early 1960s. Burton A. Weisbrod, one of its champions, was a CEA staff member who assisted in developing early antipoverty plans. In addition, sociological evidence showed a correlation between educational attainment and poverty, confirming the everyday observation that it was hard to find a highly educated person who was poor, except by choice. Yet other data suggested that attitudes acquired in the home affected receptivity to education, which might have made people skeptical about how much educational institutions could affect the young.[22]

Lampman's preference for investing in youth as the best way to fight poverty reflected faith in education and human-capital theory. It also was based on an important demographic fact, that the postwar baby boom was significantly increasing the number of poor school-age children and young adults. "Is it possible," he speculated, "that by a tremendous educational effort or family allowance or retraining programs for the children of the present poor that we would drastically improve the exit from poverty rate for the youngsters?" "Can we imagine," he wondered, "spending twice as much public money on the education and health of poor children as we do on non-poor children? Perhaps it is fair to say that until we do we aren't dedicated to the eradication of poverty."[23]

Lampman worried about the lack of a "politically workable definition of concept of poverty." Poverty, he observed, was particularly associated with the South, nonwhites, smaller cities, the old, the poorly educated, and broken families. Like Harrington, he believed it was "relatively invisible to many people in the U.S." Perhaps, he speculated, racial conflicts were making it more visible. Reflecting prevalent views about the lack of class conflict in America, he wrote that "most people see no political dynamite in the fact that our income distribution at the low end is about the same as it has always been." "The bottom fifth of income receivers," he pointed out, "get no more than 5 percent of total income."[24]

Practical political considerations discouraged Lampman and other administration economists from proposing income transfers. "Probably a politically acceptable program must avoid completely any use of the term 'inequality' or of the term 'redistribution of income or wealth,'" Lampman early advised Heller. Similarly, Lampman and James Tobin, a CEA member, discussed a negative income tax but concluded that it was a political and budgetary impossibility. In its chapter on poverty the following January, the CEA bowed to political reality when it observed that, though all the poor could be raised above the poverty line by redistributing to them an $11 billion levy on everyone else, it would not be a proper solution, for it "would leave untouched most of the roots of poverty. Americans want to *earn* the American standard of living by their own efforts and contributions." "It will be far better, even if more difficult," the council maintained, "to equip and to permit the poor of the nation to produce and to earn the additional $11 billion and more."[25]

The economists made a reasonable reading of political reality. Progressive tax reforms had originally accompanied the tax cut, but they proved to be a price the administration had to pay for tax reduction. Even after that price was paid, the tax cut, contrary to O'Donnell's confident assurances to Heller, languished in the Senate Finance Committee, chaired by Harry F. Byrd of Virginia. An apostle of the balanced budget, Byrd was fighting to hold down spending, and, in addition, he was perturbed by the administration's advocacy of civil rights legislation. Other major new spending programs with more broad-based appeal than increases in assistance to the poor, such as medical insurance for the aged under Social Security and aid to education, were also stalled in Congress. The 1962 welfare amendments, with their emphasis on rehabilitation, had been partly designed to cool off an incipient popular rebellion against welfare. This, then, hardly seemed an auspicious moment to propose significant increases in transfer payments to the poor.[26]

At best it might be possible to redirect several hundred million dollars from existing programs into a new antipoverty effort. The economists expected that the tax cut would eventually generate more revenues by increasing national income and thus produce a "fiscal dividend" which could be used to help those who had not benefited from it immediately, but that lay in the future. As practical individuals, the economists preferred a modest poverty program to none at all. As practical individuals who were serving a president up for reelection, they were looking for a program that would be both workable and popular. Their abandonment of transfers also in part reflected their belief in human-capital theory, their acceptance of the work ethic and culture-of-poverty assumptions, and their faith in society's ability to train, educate, and reform individuals. To growth- and efficiency-oriented economists, increasing the productivity of the poor was intrinsically preferable to paying them not to work. For all these reasons, practical and intellectual, they leaned toward an antipoverty strategy that favored human services over income transfers, reform of individuals rather than economic equality.[27]

Heller assigned William M. Capron, the CEA's senior staff man, to work with Lampman. Capron had played an important role in the CEA's successful campaign to win the president over to the tax cut. Although he was familiar with the field, he was not an expert in income distribution. He had been trained in public administration, not economics, specializing in the application of economic tools to policy issues. He knew the ins and outs of Washington bureaucracy and had the advantage of enjoying good relationships with Theodore C. Sorensen, a top presidential aide, and with the Bureau of the Budget, where he had once worked. Under President Kennedy, it should be noted, the Budget Bureau had become unusually involved in policy making. Over the summer, Capron and Lampman convened an informal group of staff members, largely fellow economists, from several departments and agencies to discuss ideas and proposals. In the fall, Lampman returned to the University of Wisconsin and the burden of developing a program fell largely to Capron, working closely with Budget officials Charles L. Schultze, William Cannon, and Michael March.[28]

These planners were generally unimpressed with the recommendations they received. From the departments came numerous program suggestions which had been languishing on Capitol Hill. Each department watered its own field; the Labor Department wanted a massive jobs program; the Department of Health, Education, and Welfare, educational and health programs; and so on. This confirmed the planners' skepticism toward the departments, a skepticism that permeated the upper reaches of the Kennedy administration. The departments and agencies, it was believed, were bureaucracies with their own internal agendas whose programs were often ineffectual. Experts they consulted from social work and the social sciences, meanwhile, made divergent recommendations, based on sharply differing diagnoses of the poverty problem.[29]

The planners did like the idea of local demonstration or community action projects, which they heard about from people who had been involved in such projects—David Hackett and Richard Boone of the President's Committee on Juvenile Delinquency and Youth Crime, Paul Ylvisaker of the Ford Foundation, Mitchell Sviridoff in New Haven, and George Esser in North Carolina. In a "community action project," "demonstration project," or "development corporation," as the idea was variously called, the federal government would directly fund service-oriented, coordinated efforts in localities where poor people resided in significant numbers, such as Appalachia and the nation's largest black ghettoes.

The planners were attracted to this idea because it seemed to hold out the promise of having a dramatic impact. "Rather than developing a 'program' which simply adds funds to existing across-the-board programs, or creates new programs in which a large part of the funds are spent on those whose need is marginal," one of the planners argued, "we ought to make a concentrated effort to assist those whose needs are substantial." They liked the emphasis on experimentation, for total funding was expected to be small and social welfare experts were divided about what should be done. Because of the expectations of low funding as well, they wanted to prevent the money from being spread around so thin as to negate its effects, which is what had happened to the Area Redevelopment Administration (ARA). When ARA was first considered by the Senate in 1956, it was estimated that 69 areas would qualify for assistance; in 1963, however, 780 areas qualified. Congress had sliced a small pie exceedingly thin. Each member had wanted to have a piece for himself; so everyone had received a diet portion.[30]

A coordinated and concentrated federal effort at the local level also appealed to the planners precisely because of their skepticism of federal bureaucracies. It offered a way of bypassing them or at least shaking them up. They perceived in a localized approach advantages that were partly ideological and partly political. "The program ought to be presented quite frankly in terms of the obligations which a prosperous majority owes to a submerged and desperately poor minority," one of them, probably Schultze, observed at the time. Although he wanted to highlight the practical aspects of the program, such as its impact on economic growth or on reducing welfare costs, he believed that "poverty-in-the-midst of plenty" should be the main theme. He explained:

There are two ideas which go hand-in-hand in this approach: First, the concept of equity—initial opportunities for all as close to equal as possible (Remember, even Bob Taft was strong for this.); and second, the concept of the social obligation of the "rich" to the "poor." Both of these are powerful themes in American history, and, after all the political cynicism is taken into account, may well form a more realistic approach than the alleged realism of narrow self-interest Congressional District by Congressional District. Moreover, a party division along these lines would be "duck-soup" for Democratic candidates.

Finally, this approach promised the mobilization of people at the local level, of getting previously uninvolved people to work for their communities. It therefore accorded with Kennedy's call to patriotic sacrifice in his inaugural address, his challenge to Americans to ask what they could do for their country, something the tax cut had obviously not required.[31]

Although the planners paid considerable attention to political considerations, particularly to how an antipoverty program might be framed to win united Democratic support in Congress, there is no evidence to support the Piven-Cloward thesis that community action was intended to shore up black support in the 1964 election. At a conference in 1973, antipoverty planners, though acknowledging certain political motives, challenged Piven and Cloward face to face. "We would have run it completely different if we had followed your thesis," argued Hackett. "If it had been a political program and if the administration wanted to cater to the black votes, we would have done it completely different. We didn't do it that way. We were going initially with the mayors and the establishment."[32]

Like community action, the National Service Corps, a domestic version of the Peace Corps, appealed to the planners for summoning the nation's idealism. Legislation to create such a corps was stalled on Capitol Hill, but the planners hoped they might pry it loose by including it in the president's antipoverty program. In addition, they looked forward to incorporating the recommendations of a special interagency task force the president had appointed to look into the problem of selective service rejectees. In the spring of 1964, Secretary of Defense Robert S. McNamara observed that President Kennedy himself frequently expressed his concern that "poverty was becoming an inherited trait," as evidenced by the failure of a third of the young men examined each year for the military draft to pass either mental or physical examinations. Kennedy's elusive logic reflected acceptance of culture-of-poverty assumptions.[33]

As discussion proceeded on an antipoverty program in the fall, members and friends of the Kennedy administration raised questions about the whole enterprise. Wilbur Cohen, an influential assistant secretary of Health, Education, and Welfare, and others with backgrounds in Social Security observed that programs benefiting the poor alone were bound to be impoverished ones—that is, inadequately funded. Myer Feldman, a White House counsel, pointed out to Lampman that his ideas would make good ammunition for Republicans in that they implied the failure of social welfare programs long identified with the Democrats. At a general strategy meeting on the 1964 election in November, Richard Scammon, director of the Census Bureau, in answer to a question from the president about the pending poverty program, noted that most people did not consider themselves poor. At an informal seminar in Robert F. Kennedy's home, George F. Kennan, the diplomat, departed from his topic to reflect that nothing could be done about poverty since, as the Bible said, the poor would be with us always. Heller strenuously objected and was joined in the ensuing debate by Robert F. Kennedy and Harriman against Kennan, Supreme Court Justice Potter Stewart, and Randolph Churchill, son of the former British prime minister.[34]

Criticisms like these made those planning the poverty program acutely aware of its packaging, and so they considered such titles as "Human Conservation and Development," "Access to Opportunity," and "Widening Participation in Prosperity," in order to broaden its appeal. They thought of billing it as a "domestic aid program" in order to "capitalize on some of the anti-foreign aid sentiment—especially on the part of those who continually chide us for 'sending money overseas when there is so much to do at home.'" On the other hand, they worried that whatever was gained for the domestic aid programs might be lost to foreign aid, and they were concerned about giving the Soviet Union "a well-documented stick to beat us over the head with—although this will be true of any case we make that there are important segments of the U.S. population living a submarginal existence."[35]

In considering possible constituencies for this program, some political operatives in the White House looked to the upper middle class; "suburban women" was the catchphrase. The poor themselves were assumed to be politically passive, and an antipoverty effort was therefore most likely to impress those who were among the most affluent and presumably most conscience-stricken. John F. Kennedy himself was puzzled that the poor in this country were not angrier and more demanding. "In England," he commented to Arthur M. Schlesinger, Jr., in the spring of 1963, "the unemployment rate goes to two per cent, and they march on Parliament. Here it moves up toward six, and no one seems to mind." Although there had been more agitation among the poor in the 1930s than was usually recalled in the 1950s and 1960s, it was also true that by international standards the American poor in this century were relatively quiescent. Civil rights demonstrations in the early 1960s repeatedly focused on access to the political and economic systems, not on economic inequality or poverty. Labor unions, whom socialists like Harrington thought of as allies of the poor, generally failed to beat the drum for an antipoverty program. When Heller gave a speech about poverty to the Communication Workers of America, his audience responded indifferently. It made Lampman recall a lesson that Selig Perlman, the labor economist, had taught him as a graduate student at the University of Wisconsin: that unionists regard the poor as competitive menaces.[36]

Given all the doubts expressed, the planners were sometimes uncertain whether the president would even decide to adopt an antipoverty program. A timely piece of reporting helped their cause. In October Homer Bigart wrote grippingly in the *New York Times* about the plight of impoverished miners in Kentucky. The report prompted President Kennedy to observe to Heller ''that there was a tremendous problem to be met.'' According to Heller's notes, Kennedy indicated that ''if he could get sufficient *substance* in a program to deal with poverty, he would like to make a two- or three-day trip to some of the key poverty-stricken areas to focus the spotlight and arouse the American conscience on this problem from which we are so often shielded.'' To Heller it seemed ''perfectly clear'' that Kennedy was ''aroused about this and if we would really produce a program to fill the bill, he would be inclined to run with it.'' Soon thereafter, Heller wrote the heads of several departments and agencies to tell them that the president had ''tentatively decided that a major focus in the domestic legislative program in 1964 will be on a group of programs variously described as 'Human Conservation and Development,' 'Access to Opportunity' and 'Attack on Poverty'" and to ask their help formally in devising a general framework as well as specifics.[37]

After November's election strategy meeting, the president remained interested, though circumspect. ''I'm still very much in favor of doing something on the poverty scheme if we can get a good program,'' is how Heller summed up Kennedy's attitude on November 19, ''but I also think its important to make clear that we're doing something for the middle-income man in the suburbs, etc. But the two are not at all inconsistent with one another. So go right ahead with your work on it.'' At the time of Kennedy's assassination on November 22, 1963, antipoverty plans emphasized youth, human services rather than income transfers, experimentation, selectivity, coordination, and local administration. They included a domestic Peace Corps and a remedial effort aimed at Selective Service rejectees. There is no telling, of course, what would have happened to these plans had the president not been shot.[38]

The day after the assassination Heller met with Johnson. He informed the new president, among other things, of the CEA's work in developing the ''attack on poverty,'' as his notes of the conversation termed it. He told Johnson there was enthusiasm within the government for the idea, but it was uncertain whether an attractive program could be constructed. He also reported President Kennedy's last words to him on the subject. According to Heller's notes, Johnson ''expressed his interest'' in the poverty program, and ''his sympathy for it, and in answer to a point-blank question, said we should push ahead full-tilt on this project.'' As Heller was about to depart, Johnson drew him back in and said:

Now I wanted to say something about all this talk that I'm a conservative who is likely to go back to the Eisenhower ways or give in to the economy bloc in Congress. It's not so, and I want you to tell your friends—Arthur Schlesinger, Galbraith and other liberals—that it is not so. I'm no budget slasher. I understand that expenditures have to keep on rising to keep pace with the population and help the economy. If you looked at my record, you would know that I am a Roosevelt New Dealer. As a matter of fact, to tell the truth, John F. Kennedy was a little too conservative to suit my taste.[39]

Through his service as senator from Texas and Democratic leader in the Senate, Johnson had indeed developed a rather conservative reputation, but a combination of influences—personal, political, and cultural—led him to adopt the poverty issue and make it his own. In his postpresidential memoir, Johnson noted he was always an activist, taking pleasure in getting things done. Profoundly impressed by the New Deal, Johnson believed in government, in its responsibility, and in its capacity to solve problems. For social change to occur, he reflected, three conditions had to be met: a recognition of need, a willingness to act, and someone to lead the effort. Johnson recalled that in 1963 America had the needs, the launching of Sputnik and the shock of President Kennedy's assassination had produced a popular readiness for change, and he was personally disposed to lead.[40]

Bill Moyers, Johnson's protégé and aide, has observed that, though Johnson could rationalize any decision after the fact (of course, historians do likewise with the decisions they study), he was a highly instinctual politician, whose instincts, rather than cold calculation, told him that the poverty issue was well suited to him personally and that the right moment had arrived to raise it. Some of Johnson's aides, like some of President Kennedy's, warned him not to ''get caught in the snare of a program directed entirely toward helping the poor,'' Johnson himself recalled. Horace Busby, one of his assistants, urged that he pay attention instead to Americans "in the middle," those earning between $3,000 and $9,000 a year, a majority of the country. Assistance to people like that, Busby asserted, had accounted for Franklin D. Roosevelt's great political success. On the other hand, a private survey of intellectuals that the historian Eric F. Goldman conducted for Johnson indicated widespread interest in a new national effort to help the disadvantaged. "Memo after memo," Goldman reported, "called for establishing an organization that would release the idealism of the nation, especially its youth, in an attack on poverty inside the United States. The usual specific proposal was setting up a Domestic Peace Corps or reconstituting an NYA [National Youth Administration] or CCC."[41]

Although Johnson had never been impoverished himself, his occasional claim to the contrary notwithstanding, he had seen much poverty during his youth in Texas. For a time he taught school to impoverished Mexican-Americans in Cotulla, Texas, an experience he never forgot. In his first important government post, he directed his state's NYA which gave unemployed young people jobs during the Great Depression. Roosevelt became Johnson's idol, and after Johnson became president, his model as well. Much as Roosevelt had helped those who needed help, Johnson hoped to do likewise. Soon after becoming president, he told Richard Russell, a close Senate friend, that he hoped his epitaph would someday read: "Lyndon Johnson did his best for folks who couldn't do theirs." Clearly Johnson had emotional needs that were met by helping people, but these needs also coincided with the nation's political culture, for Americans mythologized those presidents whom they perceived as helping others. "If you do good, you'll do well," Johnson often observed about politics, and poverty was unmistakably a "do good" issue. Johnson found confirmation for his general view of government in *The Rich Nations and the Poor Nations* by Barbara Ward, the eminent British economist. When Liz Carpenter went to work for Johnson, who was still vice-president, he once picked up Ward's book, which he said he had read many times. "This is what it's all about—this is what the whole government effort is all about," he said. "It's right here in one sentence —the mission of our times is to eradicate the three enemies of mankind—poverty, disease and ignorance."[42]

The particular tragic circumstances of Johnson's assumption of office also help explain his adoption of the poverty issue. During his early weeks as president, Johnson strove to show members of the Kennedy administration, the nation, and the world that there would be continuity in policy, yet at the same time to establish his own authority, identity, and constituency. The poverty issue afforded him a way of doing both. By giving Heller the go-ahead, Johnson signaled the Kennedy team that he planned to carry on as President Kennedy would have, but because Kennedy had not publicly announced the drive against poverty, Johnson could present it as his own to the nation. Since he was assuming so many of Kennedy's policy commitments, including civil rights, the tax cut, medical insurance for the aged, and federal aid to education, Johnson welcomed the chance to promote his very own cause.[43]

Finally, the poverty issue appealed to Johnson because, like many southerners, he believed that the nation's racial problems were essentially economic in nature. If blacks only had good jobs and decent incomes, whites would, in his view, respect them and let them exercise their civil rights. President Kennedy would not have disagreed, though he had felt it necessary to address racial discrimination directly. When Kennedy was contemplating his request for major civil rights legislation in the spring of 1963, Johnson had privately expressed reservations about its timing to the president's aides. He was not opposed to the legislation, he told Sorensen—indeed, he wanted President Kennedy to take a strong moral stand in favor of civil rights—but he feared that "we run the risk of touching off about a three- or four-month debate that will kill his program and inflame the country and wind up with a mouse." To Assistant Attorney General for Civil Rights Burke Marshall, Johnson recommended that the administration concentrate on solving underlying economic problems, specifically black unemployment, and harked back to his own experience with the NYA.[44]

When Johnson suddenly became president, he could not have reversed his predecessor's commitment to civil rights legislation, even if he had wanted to, for that would have violated the whole spirit of continuity that he was trying to engender and would have cast Johnson as a parochial, sectional leader, not up to national responsibilities or national office. It would have alienated the significant pro-civil rights constituency in the Democratic party. Given the political situation, his desire for continuity, and his own genuine sympathy for the civil rights cause, Johnson, in one of his first public statements as president, committed himself unequivocally to passage of President Kennedy's civil rights legislation. That legislation would be Kennedy's, a memorial to him, but the poverty issue, with its economic instead of racial thrust, would be quintessentially Johnson's. Perhaps his fellow white southerners would even forgive him his transgressions on civil rights as matters of personal loyalty to the slain president and political necessity, especially when they saw he was addressing the underlying problem on his own.[45]

Johnson worried, though, about how to identify the problem. Walt Rostow, an economist and foreign-policy aide, recounted Johnson's views at a meeting in late December on the State of the Union message: "In domestic affairs, civil rights was at the top of the list. Then the tax bill. He would move ahead with the poverty program, but he wanted it to be a positive effort to fulfill human needs and widen opportunity. Poverty was too negative a concept. (General discussion yielded no satisfactory alternative phrase.) We had to fulfill Kennedy's programs and move beyond. He wanted to see military resources shifted to education, human needs, and manpower development."[46]

In his State of the Union address to Congress on January 8, Johnson did not find a substitute for the term *poverty* when he announced his emphatic opposition to the condition it described. "This administration today, here and now, declares unconditional war on poverty," asserted the president. The analogue of war, a legacy of progressivism and World War I, had been popular during the depression and the New Deal when Johnson was young and had entered public life. The idea of invoking it once again in 1964, if not Johnson's originally—its exact paternity is uncertain—appealed to him viscerally. "It will not be a short or easy struggle, no single weapon or strategy will suffice," Johnson said, "but we shall not rest until that war is won." Alluding to the country's prosperity, he observed that "the richest nation on earth can afford to win it." But he also immediately set forth a practical, efficiency argument to justify the effort: "We cannot afford to lose it. One thousand dollars invested in salvaging an unemployable youth can return $40,000 or more in his lifetime."[47]

Lacking specific antipoverty plans, Johnson emphasized the general recommendations of the economists and budget officials who had begun to work under President Kennedy: improved coordination of existing federal programs, new efforts organized and carried out locally. "For the war against poverty will not be won here in Washington," Johnson explained. "It must be won in the field, in every private home, in every public office, from the court house to the White House." "The program I shall propose," he said, "will emphasize this cooperative approach to help that one-fifth of all American families with incomes too small to even meet their basic needs."

Beyond his new antipoverty program, Johnson called for "better schools, and better health, and better homes, and better training, and better job opportunities to help more Americans, especially young Americans, escape from squalor and misery and unemployment rolls where other citizens help to carry them." Thus Johnson went beyond mere efficiency justifications for fighting poverty to a frankly antiwelfare position. Give the poor the tools to lift themselves out of poverty, he told Congress, and working Americans would no longer have to support them on relief. Lack of money or employment, he asserted, were often symptoms of poverty, not its cause, which he speculated lay deeper, perhaps in society's failure to give everyone a fair chance. "But whatever the cause," he said, "our joint Federal-local effort must pursue poverty, pursue it wherever it exists." He requested legislative action in a wide variety of areas, including special aid to Appalachia and expansion of ARA, youth employment, a broader food stamp program, a national service corps, and a higher minimum wage. Although Johnson had essentially argued that poverty be taken out of people, his inclusion of food stamps and minimum

[1] Daniel P. Moynihan, *Maximum Feasible Misunderstanding: Community Action in the War on Poverty* (New York, 1970); Frances Fox Piven and Richard A. Cloward, *Regulating the Poor: The Functions of Public Welfare* (New York, 1971); James L. Sundquist, *Politics and Policy: The Eisen-*

hower. *Kennedy. and Johnson Years* (Washington, 1968). Social scientists have written voluminously on the causes of the War on Poverty; these are, I think, the most representative and influential works.

2 Paul H. Douglas. *In the Fullness of Time: The Memoirs of Paul H Douglas* (New York, 1972), 512-18; Sar A. Levitan, *Federal Aid to Depressed Areas: An Evaluation of the Area Redevelopment Administration* (Baltimore, 1966), 1-17; Sundquist, *Politics and Policy*, 60-76.

3 "Governor Harriman's Message to the Legislature," in New York State Department of Labor, *Industrial Bulletin* (Jan. 1956), 18-19; "Governor Harriman's Message to the Legislature," in *ibid.* (Feb. 1956), 12-14; Michael Levitas, "Progress against Poverty," in *ibid.* (July 1958), 3-7; *New York Times*, Feb. 1, 1956, pp. 1, 10, Feb. 4, 1956, p. 18, Jan. 31, 1957, p. 13, Feb. 2, 1957, p. 8, Jan. 9, 1958, p. 24, Jan. 28, 1958, p. 20, June 30, 1958, p. 21, John Bartlow Martin, *Adlai Stevenson and the World: The Life of Adlai E. Stevenson* (Garden City, 1977), 365.

4 John Kenneth Galbraith, *The Affluent Society* (Boston, 1958), 323; Henry George, *Progress and Poverty* (New York, 1931); Michael Harrington, "Our Fifty Million Poor: Forgotten Men of the Affluent Society," *Commentary*, 28 (July 1959), 19-27; H. Brand, "Poverty in the United States," *Dissent*, 7 (Autumn 1960), 334-54.

5 Douglas T. Miller and Marion Nowak, *The Fifties: The Way We Really Were* (Garden City, 1977), 106-23; Edward Berkowitz and Kim McQuaid, "Welfare Reform in the 1950s," *Social Service Review*, 54 (March 1980), 45-58; U.S. Congress, Senate, Committee on Commerce, *Freedom of Communications: Final Report* (2 vols., Washington, 1961), II, 311.

6 Charles C. Alexander, *Holding the Line: The Eisenhower Era. 1952-1961* (Bloomington, Ind., 1975), 184-293; Miller and Nowak, *Fifties*, 259-64; memorandum for speechwriters, July 23, 1960, box 26, Theodore C. Sorensen Papers (John F. Kennedy Library, Boston). For the 1960 campaign generally, see Theodore H. White, *The Making of the President. 1960* (New York, 1961).

7 Committee on Commerce, *Freedom of Communications*, I, 18.

8 "The President's News Conference of January 25, 1961," in *Public Papers of the Presidents of the United States. John F. Kennedy. 1961* (Washington, 1962), 13; Sundquist, *Politics and Policy*, 83-97, 115-34. Daniel Knapp and Kenneth Polk, *Scouting the War on Poverty: Social Reform Politics in the Kennedy Administration* (Lexington, Mass., 1971), 65-107; James T. Patterson, *America's Struggle against Poverty. 1900-1980* (Cambridge, 1981), 126-33.

9 Council of Economic Advisers panel oral history interview, Aug. 1, 1964, transcript (Kennedy Library); Herbert Stein, *The Fiscal Revolution in America* (Chicago, 1969), 372-453; Walter W. Heller interview by Carl M. Brauer, March 29, 1979 (in Brauer's possession); Gregory H. Hawley, "The Kennedy Tax Cut. A Study of the Interrelationships of Politics, Economics, and Government" (B. A. thesis, Harvard College, 1979); John Kenneth Galbraith to President, July 10, Aug. 20, 1962, box 30, Special Correspondence, President's Office Files (Kennedy Library).

10 Michael Harrington, *The Other America: Poverty in the United States* (New York, 1962); Leon Keyserling, "Two-Fifths of a Nation," *Progressive*, 26 (June 1962), 11-14; Gardner Ackley to Walter W. Heller, April 27, 1963, box 76, President's Office Files; Leon Keyserling to Galbraith, July 3, 1963, box 38, John Kenneth Galbraith Papers (Kennedy Library); Heller interview; Heller to President, Dec. 16, 1962, box 63, President's Office Files.

11 "Television and Radio Interview: 'After Two Years—A Conversation with the President, December 17, 1962," in *Public Papers of the Presidents of the United States: John F. Kennedy. 1962* (Washington, 1963), 889-904; Robert J. Lampman to Heller, March 22, 1963, microfilm roll 68, Walter W. Heller Papers (Kennedy Library).

12 Dwight Macdonald, "Our Invisible Poor," *New Yorker*, 38 (Jan. 19, 1963), 82-132; Arthur M. Schlesinger, Jr., *A Thousand Days: John F. Kennedy in the White House* (Boston, 1965), 1010; Herbert S. Parmet, *Jack: The Struggles of John F. Kennedy* (New York, 1980); Heller interview; Robert J. Lampman interview by Brauer, Jan. 24, 1979 (in Brauer's possession); William M. Capron interview by Brauer, Feb. 5, 1979, *ibid.*; Richard Goodwin interview by Brauer, June 21, 1979, *ibid.*; Theodore C. Sorensen interview by Carl Kaysen, May 20, 1964, transcript (Kennedy Library), p. 168.

13 Heller interview; Lampman interview; Capron interview; *The Annual Report of the Council of Economic Advisers* (Washington, 1964), 32; Edward S. Flash, Jr., *Economic Advice and Presidential Leadership: The Council of Economic Advisers* (New York, 1965), 176-77; Lafayette G. Harter, Jr., *John R. Commons: His Assault on Laissez-Faire* (Corvallis, Ore., 1962); Theron F. Schlabach, *Edwin E. Witte: Cautious Reformer* (Madison, 1969).

14 Lampman interview; Robert J. Lampman, "The Low Income Population and Economic Growth," in U.S. Congress, Joint Economic Committee, *Study Papers* (Washington, 1959), 1-36; Heller to President, May 1, 1963, box 76, President's Office Files.

15 Heller interview; Lampman interview; Capron interview; Walter W. Heller, *New Dimensions of Political Economy* (Cambridge, 1966), 20; Heller to Carl M. Brauer, January 23, 1980 (in Brauer's possession).

16 Carl M. Brauer, *John F. Kennedy and the Second Reconstruction* (New York, 1977), 42-43, 230-64; Heller interview.

17 Brauer, *John F. Kennedy*, 297-302; Heller interview; Heller to President, June 20, 1963, box 76, President's Office Files; Heller's notes on "Meeting in Sorensen's Office, Oct. 21, 1963," Oct. 22, 1963, box 13, Heller Papers; "Confidential Notes on Meeting with the President," Oct. 21, 1963, box 6, *ibid.*

18 Heller to Lampman, June 3, 1963, box 1, Legislative Background, Economic Opportunity Act, White House Central Files (Lyndon Baines Johnson Library, Austin, Texas).

19 Lampman to Heller, June 10, 1963, microfilm roll 37, Heller Papers.

20 *Ibid.* For a very interesting and up-to-date discussion of the debate over a culture of poverty, see Patterson, *America's Struggle against Poverty*, 115-25.

21 Lampman interview; *Annual Report of the Council of Economic Advisers, 1964*, 43, 47; James M. Morgan, Martin H. David, Wilbur J. Cohen, and Harvey E. Brazer, *Income and Welfare in the United States* (New York, 1962), 206-12. Social historians have subsequently been wrestling with the time dimension and with the question of poverty's heritability. See, for example, Stephan Thernstrom, *The Other Bostonians: Poverty and Progress in the American Metropolis. 1880-1970* (Cambridge, 1973).

[22] Lampman interview; Jacob Mincer, "Investment in Human Capital and Personal Income Distribution," *Journal of Political Economy*, 66 (Aug. 1958), 281–302; Theodore W. Schultz, "Investment in Human Capital," *American Economic Review*, 51 (Jan. 1961), 1–17; Theodore W. Schultz, "Reflections on Investment in Man," *Journal of Political Economy*, 70 (Oct. 1962), 1–8; Gary S. Becker, "Investment in Human Capital: A Theoretical Analysis," *ibid.*, 9–49; Burton H. Weisbrod, "Education and Investment in Human Capital," *ibid.*, 106–28; Morgan, David, Cohen, and Brazer, *Income and Welfare in the United States*, 371–83.

[23] Lampman interview; Lampman to Heller, June 10, 1963, microfilm roll 37, Heller Papers.

[24] Lampman to Heller, June 10, 1963, microfilm roll 37, *ibid.*

[25] *Ibid.*; Heller interview; Lampman interview; Capron interview; "Poverty and Urban Policy," transcript of conference held in Waltham, Mass., June 16–17, 1973 (Kennedy Library), p. 148; *Annual Report of the Council of Economic Advisers, 1964*, 54.

[26] Brauer, *John F. Kennedy*, 303; Stein, *Fiscal Revolution in America*, 428–53; "Poverty and Urban Policy," 148.

[27] Heller interview; Lampman interview; Capron interview.

[28] Capron interview; Lampman interview; "Poverty and Urban Policy," 138–42; Larry Berman, *The Office of Management and Budget and the Presidency, 1921–1979* (Princeton, 1979), 67–73.

[29] Capron interview; Lampman interview; "Poverty and Urban Policy," 142–45; Adam Yarmolinsky interview by Brauer, Feb. 22, 1979 (in Brauer's possession)

[30] "Poverty and Urban Policy," 142–54; C. L. Schultze, "Some Notes on a Program of 'Human Conservation,'" Nov. 1, 1964, box 1, Legislative Background, Economic Opportunity Act, White House Central Files; David L. Hackett to Heller, Dec. 1, 1963, *ibid.*; WMC [William M. Capron] to WWH [Heller] and attached memo by William Cannon and Sam Hughes, Dec. 12, 1963, *ibid.*; Heller interview; Capron interview; Lampman interview; Moynihan, *Maximum Feasible Misunderstanding*, 77–80, 168–69; Richard Blumenthal, "The Bureaucracy: Antipoverty and the Community Action Program," in *American Political Institutions and Public Policy: Five Contemporary Studies*, ed. Allan P. Sindler (Boston, 1969), 147–49.

[31] Schultze, "Some Notes on a Program of 'Human Conservation'"; "Poverty and Urban Policy," 142–54; Heller interview; Capron interview; Lampman interview.

[32] "Poverty and Urban Policy," 201.

[33] Schultze, "Some Notes on a Program of 'Human Conservation'"; Theodore C. Sorensen to Kermit Gordon et al., October 23, 1963, box 13, Heller Papers; Capron to Heller, Dec. 5, 1963, box 1, Legislative Background, Economic Opportunity Act, White House Central Files; U.S. Congress, House of Representatives, Committee on Education and Labor, *Economic Opportunity Act of 1964: Hearings on H.R. 10440*, 88 Cong., 2 sess., March 18, 1964, 110–11.

[34] Wilbur Cohen interview by Brauer, Aug. 6, 1979 (in Brauer's possession); Lampman interview; Sorensen interview, 168; Heller interview. Richard Scammon does not specifically recall the question of poverty being discussed at the general strategy meeting but accepts Sorensen's recollection since it occurred much closer to the event. Richard Scammon to Brauer, Jan. 11, 1979 (in Brauer's possession).

[35] Schultze, "Some Notes on a Program of 'Human Conservation'"; notes on "Meeting in Sorensen's Office, October 21, 1963," Oct. 22, 1963, box 13, Heller Papers; "Poverty and Urban Policy," 173–74; Heller interview; Lampman interview.

[36] Schlesinger, *Thousand Days*, 1010; Lampman interview; Heller interview; "Poverty and Urban Policy," 155–222.

[37] "Poverty and Urban Policy," 168; *New York Times*, Oct. 19, 1963, pp. 1, 18; "Confidential Notes on Meeting with the President"; Heller to Secretary of Agriculture et al., Nov. 5, 1963, box 1, Legislative Background, Economic Opportunity Act, White House Central Files.

[38] "Notes on a Quick Meeting with the President and other leading members of the Kennedy Family," Nov. 19, 1963, box 6, Heller papers; Heller interview; Lampman interview; "Poverty and Urban Policy," 169–70.

[39] Heller, "Notes on Meeting with President Johnson," Nov. 23, 1963, box 7, Heller Papers.

[40] Lyndon Baines Johnson, *The Vantage Point: Perspectives of the Presidency, 1963–1969* (New York, 1971), 70–71.

[41] Bill Moyers interview by Brauer, June 15, 1979 (in Brauer's possession); Johnson, *Vantage Point*, 71; Horace Busby to President, Dec. 30, 1963, file We9, Executive, White House Central Files; Eric F. Goldman to President et al., December 21, 1963, file SP2-4, box 133, White House Central Files.

[42] Moyers interview; Liz Carpenter, *Ruffles and Flourishes* (Garden City, 1970), 250–51; Heller interview; Otis Singletary interview by Joe B. Frantz, Nov. 12, 1970, transcript, Oral History Collection (Johnson Library). Lyndon B. Johnson, it would appear, was not quoting Barbara Ward exactly; see Barbara Ward, *The Rich Nations and the Poor Nations* (New York, 1962), 158–59. Johnson has been the subject of many books, and he will undoubtedly be the subject of many more. Among the most useful published works on Johnson are: Merle Miller, *Lyndon: An Oral Biography* (New York, 1980); Rowland Evans and Robert Novak, *Lyndon B. Johnson: The Exercise of Power* (New York, 1966); Doris Kearns, *Lyndon Johnson and the American Dream* (New York, 1976); Harry McPherson, *A Political Education* (Boston, 1972); Jack Valenti, *A Very Human President* (New York, 1975); Booth Mooney, *LBJ: An Irreverent Chronicle* (New York, 1976); T. Harry Williams, "Huey, Lyndon, and Southern Radicalism," *Journal of American History*, 60 (Sept. 1973), 267–93.

[43] Johnson, *Vantage Point*, 18–41; Moyers interview.

[44] Moyers interview; Brauer, *John F. Kennedy*, 30–37, 245–46, 314; Johnson conversation with Sorensen, June 3, 1963, Edison Dictaphone recording transcript, box 1, Office Files of George Reedy (Johnson Library); Robert F. Kennedy and Burke Marshall interview by Anthony Lewis, Dec. 4, 1964, transcript (Kennedy Library), 26–27; "Notes of Troika Meeting with President Johnson," Nov. 25, 1963, box 7, Heller Papers; Monroe Billington, "Lyndon B. Johnson and Blacks: The Early Years," *Journal of Negro History*, 62 (Jan. 1977), 26–42.

[45] Moyers interview; Harry McPherson interview by T. H. Baker, n.d., transcript, Oral History Collection, tape 2, pp. 11–12. Johnson's civil rights sympathies are in clear evidence in Johnson conversation with Sorensen. There is no indication why Johnson had this particular conversation recorded.

[46] W. W. Rostow, *The Diffusion of Power: An Essay in Recent History* (New York, 1972), 305.

47 "Annual Message to Congress on the State of the Union, January 8, 1964," in *Public Papers of the Presidents of the United States: Lyndon B. Johnson, 1963–1964* (2 vols., Washington, 1965), I, 114; Johnson, *Vantage Point*, 69–76; Heller interview; Moyers interview; Goodwin interview; Jack Valenti interview by Frantz, Oct. 18, 1969, Oral History Collection, II, 28–29. In drafts of the speech in the Johnson Library the phrase "unconditional war on poverty" was present from the beginning; the Budget Bureau evidently added efficiency justifications. "State of the Union Address," box 112, Statements (Johnson Library). For an interesting discussion of the war analogy in the depression and New Deal, see William E. Leuchtenburg, "The New Deal and the Analogue of War," in *Change and Continuity in Twentieth Century America*, ed. John Braeman, Robert H. Bremner, and Everett Walters (Columbus, Ohio, 1964), 81–143.

Kennedy, Johnson, and the Great Society
John H. Ehrenreich

A systematic and conclusive account of a period so recent as the 1960s and 1970s is not easily written. For one thing, we do not yet have the perspective that only time can bring: It is easy to determine which of the social policies of the Progressive Era or of the New Deal were lasting and significant, which transient or peripheral. But because many of the social policies of the sixties and early seventies—the heightened concerns with poverty, the urban ghetto, racial and sexual discrimination, and the new programs and laws dealing with hunger, health care, reproductive rights, and housing problems—remain matters of intense current political debate, a full history cannot yet be written.

Each period of reform in American history sheds light upon the previous period—its strengths, characteristic approaches, the issues to which it was blind, its limitations. From the perspective of the creation of the welfare state in the 1930s, the limited, regulatory approach of the Progressive Era is clearly seen; from the perspective of the emphasis on racism and hard-core poverty in the 1960s, the inability of the major New Deal welfare programs to address these issues is revealed. But the period of the sixties has not yet had its subsequent period of reform. Our judgment of it, then, must be a preliminary, anticipatory one.

Beyond this, the sixties and seventies are part of my own memories. Academic analysis and personal recollection (with all of its inescapable distortions and emotions) are inextricably mixed. I was a participant in many of the events of the sixties, in a limited way as a civil rights activist and in a more substantial fashion as an antiwar activist and a researcher and writer working with community groups on health issues. Thus my sense of what happened, why things happened, and what was important about them is shaped by my own experiences and observations as well as by subsequent academic research and analysis. Any historian is "biased," of course; one would have to be very suspect of the biases of the writer on social policy who lived through, but was *not* involved in, the ferment of the sixties. But it is well to acknowledge the sources and directions of one's biases, even if they cannot be entirely transcended.

Another problem in writing about social work and social policy in the post–World War II period is the growing disconnection between the two. In the years before the Great Depression, social work and social policy were virtually inseparable. No history of progressivism would be complete without a discussion of the settlement houses, the reform movements led by social workers, and the shift from Social Darwinist to environmentalist understandings of poverty. Equally, the retreat of the reform-oriented middle-class occupations from social concerns into a narrower professionalism is central to defining the social policy of the twenties.

By the thirties, however, the relationship between social work and social policy had become more distant. Social work was certainly powerfully affected by the social policy of the New Deal—the new institutions, new functions for social work, and new sources of funding—and in response to these new programs, the number of social workers mushroomed. The history of social work in the thirties and forties is in large measure a history of how the occupation responded to these new developments. The intensity of the reverse relationship (i.e., the significance of social work for social policy), however, diminished. Individual social workers and others with settlement-house backgrounds certainly were extremely prominent as experts, planners, and administrators. Most social work leaders enthusiastically embraced the New Deal; and New Deal programs, such as the Federal Emergency Relief Administration, were administered by social workers, who also trained many of the newly recruited social workers required by the new programs. But social workers were no longer central to the development of social policy. They were predominantly troops, not officers.

By the 1960s the relationship had become still more diffuse. Social policy continued to be vitally important in shaping social work. But to the planners of the Kennedy-Johnson poverty program, and increasingly to organized client groups as well, social work and social work agencies, far from being major sources of insight and support, seemed to be not part of the solution but part of the problem. In the thirties, the worst that could be said of social work was that it was often irrelevant to social policy. By the sixties, it was all too frequently hostile to social change. And it was the social movements of the sixties, as much as government social policy per se, that had a direct impact on the social work profession.

This changing relationship between social policy and social work (or, to put it more precisely, the growing distance between social work as a profession and its traditional concerns with social change and social reform) has been, of course, a principal theme of this book. It does, however, create a problem: in discussing the Progressive Era and even in discussing the Depression, social work and social policy can be considered an entity (although by the thirties, distinct emphases appear in the account of each, and social work responses to the New Deal have been expanded in a separate chapter). In writing about the sixties and seventies, such an integration is no longer possible. Social policy in the sixties and seventies, and social work in the sixties and seventies, require entirely separate treatments. Consequently, social policy developments, largely without reference to social work, will be the subject of the remainder of this chapter. The impact of the social movements and social policy of the 1960s on social work will be discussed in Chapter 7.

In the early days of the Kennedy administration, social unrest, both in the form of the civil rights movement and in the form of individual deviance and discontent (among both black and white poor), was growing but had not yet emerged as the fully disruptive force that would later compel action. In any case, President Kennedy was not free to respond effectively to it: his electoral margin had been razor thin, and he was dependent on the goodwill of white southern congressmen and big-city, white ethnic-dominated political machines. He was in a weak position to respond to the plight of black America.

And so, for two years, Kennedy temporized on black rights and sought solutions to social problems through a simple application of New Deal–style social policy: macroeconomic manipulation and nonracially targeted welfare measures. If economic growth could be accelerated, he reasoned, unemployment levels would drop. Unemployed young people, black and white, would return to the paid work force. Their immediate economic grievances would be reduced. At the same time, the effect of regular employment itself in structuring workers' lives would provide a basis for restored social control and community stability. The new (or strengthened) social welfare measures would also appeal to a broad constituency. Thus, he could help blacks (and gain their votes) without affronting southern whites or northern white ethnics and without creating conflict with a white ethnic-oriented city hall.

The initial Kennedy economic and welfare program had three major components: First, Kennedy proposed some modest expansions of the welfare state: an extension of unemployment insurance, an increase in the minimum wage, liberalized Social Security benefits, permission for states to provide "welfare" to families with an unemployed parent, and a housing act that would create almost a half million construction jobs. Second, he proposed measures to deal with "structural unemployment" (as the hard-core unemployment that did not respond to overall economic growth was called): a Manpower Development and Training Act to train the unemployed in new skills, Service Amendments to the Social Security Act to provide federal funds for casework and other direct services to long-term unemployed families, and an Area Redevelopment Act to funnel financial and technical aid into areas such as Appalachia, which had unusually high unemployment rates. Finally, he proposed a cut in personal and corporate income taxes to stimulate consumer spending and corporate investment.

But it quickly became apparent that these programs were insufficient. The civil rights movement continued to grow and spread, and poverty and unrest in poor communities remained undiminished.

The civil rights movement gained in intensity year by year. Daily television news programs beamed around the world scenes of blacks being clubbed, beaten, gassed, and set upon by dogs as they peacefully demanded their elementary democratic rights. Disorder was spreading to the North, too; and many of Kennedy's white liberal supporters in the North were providing funds and moral support and sometimes even risking their own lives in support of the civil rights movement.

In the spring of 1963 President Kennedy was finally forced to express direct and open support of the cause of the civil rights movement. On June 11, addressing the nation on radio and television, he told the nation: "We are confronted primarily with a moral issue. . . . The heart of the question is whether all Americans are to be afforded equal rights and equal responsibilities."[1] A few days later he sent to Congress a bill to ban discrimination in all places of public accommodation (hotels, retail stores, recreational facilities, etc.), to end discrimination in employment, and to strengthen the attorney general's authority to speed up school desegregation proceedings. "The Administration's civil rights bill . . . is designed to alleviate some of the principal causes of the serious and unsettling racial unrest now prevailing in many of the states," Attorney General Robert F. Kennedy explained.[2]

But the bill remained bottled up in Congress and the unrest continued to grow. In the summer of 1963, by one count, no less than 1,412 civil rights demonstrations occurred, including the 300,000-strong March on Washington of late summer. By early the following year, Kennedy was dead, Medgar Evers, secretary of the Mississippi NAACP, was dead, and four black children in a church in Birmingham were dead. On July 2, 1964, Congress passed the Civil Rights Act by an overwhelming vote. And yet the violent resistance to black rights continued, and the civil rights movement, North and South, continued to grow.

In November 1964 Lyndon Johnson was reelected by one of the greatest landslides in American political history, losing only Alaska and five states of the Deep South. In the black ghettos of the North, 95 percent of the vote went to the Texas Democrat. The Democrats also chalked up enormous gains in both houses of Congress, producing the most Democratic and the most liberal Congress since the Roosevelt landslide of 1936. The power of the Old South over the Democratic party had been shattered forever. And the far right, pinning its hopes on Barry Goldwater, was, for the moment at least, in eclipse. President Johnson moved rapidly and sharply to the left.

The parallel between the history just recounted and that of the early years of FDR's administration should be noted. In each case, a president sought to respond to a social crisis and to mounting social unrest by fundamentally conservative means. The initial response proved insufficient: the crisis continued, the social movements grew, and the nation's electoral politics shifted sharply to the left. Faced with this constellation of political influences, in 1935 FDR responded with the Second New Deal—the creation of the welfare state. Faced with a similar set of forces, in 1965 Lyndon Johnson responded with the measures that comprised the Great Society—the Voting Rights Act of 1965, the War on Poverty, and a dramatic expansion and extension of New Deal–style welfare-state measures.

Responding directly to the southern civil rights movement and the growing northern black movement, President Johnson sent federalized National Guardsmen to protect civil rights marchers in Selma, Alabama; made a nationwide speech in which he proclaimed, along with the civil rights movement, "We shall overcome"; and sent to Congress the Voting Rights bill of 1965. The bill, passed into law in August, abolished literacy tests for voters and empowered the attorney general to send federal voter registrars into those states still practicing discrimination, to register those who wanted to vote.

The importance of these actions for blacks was immediate and great. The 1964 Civil Rights Act led to the final dismantling of the system of legalized segregation in schools and public accommodations and, along with Johnson's 1968 Affirmative Action Order, began to open up new employment opportunities for minorities. The 1965 act led to the registration of almost a million southern blacks within three years. By the mid-seventies in the South, blacks and whites were registered in numbers proportionate to their numbers in the population. With growing numbers of black voters, blacks became a bloc that required wooing by candidates for federal, state, and local elections alike. Perhaps of most immediate importance, the local sheriffs and judges, historically the principal institutional mechanism for the violent suppression of black rights, became vulnerable to the black vote. The primacy of violence and terror as a means of social control of the black population was markedly diminished.

It needs emphasis, however, that the equal rights legislation of the sixties affected only formal, legally enforceable patterns of racial discrimination. It did not eliminate racism, racial discrimination, or de facto segregation; it did not abolish racial inequality in economic status or political power; and it did not directly affect the problem of black poverty.

With the 1965 Voting Rights Act, the period of intense, federal legal assault on racial discrimination came to an end. Black community unrest in the North continued to strengthen. But the problem underlying this activism was not the legal denial of rights but the deeply ingrained and institutionalized discriminatory patterns in housing, schooling, jobs, and the provision of social services. And underlying all of these was the continued poverty and powerlessness of the black population.

Civil rights legislation, like the New Deal–style economic programs of the Kennedy administration, remained an insufficient response to the rising tide of unrest. Neither approach made major dents in the problem of poverty, in particular as it affected racial and ethnic minorities.[3]

By 1964 and 1965 the intractability of long-term poverty, in both North and South, was forced to the center of the policy planners' thinking. They observed, for example, that many of the poor did not take full advantage of the job retraining programs or the new job opportunities opened up by economic growth. When they did, handicapped by their limited education or unaccustomed to the work rhythms and time discipline required by an urban industrial society, they often failed.[4] In any case, women with dependent children were barred from the job market by their child-care responsibilities; and blacks, men and women alike, regardless of legal strictures, still faced discrimination in hiring, promotions, wages, and layoffs. Crime, inadequate schools, deteriorated housing, malnutrition, and poor health and physical or mental disability created further stumbling blocks in the effort to bring the poor and minorities into the economic mainstream.

The explanation many federal policy planners gave for the continued failure of economic growth to trickle down to the poor was what anthropologist Oscar Lewis had labeled the "culture of poverty."[5] The theory had several versions. In its simplest form, it was nothing more than the observation that prolonged poverty leads to poor health, inadequate education, high rates of marital instability, aberrant subcultural value systems and behaviors, and ultimately to individual and community apathy, lack of self-esteem, and powerlessness; and that all of these characteristics handicap people in their efforts to improve their situation. A direct and sustained attack on poverty itself would be the key to solving the other problems.

Michael Harrington, in his best-selling *The Other America*, which played a major role in calling attention to the continuing problem of poverty, extended this argument, emphasizing that the poor were caught in a "cycle of poverty":[6] poor and therefore undereducated, undernourished, sickly mothers gave birth to unhealthy infants who grew into unhealthy children. Handicapped in already substandard schools by poor eyesight, chronic infections, and malnutrition, lacking academic support and help from their uneducated parents, these children did poorly and were disproportionately likely to drop out of school. As adults, unskilled and untrained, they were unable to compete in the job market, which condemned them to poverty, malnutrition, and poor health, completing the cycle. If the cycle was not broken, Harrington argued, it would go on producing generation after generation of poor people. And because the various aspects of the cycle (nutrition, health care, schooling, housing conditions, psychological effects) were all intertwined, trying to change only one aspect of the conditions in which poor people found themselves (e.g., just schools or just jobs or just health care) was useless; all the other components of the tangle of poverty would quickly draw the poor person down into its reach again, undoing the good done in one area.

Perhaps the most arguable version of the "culture of poverty" thesis represented among major policy planners in the sixties was that of then Labor Department assistant secretary Daniel Patrick Moynihan.[7] In his report "The Negro Family," Moynihan argued that the key to the tangle of poverty in which many of the black poor were enmeshed was family structure. Slave masters had prevented "normal" nuclear families from forming among their slaves, Moynihan noted. As a result, black boys grew up in female-headed families, without adequate adult male role models. This "aberrant" child-rearing pattern produced young men who lacked the values needed for economic success. Moreoever, they were themselves unable to form stable marital units, reproducing for their children the same crisis. To Moynihan, programs to strengthen the black family were the centerpiece of any antipoverty program.

Moynihan's report touched off a storm of controversy.[8] Critics pointed out that Moynihan failed to see that poor white families were almost as likely as black families to be "female-headed" (i.e., that the "crisis" of the black family was the consequence of poverty, not the residue of slavery); that it had been urbanization, prolonged male unemployment, and welfare regulations that forbade payments to families with a male present that had disrupted the black family; that the statistics Moynihan used were both inaccurate and misinterpreted; and that poor blacks had evolved alternative kinship structures that effectively served the functions of child rearing and economic emotional support. But despite the critics, Moynihan's argument was (and continues to be) widely influential.

Regardless of the specifics, the broad concept of the "culture of poverty" led the Johnson administration social policy planners to a new set of notions as to how to combat poverty.[9]

First, the multiple problems of the poor were interrelated. To attack the problem of poor education alone or poor health alone or lack of skills alone was to guarantee that the efforts would be swallowed up by the larger, multifaceted tangle of poverty. Instead, the problems of the poor had to be attacked in a multifaceted, coordinated, and sustained way.

Second, the agencies that had traditionally been relied on for social services, whether public agencies (e.g., schools, welfare departments) or private (e.g., private family agencies, voluntary hospitals), and the professionals who had traditionally provided services (government officials, social workers, physicians, educational administrators) had failed. For various reasons—the maintenance of political power, institutional inertia, professional jealousies, racism—they were unresponsive to the needs of the poor and especially to the needs of the black poor. To enable the poor to benefit from new federal programs, the traditional agencies and local governments had to be prodded or simply bypassed.

Third, broadly targeted programs (such as the overall policy of economic stimulation and even the Manpower Training and Development Act) did not address the "culture of poverty." If the poor lacked the motivation or the hope to complete training programs, if they had internalized a low sense of self-esteem and lacked the skills and even the cognitive abilities to make use of the training programs much less to hold down jobs, if they lacked the disciplined attitudes needed for jobs even if the jobs were available, then these "macro" approaches to solving the problem of poverty would not work. Thus, more specifically targeted interventions, aimed at particular "deficits" of the poor were needed.

That is, the goal of public policy had to go beyond the amelioration of poverty and its consequences. It had to attack the underlying causes of poverty. And the causes of poverty were understood to be not simply the lack of money or the lack of opportunities but the lack of *capacity* on the part of the poor to use opportunities. It was this deficit, rooted in the culture of poverty, that had to be the central focus of an effective War on Poverty. In the words of Adam Yarmolinsky, deputy director of the task force that wrote Johnson's antipoverty program, what the poor needed was "not a hand out but a hand up."[10]

Although this formulation sems to echo the old Charity Organization Society motto of a century ago, "not alms but a friend," there were crucial differences. To start with, the Johnson antipoverty program was accompanied by efforts to stimulate the economy to create jobs and by the creation of new welfare institutions, training programs, equal opportunity laws, health services, and so on. Beyond this, although the outlook of the new poverty warriors, like that of the old Charity Organization officials, remained focused upon individual change and based on a model that blamed the intransigence of poverty on the individual deficits of the poor themselves, the problems of individuals were nevertheless seen as a reflection of the problems of the community, of economic and political and welfare institutions. The Great Society planners ultimately had an environmentalist understanding of poverty, albeit one that focused on the adverse impact of the environment on individual personality rather than on the continued obstacles that social and economic institutions placed in the way of individual achievement.

Earlier generations of social planners and social workers, as we have seen, divided sharply over whether the social problems of individuals were best met through concentrated work with those individuals ("casework," "education") or through large-scale social reform (economic growth, protective legislation, "welfare" measures). These alternatives were sharply opposed to each other, if not outright contradictory. The conception underlying the new poverty program, however, sought to unite both approaches. It linked individual change to social reform. The mode of encouraging individual change was not to be primarily individual casework, doing things for individual poor people, or individual therapy, however. Rather the focus was to be on changing institutions, changing community patterns, changing the "structure of opportunity." And the approach to making these changes was to enlist the poor, as communities, in solving their own problems. The poor themselves would be asked to provide information and other input for planning the new programs, to participate on the boards that planned and administered programs, even to perform some of the jobs that traditionally had been done by professionals.

The programs resulting from these understandings were many.[11] First, programs directly providing income (in the forms of cash, goods, or services) to the poor were dramatically expanded. In 1964 the Food Stamp program was set up. In 1965 rent subsidies, Medicaid (health care for the poor), and Medicare (health care for the aged, poor or not) were added. Public assistance ("welfare") itself was rapidly expanded: AFDC rolls, which had gone up by only 17 percent from 1950 to 1960, rose 107 percent in the eight years from Kennedy's accession to office to Johnson's departure from office; two-thirds of the increase occurred after 1964.

But more innovative were a series of programs that evolved directly from the new theories of poverty. They were aimed at chronic poverty and despair and typically targeted on the minority ghettos (and especially on young men, reflecting both Moynihan's concern for reestablishing male-dominated families and the more realistic and urgent perception that young men in the urban ghettos were those most in need of "control.") The programs were comprehensive in scope, offering a wide range of services. They stressed the prevention of poverty as well as its amelioration. They sought to create new institutions to plan, coordinate, and deliver services in new ways. They sought to increase the ability of the poor to solve their own problems, largely through encouraging massive community participation in planning, administering, and delivering the new services. And they were based on a new relationship between the federal government and localities, one in which money from the federal government went directly to service programs, circumventing the city and state governments.

The major programs that shared all or most of this outlook were the Juvenile Delinquency and Control Act of 1961, which established grants for projects for the prevention and treatment of delinquency in inner city neighborhoods and provided the model for many of the later programs; the Community Mental Health Act of 1963, which established a network of Community Mental Health centers to provide both preventive mental health programs and community-based treatment; the Elementary and Secondary Education Act of 1965, which provided educational services and programs for disadvantaged children; the Partnership for Health Act and Regional Medical Plan Act of 1966, which provided incentives and structures for the coordination of medical services and health planning, with citizen input (combined with Medicaid, these provided the health services core of the poverty program); and the Demonstration Cities and Metropolitan Development Act of 1966, often called the Model Cities program, which provided for a concentrated and coordinated attack on the economic, social, and physical problems of selected slum neighborhoods. The Economic Opportunity Act of 1965 was the centerpiece of the entire effort. Often called the War on Poverty program (although, as I am suggesting, a number of other acts shared many of the same purposes and analyses), the Economic Opportunity Act provided for, among other programs, training and career-development programs for young people (the Neighborhood Youth Corps, the Job Corps, the New Careers programs for paraprofessionals, and the college Work-Study programs); VISTA (Volunteers in Sevice to America—the domestic Peace Corps); and, under the rubric of community action programs, neighborhood health centers, Head Start, Upward Bound, Neighborhood Legal Services, Adult Basic Educational Services, family planning services, addiction services, and a variety of other activities. The act also established the Office of Economic Opportunity (OEO), within the office of the president, to coordinate the entire effort.

The Community Action Program (Title II of the Economic Opportunity Act) was the largest, the most controversial, and the most fully characteristic exemplar of the new approach. At the local level, according to the law, a Community Action Program was "a program . . . which provides services, assistance, and other activites of sufficient scope and size to give promise of progress toward elimination of poverty or a cause or causes of poverty through developing employment opportunities, improving human performance, motivation, or productivity, or bettering the conditions under which people live, learn, and work."[12] Thus, the Office of Economic Opportunity was to provide money for a group of community organizations to set up a Community Action Agency to develop, coordinate, and mobilize a whole range of programs, services, and community development projects, existing or newly created, designed to reduce poverty. Beyond simply coordinating existing programs, the Community Action Agency was expected to plan and prod and seek to develop or alter the structure of community services to make them more integrated, more comprehensive, and more responsive to the needs of the poor. To ensure this latter function, it would encourage the "maximum feasible participation of residents of the areas and members of the groups served."

No part of the Economic Opportunity Act was more controversial than those three innocent-sounding words "maximum feasible participation." To those who drafted the law, the original idea had seemed relatively innocuous. To some, it had meant only that a mechanism should be built in to ensure that black communities in the South were not excluded from the benefits of the law by white policy-making agencies. To others, it suggested that the poor should be consulted in planning the programs and that, wherever possible, the program should employ community residents as clerical workers, custodial workers, and in paraprofessional roles.

But whatever it meant to the original planners, to militant civil rights organizations in poor black communities, it represented an opening, a chance to get some real power to force changes in the community. As soon as the first program proposals arrived in Washington, protests started flooding the desk of Sargent Shriver, OEO director: the poor, the minority organizations, residents of the target communities, had been systematically excluded from the planning process, contrary to the law's provisions. The law, insisted the community groups, meant that the poor were to play the major role in both planning and directing the services they selected. Shriver and other OEO officials quickly accepted this definition of maximum feasible participation. In fact, the level of unrest in the community and the level of organized demands upon them left little choice: either community action would fully embrace the participation of the poor, or it would not happen at all. The following year Congress formally amended the law to require that at least one-third of the board of directors of the local Community Action Agency be representatives of the poor, chosen by residents of the target area.[13]

The notion of maximum feasible participation was, perhaps, the single most innovative policy of the entire decade. It represented, implicitly at least, an important modification of the "culture of poverty" analysis: in defining "poverty," lack of *power* was as important as lack of *resources.*

Taken at face value, maximum feasible participation implied nothing less than a total restructuring of local power systems. It meant not simply "helping" the poor but empowering the poor to help themselves and to challenge anyone who got in their way. Attorney General Robert F. Kennedy told a House committee:

> The institutions which affect the poor—education, welfare, recreation, business, labor—are huge, complex structures, operating far outside their control. They plan programs for the poor, not with them. Part of the sense of helplessness and futility comes from the feeling of powerlessness to affect the operation of these organizations. The community action programs must basically change these organizations by building into the program real representation for the poor.[14]

OEO director Sargent Shriver suggested to a Yale Law School audience in 1966 that the Economic Opportunity Act was "for the poor what the National Labor Relations Act was for unions. . . . It establishes a new relationship and new grievance procedure between the poor and the rest of society."[15]

Increasing the power of the poor generated enormous opposition from those whose previously undisputed power was to be challenged by the poor—mayors, agency heads, local businessmen, local union leaders, and the like. Up to a point, OEO officials continued to support maximum feasible participation, regardless of the uproar. "I said to Congress that if our activities did not stir up a community, then Congress should investigate it," OEO director Shriver told a 1965 meeting of social workers. "In community action we are asking the various establishments to share their power with those they purport to help. We must insist that this be not a token involvement but a genuine one."[16] In the end, however, the mayors, agencies, businessmen, and unions continued to hold the reins of power. As we shall see, maximum feasible participation in any real sense was unable to survive.

Maximum feasible participation was more than a formal power-sharing arrangement, however. It became an ideology, giving a degree of reality to the "participatory democracy" of the early civil rights movement, and merging into the new demands for "community control" of schools, local businesses, hospitals, and other community institutions that community activists were beginning to develop. Maximum feasible participation was not merely an abstract idea created by policy-making intellectuals and bestowed upon a passive population, nor was it simply an attempt to co-opt community leaders. If it had any meaning, it was meaning given it solely by the struggles of community activists. When community residents besieged the mayor's office demanding more summer jobs for young people, that was maximum feasible participation. When local residents joined with paraprofessional hospital workers to demand that hospital policies be determined by the needs of patients rather than by doctors and administrators, that was maximum feasible participation. When welfare recipients, organized into the National Welfare Rights Organization (in part by VISTA and other poverty program workers), demanded financial support from social service agencies and changes in welfare regulations, that was maximum feasible participation. In short, the phrase helped generate, and was sustained by, the full range of social activism that drove the reform movements of the late sixties.

Maximum feasible participation also provided a key link between institutional changes and broad social reform, on the one hand, and individual personality change, on the other—what some called "sociotherapy."[17] Harlem Youth Opportunities Unlimited, a pioneer community action program that provided one of the models for the Economic Opportunity Act itself, explained its strategy this way:

> If concrete successes of these forms of mobilized community power are obtained, then one can expect that these will stimulate, increase, and reinforce self-confidence and pride in Negro adults and youth.
>
> Given an increase in the positive self-image of Negro youth, based upon the realities of effective social action and demonstrated social change, there should emerge a solid basis for a new cycle of greater personal and community effectiveness. . . . A positive self-image cannot be obtained by exhortation or by mere verbal demands. It must be created and reinforced by reality experiences. . . .
>
> It is not the primary objective of these programs to bring under-achieving delinquents or delinquency-prone youngsters into a helping relationship with a caseworker, group worker, or remedial specialist. . . . This aspect of HARYOU's program puts stress upon a restructured *culture*, or redirected way of life, rather than on the therapeutic problem-solving relationship with a helping person, as the source of new perspectives, motives, and behavior patterns.[18]

George Brager, an executive director of another pioneering community action program, Mobilization for Youth on Manhattan's Lower East Side, similarly argued: "We believe that the personal sense of powerlessness felt by low income people is a major cause of their isolation and apathy. . . . To encourage education and social learning, therefore, it is necessary to decrease the sense of powerlessness."[19] To the Mobilization for Youth planners, encouraging militant self-assertion by poor people would enhance their self-confidence.

Numerous observers had already noted the association between involvement in social action and improved "mental health." For example, it was reported that crime among black youths in Montgomery, Alabama, had declined sharply during the year of the bus boycott.[20] Psychologists noted that students involved in the sit-in movement used that experience of "prosocial acting out" to serve constructive developmental tasks.[21] Later in the decade, some outstanding successes in the treatment of drug addiction were achieved by the Black Muslims and by militant community groups such as the Black Panther party and the (Puerto Rican) Young Lords organization, who found that participation in militant movements for social change provided the motivation and context for startling personality change. In the same vein, participation in the women's liberation movement at the very end of the decade was to prove a powerful vehicle for personal change as well as for helping achieve social reform.[22] Thus, maximum feasible participation was central to bridging the traditional gap between "macro" and "micro" approaches to dealing with social problems.

A second enormously innovative approach taken by the Community Action Program was its response to professionals and to traditional social service agencies, public and private. The early poverty program planners realized that the existing structure of services, both public and private, was simply not working, despite the enormous amounts of money flowing through it. Sargent Shriver, scolding social workers for their failure to meet the needs of the poor, cited a study of social services in Detroit:

> There are many voluntary agencies in the group service and recreation field in Detroit, but with few exceptions they serve relatively few from low-income families. . . . Of those agencies which actively do reach the poor, all of them are extremely limited in size, and in spite of some commendable effort, their total impact is still negligible with respect to the total needs of the poor. . . .
> Public tax-supported agencies were the chief resources used by the poor. Excluding hospitals, only 10 per cent, 10.1 per cent of these poor families, reported any contact with any voluntary agency. This includes the visiting nurse service, the legal aid, the family and child welfare services, the recreation and youth services, including the YMCA and the YWCA, the Boy Scouts, the Girl Scouts, the Catholic Youth Organization, the Boys Clubs, and all the neighborhood church related programs and services.[23]

Other poverty program planners made similar charges with respect to schools, legal institutions, health institutions, and mental health services.[24]

Mitchell Sviridoff, a New Haven poverty program planner and another influential designer of the Economic Opportunity Act, described the planners' response to this problem:

> The prime problem was that the established systems were rigid and unresponsive. . . . This suggested "the social application of the art of jujitsu"—the process of bringing small amounts of resources to bear at points of leverage to capture larger resources otherwise working against (or ignoring) socially desirable ends. Community action, then, was not conceived as a new service concept. Services would be provided, of course, but mainly as a challenge to established institutions— a spur to social reform.[25]

In practice this resulted in not some orderly process of "planning" and "coordination" but an immensely vital, often uproarious process of social change.

Maximum feasible participation provided the key mechanism for developing the power to mount popular challenges to existing agencies. The community-controlled board of a Community Action Agency could make demands on participating agencies as a condition of funding them. But under the "community action" rubric, OEO also set up a variety of programs that directly challenged existing practices.

Of these, perhaps most important was the Neighborhood Legal Services Program.[26] By 1968 some 250 Legal Services offices and 1,800 lawyers were initiating more than 250,000 cases per year. Originally, Legal Services had been seen as simply a way of meeting the legal needs of poor individuals in divorce cases, criminal cases, consumer finance problems, landlord–tenant proceedings, and the like. But under the impact of maximum feasible participation and the growing radicalization of the young lawyers who staffed the offices, many Legal Services projects soon became aggressive advocates for the people of their neighborhood. They pressed legal challenges to administrative procedures in the welfare department and school systems, initiated class actions on issues ranging from consumer fraud to a patient's right to treatment in mental institutions, lobbied to reform laws that had an adverse impact on the poor, and represented neighborhood organizations and political groups formed by poor people in their dealings with the police, the city administration, and the courts.

OEO and the other similar antipoverty programs also provided money for setting up new service agencies. These were expected not only to provide more service but to provide new models for service delivery. Community Mental Health centers were expected to offer decentralized, community-based mental health services, replacing the highly centralized and bureaucratic state hospitals, to provide educational and consultative services for the community and for other community agencies, and even to initiate programs aimed at dealing with the presumed environmental sources of emotional disorder, including poor schools, exploitative landlords and employers, and racism. Neighborhood Health centers were to offer a model of comprehensive, continuous, family-centered care, as an alternative to the badly fragmented and impersonal services delivered by hospital outpatient departments. And OEO funds were expected to entice traditional social work agencies, which had long ago lost interest in serving the poor, to resume activities directed at poverty populations.

Finally, OEO underwrote experimental reorganizations of services. The most widespread and enduring form of this reorganization was the use of "paraprofessionals" (again, the maximum feasible participation concept).[27] In legal offices, health and mental health centers, welfare offices, schools, and family service agencies, local residents were trained to perform at least some of the functions previously done by professionals. The use of paraprofessionals vastly increased the manpower available for the delivery of the now-expanded services. And it provided jobs for tens of thousands of residents of poor communities. In a number of cases, "career ladders"—job advancement patterns based on mixtures of on-the-job experience, in-service training, and released-time training programs—made these positions seem to promise not a long-term dead-end job but a career.

The use of paraprofessionals posed a basic challenge to traditional models of providing services. For one thing, it rejected the assumption that only highly trained professionals could deliver human services: advocates of the use of paraprofessionals argued that the very education that created professionals also created social barriers between them and the poor populations they were to serve. Because the paraprofessional was a member of the community to be served, such social distance was minimal, and consequently, the planners hoped, the paraprofessionals would be able to provide services more effectively than professionals.

This turned the professional model on its head: traditionally, professionals had defined a knowledge base and had claimed a monopoly over the acts that sprang from that knowledge base. The use of paraprofessionals suggested replacing this model, based on formal education, with a model based on a hierarchy of competence. Beyond this, in a number of instances the paraprofessionals identified more strongly with their communities than with their employers. In institutions such as New York's Lincoln Hospital Mental Health Services, the paraprofessionals took a leading role in demanding major reorganizations and reorientations of the services themselves.[28]

Before the War of Poverty, most governmental social policies directed to the poor had been content to add new services. The poverty program, partly by design, partly through the vagueness of the law, and partly by the pressures created by community unrest, allowed the organization and delivery patterns of the services themselves to be challenged. The traditional institutions, the traditional "professional" ways in which staffs related to clients, the technology and skills on which professional monopoly and status was based, the underlying purposes of the services themselves, all came under question and often under attack. Even the schools that trained professionals came under scrutiny: professional schools were forced to reorganize their curricula to train students to respond better to the needs of poor and minority clients, open their admissions policies to recruit more minority and poor (and later female) students, and permit students a greater input into school decision making.

This picture of the poverty program is, of course, vastly oversimplified. In actuality, the process was much less orderly and systematized: it was, in Mitchell Sviridoff's words, a "long, slow, messy process"—chaotic, contradictory, disruptive, rhetorical to excess, polarizing, often extremist, occasionally violent, sometimes counterproductive. And in the end, despite the successful reorganization of many agency practices and attitudes, the poverty program failed to reform the service delivery system, much less to eliminate poverty. The central reason for this failure was the reliance of the program on "culture of poverty" theories and a corresponding inability to understand the basic politics and economics of poverty in America.

Perhaps the most important immediate reason for the failure of the poverty program was its misconception of power. The whole idea of "community action" implied there was a "community" that could be cajoled or pushed into a coordinated, cooperative effort to end poverty. The old Progressive Era idea of the ultimate harmony of interests of the rich, the middle class, and the poor was deeply embedded in the whole concept of the War on Poverty. It was assumed that no one had a vested interest in maintaining poverty and that the culture of poverty was a sufficient explanation for the persistence of poverty in the face of overall affluence.

But, in fact, the poor (black, Hispanic, Asian, and white), the middle-class professionals and local politicians, the public and private agency officials, landlords, retailers, and large employers did not constitute a "community." American society was torn asunder by war, racial polarization, growing generational tensions, tensions in the family, and class and sectional interests. Racial and ethnic minorities, women, and students were making demands on American society for power, which meant that someone else would have less power, and for resources, which meant someone else would have fewer resources. Landlords seeking exorbitant rents, merchants seeking excessive mark-ups, employers seeking low-wage labor, professionals seeking to protect their institutional power and social status, all benefited from the continued existence of poverty. There was simply no basis for the kind of social cohesion essential to the success of community action.

Nevertheless, had the economy grown at a sufficiently rapid pace, some of the needs of the poor could have been met without threatening other groups with loss of income or power. But the designers and administrators of the poverty program never came to grips with the inability of the American economy of the 1960s to provide steady employment at adequate wages for all. The War on Poverty itself represented a "service strategy": it was aimed at rationalizing and improving the delivery of services to the poor. It was not an "income strategy" designed to provide adequate incomes for all. And, in the words of John G. Wofford, an OEO official, it was "not a job creation program. We have to assume that the economy, spurred on by the tax reduction, will create the jobs."[29]

As we have seen, the poverty program was accompanied by efforts to stimulate the economy. But for the most part, these were broad efforts. They were not effectively targeted at creating jobs appropriate to the location and to the skills of the poor. To do this would have implied a direct governmental role in corporate investment decisions, a step that Johnson-era America was not ready to take and that the poor never gained enough power to demand. In fact, by the sixties the American economy was not able to create jobs and income for the poor, even at high levels of overall economic activity. Ironically, it was the war in Vietnam, not the War on Poverty and not the tax cut, that both stimulated the economy and provided "jobs" (although often fatal ones) for many of the poor.

The War on Poverty also represented a "localist" strategy: it was based on the belief that an extensive local expansion of services could meet the needs of the poor. To the policy planners, the inadequacy of local services was unconnected to the national economy's inability to provide jobs at decent wages, unconnected to the systematic power of racism, unconnected to national systems of power. The "power" that the War on Poverty proposed to give to the poor was, at best, power vis-à-vis local politicians and professionals, not power with respect to national economic and political decision making.

Even at the local level, the War on Poverty planners believed that the existing institutions and agencies—the local school boards, welfare departments, hospitals, social work agencies, and the like—could be prodded into change by the lure of funds and the pressure of organized communities. The autonomy of the agencies was never seriously questioned. In reality, the agencies strenuously resisted change while seeking the new federal funds. Sometimes quickly, sometimes after protracted struggles, they beat back the demands for change. The Community Mental Health Centers program, expected to pioneer a new mode of services more appropriate to the needs of poor clients and to provide extensive preventive mental health care and educational services, became little more than an expansion of entirely conventional outpatient services into poor communities. "Neither accountable backward to the National Institutes of Mental Health . . . nor forward to the consumers and citizens in the community they allegedly serve," noted a Ralph Nader task force, "they have often become . . . windfalls for psychiatrists who have systematically ignored the programs' directives to serve the poor."[30] The Neighborhood Health Center program of OEO was captured by the hospitals, who used the funds available for institutional expansion.[31] The social work agencies, contrary to expectations, failed to promote social change and used the federal poverty funds to expand their traditional casework services.[32] School systems accepted funds for preschool programs (the widely popular Head Start program) but failed to engage in extensive and lasting educational innovation.[33] In the end, the old power of the professionals and the old institutions was greater than the new power of the poor. The institutions bent with the wind and slowly absorbed its force.

The mayors, too, undercut the goals of the program. They fought for control of the local poverty programs, with their accompanying funds and patronage possibilities (and, conversely, with their potential for making trouble for the mayors, should the mayors lose the battle). Mayor Robert Wagner of New York told a House subcommittee hearing: "I feel very strongly that the sovereign part of each locality . . . should have the power of approval over the makeup of the planning group, over the structure of the planning group, over the plan." Mayor John F. Shelley of San Francisco complained that OEO was "undermining the integrity of local government" by organizing the poor. A resolution at the 1966 U.S. Conference of Mayors accused Sargent Shriver of "fostering class warfare."[34]

The mayors' reaction proved effective in Congress: in late 1966 Congress cut back and severely restricted the scope of the community action program. And when the Model Cities program was passed in the same year, the notion of maximum feasible participation was reduced to the idea that the community should provide advice and mayors were given firm control of the monies. By late in 1967 Congress amended the Economic Opportunity Act itself to allow community action funds to be channeled directly through the mayor's office where the local government so elected. (Ironically, only about 5 percent of the mayors chose to exercise this option. As James Sundquist, one of the original program planners, noted: "In the others, either the program was under their control already, it was so innocuous that it did not matter, or it had such power that they dared not move against it."[35])

The concerted opposition from mayors, professional organizations, and local agencies crippled the poverty program. But the death blows were delivered first by the war in Vietnam and second by the election of Richard Nixon. During the formative stages of the poverty program, the planners had accepted Defense Department predictions that the other war, the one in Southeast Asia, would be of short duration. But by 1966 it was already becoming clear that the "light at the end of the tunnel" was far away indeed. President Johnson elected not to choose between guns and butter for American society as a whole, a choice that was to distort the American economy for years to come. But he was not so solicitous of the poor: funds for the Office of Economic Opportunity virtually never rose above the 1965–66 levels, and beginning in 1968–69 they began to decline. The Vietnam War took precedence over the War on Poverty.[36]

Then, in November 1968, the American electorate, bitterly divided over the war in Vietnam and deeply disturbed by the rising tide of racial unrest and student revolt, chose, by a narrow margin, the conservative Richard Nixon to be president. The forward motion of the 1960s reform wave ground to a halt, as Nixon sought to dismantle the poverty program, to cut back funds for social welfare programs, and to shift to more repressive means for controlling community and student unrest.

The Kennedy-Johnson War on Poverty, in its broadest sense, lasted eight years, from the Area Redevelopment Act of 1961 to the dismantling of OEO by President Nixon in 1969. In the narrower sense, the full range of community action programs called for by the Economic Opportunity Act were fully funded for only two years and were virtually eliminated after only four years. The argument that the poverty program "didn't work," often heard in the years that followed, is disingenuous; for all intents and purposes the poverty program was never even tried out.

Indeed, despite their limits, the various Kennedy-Johnson antipoverty measures *did* have a significant effect in reducing poverty in the United States: in 1959 a little over 22 percent of the American population was poor; by 1969 only 12 percent remained below the official poverty standard. Nearly 20 million Americans had risen out of poverty (by the stringent official definitions, at least). The following years of cutback and economic recession brought no sustained improvement in overall poverty rates, and in the late seventies the rates began to creep upward again, reaching 15 percent in 1982.

Despite the continued massive influx of poor blacks into the central cities during the sixties, the poverty rate in central cities dropped from 34.3 percent in 1959 to 21.5 percent in 1969, rising again to the levels of the late fifties by the early eighties.[37] Some of the reduction in poverty was the result of economic growth, itself stimulated by government spending, but according to the Final Report of the National Advisory Council on Economic Opportunity, established by the Economic Opportunity Act, "virtually all of the reduction in poverty since the mid-1960s has come about through the expansion of social insurance and income transfer programs"—that is, welfare, Food Stamps, Social Security, rent supplements, and the like.[38]

The impact of the entire Kennedy-Johnson social reform effort went far beyond the immediate, quantifiable improvement of people's material well-being, however. Responding to the civil rights and black liberation movements and related movements of other minority groups, the rights and opportunities available to racial and ethnic minorities were dramatically expanded. Laws, regulations, and policies that had previously restricted these rights were eliminated; the system of legalized racial segregation in the South was entirely dismantled; and antidiscrimination legislation and affirmative action regulations and programs enormously expanded economic opportunities for minorities. The provisions of the Voting Rights Act, in concert with the growing political consciousness of minorities, enormously facilitated the entry of minorities into the political process. Black and Hispanic officeholders increased in number in the years that followed. By 1984 black mayors had been elected in, among other cities, Chicago, Los Angeles, Philadelphia, Detroit, and Atlanta, and the Reverend Jesse Jackson had emerged as a major presidential candidate.

The improved legal and social status of minority groups both stemmed from and led to a greater assertiveness on the part of these groups. Whatever the political or economic gains, the cultural change and the weakening of age-old patterns of self-hatred and lowered self-esteem are likely to have positive impacts on the mental health, as well as the political and economic health, of these groups for years to come. Participation by clients in decision making with respect to the services they receive, though far weaker now than in the heyday of maximum feasible participation, has also not disappeared. Old paternalistic patterns, if not dead, were dealt a severe and lasting blow.

Finally, the Kennedy-Johnson programs provided apparently permanent additions to the American welfare state. Social Security benefits to the aged, the disabled, and the blind were materially improved; welfare eligibility standards were simplified; and health benefits for the aged and the poor became an integral part of the Social Security System. Although the precise levels of benefits under these systems may be whittled away in the future, their existence as part of the welfare state seems fairly well assured.

I have suggested that the Kennedy-Johnson reform era came to an end with the inauguration of Richard M. Nixon in January 1969. But it is too simple to end the story of the social reforms of the sixties at this point. For one thing, the social conditions that gave rise to the Kennedy-Johnson social reforms had not gone away. That the last of the major ghetto "riots" took place in 1968 did not become evident for several years. In 1968–71 new militant organizations such as the Black Panther party sprang up in minority communities around the country. The demand for "maximum feasible *participation*" was succeeded by the more extreme demand for "community *control*" of community institutions. Student take-overs of universities, not infrequently triggered by black student or community demands as well as by antagonism to the war in Vietnam, turned into an epidemic; by the May 1970 invasion of Cambodia and killings of student protestors at Kent (Ohio) State and Jackson (Mississippi) State universities, virtually the entire college and university system of the country was closed down by a general student strike. Unrest seemed to have become a way of life. The women's liberation movement emerged as a mass movement, its maturation symbolized by a massive parade down New York's Fifth Avenue in 1970. And a growing movement of environmentalists demanded regulation of corporate destruction of the environment. Women's issues (i.e., abortion rights, day care, equality of opportunity, freedom from sexual harassment) and environmental issues were added to the nation's social policy agenda.

In this context, President Nixon's actions were forced to retain a certain ambiguity. He did seek to cut back the Great Society's social welfare programs, especially those, such as the community action program, that challenged existing power arrangements. And he did seek to destroy the community and student movements by reducing their causes through removal of American troops from Vietnam, ending the draft, and outright repression. Funds were poured into the Law Enforcement Assistance Administration instead of the Office of Economic Opportunity (which was, for all intents and purposes, dismantled). And the COINTELPRO program of surveillance and harassment of militant and radical community and student groups was radically expanded. At the same time, Nixon proposed a welfare reform program, the Family Assistance Program, which, had it been enacted, would have established a national guaranteed minimum income (albeit one at a very low level); dramatically expanded the food stamp, child nutrition, and rent supplement programs; continued to expand job training and employment programs; and extended President Johnson's affirmative action program to cover women as well as racial and ethnic minorities.

Nevertheless, the overwhelming impact of Nixon's election was to end the forward thrust of reform. To the ideologues of Nixonism, the "limits of social policy" in curing social woes seemed more evident than their benefits. What was needed, proclaimed Daniel Patrick Moynihan, who had participated in the planning of the Johnson antipoverty program, was a period of "benign neglect" of social problems.[39]

In 1972 Nixon was reelected, this time by a wide margin. The decline of the community, black, and student movements was evident. Exhaustion and frustration, internal divisions and antagonisms between adherents of different movements, the co-optation of some leaders and the jailing, killing, or frightening of others, the inability of the movements to create larger coalitions for change, the winding down of the American involvement in Vietnam, the impact of the economic downturns of 1969 and 1971—all played a role. But regardless of the precise causes, the social pressures that had forced the Kennedy and Johnson administrations to launch an attack on poverty and racism (or, as was the case with the first Nixon administration, had prevented its total dismantling) were dramatically weakened.

The major exception to the decline of the movements was the women's liberation movement, which remained able to win signal victories: the liberalization of abortion laws that culminated in the Supreme Court's abortion decision of 1973, the Nixon administration's extension of the federal affirmative action program to women, and congressional approval of the Equal Rights Amendment to the Constitution. But by 1974 or 1975 even this movement was weakening.

With the weakening of the movements and the strengthening of his own electoral mandate, Nixon was ready to sharpen the cutbacks. But his political ability to do so was soon undercut by the Watergate scandal. Nixon's own, ultimately unsuccessful, struggle for political survival came to take precedence over domestic social policies. In August 1974 Nixon resigned. His successor, Gerald Ford, the nation's first president who had never been elected to any national office (he had been appointed vice president after the resignation in disgrace of Spiro Agnew), inherited a weakened, delegitimized presidency and a deeply divided nation. It was a time for re-creating national unity, not for enforcing divisive social cutbacks. The cutbacks did continue, but the most abrupt and deep cutbacks were effected at the local level rather than nationally, as a growing "fiscal crisis" infected city after city.

Ford, in turn, was followed by Jimmy Carter. Carter's ability to put in motion a full program of cutbacks was also limited. Although a moderately conservative figure by the standards of the sixties, he was a Democrat: his slender electoral margin in 1976 depended on the votes of blacks and urban workers and on the organizational support of labor unions. The consequence was a continued political stalemate: welfare reform programs foundered, national health insurance proposals withered, and program cutbacks continued, although at a moderate rate.

With the election of Ronald Reagan in November 1980, along with a sharp shift to the right in the political makeup of the Congress, the decade-long stalemate was finally broken, however. The barriers that had limited cutbacks in social programs to a modest level fell, and the Reaganite program of massive cuts could be put into effect.

Recall, for a moment, the combined effects of the Progressive Era, the New Deal, and the sixties: the struggles and unrest among various groups—workers, minorities, women, students—had forced often reluctant governments to institue a whole series of measures to improve people's well-being (and in doing so, to restore social order, maintain social control, and meet various corporate needs). Some of these measures provided economic security: welfare, social security, minimum wages, unemployment compensation, food stamps.

18. *Youth and the Ghetto* (New York: Harlem Youth Opportunities Unlimited, 1964), pp. 36, 371–72.

19. Cited in Marris and Rein, p. 49.

20. T. Kahn, "Unfinished Revolution" (pamphlet, 1960), cited in Jacob R. Fishman and Frederick Solomon, "Youth and Social Action: Perspectives on the Sit-In Movement," in Riessman, Cohen, and Pearl, pp. 400–11.

21. Fishman and Solomon, op. cit.

22. For other examples, see Henry Gottesfeld and Gerterlyn Dozier, "Changes in Feelings of Powerlessness in a Community Action Project," *Psychological Reports* 19 (1966): 978; Louis A. Zurcher, Jr., "The Poverty Board: Some Consequences of 'Maximum Feasible Participation,' " *Journal of Social Issues* 26, no. 3 (1970): 85–107; Charles Silberman, *Crisis in Black and White* (New York: Vintage, 1964), pp. 157–59. On similar impacts of participation in the women's liberation movement, see Carol Hamisch, "The Personal Is Political," in *Notes from the Second Year: Women's Liberation* (New York: n.p., 1970), A dissenting view is Barbara Susan, "About My Consciousness Raising," in Leslie B. Tanner, ed., *Voices from Women's Liberation* (New York: New American Library, 1970), pp. 238–43.

23. Shriver, p. 59.

24. For example, Marris and Rein, pp. 58–70.

25. Sviridoff, p. 4.

26. Charles F. Grosser and Edward V. Sparer, "Legal Services for the Poor: Social Work and Social Justice," *Social Work* 11, no. 1 (Jan. 1966): 81–87; Piven and Cloward, *Regulating the Poor*, pp. 306–9; National Advisory Council on Economic Opportunity, *Final Report* (Washington, D.C.: National Advisory Council, 1981), pp. 91–101; Levitan and Taggart, chap. 6.

27. Arthur Pearl and Frank Riessman, *New Careers for the Poor: The Non-Professional in Human Services* (New York: Free Press, 1965); George Brager, "The Indigenous Worker: A New Approach to the Social Work Technician," *Social Work* 10 no. 2 (Apr. 1965): 33–40; Felice Perlmutter and Dorothy Durham, "Using Teenagers to Supplement Casework Service," *Social Work* 10, no. 2 (Apr. 1965): 41–46; Frank Riessman, "The 'Helper' Therapy Principle," *Social Work* 10, no. 2 (Apr. 1965): 27–32; Bertram M. Beck, "Wanted Now: Social Work Associates," *Social Welfare Forum, 1963* (New York: National Conference on Social Welfare, 1963), pp. 195–205; Francine Sobey, *The Non-Professional Revolution in Mental Health* (New York: Columbia University Press, 1970); Charles Grosser, William E. Henry, and James G. Kelley, eds., *Non-Professionals in the Human Services* (San Francisco: Jossey-Bass, 1969), esp. B. M. Beck's "Non-Professional Social Work Personnel."

28. Barbara Ehrenreich and John Ehrenreich, *The American Health Empire* (New York: Random House, 1970), chap. 18; Seymour R. Kaplan and Melvin Roman, *The Organization and Delivery of Mental Health Services in the Ghetto: The Lincoln Hospital Experience* (New York: Praeger, 1973).

29. Wofford, p. 73.

30. Cited in James Lieby, *A History of Social Welfare and Social Work in the United States* (New York: Columbia University Press, 1978), p. 332. Also see Robert Castel, Françoise Castel, and Anne Lovell, *The Psychiatric Society* (New York: Columbia University Press, 1982), pp. 124–69; Ehrenreich and Ehrenreich, chap. 6; Health Policy Advisory Center, *Evaluation of Community Involvement in Community Mental Health Centers* (Rockwell, Md.: National Institute of Mental Health, 1970); Felice Perlmutter and Herbert A. Silverman, "Community Mental Health Centers: A Structural Anachronism," *Social Work* 17, no. 2 (Mar. 1972): 78–85.

31. Ehrenreich and Ehrenreich, chaps. 4 and 5; "Neighborhood Health Centers," *Health PAC Bulletin*, no. 42 (June 1972): 1; "NENA: Community Control in a Bind," *Health PAC Bulletin*, no. 42 (June 1972): 3–12.

32. Rose, pp. 123–60; Camille Lambert, Jr., and Leah R. Lambert, "Impact of Poverty Funds on Voluntary Agencies," *Social Work* 15, no. 2 (Apr. 1970): 53–61.

33. Marris and Rein, pp. 58–70.

34. Donovan, pp. 54–57; Wofford, pp. 98–99.

35. James L. Sundquist, "The End of the Experiment," in Sundquist, pp. 235–51.

36. Donovan, pp. 117–20.

37. National Advisory Council on Economic Opportunity, *Final Report,* p. 36; "Poverty Rate Rose to 15% in '82, Highest Level since Mid-1960s," *New York Times,* Aug. 8, 1983, p. A-1.

38. National Advisory Council on Economic Opportunity, *Final Report,* p. 38.

39. Nathan Glazer, "The Limits of Social Policy," *Commentary* 52, no. 3 (Sept. 1971): 51–58. The Moynihan "benign neglect" speech is reported in the *New York Times,* Mar. 1, 1970, p. A-1.

40. Frances Fox Piven and Richard A. Cloward, *The New Class War* (New York: Pantheon, 1982), p. 118.

41. Ibid. Also see Frank Ackerman, *Reaganomics: Rhetoric vs. Reality* (Boston: South End Press, 1982). For statements from Reagan advisers, see Martin Anderson, *Welfare* (Palo Alto, Calif.: Hoover Institution Press, 1978); George Gilder, *Wealth and Poverty* (New York: Basic Books, 1981); William Greider, "The Education of David Stockman," *Atlantic* 248 (Dec. 1981): 27–40.

The Objectives of the Reagan Administration's Social Welfare Policy
Martin Anderson

THE REAGAN ADMINISTRATION'S SOCIAL WELFARE PHILOSOPHY

Five important elements of the Reagan administration's social welfare philosophy seem to me to define and explain its basic thrust:

1. A sound and growing economy is vital to reducing poverty and ensuring the opportunity for prosperity for everyone.

2. Eligibility standards for social welfare programs should be fair, setting reasonable limits as to who qualifies for aid.

3. Fraud, waste, and extravagance in social welfare programs should be substantially reduced.

4. In order to improve effectiveness and to lower costs, the responsibility for certain social welfare programs, together with the tax resources necessary to fund them, should be returned to the states and localities (the New Federalism).

5. A guaranteed income is unconscionable and impractical. To the extent that people are able to take care of themselves, they should do so.

A SOUND AND GROWING ECONOMY

The general level of economic prosperity largely determines the personal prosperity of those in the society who are relatively poor.

First, the level of government support and the extent of that support is largely determined by the size of government tax revenues and that, in turn, is largely determined by the size and health of the economy. There is no way that a country like India, with its weak and relatively stagnant economy, could provide—even if it wished to do so—anywhere near the extent of social welfare benefits that exist in the United States.

Second, how well the economy is functioning can have a powerful effect on low-income people. How much money they have is important, but what they can buy with the money is equally important. The devastating effect of inflation on poor people is often overlooked. One would expect that low-income people would be less able to adapt quickly to a rapidly escalating cost of living than their more financially agile brothers and sisters with higher incomes. The differences in well-being that result from not being able to adjust one's income to inflation can be very large.

For example, if sound economic policies kept the rate of inflation at zero instead of, say, 10 percent, it would mean that after just two years someone with a low, fixed income would have real purchasing power that would be roughly one fifth higher than it would have been under the higher rate of inflation. There are few social welfare programs that could expect to enjoy growth of this magnitude.

High interest rates are another manifestation of high inflation. The higher cost of borrowing money can be especially painful to those without substantial liquid assets who must borrow if they want to use and enjoy something while they pay for it, rather than wait until they have saved enough to buy it outright.

High tax rates, especially high marginal tax rates, can have a severely inhibiting effect on people's work effort. And they can be particularly discouraging to someone who is considering entering the work force at low-to moderate-income levels. Our tax system, if we look just at federal taxes, or state taxes, or Social Security taxes, is fairly reasonable. But if we look at it from the perspective of a low- or moderate-income taxpayer who must pay all these taxes simultaneously, it becomes quite irrational. The effect of federal, state, and Social Security taxes acting together often produces effective marginal tax rates of almost 30 percent for incomes only slightly above the poverty level.

A high unemployment rate, especially if it is sustained and unemployment benefits run out, can make a lot of people poor very quickly.

In sum, all the characteristics of a poorly functioning economy—high inflation and high interest rates, rising unemployment, and high marginal tax rates—produce a powerful economic effect that constitutes a double whammy on the poor. It hurts them directly by reducing the purchasing power of their money, throwing them out of work, and eroding their incentives to work if they can find work. At the same time, a poorly functioning economy reduces the tax revenues that must pay for the social welfare programs that provide aid to them.

For anyone concerned about the long-term well-being of the poor in the United States, the achievement and maintenance of a healthy, growing economy should be of paramount importance.

ELIGIBILITY STANDARDS

Another important aspect of the Reagan administration's social welfare philosophy is the determination of who should receive social welfare benefits. Over the years, as the size and scope of our social welfare programs have grown, there has been a gradual increase in income eligibility levels.

The purpose of welfare, as understood by most Americans, is to provide help and support to poor people, to those who cannot care for themselves. One of the primary reasons we developed poverty statistics was to determine what kinds and what degree of help should be provided by government social welfare programs. Unfortunately, two developments in recent years have combined to blur our understanding of poverty in the United States and to compromise the validity of those programs in the eyes of the public.

The official poverty statistics published each year by the Bureau of the Census consistently and deliberately overstate the incidence of poverty in the United States. Many years ago, when this series was first put together, it was decided to focus on cash income only, disregarding the value of in-kind services received by the poor, such as medical care or housing assistance. At the time, this was a reasonable decision because in-kind benefits were then only a small fraction of total welfare benefits received, and the loss of completeness in the statistics was more than made up by the savings in the effort of compiling those statistics.

But as the years rolled by, the value of in-kind benefits grew and grew and grew. As the relative amount of in-kind benefits increased, the validity of the poverty statistics decreased. This problem is further compounded by the consistent underreporting of income to the Bureau of the Census. The extent of this underreporting is known, but the poverty series is not adjusted to take it into account.

The benign neglect of in-kind benefits and the disregarding of underreporting of income have gradually eroded the validity of the official poverty statistics to the point where they are not only unreliable but are very misleading. The census statistics, according to estimates by the Congressional Budget Office and independent scholars, indicate that poverty is at least twice as great as it really is.

The truly regrettable part of this whole affair is that social welfare experts who have been aware of the problem for many years continue to use discredited data while efforts to correct the data proceed with "all deliberate speed." The Bureau of the Census now has a significant effort underway to correct these statistics, but for at least five or more years the numbers have been badly misleading to those who are unfamiliar with their deficiencies.

An interesting question arises as to why otherwise reputable scholars would continue to use the discredited official poverty numbers. It may be that they do not know any better or that it is too much trouble to change. But these are unlikely explanations.

As time goes on one has to give more and more credence to the suspicion that the discredited numbers continue to be used because of, not in spite of, the fact that they grossly overstate the incidence of poverty and thus buttress the ideological view shared by most scholars in the field. To the extent that this is perceived to be true, it causes injury to the professional reputation of the entire field. The time appears long overdue for a little intellectual self-policing.

As we have gradually lost track of the true nature and extent of poverty in the United States, we have also begun to slide away from a clear idea of who should be eligible for social welfare benefits. Most Americans probably share the rather uncomplicated view that by and large only poor people should be eligible for benefits. One problem with this view is that as soon as you draw a clear line between the *poor* and *nonpoor* you create an insoluble problem, namely that those a few dollars over the line are very, very close in the nature of their financial circumstances to those just below the line. Yet those above the line are not eligible, while their neighbors just below the line are eligible for many social welfare benefits.

Partly in response to this, the eligibility levels of many programs have been increased far above the poverty level, so that many individuals and families who are not classified as officially poor receive social welfare benefits. For example, a family is eligible for Food Stamps if its income is less than 130 percent of the poverty level, and for child health care if family income is less than 185 percent of the poverty level. To qualify for certain rent subsidies, income must be less than 50 percent of the area median income (it used to be 80 percent but was recently changed). Families asking for student financial aid at one time had no income restrictions at all, and the spectacle of wealthy students investing their subsidized loans in the financial markets finally resulted in a rather generous ceiling of $30,000 being placed on "countable" family income.

These and other expansions of eligibility standards have greatly blurred our common understanding of who is poor and who should be eligible to receive government aid. As the eligibility levels are raised, the number of people at the margin who qualify for social welfare programs increases rapidly and this, in turn, sharply boosts the cost of these programs. At the same time, the public sees more and more people receiving aid whose justification for receiving that aid becomes increasingly questionable as the income eligibility levels rise.

There is no easy way to draw the line on eligibility. What the Reagan administration has done as one of the main thrusts of its social welfare policy has been to restore more of a sense of balance and fairness in federal programs designed to aid the poor. In proposing slower rates of spending growth—and, in some cases, reductions—for certain social welfare programs, the guiding principle has been that the adjustments be made primarily at the expense of those people at the upper end of the eligibility scale. To use one of the most glaring examples, it was felt to be somewhat unseemly for people with six-figure incomes to be bellying up to the federal bar for their share of the guaranteed student loan money for their precocious offspring, especially when many low- and moderate-income taxpayers were paying the bill.

A major objective of the Reagan administration's social welfare policy is to restore fairer standards of eligibility so that the available resources can be focused on those least able to take care of themselves.

The extent to which this has been achieved is still unclear, but there are some signs it is working. Last year *New York Times* reporters interviewed state welfare officials in all fifty states in an effort to ascertain the consequences of the Reagan administration's adjustments to the social welfare budget. They were expecting reports of "protests, demonstrations, and lobbying campaigns in behalf of the poor." What they found was silence—no protests, no demonstrations, and no lobbying campaigns. And the major reason for this may be found in the explanation given by John T. Dempsey, director of the Michigan Department of Social Services, who was reported to have "said that he thought Mr. Reagan had cut benefits in a way that minimized the effect on the poorest people, by reducing welfare benefits for those who could work or who had income exceeding 150 percent of the subsistence income level set by each state."

FRAUD, WASTE, AND EXTRAVAGANCE

While past studies by the General Accounting Office, the Department of Health and Human Services, and various state governments have shown massive amounts of fraud and mismanagement in social welfare programs, there has been very little rigorous analysis by social welfare scholars of the extent and causes of this phenomenon. But this has done little to deter the problem from continuing in the real world.

One of the major objectives of the social welfare policy of the Reagan administration is to reduce and some day eliminate the massive fraud and abuse that characterizes so many of those programs. There are two basic reasons for doing so. The obvious one is to save a considerable amount of money, money that could be given to those who qualify and money that would not have to be spent at all. Another reason is to remove the stigma that attaches to all people receiving social welfare benefits, because those who are cheating and getting away with it have convinced the vast majority of the American public that fraud is widespread in social welfare programs. Not knowing which recipients are fraudulent, the public tends to be suspicious of them all. If there is anything that infuriates the American taxpayer it is the idea that someone is getting his tax money who should not be.

THE NEW FEDERALISM

The question of the proper division of responsibility for government social welfare programs between the federal government and the states and localities is one that has been with us for a long time. What has been called the *New Federalism* of the Reagan administration is, for the most part, an old federalism concept that has been discussed for decades. Over thirty years ago President Eisenhower established the Commission on Intergovernmental Relations. The commission, which included such distinguished Americans as Marion B. Folsom, Oveta Culp Hobby, Clark Kerr, Wayne Morse, and Hubert Humphrey, deliberated for two years and delivered a far-reaching report that concluded that we should:

1. Leave to private initiative all the functions that citizens can perform privately.

2. Use the level of government closest to the community for all public functions it can handle.

3. Utilize cooperative intergovernmental arrangements where appropriate to attain economical performance and popular approval.

4. Reserve National action for residual participation where State and local governments are not fully adequate, and for the continuing responsibilities that only the National Government can undertake.

A major objective of the Reagan administration is to systematically transfer authority and responsibility for some social welfare programs to the states and localities along with the tax resources necessary to finance them. This is the thrust of the New Federalism.

The objective is not to eliminate the programs.

The objective is not to dump the programs on the states and localities, forcing them to raise taxes to whatever extent they can in order to continue programs.

The objective is to improve the operation of those social welfare programs, and to reduce their costs, by returning responsibility and resources to a level of government that is more appropriate for these programs. There is a good deal of sympathy for the view that Dan Lufkin expressed after serving for two years as Connecticut's first commissioner of environmental protection: "The more the administration of policies and programs is brought down to the state and local level, the better the people will be able to judge who is fair, who is honest, who is creative, and who is productive and efficient."

OPPOSITION TO A GUARANTEED INCOME

Sometimes what is not said or done is just as important as what is said and what is done. Before President Reagan took office there had been a string of administration efforts—both Republican and Democratic—to radically change the existing welfare system and to establish guaranteed income for all Americans. President Nixon proposed the Family Assistance Plan. President Ford explored the Income Supplementation Plan. And President Carter tried the Program for Better Jobs and Income.

All these programs were spawned by a small, largely liberal, intellectual elite, some of whom were well aware that what they were trying to foist on an unsuspecting public was a guaranteed income. Unfortunately for the programs, the public, which has a keen abhorrence of any guaranteed income scheme, sensed the true nature of these programs and our elected representatives thoroughly drubbed those proposals when they reached the Congress.

One of the more important social policy objectives of the Reagan administration is *to not propose any disguised guaranteed income programs*. This deliberate neglect of one of the hallowed canons of social welfare policy in this country for the last twenty years or so is, and I believe will continue to be, a major social policy objective of the Reagan administration.

The Conservative Program Is
a Women's Issue
Mimi Abramovitz

ABSTRACT

The Conservative program strikes deeply at the
institutions that support the economic independence
and security of women. This paper reviews social
welfare budget cuts, the relaxation of affirmative
action and workplace health and safety rules, and
the social issues agenda of the New Right for their
impact on women's economic, social and political
status. It describes how the Reagan Administration's
economic recovery program victimizes women, especially minority women. Not only is the "feminization"
of poverty intensified, but women are sent from the
paid labor market back to unpaid labor in the home,
aided and abetted by the social issues agenda of the
New Right. The Administration's domestic program is
analyzed in the context of its broader strategy for
coping with the current economic crisis. It is
viewed as part of a long range plan to redirect capital into the private sector by redistributing income
upwards and weakening the political power of women,
minorities and organized labor whose empowerment and
demands for an improved standard of living have become too costly for business and government.

The conservative program is a women's issue. The social welfare
cuts, the relaxation of workplace protections and rights and the
social issues agenda of the New Right, all strike deeply at institutions that support the economic independence and security of women.
They also reverse gains that women, along with minorities and organized labor have fought for and won since the 1930s.

The domestic features of the conservative program, to be discussed here, are best understood as part of a broader strategy designed to combat the deepening economic crisis facing the United
States since the mid-1970s. Like Nixon, Ford and Carter before him,
Reagan is trying to promote economic recovery by directing larger
amounts of capital into the private sector. Known as Reaganomics,
the plan includes: (1) tax and spending policies that redistribute
income upwards from the poor and middle classes (Pear, 1982c) and
(2) efforts to curb the political power of women, minorities and
organized labor, whose empowerment and demands for a better standard of living have become too costly for business and government
(Weisskopf, 1981; Campen, 1981).

Few today deny that Reaganomics benefits the "haves" at the
expense of the "have-nots." Less widely understood are the ways
in which the conservative program undermines the economic and social condition of women. This paper argues that women are primary,

women are

but not exclusive, victims of the Administration's strategy to cope with a seriously troubled economy. Part I examines how social welfare budget cuts promote an upward redistribution of income by lowering the standard of living of many women. Part II explores how the relaxation of anti-discrimination, affirmative action, workplace health and safety rights, along with the social issues agenda of the New Right weakens the political power of women, minorities and organized labor, and reinforces patriarchial values and institutions.

SOCIAL WELFARE BUDGET CUTS

Reaganomics includes both supply-side tax cuts and domestic budget cuts. Both redistribute income from the poor and working class to wealthy individuals and large corporations. The tax cuts intentionally favor the wealthy whom it is believed are most likely to save and invest. Social welfare cuts reduce the economic resources of the poor, in hopes that larger amounts of capital will flow into the private sector.

SW cuts → in hopes that amounts of $ will flow into private sector

Indeed, Wall Street and many politicians see domestic cuts as the best way to cut government costs, but also to limit the federal government as a competitor with private enterprise for investment capital believed to be scarce (Friedman, 1981; "Why Wall Street Worries," 1981; "Why Moneymen Worry," 1981). The cuts, it is argued, will reduce government spending and shrink the federal deficit. A smaller deficit in turn limits the need for federal borrowing to finance it, causing interest rates to fall and making more and cheaper money available for investment by private corporations. That is, less government spending will make room for more private economic activity and greater profits.

→ domestic cuts the best way to cut gout. costs

cuts ↓ reduce gout. spending ↓ shrink fed. deficit ↓ small deficit limits need for fed. borrowing ↓ int. rates ↓ ↑ $ avail. for invest. by private cap.

Less gout. spending (welfare prog) will make room for more private econ. activity and greater profits.

Whether or not social welfare cuts actually stimulate more private economic activity, they are lowering the standard of living of the poor. The Congressional Budget Office (CBO) reported recently that more than half of the 16 million families living near or below the poverty line will lose some income as a result of Reagan's budget cuts (Crittenden, 1981). When spending cuts are combined with supply-side tax cuts, the CBO predicts that by 1985, the net effect of the Administration's economic recovery plan will be to reduce the income of the poor while increasing that of the well-to-do (Pear, 1982c).

This upward redistribution of income helps lower women's standard of living by (a) furthering the "feminization" of poverty and (b) channeling women from the paid labor market back to unpaid labor in the home.

The Feminization of Poverty

Women are especially victimized by the upward redistribution of income achieved through domestic tax and spending cuts as they are already overrepresented among the poor and working poor. The 1980 Report of the National Advisory Council on Economic Opportunity observed that "the feminization of poverty has become one of the most compelling social facts of the decade." It predicted "that by the year 2000, the poverty population will be comprised solely of women and their children" (National Advisory Council on Economic Opportunity, 1981).

In 1980, women were twice as likely as men to be poor, and female-headed households were five times as likely as two-parent households to have incomes below the official poverty line of $8414 for a family of four. One fourth of white female-headed families and half of those headed by minority women fell below the poverty line (U.S. Bureau of the Census, 1980c: 27).

Older women are the fastest growing poverty group in the country. While only 59 percent of the population over 65 is female, 72 percent of the elderly poor are women. The poverty rate for women over 65 is 60 percent higher than that for men of the same age (U.S. Bureau of the Census, 1979, 1980b).

Even among the 51.1 percent of women over 16 who work, the risk of poverty is high. The 1981 median income of women ($11,591) employed full-time and year-round was 60 percent that of men ($19,173) (U.S. Bureau of Census, 1980c: 19-20). Despite equal opportunity laws, this gap has widened since 1965 when women earned 65 cents for every dollar earned by men (NASW, 1980). Moreover, fully-employed women with one-to-three years of college earn less, on the average, than men who have not graduated from elementary school (U.S. Women's Bureau, 1980). Throughout the post-war period unemployment among women of all races has exceeded that of men. It is greater for minority women, who are twice as likely as white women to be jobless (U.S. Department of Labor, 1980a: 67-80).

Given this "feminization" of poverty, it is not surprising that the majority of social welfare recipients are women. In recent years, 80 percent of Aid to Families with Dependent Children (U.S. Department of Health and Human Services, 1980a: 1), 70 percent of Food Stamp (U.S. Department of Agriculture, 1980: 16), 66 percent of Supplemental Security Income (U.S. Bureau of Census, 1980d: 358), Social Security (U.S. Department of Health and Human Services, 1980b: 127-128), Medicaid (U.S. Bureau of Census, 1980a: 7), and Public Housing (U.S. Bureau of Census, 1980a: 5), 45 percent of CETA (Title VI) (U.S. Department of Labor, 1980b: 174) and 35 percent of Unemployment Compensation (U.S. Department of Labor, 1979b: 56) recipients were women.

All of these programs, on which millions of women rely for minimum levels of income of food, shelter, clothing, jobs, and health care, were cut sharply in Reagan's fiscal 1982 budget and are likely to be cut further in 1983.

Aid to Families with Dependent Children (AFDC) originated in 1935 to help maintain and strengthen family life. By 1981 this $11 billion program provided cash benefits to 3.5 million families, more than 80 percent of whom were female-headed. Although benefits vary widely by state, the average AFDC family receives $271 a month or $3,253 a year (U.S. Bureau of the Census, 1980d: 354).

The fiscal 1982 budget lowered AFDC expenditures by $1.2 billion or 11 percent (Congressional Quarterly, Inc., 1981c). Since entitle-
ments .... reduced by lowering appropriations,
.... tightening eligibility requirements,
.... ing work incentives and otherwise re-
.... program. As a result, nearly 700,000
.... their benefits or have them reduced
.... fiscal 1983 proposals to convert AFDC
.... grant and/or further lower its support
.... shrink even more.

.... ogram was enacted in 1964 to feed the
.... up surplus agriculture products. In
.... se of food by 22.5 million low-income
.... es (Pear, 1981a; Roberts, 1981). Again,
.... ectly, program rules were changed to cut
.... lion Food Stamp program in 1982. Tighter
.... ial of aid to boarding house residents
.... on people off the program (Congressional
.... rly all the remaining recipients had
.... lans to defederalize food stamps succeed,
.... be expected (Raines, 1982).
.... and other food programs further assaulted
.... ree million children and 400 hundred
.... hool lunch program after $1.4 billion in
.... ll Cutting School Lunch Corners," 1981).
.... the $1 billion Supplemental Program for
Women, Infants and Children (WIC) was capped (Congressional Quarterly, Inc., 1981c).

Medicaid enacted in 1965 to finance the purchase of medical services by the poor and working poor served 18.3 million people and cost of $18.5 billion in 1981. The fiscal 1982 budget reduced Medicaid payments to the states by $1 billion and another $2.1 billion cut was requested for 1983 (Congressional Quarterly, Inc., 1981e). Women and children will be especially hard hit. Although two-thirds of Medicaid recipients are women and 36 percent of households enrolled in the program are female-headed, 65 percent of all Medicaid payments go to a minority of elderly recipients in nursing homes and hospitals (U.S. Bureau of Census, 1980a: 7; Weinraub, 1981b). The states are less likely to reduce aid to this minority of program recipients, leaving women and children to take the brunt of the cuts.

Support for other health care programs also fell when the Administration converted many of them into state administered block grants and cut them by 25 percent across the board. Fiscal 1983 budget proposals intensify this trend (Raines, 1982). Ironically, health care cuts, like many others may cost the federal government more than it saves. A 1978-1979 Harvard study found that for each $1 spent on prenatal care, $3 was saved in hospital costs because fewer babies were born at low weights (Burros, 1981). More recently the New York City Task Force on Adolescent Pregnancy reported that "for every dollar spent on Family Planning, three are saved from other human service programs" (Brozan, 1981).

Until the Reagan cuts made $11.6 billion fewer federal dollars available for public housing and subsidized rents, these programs served 2.4 million families, two-thirds of whom were female-headed (U.S. Bureau of Census, 1980a: 15). Fiscal 1982 cuts sharply limited the construction of new public housing units, reduced Section 8 low-rent subsidies, restricted eligibility for public housing and raised rents from 25 percent to 30 percent of family income (Congressional Quarterly, Inc., 1981b).

Proposals for 1983 redirect federal housing aid from the construction of low-income housing units to "vouchers" which aid individuals to secure shelter on the open market ("Panel Urges Shift in Housing Policy," 1981; Pear, 1982d). Critics fear that families who qualify for vouchers because of their low income, may have no place to use them due to discrimination against poor, minority and female-headed families, housing shortages and/or high rents (Pear, 1982d).

Elderly women, who are 72 percent of the aged poor, face cuts in Supplemental Security Income (SSI), Social Security and Medicare benefits, as well as a loss of Food Stamps. Although the Administration failed to eliminate the $122 minimum Social Security payment for current recipients, it succeeded for those eligible after January 1982. About 75 percent of those affected are women, almost 90 percent if survivors and dependents are included (Miller, 1981). The Administration suggests they apply for SSI, a public assistance program for the aged, blind and disabled poor whose already low monthly benefits were also cut (Congressional Quarterly, Inc., 1981d). But analysts predict that many will not (Miller, 1981).

The Administration also wants to lower retirement benefits for 1.4 million Social Security early retirees, the majority of whom are women (Weaver, 1981; Miller 1981). Although temporarily postponed, these and other changes in the Social Security program are under review by a task force appointed to investigate the solvency of the Social Security Trust Fund.

Medicare cuts increase the cost and reduce the availability of health care services to the aged by limiting federal reimbursement for both hospital and physician services (Congressional Quarterly, Inc., 1981d). Backburner plans exist to replace Medicare with a voucher to be used for the purchase of private health insurance or enrollment in a Health Maintenance Organization (HMO). Since vouchers may not cover all HMO costs, this promises to further restrict the ability of the aged to secure necessary health care services (Demkovich 1982).

The fiscal 1982 and 1983 budget cuts cannot be taken lightly, even though the Administration's political support seems to be waning. Indeed, the conservative legacy of Reaganomics may outlast Reagan's presidency. From the outset, the Administration made its antipathy to entitlement programs clear. In the Spring of 1981, David M. Stockman, Director of the Office of Management and Budget stated:

> The idea that has been established over the last ten years, that almost every service that someone might need in life ought to be provided and financed by the government as a matter of rights is wrong. We challenge that. We reject that notion (Rosenbaum, 1981b).

Since then tax revenues have been lowered and entitlement programs restructured in unprecedented ways and amounts, leaving domestic programs smaller and more vulnerable. Eligibility restrictions now limit social programs to the poorest of the poor, while lowered benefit levels increase both program and recipient stigma. Both smaller and weaker constituencies and heightened stigma make social welfare programs more difficult to defend against future cuts. So does the transfer of federal responsibility for social welfare to the states which have historically been unresponsive to the needs of minorities and the poor and whose currently ailing treasuries leave little room for change (Herbers, 1981). If these and other plans succeed in undermining the concept of entitlement, social welfare programs will be even more vulnerable to future attacks.

Moreover, as was noted above, many social welfare cuts were made by enacting new laws rather than merely reducing program funds. Since cuts made by lowered appropriations can be restored more easily than those achieved through statutory change, the recent cuts are more likely to persist. The combined effect of increased vulnerability to future cuts and statutory change suggests that the impact of Reaganomics may be difficult to reverse (Abramovitz and Hopkins, 1982).

Channeling Women From Paid Labor Back to Unpaid Labor in the Home

The social welfare cuts not only further the "feminization" of poverty but they encourage women to leave paid work for unpaid labor in the home. Although the Administration holds that economic recovery requires an increased work effort by all, the call seems to be aimed primarily at men. Many features of the conservative program actually discourage paid employment among the 44 million working women who are nearly 50 percent of today's labor force (U.S. Department of Labor, 1980a: 6, 9).

Regulating women's labor force participation to solve other problems is not new. Indeed, women frequently have been called upon to work and sent back home on an as needed basis (Grossman, 1981). It is well known that during World War II, when more women were needed to work in the defense plants, the federal government subsidized day care centers and Rosie the Riveter became a wartime heroine. Immediately after the War, when the returning soldier needed work, the nurseries were closed and Rosie the Riveter was displaced by the "feminine mystique."

Sharp economic fluctuations also create strong pressures for and against women's employment. This helps explain the rapid growth of the female labor force in the generally prosperous years following World War II. The simultaneous expansion of social programs, fast food chains, laundramats and other commercial domestic services employed many women and helped to free others for paid labor outside the home (Rothchild, 1981).

But in periods of economic difficulty when the economy cannot use all available workers or when cheap and available (i.e., unemployed) labor helps keep wages from rising, forces often combine to channel women back into the home. Back in the home they raise children, keep employed husbands ready for work and stabilize the family system (Sokoloff, 1974: 14-15). Moreover, their child care, housekeeping, food preparation, health care, teaching, counseling and other services, previously paid for by the government or private enterprise, command no wage at all. This unpaid labor of women lessens the charge upon industry for male wages and lowers the cost to government of providing comparable services (Gardiner, 1978). The savings are not inconsequential. The market value of women's domestic labor is estimated at one-quarter of the GNP (Kreps, 1971: 67-69) or one-half of the income of her employed spouse (Kreps and Clark, 1975: 72).

The Administration's economic recovery program discourages women's paid employment through policies that (a) increase unemployment rates of all workers, especially those in the public sector, (b) weaken work incentives contained in income maintenance programs, and (c) intensify women's household responsibilities by shrinking social services that free them for paid work outside the home.

Greater Unemployment. Reaganomics includes expansionary supply-side tax cuts but also restrictive monetary policies which seek to squeeze inflation out of the economy by inducing a recession. Because women are not employed in industries most sensitive to swings in the business cycle, their unemployment rates do not increase as fast as those of men during recessions. But Department of Labor employment data (payroll and household surveys) suggest that during recessions women employed in manufacturing industries [2] and blue collar occupations, lose their jobs disproportionately, the 1980 recession excepted. Minorities and youth are similarly vulnerable in these recession-sensitive industries (Bowers, 1981).

The attack on big government also increases female unemployment as large numbers of women have found work in the public sector since the early 1960s (U.S. Bureau of Census, 1980d: 279, 320). Although the final figures on public sector layoffs are far from known, in the fall of 1981 the National Association of Social Workers reported that 7,000 Health and Human Service workers and 1,000 from the Community Services Administration were scheduled to lose their jobs. So were thousands of state and local government employees. In Massachusetts, for example, 40-60 percent of the school social workers, 20 percent of those in the Department of Public Health and many employed by private agencies dependent on state contracts have already been laid off (NASW, 1981).

Women lost still other jobs when 300,000 CETA public service slots were eliminated. Low income women trying to move from welfare into the labor force held close to 45 percent of these jobs (U.S. Department of Labor, 1979a: 42; 1980b: 177). CETA cuts also mean fewer services for women as CETA workers staffed many rape crisis centers, battered women's shelters, day care and senior citizen programs.

The Administration's argument that public sector cuts release employees for work in the more productive private sector is belied by mounting unemployment rates, but also business's response to the cuts. Early on, The Wall Street Journal reported that despite newspaper ads exhorting New Jersey's businessmen to hire 16,000 displaced CETA workers, "only 18 employers offered a mere 20 job leads." The private sector, says the business press, "has been slow to come to the rescue" (Lubin, 1981).

Weakened Work Incentives. Ironically, the conservative program also discourages women's employment by relaxing work incentives built into income maintenance programs. Until now, AFDC mothers who worked kept the first $30 of earned income and one-third of the remainder. Moreover, welfare agencies deducted itemized work and child care expenses before the AFDC benefit was calculated. To save dollars, the fiscal 1982 budget limited the $30 and one-third formula to the first four months of work and replaced itemized work and child care expenses with a flat $75 deduction. As a result, many employed AFDC mothers

are left little better off than those who do not work (Rosenbaum,
1981a). Proposals for 1983 worsen this disincentive to work. The University of Chicago reported that while "last year's changes reduced the
income differential between working and non-working welfare recipients,"
the proposed 1983 changes "would make it clearly more profitable for
most poor people to rely entirely on welfare and food stamps than to
work at the low wage jobs available to them" (Pear, 1982b). Likewise,
work incentives are threatened in the 1983 Food Stamp program proposals
(Pear, 1982a).

While discouraging paid employment, AFDC regulations now permit
states to re-introduce "workfare." Workfare requires welfare recipients
aged 15-65 (except mothers of young children and full-time students) to
"work-off" their benefits without additional pay. Clients who refuse
assigned jobs can be denied benefits. Workfare is neither new nor known
to be effective. Not only are many AFDC clients unsuitable workfare
candidates,[3] but both clients and workers have resisted the coercion
involved ("Workfare and the Work Ethic," 1981).

More Household Responsibilities. Whether they work or not, women
carry the primary responsibility for children and housework. The time
involved is enormous. Although the gap has declined somewhat, it is
estimated that women spend over 25 hours a week doing unpaid domestic
labor compared to 10 hours for employed men (Stafford, 1980). Social
service programs reduce the household burdens of women, enabling them
to combine work and family tasks more easily. Thus, today's cutbacks
also effectively discourage women's employment.

Day care services are clearly most critical. Over 8 million children under age 6, or 45 percent of all preschoolers had a working mother
in 1981. Fifty percent of single mothers of children under age 6 were
employed (Grossman, 1982). Even though day care is currently available
to only a minority of these women, the Administration did not spare child
care centers (Twentieth Century Fund, 1975; U.S. Bureau of Census, 1980:
360, 403). The 25 percent cut in Title XX funds will shrink day care
centers by one-third, leaving 700,000 current users with no place to go.
Other children will be withdrawn due to higher fees and/or curtailed
services. The elimination of CETA jobs, 25 percent of which were in day
care centers, also deprives an estimated one million working mothers
and their children of needed services (Pear, 1981a; Bedell, 1981a).
Meanwhile, the maximum $75 child care deduction for employed AFDC
mothers falls far below day care costs, estimated by the government
to be $30 per child per week (Pear, 1981a; Bedell, 1981a).

The work disincentive is clear. A New Jersey mother of three
had planned to take a full time job as a sales clerk in a women's
department store, but had to forgo it when her neighborhood day care
center closed. "The closing of the center," she told the New York
Times, "will just make me stay home and collect welfare" (Pear,
1981b).

Food program cuts will make it more difficult for low-income
mothers to provide nutritional family meals. Shopping for a nutritional diet on a poverty income already requires ingenuity beyond
the capabilities of a skilled dietician. Fewer food stamp dollars,
more expensive school lunches, lowered WIC funding can only make it
more difficult. The daily per capita intake of key nutrients by the
poor, already below that of the non-poor, will fall (U.S. Bureau of
the Census, 1980d: 132). The deferred social costs of poor nutrition will show up in poor school performance, more illness and greater
health care expenses years from now. More immediately, these problems
will intensify the work women must do in the home, making employment
more difficult to seek or sustain.

Less obvious is the likelihood that food program cuts will adversely affect local economies and increase the time and cost that
daily shopping takes. Food Stamp purchases now account for 35 percent
of the food sold in the poorest neighborhoods, reports John Loeb,
chairperson of Hillmans, a Chicago supermarket chain. Loeb predicts
that food stamp cutbacks will force many small neighborhood groceries

to close (Rosenbaum, 1981b). With fewer neighborhood stores to shop at, shopping will take longer and/or travel and child care costs will be added to the already high cost of food. A New York Times reporter recently accompanied a welfare mother through a typical day. She observed that:

> The 40 year old mother scoured advertisements for the coupons she clips, picked through bins of damaged goods at bargain stores for clothing for her children and walked more than a mile for a bargain on detergent (Rule, 1982).

Mothers of the millions of children denied school lunches will also have to spend more time and money preparing lunch and assuring nutrition.[4]

Medicare and Medicaid cuts increase the cost of and decrease access to medical services (Pear, 1981a, Hildredth, 1981). Since mothers and wives traditionally care for family members who become ill and arrange for medical care, these cuts too will intensify women's household responsibilities. This is compatible with the Administration's philosophy. Prior to becoming Secretary of Health and Human Services, Richard Schweiker stated that, "Medicare could save money if more people were looked after at home" (Rothchild, 1981).

Similarly, public housing cutbacks which reduce the stock of low-income housing and raise rents promise to increase women's work in the home. Affordable housing for the poor already is scarce, since each year one million low-income units disappear due to rent inflation, condominium conversions and the abandonment of older buildings (Congressional Budget Office, 1981). A smaller housing stock, discrimination against poor, minority and female-headed households (Pear, 1982d), and the growing unwillingness of many landlords to rent to families with children (Institute for Social Research, 1980), will make finding a suitable place more burdensome. In many families, women will absorb this time-consuming task along with that of managing a household budget shrunken by newly raised rent [5] and caring for family members whose physical and emotional health may suffer due to increased dangers and health hazards that typically accompany poor housing.

Finally, reduced community health and mental health services, citizen centers and social service programs used by families under stress can only increase women's "emotional work." As stress among women themselves grows, the social service cuts leave them with few or no places to go for relief.

RELAXING GOVERNMENT PROTECTIONS

If channeling women back into the home undermines their economic security and challenges their economic independence, the Administration's systematic relaxation of civil rights, affirmative action and workplace health and safety regulations risks lowering women's standard of living and eliminating needed protections against the dangers and inequities of living and working in a capitalist economy. This "de-regulation" of the workplace, along with the domestic budget cuts, promises to reverse many political and economic gains fought for and won by organized labor, civil rights organizations and women's liberation groups since the 1930s.

Social welfare benefits and government protections strengthen the political power of women, minorities and organized labor. They provide both a minimum level of economic security and a sense of entitlement. Perhaps more significantly the fight for these benefits and protections, over the years, gave rise to trade unions, civil rights groups and women's liberation organizations. These groups pressed for a larger share of available resources and politicized the process of income distribution through collective bargaining and government and tax and spending programs (Weisskopf, 1981).

While the economy grew and prospered, it was not difficult to accommodate the claims of all classes. Moreover, meeting them helped assure the social peace. But since the economic crisis surfaced in the mid-1970s, demands for a rising standard of living by empowered groups have become too costly for both business and government to meet. To reduce corporate costs and limit resistance to the entire conservative program, social welfare programs and government regulations are under attack; and the political strength of women, minorities and organized labor is being curbed (Weisskopf, 1981). The weakening of civil rights, affirmative action and workplace health and safety laws is a step in this direction.

Among the first to go were provisions of Executive Order 11246 which outlaws discrimination by employers receiving federal contracts and requires approval of affirmative action plans prior to receipt of federal funds. The Office of Federal Contract Compliance (OFCCP), which previously covered companies with 50 or more employees and contracts of $50,000 or more, now exempts firms with fewer than 250 employees and contracts of less than one million dollars from these affirmative action standards. Nearly 4,000 of 17,000 companies doing business with the federal government will no longer have to report on women and minorities in their work force or show plans for corrective action if they are underrepresented. Larger contractors must still affirm they are equal opportunity employers, but less often and in abbreviated form (Shribman, 1981; Hunter, 1981; Congressional Quarterly, Inc., 1981f). In addition, the budget of the OFCCP was cut by 20 percent further limiting the agency's ability to enforce its rules (Stasz, 1982).

These and other changes substitute voluntary compliance for government enforcement of anti-discrimination policies and reduce fears of losing a federal contract or facing a law suit among employers who discriminate. The exemption of government contractors from affirmative action rules, contends Karen Nussbaum, director of Working Women, a national organization of office workers, "will exempt hundreds of thousands of employers from compliance, lessen hiring and promotional standards and cut back protections against sex discrimination" (Stasz 1981).

Redress for victims of sex and race discrimination will be more difficult now that the budget of the Equal Employment Opprotunity Commission (EEOC) has been cut by 12 percent (Stasz, 1981). Plans also exist to freeze the filing of new lawsuits and the issuance of new guidelines; to remove restrictions on employer use of pre-employment and biographical histories; and to require complainants to present proof of their employers intent to discriminate (Affirmative Action Coordinating Center, 1981). If approved, such changes will effectively nullify a host of laws passed to ensure equality of employment in the U.S.

Workplace rights are also jeopardized by efforts to weaken both the standards and the enforcement power of the Occupational Safety and Health Administration (OSHA). While not well enforced, OSHA regulations did establish a legal right to a safe and healthy work environment and stimulated unionization around the nation ("Deregulating Workers Health," 1981). Occupational health hazards are commonly associated only with "mens" work. But many women are employed in industries with higher than average injury rates and work day losses. Almost two million women work in the fifty industries where a substantial number of hazardous substances are commonly used ("Facts About Women Workers," 1979). Moreover accidents, infections, chemical poisoning, and physical dangers are common in the hospitals, offices and laboratories where women traditionally are employed (Stillman, 1977).

Nonetheless, Secretary of Labor Donovan, hopes to exempt thousands of manufacturing firms from routine safety inspections, concentrating only on those with above average injury rates. Some of the most effective enforcement procedures, such as surprise visits and fines for hazards, will be limited (Bedell, 1981b).

The Administration's outright assault on these government protections makes more sense when it is remembered that women, minorities and organized labor are being asked to bear the brunt of the economic recovery programs. If production costs of business are to be lowered by cutting the standard of living of workers, minorities and women, their resistance to cutbacks must be forestalled and delegitimized. Current policies are having this effect. High rates of unemployment and fewer social benefits to rely on make these groups more vulnerable. Joblessness becomes a more effective mechanism of employer control of labor and weakens the bargaining power of unions as the recent contract negotiations in steel, rubber, automobile, airlines, printing and trucking industries demonstrate (Raskin, 1982).

Civil rights and women's groups have also been placed on the defensive leaving them less able to protect their constituencies. Rather than continuing to identify and combat institutional sexism and patriarchial practices in new arenas, the National Organization of Women, the National Abortion Rights Action League, and other women's organizations must devote scarce resources just to protect previously won rights. They are fighting to enact the ERA and against the loss of Medicaid abortions, the constitutional amendment banning all abortions, erosion of gay and lesbian rights and the Family Protection Act. Since these issues constitute the core of the social issues agenda of the New Right, its role in supporting Reaganomics, both practically and ideologically, needs to be understood.

PROMOTING PATRIARCHY: THE AGENDA OF THE NEW RIGHT

The New Right's program which favors economic retrenchment and military build-up supports the Administration's economic recovery policies that redistribute income upwards and redirect capital into the private sector. It's social issues agenda, yet to receive full attention by Reagan, also reinforces the Administration's assault on the rights of women, minorities and labor. Not only does the New Right encourage domestic cutbacks, but it legitimizes them by arguing that "big government" and the gains women have made are threatening to the stability of American family.

The social issues agenda of the New Right is embodied in the Human Life Amendment (HLA) and in the Family Protection Act (FPA). The Human Life Amendment seeks to reverse the 1973 Supreme Court decision legalizing abortion in the early months of pregnancy. It states that "the paramount right to life is vested in each human being from the moment of fertilization without regard to age, health, or condition of dependency." If it succeeds, abortion will be murder in the eyes of the law and "women's bodies, health, work and even lives," would be subordinated to "fetal survival" (Copelan, 1981). Not only could doctors and hospitals refuse to do abortions, but many forms of contraception such as the IUD and diagnostic procedures such as amniocentesis could become illegal.

The FPA, a melange of provisions intended to "protect" the American family was first introduced into the Senate in 1979 by Paul Laxalt, a leader of the Moral Majority and twice chair of the Reagan for President Committee. The FPA was re-introduced to Congress in 1981 by Senator Roger Jepsen (R-Iowa) who stated the act "marks another major step in the vital process of strengthening the traditional family structure in America and minimizing the harmful Federal intrusion in our nation's churches, schools and families" (U.S. Congress, 1981, S6344).

For the New Right, the traditional two-parent family is "the bedrock upon which our whole nation as well as our society is based" (U.S. Congress, 1979: S13579). Not surprisingly, it sees the rise of female-headed families, teenage sex, unmarried couples, open homosexuality and greater employment and autonomy among women as problematic. Seeking political support from sectors of the white

middle class who may feel that these changes threaten their traditional values, the New Right claims that the family is "breaking down"
rather than restructuring itself in response to changing economic
conditions. According to Congressman McKay from Utah, the family as
a societal "keystone" has been slipping.

> ...and America has been reaping the results of the
> slippage. Predictably aimless children raised in
> fragmented homes--often become aimless adults.
> Many become social deficits, costing society vast
> sums of money, time and talent spent on programs
> designed to clean up the mess that failed homes
> left behind (U.S. Congress, 1980: H4527).

The FPA strives to strengthen the American family in various
ways. All involve reducing government involvement in family life.
One way the FPA hopes to strengthen the family is to increase parental authority. To this end the Act, (a) bans federal funds for
any program or organization that gives contraceptive devices or
abortion services to any unmarried minor, unless the parent or
guardian is notified; (b) permits parental review of textbooks
prior to their classroom use, (c) cedes federal responsibility
for monitoring child abuse and wife abuse to the states and (d) re-
defines child abuse to exclude corporal punishment applied by a parent or someone authorized by the parent to perform this function
(U.S. Congress, 1981, S6324-S6344). By strengthening parental authority over children and weakening child abuse and wife abuse laws,
the FPA creates support for a more authoritarian, male dominated
household.

The New Right also hopes that less government intrusion in
family life will strengthen it by promoting family cohesion. Ex-
plaining the need for the FPA, Senator Laxalt stated, "it is becoming increasingly apparent that the federal government itself, although ostensibly aiming at helping the family, is often working
counter to its best interests" (U.S. Congress, 1979: S13549).
Government involvement in family life is "frequently disruptive,"
Laxalt argued, citing that federal health and welfare programs reduce interaction between elderly parents and children and encourage
placement of aging relatives in nursing homes away from their families. Likewise, federal aid to schools has removed parents from
their children's learning process.

Therefore, the FPA replaces reliance on government programs
with reliance on one's own family or the market. For example, it
offers a $250 tax credit for families who care for aging relatives
at home instead of placing them in a nursing home and a $1,500 tax
deduction for establishing a retirement fund for a non-salaried
spouse, an incentive for women to remain in the home. In these
ways Senator Laxalt suggests that the FPA encourages family members,

> ....to decide crucial issues for themselves instead
> of leaving them to government. Parents will be en-
> couraged to stay with their children, to actively
> participate in their children's educational, moral
> and religious upbringing. Children will be encour-
> aged to care for their aged parents. All generations
> will be encouraged to live together and share living
> experiences, enriching the lives of each member (U.S.
> Congress, 1979: S13550).

These means of strengthening the family assume that and/or provide incentives for women to be in the home. Who else will supervise children's educational, moral and religious upbringing and care
for aging parents. Jepsen confirmed this expectation when he told
Congress that,

> ...with the eroding away of the values of the man-wife,
> the mother-father, sister-brother relationship, the
> family as a basic unit, there is also the eroding away

of the value and the beauty of women being a mother and homemaker (U.S. Congress, 1981: S6328).

Still another way the FPA seeks to support the traditional family is to restrict information about other ways of living. It is disturbed by new broader definitions of the family when they extend its meaning "to include anyone and anything from group marriage to homosexual and lesbian couples who want to adopt children" (U.S. Congress, 1981: S6327). The Act bans federal funding for educational materials that "denigrate, diminish or deny role differences between the sexes;" and to individuals or programs that "present male or female homosexuality as an acceptable life style." However, schools may "limit or prohibit the intermingling of the sexes in any sport or other school related activity" (U.S. Congress, 1981: S6326). The FPA also denies federal funds to Legal Aid Programs that litigate cases dealing with divorce, gay or lesbian rights, abortion and school segregation. (Not discussed here are other ways in which the FPA attacks the civil rights of minorities). Combined with the Human Life Amendment and the New Right's general opposition to social welfare programs, the FPA makes it clear that the New Right not only wants women back in the home, but defines the family in traditional patriarchial terms --comprised of a dominant male breadwinner and a passive female wife and mother. As Laxalt says, the FPA will cause a "rebirth of the American family."

> With just a little help--just removing the governmental barriers and allowing the traditional family roles to reassert themselves--I am convinced that we will see a renaissance of the family and the resultant gains for all Americans (U.S. Congress, 1979: S13550).

The rationale for the FPA, including its patriarchial underpinnings has been widely publicized in Wealth and Poverty (1981) written by George Gilder, New Right and supply-side theorist. In addition to arguing that biological differences between the sexes condition social role behavior (Gilder, 1981: 89, 164-165) Gilder, blames the gains women have made for the problems faced by American families today.

For example, Gilder argues that because "men make the sacrifices necessary to reach the higher reaches in the American economy chiefly to support the wives and families," when "the wives earn more, the men feel a decline of urgency in their work and a loss of male nerve and drive" (Gilder, 1981: 180). Employment by women is also responsible for rising divorce rates and other social problems. When women accept full-time work, Gilder maintains,

> ...both husbands, and wives suffer new strains of pure fatigue together with tension over the change in formerly settled sex roles. These strains are not an illusion as is attested by an increasing body of census statistics that show a sharply rising rate of divorce and separation after wives submit to full time work responsiblity (Gilder, 1981: 17).
> (emphasis added)

When marriage fails, Gilder continues, "the man often returns to the more primitive rhythms of singleness. On the average, his income drops by one-third and he shows a far higher propensity for drink, drugs and crime" (Gilder, 1981: 90). Since women's employment causes divorce, it implicitly is responsible for this male degeneration.

Similar consequences obtain when women rely on social welfare benefits. This Gilder asserts, "destroys the father's key role and authority." Unable to feel "manly in his own home" he "turns to the street for male affirmation." In the street men "find an atmosphere that does not make the larger and deeper claims of familial and sexual love which are hard for men to meet without a sense of male dominance (Gilder, 1981: 164). Nothing, Gilder observes, is so destructive to male confidence, authority, sexual

potency, respect from his family and motivation to work than "the
growing imperious recognition that when all is said and done his
wife and children can do better without him." The man has the

> ....gradually sinking feeling that his role as
> provider, the definitive male activity from the
> primal days of the hunt through the industrial
> revolution and on into modern life has been large-
> ly seized from him; he has been cuckholded by the
> compassionate state (Gilder, 1981: 140).
> (emphasis added)

The implication of both these views and the provisions of the
Family Protection Act is that if women would just return to their
traditional roles in the family, sacrifice essential social services
and newly won rights, stop working, stop demanding control over their
bodies and stop pursuing sexual and sex-role freedom, their families
would be happy, would restabilize and male productivity would not decline. Indeed, women are being asked to bear responsibility for the
economic crisis that neither business nor government can resolve, by
"taking up the slack" through acceptance of stereotyped sex roles and
economic dependency. By encouraging the belief that family problems
and the current economic crisis are the fault of individuals, the New
Right "blames the victim." In so doing, it diverts attention from the
underlying causes of the problems faced by each and provides an ideological rationale for the Administration's economic recovery program.

                          CONCLUSION

The Conservative program is consistently anti-women. It undermines their economic independence and security, abolishes painfully
won rights and protections, and subscribes to the view that a woman's
place is in the home. This is not the first time that sexism (the
unequal treatment of people on the basis of sex) and patriarchy (the
acceptance of male supremacy) have contributed to a definition of
women's labor as marginal to the economy. 6 Both posit differences
between the sexes that inevitably determine the roles and behaviors
of each. Together they define women as inferior, subordinate and dependent. These "biology-as-destiny" arguments condone violence
against women, permit women to be relegated to accessory and dependent roles in the family and the economy and to be denied full and
equal rights in society. They encourage the channeling of women out
of the labor market into the home and/or into low-paid, low status
often part-time "women's" jobs.

Although consistently anti-women, the Conservative program contains numerous contradictions. If implemented as planned, it cannot
fulfill its own stated objectives. The budget cuts, meant to reduce
the federal deficit, promise increased federal costs as cuts in one
area produce new needs and expenditures elsewhere. Not only is the
government-induced recession raising unemployment compensation and
welfare costs, but public sector cutbacks are making more women eligible for welfare and other income maintenance programs. Meanwhile,
massive military expenditures and supply-side tax cuts deflect funds
needed to offset the mounting federal deficit.

Likewise, the Administration's program for protecting the
family actually threatens its viability. Cuts in income maintenance,
food, health, family planning, housing and social service programs
can only generate greater economic pressures, more child care responsibilities, increased care for the aged and an intensification of
women's household management tasks. Unwanted pregnancies, child and
wife abuse and certainly more family stress can be predicted. In
today's economy, weakened social welfare programs, subject many
American families to greater economic distress and possible dissolution (National Advisory Council on Economic Opportunity, 1981: 38).

Similarly the Administration's belief that an increased work effort by all is needed to stimulate production is contradicted by its programs which discourage women's employment. A shrunken public sector, the elimination of CETA jobs, and weakened affirmative action programs will remove literally thousands of women from the labor force and prevent others from entering it. Loss of day care centers, a smaller AFDC child care allowance and lowered benefits for employed AFDC mothers are causing many welfare mothers to stop working. Likewise, income maintenance and social service cuts, by requiring women to spend more time caring for family members and managing their households, will prevent them from looking for or sustaining full-time work. At home, women will once again provide, without pay, services similar to those they previously delivered as government and private sector employees.

Loss of workplace safety and anti-discrimination protections can only lower women's employment opportunities and status. Those who remain at work, will be promoted less often, occupy more part-time jobs and continue to be concentrated in low-paid, low-status, dead-end women's occupations.

These contradictions "make sense" once it is recognized that the domestic budget cuts and the regulation of women's labor force participation is part of a broader plan. To cope with the current economic crisis, the Administration is: (a) directing larger amounts of capital into the private sector through tax and spending policies that redistribute income upward; and (b) trying to curb the political strength of women, minorities and labor to restrict them from increasing their claims upon social resources and/or resisting policies that undermine their standard of living.

The social issues agenda of the New Right, reinforces the Administration's social welfare strategy pragmatically. More importantly, it justifies it ideologically. By arguing that a woman's place is in the home, and blaming women for the problems faced by both the family and the economy, it diverts attention away from the underlying causes of each. In so doing, the conservative program fails to recognize that the re-emergence of feminism in the late sixties was a consequence not a cause of economic change and that as a result, feminism cannot be made to disappear.

To the extent that the Administration's program is implemented, many women, minorities and workers will suffer badly. Perhaps they will also resist. Signs of both are appearing as more people fall below the poverty line, and as the militance of organized labor, civil rights organizations and women's liberation groups re-surfaces. The time may be right for these traditionally isolated groups to submerge their special interests and join forces against the conservative assault which jeopardizes them all. Should this occur, it may be the conservative program's most serious contradiction of all.

1. At the time of this writing, the Fiscal 1983 budget was stalled in Congress.
2. In 1979, 30.6 percent of all workers in manufacturing were female (U.S. Department of Labor, 1980a: 151, 159).
3. In 1977, for example, 50 percent of AFDC clients in the nation were at home as full-time homemakers or were incapacitated. Of the 27 percent already in the labor force, 15 percent were employed, 11 percent were actively seeking work and one percent was awaiting recall from layoffs (U.S. Department of Health and Human Services, 1980a: 2).
4. The Department of Agriculture reports that needy children rely on school lunch programs to supply one-third to one-half of their basic nutrients compared to one-quarter for children of the middle class (Brody, 1981).

5. The New York City welfare mother described earlier, pays $110 of her $370 AFDC check for rent in public housing, leaving her $2.55 in cash plus $1.28 in food stamps a day for each member of her family of three (Rule, 1981).

6. Likewise, the labor force participation of minorities is marginalized using racial and/or ethnic distinctions.

REFERENCES

1. Abramovitz, Mimi and Hopkins, Tom, "Reaganomics and the Welfare State, "Journal of Sociology and Social Welfare 1982 (forthcoming)

2. Affirmative Action Coordinating Center, AACC News, Vol. 2 (4), April/May 1981, p. 12.

3. Bedell, Ben, "Reagan Budget Hides Attack on Families," The Guardian, July 17, 1981, p. 7. (a)

4. _____, "Reagan's Labor Policy," The Guardian, September 2, 1981, p. 2. (b)

5. Bowers, Norman, "Have Employment Patterns in Recession Changed," Monthly Labor Review, February 1981, Vol. 104 (2), pp. 15-28.

6. Brody, Jane E., "School Food: New Intent," New York Times, 9/14/81.

7. Brozan, Nadine, "Cuts in Aid to Young Mothers Deplored," New York Times, October 14, 1981.

8. Burros, Marian, "Feeding Program Reported at Risk," New York Times, September 23, 1981.

9. Campen, Jim, "Economic Crisis and Conservative Economic Policies: U.S. Capitalism in the 1980's," Radical America, September 1981, Vol. 15 (1,2), pp. 33-54.

10. Cole, Nancy, and Stacey, Sue, "Blueprint for a Moral America?" Guild Notes, Vol. X, #5, September/October 1981, p. 7.

11. Congressional Budget Office, The Tax Treatment of Home Ownership: Issues and Options, September 1981, p. xiii.

12. Congressional Quarterly, Inc., "Child Nutrition Programs Cut by $1.5 Billion," Congressional Quarterly Weekly Report, July 25, 1981, p. 1331. (a)

13. _____, "Reagan Housing Plans Generally Approved," Congressional Quarterly Weekly Report, August 15, 1981, pp. 1471-1472. (b)

14. _____, "Congress Orders Changes in Food Stamp Program Designed to Save Billions," Congressional Quarterly Weekly Report, August 15, 1981, p. 1489. (c)

15. _____, "Working Mothers' Benefits Cut in New AFDC Provisions in Reconciliation Measure," Congressional Quarterly Weekly Report, August 15, 1981, pp. 1493-1494. (d)

16. _____, "Medicaid Spending Cut, 'Cap' Rejected," Congressional Quarterly Weekly Report, August 15, 1981, p. 1499-1502. (e)

17. _____, "Use of Affirmative Action Tool," Congressional Quarterly Weekly Report, September 12, 1981, p. 1750-1753. (f)

322

18. Copelan, Rhonda, "Human Life" Amendment," Union of Radical Political Economists Newsletter, March/June, 1981, p. 13.

19. Crittenden, Ann, "Rich and Poor in U.S. today," New York Times, December 16, 1981.

20. Demokovich, Linda, "Relying on the Market, The Reagan Approach to Containing Medical Costs," The National Journal, January 30, 1982, pp. 194-197.

21. "Deregulating Workers' Health," Dollars and Sense, October 1981, (#70) pp. 3-4.

22. "Facts About Women Workers," Women's Occupational Health Resource Center News, January/February 1979, Vol. 1, (1), p. 1.

23. Friedman, Thomas, L., "Wall Street Asks New Budget Trims and Changes in Reagan's Program," New York Times, September 15, 1981.

24. Gardiner, Jean, "Women's Domestic Labor," exerpted in The Capitalist System, R. C. Edwards, M. Reich, and T. E. Weisskopf (EDS), (Englewood Cliffs: Prentice Hall, 1978), p. 353.

25. Gilder, George, Wealth and Poverty (Toronto: Bantam Books, 1981)

26. Grossman, Allyson, S., "Working Mothers and Their Children," Monthly Labor Review, May 1981, Vol. 104 (5), pp. 49-54.

27. _____, "More Than Half of All Children Have Working Mothers," Monthly Labor Review, February 1982, Vol. 105 (2), pp. 41-43.

28. Herbers, John, "Shift to Block Grants Raising Issue of States Competence," New York Times, September 27, 1981.

29. Hildreth, James, "Now the Squeeze Really Starts," U.S. News and World Report, October 5, 1981, p. 23.

30. Hunter, Majorie, "Plan to Ease Fight on Jobs Critized," New York Times, 10/8/81.

31. Institute for Social Research, "No Children Allowed Has Become A More Frequent Policy in Rental Housing Market," ISR Newsletter, August 1980, pp. 7-8.

32. Kreps, Juanita, Sex in the Marketplace: American Women at Work, (Baltimore: Johns Hopkins Press, 1971).

33. Kreps, Juanita, and Clark, Robert, Sex, Age and Work: The Changing Composition of the Labor Force, (Baltimore: Johns Hopkins Press, 1975).

34. Lublin, Joann S., "Business Slow To Hire From CETA, Frustrating 'Reemployment' Plans," The Wall Street Journal, August 17, 1981.

35. Miller, Dorothy, "The Feminization of Poverty: Women and the Proposed Social Security Cuts," Washington Social Legislation Bulletin, August 24, 1981, Vol. 27 (16), p. 62.

36. National Advisory Council on Economic Opportunity, "No, Poverty Has Not Disappeared," Social Policy, January/February 1981, Vol. II (4), p. 28.

37. NASW, "Women's Work: Chipping Away At Chauvinism," Woman Power, September 1980, p. 1.

38. NASW, "Budget Cuts and State Fiscal Crises Causing Social Work Unemployment," NASW News, October 1981, Vol. 26 (9), p. 6.

39. "Panel Urges Shift in Housing Policy," New York Times, November 1, 1981.

40. Pear, Robert, "Confusion on October 1 Welfare Cuts Is Expected to Delay Their Impact," New York Times, September 21, 1981. (a)

41. _____, "Federal Cuts Forcing States to Curb Day Care Services for Poor," New York Times, October 22, 1981. (b)

42. _____, "Proposed Food Stamp Cuts Are Assailed," New York Times, February 23, 1982. (a)

43. _____, "Incentives Not Working Is Found in Study of Budget," New York Times, February 25, 1982. (b)

44. _____, "Study Confirms Tax Plan's Effect," New York Times, February 28, 1982. (c)

45. _____, "Housing Aid For Poor," New York Times, March 6, 1982. (d)

46. Raines, Howell, "Reagan Vows to Keep Tax Cuts; Progress $47 Billion Transfer of Social Programs to States," New York Times, January 27, 1982.

47. Raskin, A. H., "The Cooperative Economy," New York Times, February 14, 1982.

48. Roberts, Steven V., "Food Stamps Program: How It Grew And How Reagan Wants to Cut It Back," New York Times, April 4, 1981.

49. Rosenbaum, David E., Study Shows Planned Welfare Cuts Would Most Hurt Poor Who Work," New York Times, March 20, 1981. (a)

50. _____, Reagan's Thesis: Issue is Entitlement," New York Times, March 23, 1981. (b)

51. Rothchild, Emma, "Reagan and the Real Economy," The New York Review of Books, February 5, 1981, Vol. 27 (1), pp. 12-18.

52. Rule, Shelia, "Family Tries With Welfare To 'Make Do,' New York Times, March 23, 1982.

53. Shribman, David, "U.S. Easing Rules on Discrimination By Its Contractors," New York Times, 8/25/81.

54. Sokoloff, Natalie J., "The Economic Position of Women in America," paper delivered at the American Sociological Association, Montreal, Canada, August 1974, p. 14-15.

55. Stafford, Frank P., "Women's Use of Time Converges With Men," Monthly Labor Review, December 1980, V. 103 (12), pp. 57-59.

56. Stasz, Clarice, "Room at the Bottom," Working Papers, January/ February 1982, Vol. IX (1), pp. 28-41.

57. "Still Cutting School Lunch Corners," New York Times, November 2, 1981.

58. Stillman, Jeanne Mager, Women's Work, Women's Health: Myths and Realities, (New York: Pantheon Books, 1977), ch. 3

59. "The 'Right' Kind of Family," Fight the Right, May 1981, Vol. 1, pp. 15-16.

60. Time Magazine, "To the Right, March!," September 14, 1981, p. 36.

61. Twentieth Century Fund, Exploitation from 9-5: Report of 20th Century Fund Task Force On Women and Employment, (New York: Lexington Books, 1975) p. 28.

324

62. U.S. Bureau of the Census, Current Population Reports, Series P-23, No. 85, "Social and Economic Characteristics of the Older Population: 1978," U.S. GPO, Washington, D.C., August 1979.

63. U.S. Congress, "The Family Protection Act - S1808" Congressional Record, 96th Congress (1st Session), September 27, 1979, Vol. 125 (127), pp. S13549-13550.

64. U.S. Congress, "Success in The Home" Congressional Record, 96th Congress (2nd Session), June 4, 1980, Vol. 126 (90), pp. H4527-4528.

65. U.S. Congress, "S1378 - The Family Protection Act" Congressional Record, 97th Congress, (1st Session), June 17, 1981, Vol. 127 (92), pp. 6324-6344.

66. U.S. Bureau of the Census, Current Population Reports, Series P-23, No. 110, "Characteristics of Households and Persons Receiving Non-Cast Benefits, 1979," (preliminary data), U.S. GPO, Washington, D.C., March 1980. (a)

67. _____, Current Population Reports, Series P-14, No. 870, "Estimates of Population of the U.S. by Age, Race and Sex--1976-1979," U.S. GPO, Washington, D.C., January 1980. (b)

68. _____, Current Population Reports, Series P-60, No 127, "Money Income and Poverty Status of Families and Persons in the U.S.: 1980," (advance data), U.S. GPO, Washington, D.C., 1980. (c)

69. _____, Statistical Abstracts of the U.S.: 1980, (101st. ed.), Washington, D.C., 1980. (d)

70. U.S. Department of Agriculture, Food and Nutrition Service, "Characteristics of Food Stamp Households, February 1978," U.S. GPO, Washington, D.C., February 1980.

71. U.S. Department of Health and Human Services, Social Security Administration, "AFDC-1977 Recipient Characteristic Study," U.S. GPO, Washington, D.C., June 1980. (a)

72. _____, Social Security Administration, Social Security Bulletin, (Annual Statistical Supplement 1977-1979), September 1980. (b)

73. U.S. Department of Labor, Annual Report--1978, GPO, Washington, D.C., 1979. (a)

74. _____, Unemployment Insurance Statistics, GPO, Washington, D.C. May/June 1979. (b)

75. _____, Handbook of Labor Statistics, (Bulletin 2070), GPO, Washington, D.C., December 1980. (a)

76. _____, Annual Report--Fiscal Year 1980, GPO Washington, D.C., 1980. (b)

77. _____, Employment and Unemployment: A Report on 1980, (Special Labor Force Report #244), GPO, Washington, D.C., April 1981

78. U.S. Women's Bureau, "Facts on Women Workers," GPO, Washington, D.C., 1980.

79. Weaver, Warren, Jr., "Congress Returning to Issue of Social Security Solvency," New York Times, 9/8/81.

80. Weinraub, Bernard, "Reagan Cut Held to Affect 20 Percent of Welfare Families, "New York Times, March 24, 1981. (a)

81. _____, U.S. Limits on Medicaid Would Shift Burden to
       States," <u>New York Times</u>, April 6, 1981. (b)

82. _____, "Welfare Roles to Shrink by 11 Percent Next Month,"
       <u>New York Times</u>, September 8, 1981. (c)

83. "Workfare and the Work Ethic," <u>New York Times</u>, March 5, 1981.

84. Weisskopf, Thomas, "The Current Economic Crisis in Historic Per-
       spective," <u>Socialist Review</u>, #57, (Vol. 11, No. 3), May/June,
       1981.

85. "Why Wall Street Worries," <u>Newsweek</u>, September 21, 1981, pp. 29-31.

86. "Why Moneymen Worry," <u>Newsweek</u>, October 12, 1981, p. 75.